Trinity and Election in Contemporary

# Trinity and Election in Contemporary Theology

*Edited by*

Michael T. Dempsey

*William B. Eerdmans Publishing Company*
*Grand Rapids, Michigan / Cambridge, U.K.*

Published 2011 by
Wm. B. Eerdmans Publishing Co.
2140 Oak Industrial Drive N.E., Grand Rapids, Michigan 49505 /
P.O. Box 163, Cambridge CB3 9PU U.K.

Printed and bound in Great Britain by
Marston Book Services Limited, Didcot

17  16  15  14  13  12  11        7  6  5  4  3  2  1


**Library of Congress Cataloging-in-Publication Data**

Trinity and election in contemporary theology / edited by Michael T. Dempsey.
         p.        cm.
    ISBN 978-0-8028-6494-9 (pbk.: alk. paper)
    1. Trinity — History of doctrines — 20th century.
    2. Election (Theology) — History of doctrines — 20th century.
    3. Barth, Karl, 1886-1968.    4. Theology, Doctrinal — History — 20th century.
    I. Dempsey, Michael T.
    BT111.3.T735   2011

    234 — dc22

                                                          2011005887


www.eerdmans.com

*To Jackson and Lillian*

# Contents

## Part II: Roman Catholic Perspectives

## Part III: Implications for Ethics Today

# Acknowledgments

Projects such as this always involve the work and generosity of so many people that it is often difficult to know where to begin. I will begin with the contributors to this volume to whom I am especially grateful. Among these, I must extend special thanks to Bruce McCormack and George Hunsinger for agreeing to participate in this volume. I am also grateful for the kind help and participation of Paul Nimmo and Matthew Levering, as well as Paul Dafydd Jones and Paul Louis Metzger. My colleagues at St. John's University in New York have also been an invaluable resource and source of support, especially Nick Healy, Dave Haddorf, and Matt Sutton, and I thank Andy Russakoff, Rex Thomas, and Mergim Cahani for technical assistance. I am grateful to each of them for the various forms of support and friendship they have offered over the years.

I must also make special mention of my good friend and colleague Paul Molnar for supporting this project from the beginning and for encouraging me to think these issues through for myself with clarity and depth. I have enjoyed countless hours of theological exchanges with him and remain profoundly grateful for his erudition, patience, and enthusiasm in sharing the great depth of his theological learning. Most new hires in theology should be so lucky to have a colleague as kind and generous as he. Thanks also to my dean at St. John's University in the College of Professional Studies, Kathleen Vouté MacDonald, for providing me with a research grant during the summer of 2008 to help this project along.

The people at Eerdmans also deserve special appreciation for their great care and expertise, especially Linda Bieze for her assistance and Bill Eerdmans for agreeing to undertake this worthy project in the first place. I am grateful to Jenny Hoffman, Reinder Van Til, and Victoria Fanning for their assistance as well.

Several of the essays included in this volume have previously appeared elsewhere. I would like to acknowledge permission to include them. Kevin W. Hector, "God's Triunity and Self-Determination: A Conversation with Karl Barth, Bruce McCormack, and Paul Molnar," *International Journal of Systematic Theology* 7, no. 3 (2005): 246-61; Paul D. Molnar, "The Trinity, Election, and God's Ontological Freedom: A Response to Kevin W. Hector," *International Journal of Systematic Theology* 8, no. 3 (2006): 294-306; and George Hunsinger, "Election and the Trinity: Twenty-Five Theses on the Theology of Karl Barth," *Modern Theology* 24, no. 2 (2008): 179-98, are reprinted by permission of John Wiley and Sons, Ltd. Bruce L. McCormack, "Election and the Trinity: Theses in Response to George Hunsinger," *Scottish Journal of Theology* 63, no. 2 (2010): 203-24, and Aaron T. Smith, "God's Self-Specification: His Being Is His Electing," *Scottish Journal of Theology* 62, no. 1 (2010): 1-25, are reprinted by permission of Cambridge University Press. Paul D. Molnar, "Can the Electing God Be God Without Us? Some Implications of Bruce McCormack's Understanding of Barth's Doctrine of Election for the Doctrine of the Trinity," *Neue Zeitschrift für Systematische Theologie und Religionsphilosophie* 49, no. 2 (2007): 199-222, is reprinted by permission of de Gruyter.

I also wish to extend my gratitude to my parents for their continued support: my father, Thomas Dempsey, and my mother, Susan Dempsey, who helped me search through thousands of houses in the New York City area so I could work on this project. None of this would have been possible without them. Finally, and most importantly, I wish to extend my deepest gratitude to my children, Jackson and Lillian Dempsey, who have inspired me in hitherto unknown ways and have remained a constant source of joy and wonder. With great love and affection, I dedicate this book to them.

# Introduction

*Michael T. Dempsey*

"Those who are at loggerheads here can neither understand nor convince one another. They not only speak another language; they speak out of a different knowledge. They not only have a different theology; they have a different faith."

Karl Barth[1]

"Iron sharpens iron."

Proverbs 27:17

Karl Barth once described his theological relationship with Rudolf Bultmann as an impossible conversation between an elephant and a whale.[2] In many ways this might be an apt metaphor for another theological debate that has been heating up between some of the most formidable authorities on the theology of Karl Barth in the English-speaking world today. The debate itself centers on the question of the relationship between Trinity and election: Is the Trinity complete in itself from all eternity and apart from God's determination to become incarnate in Jesus Christ, or is it constituted by the eternal decision of election? On the one side stands Bruce McCormack, author of the acclaimed *Karl Barth's Critically Realistic*

---

1. Karl Barth, *Church Dogmatics*, 4 volumes in 13 parts, ed. G. W. Bromiley and T. F. Torrance (Edinburgh: T & T Clark, 1956-1975), I/1, p. 422 (hereafter, volume, part, and page references to the *CD* appear in parentheses in the text and footnotes).

2. *Karl Barth–Rudolf Bultmann: Letters, 1922-1966*, ed. Bernd Jaspert, trans. G. W. Bromiley (Grand Rapids: Eerdmans, 1981), p. 105.

*Dialectical Theology* (among other works), who presents an original and provocative interpretation of Barth's theology of Trinity and election as he developed it in the *Church Dogmatics,* in which the Trinity itself is a result of the primordial decision of election. On the other side stand two other pillars in the interpretation of Barth's theology, George Hunsinger and Paul Molnar, both of whom take issue with McCormack's interpretation and defend a more traditional understanding of the doctrines and their place within the *Church Dogmatics.*

For McCormack, the issues involved in this debate are essential for understanding the full development of Barth's later theological ontology; for Molnar and Hunsinger, nothing less than the consistency and orthodoxy of Barth's theology are on the line. This book's collection of essays, contributed by Barth's contemporary interpreters from both Protestant and Roman Catholic perspectives, seeks to address this rift through rigorous and critical treatment of selected topics in Barth's theology.

## Background to a Theological Debate

The origin of this debate has its roots in Bruce McCormack's magisterial 1995 study of the historical development of Barth's theology between the years 1909 and 1936. In the final pages of *Karl Barth's Critically Realistic Dialectical Theology,* McCormack discusses a paper Barth presented in September 1936 in Debrecen, Hungary, entitled "God's Gracious Election," in which he took an insight from a paper given by Pierre Maury earlier that summer at the International Calvin Congress in Geneva on Calvin's doctrine of predestination. According to McCormack, it was Maury's paper that first awakened in Barth the idea that predestination or election must not be understood in the anthropocentric terms of the individual's election or rejection in the moment of the revelation event, but must be discovered as already decided in Jesus Christ.[3] This key insight led Barth to consider whether God's will in Christ was not simply the ground of election but also the very basis of God's triune being. From this point on, according to McCormack, Barth began to think with a more radical and consistent christological concentration in which "the being of God is itself established in the act of revelation."[4]

---

3. Bruce L. McCormack, *Karl Barth's Critically Realistic Dialectical Theology: Its Genesis and Development 1909-1936* (Oxford: Oxford University Press, 1995), p. 459.

4. McCormack, *Barth's Dialectical Theology,* pp. 460-61.

The full implications of McCormack's final pages escaped all but the most perspicacious readers of his book. Only with the publication of McCormack's contribution to *The Cambridge Companion to Karl Barth* in 2000 did the broader implications of his thinking begin to emerge. In his essay "Grace and Being: The Role of God's Gracious Election in Karl Barth's Theological Ontology," McCormack explains what it means for Barth to say that Jesus Christ is not simply the object of election but also its subject as well, electing God and elect human.[5] Such a statement, he argues, entails a "massive correction" of the classical Reformed teaching on predestination and a clear break with the metaphysical presuppositions of the tradition.[6] Situating Barth's theology of election within the context of the Reformed debates of the seventeenth century, McCormack argues that Barth became critical of the essentialist, metaphysical presuppositions of the traditional distinction between the *Logos asarkos* and the *Logos ensarkos,* the *Logos incarnandus* and the *Logos incarnatus,* that is, between the *Logos* apart from the flesh and the *Logos* in the flesh, the *Logos* to be incarnate and the *Logos* incarnate. Since, for the tradition, the decision for incarnation was made *after* the decree to predestine the elect and the reprobate, that decision had no direct bearing on the specific identity of God's eternal being. The being of God was thus conceived in abstraction from the incarnation, complete in and for himself, which meant that election "tells us nothing about who or what the Logos is in and for himself. It is merely a role he plays, something he does; but . . . has no significance for his eternal being" (p. 97). As a result, a gap is opened up between God's being *a se* and God's act *pro nobis.*

Thus, when Barth writes in his doctrine of election that Jesus Christ, the God-man, is the subject of election, he is not only rejecting the *decretum absolutum* of the Reformed tradition and its metaphysical presuppositions about the being of God; he is also applying his radical christological concentration and its concomitant actualism to the doctrine of God in a way that should have important implications for the structure of the *Church Dogmatics* itself. Election, then, is not only the "sum of the

---

5. Bruce L. McCormack, "Grace and Being: The Role of God's Gracious Election in Karl Barth's Theological Ontology," in *The Cambridge Companion to Karl Barth,* ed. John Webster (Cambridge: Cambridge University Press, 2000), pp. 92-110, reprinted with slight revisions in *Orthodox and Modern: Studies in the Theology of Karl Barth* (Grand Rapid: Baker Academic, 2008), pp. 183-200. References in this chapter will be to the *Cambridge Companion.*

6. McCormack, "Grace and Being," p. 97 (hereafter, page references to this essay appear in parentheses in the text).

Gospel" in which God chooses to be in covenant relationship with humans, but belongs to the very doctrine of God itself and thus *should* have been placed before Barth's doctrine of the Trinity. As McCormack argues, election is not simply the work of the triune God, but is the free decision whereby God constitutes God's own being as triune. "God in himself *is* God 'for us'" (p. 99), McCormack argues, which means that "there is no *Logos asarkos* in the absolute sense of a mode of existence in the second 'person' of the Trinity which is independent of the determination for incarnation" (p. 100). To take Jesus Christ as the *subject* of election means that we must bid farewell to the essential distinction between the *Logos asarkos* and the *Logos incarnandus* and acknowledge that God's being in itself is constituted in the act of election.[7]

In saying this, McCormack argues that Barth overcomes the metaphysical gap in the tradition between the immanent and the economic Trinity. No longer is God being regarded as complete in God's own eternity, but is now regarded as complete *by way of anticipation* of the event in which God's being and life are constituted in history. Therefore, McCormack argues, against the tradition, that "the works of God *ad intra* (the Trinitarian processions) find their ground in the *first* of the works of God *ad extra* (viz. election)" (p. 103, emphasis in original), which means that, logically, the doctrine of election cannot be postponed until after the doctrines of Trinity and divine perfections, but should precede them, for it is precisely the works of God *ad extra* that define, in the simultaneity of God's eternal being, who God is *ad intra*.[8]

In his more recent works, McCormack has been quick to defend his interpretation that, even as God's essence is determined in the primal decision for the covenant, election is nonetheless a free decision grounded in God alone. In his 2007 response to criticism raised by Edwin Chr. van Driel and Paul Molnar, McCormack emphasizes that for Barth, unlike

---

7. McCormack, *Orthodox and Modern*, p. 217.

8. For reference to the eternal simultaneity of God's being and work, see Bruce L. McCormack, "Seek God Where He May Be Found: A Response to Edwin Chr. Van Driel," in *Scottish Journal of Theology* 60, no. 1 (2007): 62-79 (reprinted in a slightly revised version in *Orthodox and Modern*, pp. 261-77, esp. 265). So consistent is McCormack in following God's acts to understand God's being that he also insists that even God's power cannot be known to be more than what is necessary to carry out the covenant. Anything more than this we cannot say. It simply falls outside the spectrum of revealed knowledge and represents the kind of metaphysical thinking that was the bane of early church theology. See *Orthodox and Modern*, p. 60.

Hegel, creation and incarnation are not necessary or essential to God.[9] What is essential is only what is determined freely by God. And since God's being is itself the result of God's free will and not a matter of necessity, as the tradition holds, it is not the case that God is bound by the being of the world in any regard whatsoever.[10] In fact, God's freedom is upheld to an even greater extent in that God as a single divine subject freely determines his own being "not [to] exist as such outside or behind or above these modes of being."[11] God wills his own being in threefold repetition, but not in the temporal sequence of a "before" and an "after," as implied by the traditional concept of God. Rather, in the unity of a singular and eternal act, God freely decides to be God in this way and no other.

In addition to understanding the self-constitution of God's being and essence in history, McCormack also explores the constitution of human being and essence in terms of its shared participation in the life and history of God.[12] Since Jesus Christ is not only the subject of election, but also its object, he also reveals the true nature of human beings as the active recipients of God's grace. Just as the essence of God is determined through the obedience and humiliation of the history of the Son, so too is the essence of human being determined in the exaltation of Jesus Christ through receiving the free overflow of God's grace.[13] The sovereignty of grace thus finds its corresponding and analogous agency in the lived human response of faith, obedience, and prayer as the human history of Jesus "is so taken up into God's own life that it constitutes the fulfillment of the divine Self-determination to be God only in and through it" (p. 229; cf. p. 223). Both the divine and human essence is "constituted in and through the same his-

---

9. See McCormack, "Seek God Where He May Be Found," in *Orthodox and Modern*, p. 268. See also Edwin Chr. Van Driel, "Karl Barth on the Eternal Existence of Jesus Christ," *Scottish Journal of Theology* 60, no. 1 (2007): 45-61. For Paul D. Molnar's criticism, see his *Divine Freedom and the Doctrine of the Immanent Trinity: In Dialogue with Karl Barth and Contemporary Theology* (London: T. & T. Clark, 2002), pp. 61-64, 81.

10. McCormack, *Orthodox and Modern*, pp. 268-69.

11. *CD* IV/1, p. 205, as cited by McCormack, *Orthodox and Modern*, p. 271.

12. See the landmark McCormack essays "Karl Barth's Historicized Christology" and "Participation in God, Yes; Deification, No," in *Orthodox and Modern*, pp. 201-33 and 235-60, respectively; see also "Divine Impassibility or Simply Divine Constancy: Implications of Barth's Later Christology for Debates over Impassibility," in *Divine Impassibility and the Mystery of Human Suffering*, ed. James F. Keating and Thomas Joseph White, O.P. (Grand Rapids: Eerdmans, 2009), pp. 150-86.

13. McCormack, *Orthodox and Modern*, p. 239 (hereafter, page references to this work appear in parentheses in the text).

tory" (p. 246). Ever against the metaphysical abstraction of the tradition, McCormack thus follows the concrete revelation of Jesus' life to bring forth one of the most original and provocative interpretations of the development of Barth's later theological ontology and anthropology.

Long before McCormack fully developed his interpretation of Barth's doctrine of election, Paul Molnar was working (since 1989) on Barth's doctrine of the Trinity.[14] In 2002, he published his own monumental study on the immanent Trinity with in-depth analyses of more than sixteen contemporary voices in dialogue with Karl Barth. Although he offers only a few dense pages on McCormack, Molnar nonetheless puts forth a robust argument that sets Barth's thought in dramatic opposition to McCormack, with a strong defense of the immanent Trinity as the basis of divine and human freedom.[15]

Simply stated, Molnar argues that the immanent Trinity is vital to any theological endeavor that seeks to uphold God's freedom and secure a solid foundation for theological discourse in the being and action of God and not in human thought or experience. He argues that, if our knowledge of God is not grounded wholly in God's act, and not partially in God and partially in ourselves, then our thoughts are inevitably going to say more about ourselves than they do about God.[16] They will simply be the product of the mind's ability to construct a doctrine of God either on the basis of human experience, leading to an Ebionite Christology, which fails to allow Jesus to be authentically and definitively God himself incarnate in history; or on the basis of human thoughts, leading to a Docetic Christology, which refuses to allow the man Jesus himself to dictate our understanding of the Trinity.[17] Such thinking will inevitably be subject to the distortions of the natural intellect, which projects its own images onto God, as we think from a center within ourselves, but not from a center in God, as God acts for us within history in his Word and Spirit. As a result, such thinking will never be able to differentiate human thoughts about God from God's own thoughts about God, which then reduces theology to anthropological speculation.

No doubt, as Molnar insists, human thoughts and experiences are al-

14. See Paul D. Molnar, "The Function of the Immanent Trinity in the Theology of Karl Barth: Implications for Today," *Scottish Journal of Theology* 42, no. 3 (1989): 367-99.

15. Molnar, *Divine Freedom*, pp. 61-64, 81.

16. See, e.g., *CD* II/1, p. 281.

17. For Molnar's discussion of Ebionitism and Docetism in contemporary theology, see *Divine Freedom*, pp. 35-43. For Barth's, see *CD* I/1, pp. 402-6.

ways important, because all faith and theology arise out of one's lived experiences and are expressed in human thought and action. His point is that the *truth* of Christian faith does not rest on our experiences or concepts per se, but on the being and action of God, which is complete in itself and thus operates apart from the strengths or weaknesses of human perception as the enabling condition of all genuine knowledge and experience of God. While Molnar readily admits that all our knowledge of God comes from God through the economy of grace, he nonetheless insists with Karl Barth that our theological knowledge must always be grounded in God's being and act if we are truly to have assurance of its inviolable truth. If, in our understanding, God's being and act are limited to our experience of God in the economy of grace, then our understanding of God depends in some sense on the abilities of human thought and perception and is inevitably reduced to a description of human ideas and experiences. But for Barth, Molnar argues, our knowledge of God can never explain *how* we can know God, as if we could arrive at such knowledge through a synthesis of our thoughts and experiences of God or according to the logical relationship of election and triunity. Rather, our knowledge of God is always miraculous in that it comes to us from God as God reveals himself to us as he truly is in himself, even as God remains incomprehensible in his revelation. While the immanent Trinity is indeed identical in content with the economic Trinity, it cannot be collapsed into the economic Trinity without remainder if we are to preserve God's freedom to exist and act apart from human thoughts and perceptions and therefore within our thoughts and experiences *as* God for us. Molnar summarizes in the opening pages of his book with the words of Karl Barth:

> [T]he content of the doctrine of the Trinity . . . is not that God in His relation to man is Creator, Mediator and Redeemer, but that God in Himself is eternally God the Father, Son and Holy Spirit . . . . [God acting as Emmanuel] cannot be dissolved into His work and activity.[18]

Therefore, it is not surprising that Molnar would object to McCormack's proposal that Barth ultimately makes the immanent Trinity a product of God's will to be God for us in the economic Trinity. According to Molnar, if God's work *ad extra* is constitutive of God's being *ad intra*, a series of theological problems follow. Most notably, it means that

---

18. See Molnar, *Divine Freedom*, p. x, citing *CD* I/2, pp. 878-79.

God would be dependent on the world, for God would simply not be tri-une without a world in need of saving. If God's essence were eternally de-termined in the act of election, God would not exist as such without that toward which God determined himself in that eternal decision. Even as the free decision of God, whose being would be complete by way of anticipa-tion, Molnar argues, such thinking binds the being of God to the world in a way that Barth would never have allowed.

Moreover, if God's being were constituted by the incarnation and out-pouring of the Spirit, then that would even go so far as to undermine the gratuity of grace at the heart of Christian faith. By reversing the order of God's being *ad intra* with God's work *ad extra*, Molnar argues that McCormack makes creation, reconciliation, and redemption a *necessary* component of God's relative and conditioned being.[19] As Barth himself argues (in *CD* I/1)[20] against the Protestant modernists who, like McCor-mack, are suspicious of our ability to say anything about God's being in himself and thus limit our theological knowledge to the economy alone, if our thought and speech about God can only describe God in his relation-ship to us and not antecedently in himself, then

> we turn. . . His being God for us, into a necessary attribute. God's being is then essentially limited and conditioned as a being revealed, i.e., as a relation of God to man. Man is thus thought of as indispensable to God. But this destroys God's freedom in the act of revelation and reconcilia-tion, i.e., it destroys the gracious character of this act. It is thus God's nature . . . to have to forgive us. And it is man's nature to have a God from whom he receives forgiveness.[21]

For this reason, Molnar reminds us why Barth resolutely and repeat-edly refused to reduce God's being to God's work without distinction, even as God always reveals himself to us as God is in himself, for otherwise God would reveal himself as something other than who God essentially is.[22] If

19. Molnar, *Divine Freedom*, p. 63.
20. See *CD* 1/1, pp. 414-24, esp. 419-21.
21. *CD* I/1, p. 421. For a discussion of this, see Molnar, *Divine Freedom*, pp. 152-54.
22. See *CD* II/1, p. 330. Citing G. Thomasius, Barth explains: "If God exists only in a re-lation to the world, then all His attributes are only relations, revelations and effects in the world — and such a view imperils God's independence of the world; for in that case He be-comes what He is only through His relationship to the world. . . . But there is a relationship of God to Himself . . . and in this is grounded the justification for affirming immanent or es-sential attributes in God."

God's being were actualized or complete *only* in relation to the world, or if God's work were necessary to constitute God's triune being in history as such, then it is simply inconceivable for God to exist in God's very essence without the world. This not only undermines God's ontological independence and the gratuity of grace, but also blurs the distinction between God and the world and makes human beings a predicate of God's existence, all of which Barth had always famously sought to avoid. Therefore, it is the immanent Trinity that not only safeguards the freedom and love of God but also prevents what Barth refers to as the "untheological speculation" of the Protestant modernists who limit our knowledge of God to the economy of grace (*CD* I/1, pp. 419-20). Indeed, if our knowledge of God is limited exclusively to God's being toward us, then we cannot, strictly speaking, be certain that God exists apart from human thought and experience, as in, for example, Docetism and Ebionitism.

We cannot be certain that what we know about God in faith is truly based in the being and reality of God or whether it is a product of our own thought and experience. And if our knowledge of God is limited in this way, Barth asks, "what standard and criterion can there be for this understanding . . . ? Obviously the criterion will have to be something man himself has brought. It may thus be, within the limit of our capability, either the evaluation of human greatness or the evaluation of the idea of God or a divine being" (*CD* I/1, p. 421). This is precisely why, Molnar contends, Barth always insisted on a clear and sharp distinction between the immanent and the economic Trinity to preserve the gratuity of grace and secure our talk about God against all forms of anthropocentric speculation (*CD* I/1, p. 420).[23]

Thus, for Molnar, everything depends on not conflating or collapsing the immanent into the economic Trinity or identifying the two without remainder. If God is *a se* only as God is *pro nobis,* then the being of God is conceived, quite explicitly, in terms of human beings (anthropocentrism), but not in terms of the inconceivable perfection and glory of God to reveal himself to us as God is in himself. It is thus essential that, in order to understand and appreciate what it means to say that God is for us, we must also understand what it means for God to be Father, Son, and Holy Spirit in himself. "The covenant of grace is a covenant of *grace*," Molnar writes,

---

23. "It is strange but true," Barth writes, "that the Church dogma of the true and eternal deity of Christ with its 'antecedently in Himself' is the very thing that denies and prohibits an untheologically speculative understanding of the 'for us.'"

"because it expresses the free overflow of God's eternal love that takes place in pre-temporal eternity as the Father begets the Son in the unity of the Holy Spirit."[24] The being of God must be understood as complete in the perfection of God's own eternal, inner-Trinitarian life and would remain so even if there had been no creation, reconciliation, or redemption. And it is precisely this that constitutes the truth of Christian faith and the gratuity of grace.

Molnar's critique of McCormack was soon followed by an article by George Hunsinger, who also takes issue with McCormack for advocating positions that he argues were never espoused by Barth and that contradict some of his most important theological insights.[25] According to Hunsinger, when Barth says that Jesus Christ is the subject of election, he is not claiming that the eternal Son had no existence apart from election, but that the eternal Son elects to be *incarnandus* in Jesus Christ in his obedience to the Father. To help us understand what this means, Hunsinger refers to the grammar of the *perichoresis* to explain how the eternal Son and the Son *incarnatus* mutually coinhere with one another without losing their real distinctiveness: God remains Father, Son, and Holy Spirit in the perfection of his own pre-temporal, supra-temporal, and post-temporal eternity and yet chooses for himself to be in covenant relationship with the world (p. 98 below). This does not mean that the being of the Son was constituted by this decision, but that the decision for election was made out of the abundance of God's perfect and complete triune being, in which God's eternal self-relationship as Father, Son, and Spirit is reiterated in time. The immanent Trinity remains necessary in itself as the ground of God's free and loving temporal work *ad extra,* even as God in himself simultaneously remains fundamentally incomprehensible and incommunicable to us (pp. 105-6 below). God simply reveals himself to us as the one he is eternally.

Hence, it is not the case that election is the ground of God's triunity; rather, the being of God is the ontological and logical ground to God's work *ad extra.*[26] Indeed, according to Hunsinger, if God's triunity were

---

24. Molnar, *Divine Freedom,* p. 63.

25. George Hunsinger, "Election and the Trinity: Twenty-Five Theses on the Theology of Karl Barth," *Modern Theology* 24, no. 2 (2008): 179-98; repinted in this volume, pp. 91-114 below (hereafter, page references to the essay in this book appear in parentheses in the text).

26. Hunsinger, it should be noted, denies that, for Barth, being is prior to act. He says that, for Barth, "being" and "act" are equally primordial. He argues that, for Barth, God is always the living God, and therefore the God whose being is always eternally in act as Father, Son, and Holy Spirit. God is not first some sort of metaphysical "substance" whose act could

constituted by election, then, strictly speaking, it would be the Father alone, and not Jesus Christ, who would be the active subject of that decision, for the very processions of the Son and the Holy Spirit would not take place without the prior decision of the Father for election. The very existence of the Son and the Spirit would then be subordinated to the Father's will and could not possibly exist as such in pre-temporal eternity, as Barth had always maintained. If the Father generates the Son and the Spirit for the purpose of pre-temporal election, then the Holy Trinity itself would be dependent on the being of the world. Only the Father would be independent of the world, while the processions of the Son and Spirit would depend on the Father's decision alone (p. 110 below). There would then be no eternal *koinonia* within the Godhead that the Son and the Spirit would enjoy with the Father, for their existence would only be instrumental to the Father's decision of election. Thus, "Jesus Christ would not be the subject but merely the consenting object of the decision" (p. 110 below), as there would be no inner-Trinitarian act of election that would involve three persons in one eternal divine being. For these reasons, Hunsinger concludes, we must follow Karl Barth and insist that Barth never changed his mind in affirming that God exists as three persons in one eternal being with two simultaneous modes of existence: God exists first in himself and then reiterates his prior triune being in a free and gracious act of self-determination for the sake of the world.

In order to appreciate the force of these criticisms, as well as the radical nature of McCormack's interpretation of the later Barth's departure from the classical tradition, let us briefly survey Barth's early and later thought. As many readers familiar with Barth's thought already know, he raises many of these concerns in the early volumes of the *Church Dogmatics.* In his discussion of the divine triunity, for instance, he argues at length about the essential unity and distinction of God's being or essence and God's work for us. "To the unity of Father, Son, and Spirit among themselves corresponds their unity *ad extra*," he writes. For "God's work is His essence. . . . God gives himself entirely to man in His revelation, but not in such a way as to make Himself man's prisoner. He remains free in His working, in giving Himself." Even as God remains free both in his works and apart from them, God nonetheless reveals himself to us as he is in

---

only be secondary. According to Hunsinger, just as there is no God, for Barth, who is not already the Holy Trinity, so also there is no divine being that is not already in act, and no divine act that does not already belong to the self-existent being of the eternal Trinity.

himself, such that there remains an essential identity and distinction between God's being and work, as well as a "true knowledge of God's essence" in revelation (*CD* I/1, p. 371).The same distinction is found throughout Barth's discussion of the divine persons in *CD* I/1. As the bold headings atop each major section indicate (§§ 10, 11, 12), the one God reveals himself in Scripture in three distinct forms of one divine essence as Creator, Reconciler, and Redeemer, because God is so in himself as Father, Son, and Holy Spirit.[27] It is not the case, then (at least at this point in Barth's career), that God's being is determined, constituted, actualized, or completed by God's relationship with the world *ad extra*, but is rather revealed to us as such because God is in himself eternally Father, Son, and Holy Spirit (*CD* I/1, pp. 414-15).[28]

Similar arguments are also found throughout Barth's theology of the divine perfections, where Barth says that we have "exact parallels to the Trinity" (*CD* II/1, p. 326). The being and perfections of God are not limited or conditioned by God's relationship to the world, even as God allows himself to be conditioned by the world (*CD* II/1, pp. 313-15). Rather, the divine perfections constitute God's being because God is so antecedently in himself and not simply in relationship to creation.[29] God does not "assume [these perfections] merely in connexion with His revelation," Barth repeats, "but they constitute His own eternal glory," because God is so antecedently in himself (*CD* II/1, p. 327).[30]

27. "The one God reveals Himself according to Scripture as the Creator, that is, as the Lord of our existence. As such He is God our Father because He is so antecedently in Himself as the Father of the Son" (*CD* I/1, p. 384). "The one God reveals Himself according to Scripture as the Reconciler, i.e., as the Lord in the midst of our enmity towards Him. As such He is the Son of God who has come to us or the Word of God that has been spoken to us, because He is so antecedently in Himself as the Son or Word of God the Father" (*CD* I/1, p. 399). "The one God reveals Himself according to Scripture as the Redeemer, i.e., as the Lord who sets us free. As such He is the Holy Spirit, by receiving whom we become the children of God, because, as the Spirit of the love of God the Father and the Son, He is so antecedently in Himself" (*CD* I/1, p. 448).

28. "He does not first become God's Son or Word in the event of revelation. On the contrary, the event of revelation has divine truth and reality because that which is proper to God is revealed in it, because Jesus Christ reveals Himself the One He already was before, apart from this event, in Himself too. . . . But revelation and reconciliation do not create His deity. His deity creates revelation and reconciliation" (*CD* I/1, pp. 414-15).

29. Again, see the bold thesis statements in *CD* II/1, pp. 257, 322, 351, and 440.

30. We must also note that Barth does not consider at this point the affirmation of God's perfections in himself to be a matter of abstract or metaphysical speculation. "We have to take revelation with such utter seriousness that in it as God's act we must directly see

For McCormack, however, such statements are clear evidence of the essentialist metaphysical presuppositions of the tradition from which Barth increasingly sought to extricate himself. Despite Barth's repeated assertions of the unity of God's being and work, there remains an independent and separate doctrine of the Trinity that perpetuates speculation about an "unknown" God behind the revelation of Jesus Christ (see, e.g., *CD* I/1, p. 484). Moreover, this metaphysical gap between the being of God in himself and for us also raises the question of Nestorianism, which holds that the being of God in himself is separated from the being of God made available through the revelation of Jesus Christ. Indeed, if God's basic identity as Father, Son, and Holy Spirit is separate from who God reveals himself to be in the incarnation, then we have even derived our understanding of God's freedom in abstract isolation from the very freedom of God in the covenant of grace, which McCormack criticizes in the thought of Paul Molnar. All theological knowledge, McCormack insists, must be derived from the act of revelation which precludes the possibility of ever having genuine knowledge of God in himself.[31] Although there are hints that Barth began to change his mind on these basic themes of his doctrine of the Trinity and divine perfections, McCormack believes that Barth's real change of mind comes with the doctrine of election and his mature Christology, even as Barth does not always follow his deepest insights through with complete consistency.

Of special importance here are the many statements in *CD* II/2 where Barth speaks of God's being as "its own, conscious, willed and executed decision" (*CD* II/1, p. 271; cf. *CD* II/2, p. 175), with the result that there is no "godhead in himself . . . there is no such thing as a will of God apart from the will of Jesus Christ" (*CD* II/2, p. 115). As Barth argues, no other being is its own decision; no other being freely determines its own being and es-

---

God's being too" (*CD* I/1, p. 428). "The path is first from below upwards, from the *natura humana Christi* to the *cognitio Dei*. But it does really lead upwards and therefore it leads downwards again too" (*CD* I/1, p. 419). Therefore, it is the revelation of Jesus Christ that always tells us who God is in himself as Father, Son, and Holy Spirit: "Revelation in so far as it is the revelation of God the Creator and our Father, and in so far as this its content is not to be separated from its form as revelation in Jesus, leads us to the knowledge of God as the eternal Father" (*CD* I/1, p. 394). "He posits and makes known Himself exactly as he posits and knows Himself from and to all eternity" (*CD* I/1. p. 416). "For this reason and in this way and on this basis He is so in His revelation. Not *vice versa!* We know Him thus in His revelation. But He is not this because He is it in His revelation; [rather] because He is it antecedently in Himself, He is it also in His revelation" (*CD* I/1, p. 471, emphasis in the original).

31. McCormack, "Grace and Being," p. 102.

sence. And to suggest, as the tradition does, that God's being as Father, Son, and Holy Spirit comes to God as a matter of necessity is not only to limit God's freedom to constitute his own being but also perpetuates the mistake of understanding God's being as prior to and apart from the act of election. For the later Barth, however, "God Himself does not will to be God, and is not God, except as the one who elects" (*CD* II/2, p. 77)."There is no height or depth in which God can be God in any other way" (*CD* II/2, p. 77). At the innermost depths of God's being, God reveals and determines his own essence as God for us in the decision to give himself to us and even to surrender his own being in his experience of death on the cross. Thus, there is no abstract divine freedom that can be considered without explicit reference to God's being in the act of the incarnation and in the life of Jesus Christ.

This line of interpretation becomes unavoidable, McCormack argues, when we consider the precise language of Barth's later doctrine of reconciliation. Here Barth not only speaks of the essential humility, obedience, suffering, and subordination of Jesus Christ but also understands them as determinative of God's triune being. As Barth writes, "We have not only not to deny but actually to affirm and understand as *essential* to the being of God the offensive fact that there is in God Himself an above and a below, a *prius* and a *posterius,* a superiority and a subordination"(*CD* IV/1, pp. 200-201, emphasis added).[32] If these features belong to the very inner life and essence of God, as Barth repeatedly claims in this section, then we cannot avoid the fact that in God's innermost essence, God is always a being-for-incarnation, with the result that there is no abstract Godhead or eternal Son apart from this decision. By going back to the biblical witness of Jesus' human life of obedience and not beginning with the essentialist presuppositions of the classical tradition of Chalcedon regarding Jesus' two natures, McCormack argues that Barth regards Jesus' human obedience as constitutive of God's own life. In reversing the theology of Cyril of Alexandria, in which the eternal Son is the operative agent in the life of Jesus, McCormack argues that Barth understands the man Jesus to be the operative agent in the works of God in history. So free is God in covenant relationships that God gives himself to us even to the depths of his very essence in Jesus Christ. "The only act of the Son of God in relation to his humanity," McCormack writes, "is the act in which he gives it existence in his

32. For a discussion of this, see McCormack, "Divine Impassibility," p. 169 (hereafter, page references to this essay appear in parentheses in the text).

own being and existence. All subsequent acts of the God-man made possible by *this singular act* are acts performed by the man Jesus" (p. 177, emphasis in original). Therefore, since the human life of Jesus constitutes his divinity, McCormack argues that

> [t]he second "person" of the Trinity is the God-man. So even in the act of hypostatic *uniting*, the "subject" who performs that action is the God-man, Jesus Christ in his divine-human unity. What happens in time in the historical enfleshment is simply the actualization in history of that which God has determined for himself and which, therefore, is already real in him. (p. 178, emphasis in original)

Properly conceived, then, McCormack does not collapse the immanent into the economic Trinity, as Molnar contends, but rather identifies the being of God strictly with his revelation in the acts of Jesus in history. McCormack thus affirms the being of God as already complete in anticipation of what God will become in time, thus eschewing any abstract speculation about God's freedom apart from what God has done in Jesus Christ, and avoids separating God's being and action, and yet does so in a way that is "thoroughly modern in character" at the same time (p. 180).

From Molnar's perspective, however, such historicized thinking overtly collapses the immanent into the economic Trinity, the eternal processions into the temporal missions in a way that deprives the eternal Son of his essential divinity.[33] If it is the case, he argues, that the acts of Jesus are *constitutive* of the being of God, then it is not only difficult to imagine what existence the eternal Son can have prior to the historical enactment of that being by the human life of Jesus, but it also reverses the traditional understanding of the hypostatic union, in which the eternal Son *unites himself* with the man Jesus in assuming human nature. Indeed, if his human history is constitutive of Jesus' divinity, then there is, as Molnar and Hunsinger have argued, no second person of the Trinity existing in eternal relation with the Father and the Spirit. Moreover, if the human suffering of Jesus is essential to the being of God, and not just an expression of God's

---

33. See Paul D. Molnar's article review of McCormack's *Orthodox and Modern* in *Theology Today* 67 (2010): 51-56, with a response by McCormack, "Let's Speak Plainly: A Response to Paul Molnar," pp. 57-65. See also Paul D. Molnar, "Can Jesus' Divinity Be Recognized as 'Definitive, Authentic and Essential' If It Is Grounded in Election? Just How Far Did the Later Barth Historicize Christology?" in *Neue Zeitschrift für Systematische Theologie und Religionsphilosophie* 52, no. 1 (2010): 40-81.

freedom to suffer in the sending of his eternal Son, such that God is not free to be God without Jesus, then does this not make God dependent on the world and on human sin at the very depths of God's being? If so, how, Molnar asks, can we be sure that God has the power to save us from sin and suffering in the first place if God is not free from suffering at the depths of his being?[34] Rather, is it not the case that God is free to send the Son and to suffer in our place at the same time as God remains free and glorious in himself without abandoning his essential divinity?

From Molnar's perspective, therefore, McCormack's interpretation bids farewell not only to the important distinction between the immanent and the economic Trinity, but also reads into Barth's thought an actualistic ontology that goes against many of the most important features of Barth's entire theological corpus by collapsing and limiting the being of God into his work *ad extra,* denying the full divinity of the eternal Son, and reducing the being and glory of God to a function of God's relationship to history that is then conditioned, determined, and actualized in relationship to the world.[35]

How, then, are we to navigate the difficult terrain of Barth's early and later thought on these most difficult and pressing issues? How are we supposed to acknowledge and appreciate the expertise and truth of both sides of this debate in order to mine the rich depths of Barth's thought, while maintaining his most basic theological axioms and the delicate nuances of his later Christology? Is there a middle way between these divergent paths, or are we forced to choose between mutually exclusive positions that can only accuse the other side of heterodoxy or unintelligibility? The answers to these questions remain before us and likely will occupy the interpretation of Karl Barth for some time to come. At the very least, this book hopes to offer a rigorous and irenic attempt to present an important foundation

---

34. See Molnar, "Can Jesus' Divinity Be Recognized?" p. 71. See also *CD* IV/2, p. 357.

35. See, e.g., the discussion of Barth on the essential subordinationism within the Godhead at *CD* IV/1, 201, which McCormack regards as fundamental to his argument that incarnation is essential to the constitution of God's triunity. On that very page Barth continues to affirm that "God did not need this otherness of the world and man. In order not to be alone, single, enclosed within himself, God did not need co-existence of the creature. He does not will and posit the creature necessarily, but in freedom, as the basic act of his grace. . . . Without the creature he has all this originally in Himself, and it is His free grace, and not an urgent necessity to stand in a relationship of reciprocity to something other outside Himself, if He allows the creature to participate in it. . . . In superfluity — we have to say this because we are in fact dealing with an overflowing, not with a filling up of the perfection of God which needs no filling."

and reference for future debates without making hasty attempts at theological compromise. For what is at stake in this debate is not simply who will inherit the mantle of Karl Barth in the English-speaking world, but the being and glory of God as the one who is loving and free both in himself and for us. How we interpret this, of course, is a matter of debate.

## The Plan of this Book

The chapters in this book will be divided into three sections. We will first follow the historical development of the debate with chapters by Kevin Hector, Paul Molnar, George Hunsinger, and Bruce McCormack. We will then turn to the contributions pertaining to various theological *loci*, with chapters by Paul Nimmo, Paul Dafydd Jones, Christopher Holmes, and Aaron Smith. We shall then consider Roman Catholic perspectives in the chapters by Nicholas M. Healy and Matthew Levering, before concluding with an essay by Paul Louis Metzger on the social and ethical implications of Barth's doctrine of the Trinity and election for a theology of culture in the world today.

## Part I: The Debate

After the initial challenges put to McCormack by Paul Molnar and Edwin Chr. van Driel, the first public response comes from Kevin W. Hector, who attempts a middle way between these two paths of Barthian interpretation, while aligning himself more closely with the views of Bruce McCormack. This chapter offers an excellent point of departure, for it not only introduces the issues at stake for both sides of the debate, but also evinces strong sympathies and criticisms of both McCormack and Molnar. Essentially, Hector argues that since God reveals himself to us eternally as God-for-us, the being of God must always be oriented toward incarnation. The *Logos asarkos* must be identical with the *Logos incarnandus,* since there is no God apart from or prior to this eternal self-determination. Yet Hector stops short of affirming McCormack's more controversial thesis that election constitutes God's triunity, preferring instead to speak of the eternal simultaneity of triunity and election in a way that upholds the logical priority of election with the ontological priority of triunity, even if this seems to make creation "contingently necessary" to God.

In chapter 2, Paul Molnar responds to Hector's invitation for a conversation, arguing that despite Hector's best efforts to offer a critical appraisal of both sides, his views do not differ substantially from those of McCormack. Molnar rejects Hector's criticism that he has incorporated an abstract understanding of God's freedom, arguing that Barth always understood God's freedom dialectically in terms of God's positive and negative freedom: God's freedom *from* creation as well as God's freedom *for* creation in the incarnation and outpouring of the Spirit. If God's being is understood undialectically, Molnar argues, that is, only as God's covenantal freedom *for* us but not *from* us, then God's ontological independence and aseity have been lost, and the collapse of the immanent into the economic Trinity has already begun. That this is happening is evident in Hector's open admission that creation is "contingently necessary to God." Instead, we must maintain a clear and sharp distinction between God's immanent and economic Trinity if we are to avoid collapsing God's being into God's work and thus reducing God's omnipotence to omnicausality.

Molnar expands and sharpens his criticism in chapter 3 by focusing on Barth's later interpretation of divine freedom and several deleterious consequences that follow from McCormack's proposal. After citing numerous passages that contradict McCormack's reading of Barth by reiterating the crucial distinction between God's being and work, Molnar carefully argues that we cannot confuse or conflate the *Logos asarkos* with the *Logos incarnandus* into a single, undifferentiated divine act without making God dependent on the world and misconstruing the divine freedom at the heart of the Christian theology of grace. Of great importance here is Molnar's nuanced argument for Barth's understanding of the identity *and* distinction between the *Logos asarkos* and the *Logos incarnandus,* as well as the key issues surrounding Barth's thought on God's omnipotence and omnicausality and the relationship between eternity and time. A proper understanding of all of these issues, Molnar contends, is fundamental to retaining God's positive freedom to be self-moved *and* to bind himself freely in covenantal relationships as the one who loves in freedom.

Molnar also raises the critical question of whether God's being can truly be the product of God's will, as McCormack and others claim in opposition to the tradition. This cannot possibly be the case, he argues, without positing the existence of an abstract indeterminate deity who precedes God's triunity and makes that primal decision possible. If this were the case, he argues, there would be a clear subordination of the Son and the Spirit to the elective will of the Father alone. And if that is true, Molnar argues, it is

McCormack who has incorporated abstract metaphysical speculation about an indeterminate deity who preexists God's self-determination to be triune for the sake of the covenant. As Molnar argues, Barth always maintains that God's being must not be understood according to the logic of election, but according to the revelation which discloses to us God's pre-temporal, supra-temporal, and post-temporal eternity in a way that holds together, in differentiated unity, the simultaneity of God's being and work both in himself and for the world without reducing God's being to God's work or undermining the freedom of God to exist in and of himself apart from the world he created.

The complex distinction and unity of God's being and work takes center stage in the contribution of George Hunsinger in chapter 4. In what can only be described as a tour de force defense of the traditional interpretation of Barth, Hunsinger attacks the claims of many passages of McCormack, arguing that such views contradict some of the most axiomatic features of Barth's theology. For Hunsinger, Barth never repeals his affirmation of the self-sufficient being and activity of God, who freely determines to be for the world in Jesus Christ. Nowhere does Barth declare that God's being is determined as a result of his elective will; or that God's essence is a consequence of God's act; and certainly not that God is triune for the sake of his revelation. Always and everywhere, Barth maintains the absolute ontological priority of God's triunity from all eternity, who then determines in himself to be for the world. Key to his argument is the nuanced dialectic of the unity-in-distinction and distinction-in-unity of God in himself and for us. After explicating more than forty passages to bolster his argument that Barth never simply equates triunity with election, Hunsinger goes on to explain how this interpretation would subordinate the Son and the Spirit to the Father and thus make the Father alone the subject of election. If this were the case, then the Son would be the object, not the subject of election, for the decision of election in which God is said to constitute his own being would rest with the Father alone and could not possibly be an intra-Trinitarian decision of the triune God from eternity to eternity. Rather, if we properly understand Barth's most difficult dialectical moves, we will clearly see that Barth maintains the eternal simultaneity of the Father, Son, and Spirit in a way that respects the unity and distinction of persons in one eternal Godhead, while allowing the triune God to act in history as God remains grounded in his eternal being. Therefore, there is a "double historicity" in which the triune God enjoys two simultaneous modes of existence, both in himself and for us, as *Logos asarkos* in eternity and *Logos ensarkos* in time, such that God is free to reiterate himself in time precisely because God is always already as such in eternity. God's being thus remains the necessary ground for God's actions *ad extra* as the free and temporal expression of who God is in himself as Father, Son, and Holy Spirit in threefold repetition in God's being and revelation.

In chapter 5, Bruce McCormack responds to Hunsinger's theses and outlines his own constructive interpretation and attempt to move beyond Barth. After rejecting Hunsinger's characterization of this debate as one between traditionalists and revisionists, McCormack situates his thinking in the German tradition of Eberhard Jüngel and goes on to critique Hunsinger for being too closely aligned with the "substance metaphysics" of classical theism, which perpetuates the myth of the neo-orthodox Barth. According to McCormack, it is Hunsinger's interpretation that is revisionist insofar as it revises the traditional German interpretations of Barth by following classical theism's insistence on God's being as complete in and for itself, sheer actuality with no unrealized potentiality *(actus purus)*. The result of this move, McCormack argues, is that Hunsinger's reading of Barth's doctrine of God is fundamentally incoherent. On the one hand, argues McCormack, Hunsinger speaks of the Trinity as ontologically prior to election, which clearly means that God's being precedes act. On the other hand, however, he wants to maintain with Barth that God's self-determination is an act of God's being, that is, an act in pretemporal eternity when God in himself decides to be *incarnandus*. This, then, sets up the problem of affirming a traditional doctrine of God with no unrealized potentiality at the same time as agreeing with Barth that God is God in his self-revelation in time. Hunsinger's appeal to Jüngel is also of no avail, McCormack argues, because Jüngel says that we can think of God's being in revelation as it corresponds to God's being in eternity. The twofold historicality includes God's being as *decision,* in which the being of God is constituted *(konstituiert)* through historicality, so that, while Trinity logically precedes election, there is no hidden God behind the event of revelation. God's being is thus an event in history and eternity that requires no gap or separation between God's being and work.

In the second half of his essay, McCormack offers his own interpretation of Barth, noting that Barth himself uses the verbal form of the noun "essence" *(Wesen)* to substantiate his argument that God "essences" himself *(west)* as a person in a single, simultaneous act from eternity to eternity. On this basis, McCormack then demonstrates that since God's being is in the act of revelation, God's essence is freely determined in the decision of the election. This explains why obedience and humility (in *CD* IV/1) belong to the "inner moments" of the divine life and thus require us to abandon any traditional talk of the "ontological priority" of the immanent Trinity and the distinction between the eternal processions and the temporal missions of the Trinity. For McCormack, there is no option but to recognize with Barth that the inner processions of God's being must now be "collapsed," as McCormack himself now admits, into God's missions in a single and eternal event in God's life with and for the world. McCormack concludes by going through many of Barth's early and later statements to see whether these may be retained after his mature doctrine of election has been put in place.

In chapter 6, Paul Dafydd Jones offers an interpretation of Barth's Christology in a different key. Against the tendency to insist on one correct interpretation of Barth's multilayered *Church Dogmatics* over another, Jones invites scholars to view this debate as an opportunity to embrace a new theological sensibility that recognizes the need for interpretive open-mindedness and creative engagement with Barth's text for a new theological situation after neo-orthodoxy. Taking a close reading of Barth's Christology in § 59, Jones argues that Barth clarifies earlier claims about the relationship between the Father and the Son. Here the history of Jesus Christ no longer simply reveals the Son in obedience to the Father, but stands as an event with ontological consequences for God's own life. As the Father specifies the way of the Son, so too does the Son — in eternity *and* in time — obey the Father's command. The obedience of the Son is thus evident both in the immanent triune life of God, in which the Son goes into the far country, and in a maximally actualistic manner in the history of Jesus Christ on earth. The mutual compatibility of both interpretations is possible and necessary, Jones argues, if we are to respect the manifold possibilities for interpreting a text as rich as Barth's *Dogmatics*. This includes both the anterior being of God, with a modest role for the *Logos asarkos*, and the historical revelation of Jesus' life as participatory and constitutive of God's own life without reducing the immanent being of God to God's activity *ad extra* or denying the difference that Jesus' human life makes for God. Jones's chapter concludes by considering some implications of Barth's theological ontology for a theological anthropology after neo-orthodoxy, in which human being is no longer understood in essentialist categories but in the dynamic correspondence to the becoming of God.

In chapter 7, Paul T. Nimmo turns to the seldom-discussed pneumatological dimensions of Barth's doctrine of election. Since the heart of Barth's doctrine of election is the act whereby God determines himself in Jesus Christ to be the covenant partner of humanity, Nimmo considers the work of the Holy Spirit as electing God and elected Spirit. Since election is the primal, self-constituting decision of God that is worked out in time and history through the incarnation, so too is the eternal decree in God the Spirit worked out in covenant relation with humanity. Just as there is no *Logos asarkos* that is not always *logos incarnandus,* so too is there no Spirit in pretemporal eternity apart from the gathering of the community of God: that is, there is no *pneuma anecclesion,* no Spirit apart from the community of faith, without the *pneuma inecclesiandus* at the same time. The being of God as Spirit cannot be abstracted from the concrete "enchurched Spirit." Barth's doctrine of election thus includes not only a radical actualization of God's immanent being in the economy of grace, but also an actualistic enchurchment of the Spirit as basic to Barth's pneumatological ontology.

In chapter 8, Christopher Holmes expands the bounds of the discussion beyond Christology and pneumatology to consider the role of God's triune aseity for theological ethics. Turning to Barth's account of human vocation as obedience, Holmes discovers a traditional defense of God's sovereign being *a se* in the later Barth in order to secure for human ethical agency a particular status. According to Holmes, ethics, for Barth, does not so much actualize or constitute the essence of the human, but is rather reiterative of God's eternal determination to be God for us. The divine freedom and aseity thus remain fundamental to Barth's later thinking, which reiterates that human love and freedom in Barth's theological ethics are founded on the dynamic being and action of God in himself as Father, Son, and Holy Spirit, who gives of himself to human beings in their own corresponding freedom and love. As such, human essence is not constituted in one's attempt to correspond to God's command, but through receiving in faith that which God *is,* eternally in his own being as the one who loves in freedom.

Our final offering in this section comes from Aaron T. Smith, who probes the relationship between God's being and will in Barth's doctrine of election. In accordance with Bruce McCormack, Smith argues that we cannot speak of God apart from his will for humanity, yet this does not entail the logical priority of grace to being. Rather, if we are to do justice to the concerns of both McCormack and Molnar, we shall have to affirm the eternal simultaneity and reciprocity of God's being and will in Jesus Christ without prioritizing one over the other. The result of this construal is thus to acknowledge with McCormack that if Jesus Christ is the subject of election, then there is no abstract deity of God in himself apart from creation. Yet such an assertion must always maintain with Paul Molnar the freedom and love of God to exist apart from his creation in the eternal simultaneity of God's triune being.

## Part II: Roman Catholic Perspectives

In chapter 10, Nicholas M. Healy offers a criticism of the modern German-language tradition of Barthian interpretation and a defense of the premodern Catholic tradition and the Yale School of Hans Frei and George Lindbeck. Healy puts to rest the notion that classical Christian thinkers such as Aquinas were engaged in a kind of abstract speculation about the being and attributes of God on the basis of general philosophical arguments apart from the normative guidance of Scripture. Rather, according to Healy, thinkers such as Aquinas took Scripture as their starting point and then developed arguments to clarify and deepen the understanding of God revealed therein. Yet the motive of classical theologians, unlike that of most modern theologians, was not to seek rational demonstrations or deduce necessary transcendental and epistemological arguments, but to deepen the knowledge and love of God in order that others, such as the beginners to whom Thomas's *Summa* is addressed, may know and love the truth and align their lives accordingly. As Healy argues, it is the modern, German tradition (to which McCormack's thought belongs) that sees the knowledge of God as a problem to be solved within the limits of human comprehensibility, not as a mystery to be adored and revered above and beyond human comprehension. This, in part, explains why McCormack seems preoccupied with epistemological quarries and limitations as he seeks, in straightforward modern fashion, the necessary preconditions for the possibility of revelation in Jesus Christ and then defines the being and action of God accordingly.

In the generous and charitable spirit of Saint Thomas, Matthew Levering offers a contribution in chapter 11 on the relationship between Trinity, Christology, and predestination in a dialogue between Bruce McCormack and Thomas Aquinas. Eager to seek the truth in all quarters and to use McCormack's provocative insights as an opportunity to explore Thomas's christological doctrine of predestination, Levering praises what he considers McCormack's greatest achievement, namely, to identity the triune God with the eternal being of Jesus Christ, which is so often missed in the philosophical work of the tradition. Yet, in making this claim, Levering offers an invaluable contribution to this debate from the perspective of the much-maligned tradition of classical theism. After a close reading of McCormack's response to Edwin van Driel, Levering notes that Thomas Aquinas also understands God's eternal election to include the humanity of Jesus Christ, yet not in the way envisioned by Bruce McCormack. Rather, according to Levering, Aquinas always insists that the Word of God in Jesus Christ expresses not only the fullness of God, but also contains every created effect that is caused by God as well. Thus, in knowing himself, God knows all creatures through himself, which means election belongs within the eternal processions of God, yet without constituting God's being according to his temporal relations. God is always *pro nobis* in Jesus Christ, he argues, insofar as in one eternal act God comprehends himself and all creatures and their effects as well. This is possible, Levering shows, because Thomas understands God's one eternal act of being to include two different "terms" of the eternal processions and temporal missions of the Trinity. In one simultaneous act of existence, two processions flow forth from God, so that God is able to send the Son and Holy Spirit in the temporal missions of the Trinity for creation and incarnation. In this one differentiated divine act, God has predestined or elected that Jesus' human nature be united with the person of the Word of God without mixture or confusion of natures, which would be the case if God's essential divinity included the humanity of Jesus Christ in one undifferentiated eternal act (i.e., Eutychianism).

## Part III: Implications for Today

Our final contribution, the chapter by Paul Louis Metzger, moves beyond the hermeneutical implications of understanding Barth's thought and into the area of the theology of culture. Given Barth's adamant insistence on the *specificity* of the gospel and its demands on human action and obedience, it is only fitting that a book dedicated to the relationship between the being and action of God should conclude with consideration of the practical implications of this debate for individual and social ethics. In critical dialogue with the widely popular "prosperity gospel" movement of Joel Osteen, Metzger argues that a proper theological account of "true prosperity" must be grounded in God's loving freedom as the only secure basis for human love and freedom in the contemporary world. Metzger offers a critique of the individualism, consumerism, and escapism of the prosperity gospel movement, arguing that the libertarian account of freedom encourages freedom *from* the poor and uses faith and social outreach as a means to merit increases in one's social standing.

The result of the prosperity gospel, he argues, is not only that it breeds insecurity by focusing on faith in positive thinking for individual advancement, but also that it ignores the concrete demands of the gospel to stand in solidarity with the poor. A true theology of prosperity must be grounded in God and must engender relationally and communally based existence, in which human value and self-worth do not arise from material accumulation, but from what we receive in covenantal relationship with the electing grace of the triune God. Therefore, it is the love and freedom of God that leads us, not to escape the reality of suffering, but to stand in sacrificial solidarity with the sufferer, so that what begins with the love and freedom of God in himself concludes with the corresponding love and freedom of human beings for God and for others. In terms of this debate, then, Metzger shows that God's freedom must be dialectically construed in himself and for others, so that human action may itself be grounded in God and for others without isolationism or codependence, which would be the case if God's freedom were understood in an undialectical way as either freedom from or freedom for the world. Metzger reminds of Karl Barth's claim that the glory of God, while sufficient in himself, overflows into the glorification and salvation of the creature.

# I. The Debate

# 1. God's Triunity and Self-Determination: A Conversation with Karl Barth, Bruce McCormack, and Paul Molnar

*Kevin W. Hector*

## Introduction

Though Bruce McCormack and Paul Molnar agree with Karl Barth's insistence that God's immanent triunity is known only by way of God's economic triunity, they disagree sharply in regard to its implications. What, for instance, is the relationship between God's triunity and God's self-determination to be God-with-us? What does "freedom" mean when predicated of God? What is the identity of the *Logos asarkos*? Though they (appear to) agree that answers to these questions must be found in God's economic triunity, McCormack and Molnar disagree on what conclusions this entails. McCormack claims that God's economic triunity reveals that God is eternally self-determined to be God-with-us, such that God's being is eternally being-toward the economy of grace. From this, McCormack infers that (a) the Son must be identified as eternally toward-incarnation, and that (b) God's self-determination is logically prior to God's triunity, in the sense that God constitutes Godself triunely for the sake of being with humanity. Over against McCormack, Molnar contends that God's immanent triunity prevents such interpretations: on Molnar's account, God's immanent triunity is what guarantees God's freedom even in the economy of grace. As such, Molnar rejects the idea that the Son is eternally toward-incarnation and that God's self-determination is logically prior to triunity. (In fact, Molnar also appears to reject the eternality of God's self-determination.)

The agreement of McCormack and Molnar with regard to the starting point does, however, provide a helpful means by which to adjudicate between their respective claims: would either one, on the basis of their admitted starting point, need to reconsider his conclusions? In this chapter I claim that Paul Molnar's response to Bruce McCormack contains within itself the refutation of his own position, but that McCormack's position may move too far in the opposite direction. Toward this end, I will examine (a) the common ground between them; (b) where they disagree; (c) the relationship between their disagreement and the theology of Karl Barth (with which each claims to be in continuity); and (d) the implications that follow from this examination. On this basis, I will argue that (a) the *Logos asarkos* should indeed be understood as *Logos incarnandus;* (b) God's self-determination must be understood in terms of the concrete act of Father, Son, and Spirit, and thus not as the act that *constitutes* God's triunity (whereas McCormack seems to suggest that election is necessary and triunity contingent, I will argue that the reverse is true); and, (c) given that God eternally determined Godself to be-with-us and that God's freedom is freedom-for the covenant with humanity, there is a sense in which humanity is contingently necessary to God.

## Agreement between McCormack and Molnar

Assessing the claims of McCormack and Molnar is simplified by the fact that each (a) affirms that theology must be nonspeculative (and each agrees that this means starting with God's economic triunity), and (b) affirms that his theology represents a faithful continuation of Karl Barth's.

Both McCormack and Molnar argue that theology must reject speculative claims about God and, furthermore, that the antidote to such speculation lies in relating God's immanent and economic triunity. In other words, for a theological claim to be nonspeculative, it must be based on God's self-revelation in the economy of God's work *ad extra*. Though McCormack spends little time defending this position in isolation from his argument, he makes it clear that he is taking up Barth's insistence on doing theology *"without engaging in speculation."*[1] For his part, Molnar argues at length for this same rejection, insisting that "a contemporary doctrine [of God] should eschew irrelevant speculation about God's inner nature." Therefore, theologians must "adhere to the economic Trinity for our

---

1. Bruce L. McCormack, "Grace and Being: The Role of God's Gracious Election in Karl Barth's Theological Ontology," in *The Cambridge Companion to Karl Barth*, ed. John Webster (Cambridge: Cambridge University Press, 2000), p. 92 (emphasis in original).

information about the immanent Trinity."[2] From this point of view, Molnar contends that there are only two theological options (and McCormack would agree): "If our knowledge of God is not grounded in the very being and action of God himself — and consequently in his Word and Spirit — then it is in fact nothing more than our own religious or irreligious speculation grounded in our self-experience."[3] If claims about God are not based on God's work, they are ipso facto based on a human projection of "God." As both McCormack and Molnar agree, then, a doctrine of God must be based on God's economic triunity.

McCormack and Molnar also converge in identifying their projects as continuous with the theology of Karl Barth; in particular, both recognize that their rejection of speculation — and specifically theology's necessary basis in God's economic triunity — owes much to Barth. Though McCormack suggests that some elements of Barth's theology require revision, this is the result of McCormack's attempt to think through Barth's own positions; therefore, both McCormack and Molnar see their stances as the continuation of Barth's project.

In light of these convergences, we may fairly apply two criteria in adjudicating between their claims: (a) Do their arguments include any of the "speculation" that each eschews? (b) Whose project represents the continuation of Barth's? In order to address these questions, we must first outline the claims made by each.

## Disagreement between McCormack and Molnar

McCormack and Molnar disagree with regard to (a) the relationship between God's economic and immanent triunity; (b) the relationship between God's triunity and self-determination; (c) the nature of God's freedom; and (d) the character of God's *Logos*. Whereas McCormack emphasizes that God's economic triunity reveals God's eternal being, Molnar stresses that this same economic triunity discloses the absolute freedom with which God acts.

Following Barth, McCormack's claims take the form of an answer to the question "If God is truly revealed in God's triune economy, who must God be antecedently in Godself?" In other words, what must be eternally

2. Paul D. Molnar, *Divine Freedom and the Doctrine of the Immanent Trinity: In Dialogue with Karl Barth and Contemporary Theology* (Edinburgh: T. & T. Clark, 2002), p. x.

3. Molnar, *Divine Freedom*, p. 15.

KEVIN W. HECTOR

true of God if God has revealed Godself in Christ? To answer these questions, McCormack argues (a) that the triune God is eternally God-for-and-with-us; (b) that the *Logos asarkos* must be identified as the *Logos incarnandus;* and (c) that God's self-determination to be God-with-us is logically prior to God's triunity.

Because Christ reveals God, and because we see in Christ that God is God-with-us, we must conclude that, from all eternity, God determined to be God-with-us. "The electing God," McCormack argues, "is not an unknown 'x.' He is a God whose very being — already in eternity — is determined, defined, by what he reveals himself to be in Christ."[4] If God reveals Godself, then we cannot speculate about a God behind God," a *deus absconditus;* we must trust that God is eternally who God reveals Godself to be. Moreover, the God revealed in Christ is *this* God — God-with-us — such that we must recognize this as eternally characteristic of God. God's self-determination to be God-with-us is accordingly an *eternal* self-determination.

Therefore, in order to understand God correctly — "correctly" here meaning "according to God's revelation in Christ" — we must do so in light of God's eternal self-determination to be God-with-us; any God other than *this* God is the product of our religious imagination. There is, according to this account, no "neutral" God, a God other than the one who has already determined Godself in this particular way. What, then, does this entail for an account of the *Logos asarkos*? If the "second identity" of God's triune life is an identity of *this* God, we cannot speak as though this identity were "neutral," or of an unknown determination.[5] In light of God's eternal self-determination to be God-with-us, McCormack insists that the *Logos asarkos* (the pre-incarnate Son) must be identified as the *Logos incarnandus* (the Son who was to become incarnate).[6] The second

4. McCormack, "Grace and Being," p. 97.

5. Let it be stipulated that all references to the triune hypostases are problematic and that I prefer "identity" here on a somewhat arbitrary basis. I borrow the term from Robert W. Jenson, *The Triune Identity: God According to the Gospel* (Philadelphia: Fortress Press, 1982); but the fact that I am borrowing something from Jenson should not be taken as a clue that "crypto-social-Trinitarianism" underlies the claims I am making in this chapter.

6. Note carefully that McCormack rejects an unknown or indeterminate *Logos asarkos,* but not a *Logos asarkos* altogether. Molnar's characterization of McCormack's position as a "thoroughgoing rejection of a *Logos asarkos*" is simply inaccurate. (For this claim, see Molnar, *Divine Freedom,* p. 81.) McCormack denies a *Logos absconditus,* but this is certainly not the same thing as denying the *Logos asarkos.*

triune identity is eternally self-determined to be with us, such that we must speak of this identity as being-toward-incarnation. McCormack observes: "If we were to posit the existence of a *Logos asarkos* above and prior to the eternal decision to become incarnate in time, Barth feared that we would be inviting speculation." Accordingly, he must deny to the Logos a mode or state of being above and prior to the decision to be incarnate in time. He must, to use the traditional terminology, say that there is no Logos in and for himself in distinction from God's act of turning toward the world and humanity in predestination. Given that God is eternally God-with-us, the second triune identity must be identified as *Logos incarnandus* — the Word who would become incarnate.

The second triune identity must be so identified not only because God is eternally God-with-us, but also because any other way of identifying the *Logos* entails that the incarnation introduces a radical change in God's very being. In addition to ruling out speculation about a "neutral," indeterminate God, McCormack's characterization of the *Logos* as *Logos incarnandus* guards against the suggestion that the incarnation was discontinuous with God's being, such that prior to the incarnation God was one kind of God, but afterward a different kind. "How is it possible," McCormack asks, "for God to *become*, to enter fully into time as One who is subjected to the limitations of human life in this world, without undergoing any *essential* (i.e., ontological) change?" The answer, according to McCormack, is that the *Logos* must be eternally *Logos incarnandus*, such that "who or what the Logos is in and for himself (as the Subject of election) is *not* controlled by the decision to become Mediator in time; that the identity of this Logos is, in fact, *already established* prior to that eternal act of Self-determination by means of which the Logos *became* the *Logos incarnandus*."[7] If God has always been the God who is (and thus could and would be) God-with-us, then the incarnation introduces nothing *essentially* new into God's being; rather, in the incarnation God takes to Godself that for which God has always been prepared.[8] In light of God's eternal self-determination, God's being can be seen as eternally "fit" for the incarnation.

---

7. McCormack, "Grace and Being," pp. 94-97.

8. There are two ways of construing the fact that God's "essence" was unchanged by the incarnation: either (a) God's triune being is eternally being-toward the incarnation, such that the triune identities anticipate in eternity what they will be in the economy of grace; or (b) God's essence precisely *is* God's act of election, such that the only divine "essence" that could be changed in the incarnation is the essence of turning toward humanity — which is exactly what happens in the incarnation and cannot therefore be construed as a "change" in

From these reflections on God's eternal "fitness" for the incarnation, McCormack identifies two ways in which Barth's theology would, according to Barth's own strictures, need revision: first, Barth's occasional talk about an "unknown" *Logos asarkos* would need to be corrected; second, Barth's (non-)discussion of the relationship between God's triunity and self-determination as God-with-us would need to be amended. With regard to the first concern, McCormack argues that statements such as the following appear to be lapses in Barth's theology: "The second 'person' of the Godhead in Himself and as such is not God the Reconciler," Barth claims. "In Himself and as such He is not revealed to us. *In Himself and as such He is not* Deus pro nobis, *either ontologically or epistemologically.*"[9] Whereas Barth had earlier insisted that, on the basis of God's eternal self-determination, God *is* God-with-and-for-us, he now appears to posit a God above or prior to this God. If God is eternally self-determined as God-with-us, how can Barth now suggest an "unknown" or indeterminate second triune identity? McCormack contends that this assertion of an "unknown *logos*" represents a departure from Barth's own project and must therefore be revised.

In addition to this lapse, McCormack maintains that Barth's theology needs revision in another area as well: the relationship of God's triunity and self-determination. McCormack contends that God's being is not imposed on God but freely chosen: God is thus "a Subject insofar as he gives himself (by an eternal act) his own being."[10] If it is true that God freely (though eternally) assigns God's eternal being to Godself, do we have any insight into the basis of this decision? McCormack argues that we do: God's eternal decision to be God-with-us. McCormack reiterates that "God determines to be God, from everlasting to everlasting, in a covenantal relationship with human beings and to be God in no other way." This determination, according to McCormack, includes ontological implications: "This is not a decision for mere role-play," McCormack insists, but "it is a decision which has ontological significance. What Barth is

---

God's essence. One way of differentiating my position from McCormack's, if I am reading him correctly, is to say that mine corresponds with (a) and his with (b). This should become clear in this chapter's fourth section.

9. Karl Barth, *Church Dogmatics,* ed. G. W. Bromiley and T. F. Torrance (Edinburgh: T. & T. Clark, 1956-1975), IV/1, p. 52 (hereafter, volume, part, and page references to the *CD* appear in parentheses in the text); cited in McCormack, "Grace and Being," p. 102, though the emphasis is mine.

10. McCormack, "Grace and Being," p. 104.

suggesting is that election is the event in God's life in which he [God] assigns himself the being he will have for all eternity."[11] Though God's self-determination and God's triunity are both eternal, self-determination must be seen as logically prior to triunity; triunity, according to this account, is the being that God assigned Godself *for the sake of* and *as a result of* God's determination to be God-with-us. In other words, while triunity and self-determination are each eternal, self-determination is necessary while triunity is contingent.

If this is the case, McCormack argues, several elements of Barth's *Church Dogmatics* need to be revised: "Election," McCormack concludes, "must not be postponed until after the Trinity and certainly not until God's existence, nature and attributes (*CD* II/1) have been treated."[12] McCormack suggests, for example, that statements such as the following would need to be corrected in light of God's eternal self-determination: in *CD* I/1, for example, Barth had written: "We are not saying, then, that revelation is the basis of the Trinity, as though God were the triune God only in His revelation and only for the sake of His revelation."[13] If McCormack's claim is correct — that God's triunity must be understood as flowing from God's self-determination to be God-for-us — then this is precisely the sort of thing that Barth *would* need to say: God assigned Godself a being that is "fit" for being-with-us, such that it is not inappropriate to suggest that God is triune *for the sake of* revelation, reconciliation, and redemption. Though Barth failed to draw out these implications, McCormack argues that this is the direction in which his theology points.

Whereas McCormack suggests that this is the logical outworking of Barth's theology, Paul Molnar insists that the opposite is in fact the case. Given Barth's concern for God's freedom, Molnar argues, Barth would never have allowed such freedom-compromising moves as those outlined by McCormack. What McCormack identifies as inconsistencies in Barth's theology, Molnar sees as evidence that Barth was primarily concerned with affirming God's independence. Molnar worries that, in McCormack's formulation, "the economy, rather than God himself, defines his eternal be-

11. McCormack, "Grace and Being," p. 98. McCormack does note that "Barth never put the question to himself in this precise form; act and being, yes, but never with the specific content of election and trinity. He should have, but he did not" (p. 101). McCormack reiterates this argument in "Karl Barth," in Adrian Hastings et al., eds., *The Oxford Companion to Christian Thought* (New York: Oxford University Press, 2000), p. 66.

12. McCormack, "Grace and Being," p. 103.

13. *CD* I/1, p. 312; cited in McCormack, "Grace and Being," p. 101.

ing."[14] Though Molnar recognizes that McCormack is not suggesting that God *becomes* triune in the incarnation and the outpouring of the Spirit, Molnar contends that McCormack starts with the incarnation and outpouring and simply eternalizes them, with the effect that the economy is seen as determinative of God's being rather than the other way around. Molnar observes that "McCormack wishes to argue that both the incarnation and outpouring of the Holy Spirit are in some sense 'constitutive' of God's eternal being, by way of anticipation." The problem with this, according to Molnar, is whether "such an interpretation of Barth respect[s] God's freedom" (p. 62). In the name of this freedom, Molnar disagrees with McCormack's assertions about (a) the *Logos asarkos,* (b) the connection between God's economic and immanent triunity, and (c) the relationship between God's triunity and self-determination.

Molnar rejects McCormack's identification of the *Logos asarkos* as the *Logos incarnandus,* because in so doing McCormack "blurs the distinction between the immanent and economic Trinity" (p. 58). Molnar argues that, if the *Logos asarkos* is the *Logos incarnandus,* then God's immanent triunity has been eternally tied to God's economic triunity, such that God is no longer free. God cannot be free, in other words, if God's being has been eternally determined as being-for Christmas and Pentecost. In that case, God would not — *could* not — be God without us. God's being would in some sense require God to create, would require God to be incarnate, and would require God to pour out God's Spirit. How, Molnar asks, can a God with so many "requirements" be free? For this reason, Molnar rejects the idea that the *Logos* is eternally *Logos*-toward-incarnation, and that the Spirit is Spirit-toward-outpouring. Contrary to McCormack, Molnar suggests that God's incarnation is something truly *new* for God — an expression of God's freedom "to be God in a new way as God for us" (p. 63). This must be the case, according to Molnar, because (as we have seen from McCormack) the suggestion that the *Logos asarkos* is eternally-in-Godself the one who would be incarnate leads to a compromised view of God's freedom. In order to understand God as the God who could have been without us, then, Molnar insists that the *Logos asarkos* must be understood as *Logos absconditus.* Because any other formulation entails that God is not truly independent from what is not-God, he insists that the *Logos*'s identity prior to the incarnation is unknown to us.

---

14. Molnar, *Divine Freedom,* p. 58 (hereafter, page references to this work appear in parentheses in the text).

Thus, while McCormack and Molnar formally agree that God's economic triunity must be the source of our understanding of God's immanent triunity, it would appear that this formulation means something different to each. One way of identifying this difference might be to suggest that McCormack's account of God's immanent triunity is an answer to the question "What must be eternally true of God if God is genuinely revealed in God's economic triunity?" On the other hand, Molnar's account answers the question "What must be eternally true of God if God is to be seen as the free Subject of God's economic triunity?" Accordingly, whereas McCormack looks at God's economic triunity and concludes that God must always have been God-with-us, Molnar looks at that same economic triunity and concludes that God must always have been the triune God — but could have been otherwise-than-with-us. In sum, the apparent agreement between McCormack and Molnar with respect to starting with God's economic triunity leads them in widely divergent directions.

This difference — particularly Molnar's emphasis on God's independence — occasions Molnar's critique of McCormack's reformulation of the relationship between God's self-determination and God's triunity. Because (according to Molnar's account) McCormack identifies God's immanent triunity as an eternalization of God's economic triunity, McCormack is "misled into believing that God became triune only by virtue of his self-determination to be our God" (p. 64). While the lesser consequence of McCormack's method (of moving to God's immanent triunity simply by eternalizing the economic) is the identification of the *Logos* as *Logos incarnandus,* this is symptomatic (to Molnar) of McCormack's total failure to account for God's freedom, a failure made apparent in McCormack's suggestion that God's self-determination to be God-with-us is constitutive of God's triunity. According to Molnar, "For Barth, God exists eternally as Father, Son and Holy Spirit and would so exist even if there had been no creation, reconciliation or redemption." This is crucial for the affirmation of God's freedom, in that "the order between election and triunity cannot be logically reversed without in fact making creation, reconciliation and redemption necessary to God" (p. 63). If God's self-determination precedes God's triunity, Molnar reasons, then God must eternally have been the God who would be Creator, Reconciler, and Redeemer, and if this is the case, God cannot be seen as the God who could have been God-without-humanity. Given that this is, to Molnar, an illicit compromise of God's freedom, he rejects the notion that God's self-determination logically precedes God's triunity.

It should be noted, however, that Molnar's concern for God's freedom leads him to reject not only McCormack's proposed connection between God's self-determination and triunity, but also to reject the *eternality* of this self-determination. If, as Molnar insists, the freedom of God to be other-than-with-us must not be compromised, it would seem to follow that God could not have *eternally* determined to be God-with-us. Molnar puts it this way: "If God's election has always taken place, how then can it be construed as a decision; does it not then become a necessity (a logical necessity at that), that is, the very opposite of what Barth intended with his doctrine of the immanent Trinity?" (p. 62). Molnar construes God's immanent triunity as the guarantee that God could have been other than God is in the economy of grace. If God has decided from all eternity to be God-with-us, however, how can God be free in the way Molnar requires? In order to preclude God's dependence on what is not-God, Molnar insists that God could have been God-without-us; but if God has eternally determined Godself to be God-with-us, such independence is ruled out, which leads Molnar to reject the eternality of God's self-determination. It would seem, then, that Molnar is concerned not only with McCormack's assertion that God's self-determination is constitutive of God's triunity, but with the eternality of this self-determination. To protect his overriding concern — that "God must have been free to remain himself had there been no creation or salvation" — Molnar must reject the idea that God's determination to be God-with-us is an *eternal* determination (p. 69).

McCormack and Molnar thus move in nearly opposite directions: though both agree that God's economic triunity must be the starting point for claims about God's immanent triunity, each sees something different in this economy. For McCormack, God's economic triunity discloses the fact that God's being is eternally oriented toward being-with-humanity; for Molnar, on the other hand, the economic Trinity reveals that the God who is with us is *freely* with us, such that God could have been otherwise. Hence, their formal agreement on starting with God's economic triunity points them in opposite directions. However, this does not render their positions inadjudicable; in addition to this formal agreement, each additionally argues that his project represents the substantive continuation of Karl Barth's theology. Therefore, we may shed more light by investigating Barth's concept of (a) the relationship between God's economic and immanent triunity; (b) God's self-determination; and (c) God's freedom. Accordingly, we now turn to this investigation.

## Karl Barth on Triunity, Election, and Freedom

An investigation of Karl Barth's *Church Dogmatics* suggests the source of McCormack and Molnar's divergent claims to Barth's theological mantle: some texts point to God's triunity as the guarantee of God's freedom, whereas others point to God's triunity as the disclosure of God as eternally God-with-us. *CD* I/1, for instance, emphasizes the fact that God's triunity is the guarantee that God remains subject in God's interaction with humanity: because God's grace is God's *grace,* it depends on God alone for its effectuation. There Barth says that "Lordship is present in revelation because its reality and truth are so fully self-grounded, because it does not need any other actualization or validation than that of its actual occurrence, because it is revelation through itself and not in relation to something else. . . . Lordship means freedom" (*CD* I/1, p. 306). Because knowledge of God exists by God's grace alone, it must be the case that God is and remains the free subject in giving this knowledge. In this light, God's immanent triunity is what protects this free subjectivity, in that God as Father, Son, and Spirit requires nothing from God's creatures in order to reveal Godself. God's immanent triunity, it would appear, points in Molnar's directions — as that which affirms God's freedom and independence from that which is not-God.

In addition to this connection between God's triunity and freedom, however, Barth also emphasizes the connection between God's triunity and self-determination to be God-with-us. Barth insists that the doctrine of election must be understood not abstractly but in Christ, and that, from this point of view, we see that God eternally predestines Godself to be God-for-us. Barth maintains that: "In the beginning, before time and space as we know them, before creation, before there was any reality distinct from God which could be the object of the love of God or the setting for His acts of freedom, God anticipated and determined within Himself . . . that the goal and meaning of all His dealings with the as-yet nonexistent universe should be the fact that in His Son He would be gracious towards man, uniting Himself with him" (*CD* II/2, p. 101). If we combine the premises that (a) God reveals Godself in Christ and (b) in Christ God is unreservedly God-with-and-for-us, we see that (c) God in Godself (and thus eternally) is determined to be God-with-and-for-us. And because God has so determined Godself, "there is no height or depth in which God can be God in any other way" (*CD* II/2, p. 77). Thus God's economic triunity reveals that God eternally (and thus immanently) determines to be God-with-us.

On the one hand, Barth has affirmed that God's immanent triunity is the guarantee of God's freedom; on the other hand, he has suggested that God's immanent triunity is tied together with God's creatures. Are we thus to conclude that, at this point, there is an aporia in Barth's theology that leads to the divergence between McCormack and Molnar? No, the apparent aporia is just that: *apparent*. In order to see why this is the case, we must pay careful attention to Barth's definition of "freedom." In this light, it will become clear that Molnar's position diverges from Barth's.

As with any term that might be predicated of God, "freedom" must be defined with respect to God rather than God's being defined with respect to "freedom" (see *CD* II/1, § 29).[15] What, then, is the "freedom" that is characteristic of God? What freedom is affirmed in the affirmation of God's immanent triunity? This freedom, for Barth, includes the fact that God's work "is absolutely God's own, in no sense dictated to Him from outside and conditioned by no higher necessity than that of His own choosing and deciding, willing and doing." God is thus free in the sense of being self-moved and thus "independent." This freedom is, however, "more than the absence of limits, restrictions, or conditions" (*CD* II/1, p. 301), because "God has the prerogative to be free without being limited by His freedom from eternal conditioning, free also with regard to His freedom, free not to surrender Himself to it, but to use it to give Himself to this communion [i.e., the covenant-community between God and humanity] and to practice this faithfulness in it, in this way being really free, free in Himself. God must not only be unconditioned but, in the absoluteness in which He sets up this fellowship, He can and will also be conditioned" (*CD* II/1, p. 303).

Because God is the *God* of the covenant, God is free; but because God is the God of the *covenant*, God's freedom is precisely freedom-for-this-covenant. To put the matter otherwise — to suggest that God cannot use God's freedom to bind Godself — would be to make God a servant of God's freedom and thus "God" a predicate of "freedom" rather than vice versa. Therefore, over against Molnar's account of freedom, Barth maintains that "the freedom of God is primarily and fundamentally defined as God's freedom in Himself, and only from that point of view understood as His independence of the world, and therefore His absoluteness in the usual sense of the term. In this case the absoluteness of God — that which makes it genuine absoluteness — does not derive primarily from the mode of His

---

15. This is axiomatic for Barth's treatment of divine perfections.

relationship to the world. For this very reason, He can enter into a real relationship with the latter" (*CD* II/1, p. 309). Rather than starting with an abstract assertion of God's independence, Barth insists that God's independence must be seen in light of God's revelation in Christ: from this standpoint, God's independence from the world is not absolute independence, but precisely the independence necessary for God to be God-with-us in spite of the fact that we are unfit to be God's covenant-partners (*CD* II/1, p. 312). In other words, God is free *from* the world in order to be free-*for* it. God's freedom is "the freedom to be present with that which is not God, to communicate Himself and unite Himself with the other and the other with Himself, in a way which utterly surpasses all that can be effected in regard to reciprocal presence, communion and fellowship." Thus must God's freedom be seen in light of God's love (*CD* II/1, p. 313). Rather than being at odds with the eternality of God's self-determination to be God-with-us, God's freedom (in *this* sense) corresponds with it: the God who so determines Godself must be free from external limits *on God's ability to be with us* (as opposed to the abstract freedom from anything external to God) so that God's grace alone may be sufficient. Therefore, God's freedom must be understood in light of God's decision to be God-with-us.

If the preceding account of Barth's understanding of God's triunity, self-determination, and freedom is accurate, what light does it shed on the disagreement between McCormack and Molnar? On the whole, it would appear that McCormack's position is more in keeping with Barth's, with one significant exception.

Barth's theology points away from Molnar's position because, first of all, Molnar confuses God's freedom with an abstract account of freedom as absolute independence. While Molnar is correct in positing that God is free from external compulsion, this does not entail that God cannot bind Godself to humanity in such a way that God is eternally God-with-humanity — and never God-without-humanity. Though this compromises God's freedom in Molnar's sense, it does not in Barth's, because for Barth, God's freedom is freedom *for* humanity — not freedom *from* it. If God has disclosed God's freedom as freedom-for-us, we have no theological grounds for asserting that God must have some freedom "above" this. To do so would be to engage in the kind of anthropocentric speculation that Molnar deplores.

Because God's freedom is *this* freedom (freedom-for rather than freedom-from), there is no conceptual cleavage between God's freedom and eternal self-determination. Molnar is correct, of course, that such a move makes creation appear (contingently) necessary to God, such that God cannot (on God's own choosing) be God-without-us, and this is precisely what Barth (and McCormack) affirm. Barth insists that, in electing to be God-for-us, God "ordains that He should not be entirely self-sufficient as He might be" (*CD* II/1, p. 10). God — not self-sufficient? From eternity?! If Barth's account of election is correct, this is precisely the case: God has freely determined Godself from all eternity to be God-with-us, such that God's triune being is eternally being-toward this being-with. Though this was a free decision in the sense of freedom from external compulsion, it is also an eternal decision, such that God has never been other than this God — and thus never other than the God who would be with us.

If God has determined Godself eternally to be God-with-us, then God's being is never of an *in*determinate character; as such, the second triune identity must be identified (as McCormack insists) not only as *Logos asarkos* but as *Logos incarnandus*. God's being is eternally being-toward-covenant, which means that the being of the *Logos* must be eternally toward-incarnation *(incarnandus).* Indeed, Barth implies this very thing: God's eternal election, he argues, "is made with a view to the sending of His Son," such that the second triune identity is "the One who in the will of God was to be, was, is, and will be both very man and very God" (*CD* II/ 2, pp. 26, 92). Here, it would seem, in the immediate context of the doctrine of election, Barth recognizes what McCormack claims, that the *Logos* is eternally the *Logos incarnandus*. Accordingly, McCormack is justified in characterizing as a lapse Barth's later suggestion that the *Logos* is unknown or that the pre-incarnate identity of the *Logos* remains a mystery. As Barth himself saw, the fact that God is eternally God-for-us entails that the *Logos* is eternally *Logos incarnandus*.

While Barth's theology appears to point in McCormack's direction with regard to the identity of the *logos incarnandus,* the same cannot be said with regard to McCormack's suggestion that God's self-determination is logically prior to triunity. Barth and McCormack would both affirm that (a) God is eternally triune; (b) God eternally determines Godself to be God-with-humanity; and even that (c) God wills God's being. But it is unlikely that Barth would agree with McCormack's suggestion that God's eternal self-determination *constitutes* God's triunity. However, this is not because of the problems it entails for God's "freedom"; God's freedom is freedom-for this being-with, such that eternal self-determination poses no problems. The problem, rather, is that McCormack's move appears to make God's self-determination into an *abstraction*. Whereas Barth identifies God's self-determination in the concrete interaction between Father, Son, and Spirit, McCormack abstracts this self-determination from this relationship and makes it into a "thing-in-itself." Divorced from the concrete relationship of Father, Son, and Spirit, God's decision to be God-with-us becomes an "absolute will" rather than God's eternal triune act.

Barth, on the other hand, insists that election is the particular decision of God in the movement of Father, Son, and Spirit, such that triunity is *logically necessary* to this self-determination. In this sense, triunity is logically prior to election. The only election we know of is what exists in the relationship of Father, Son, and Spirit, which means that we have no warrant for identifying an election prior to these relationships. However, because God is *eternally* God-with-us, we cannot ignore the fact that God's triune being coincides eternally with God's decision to be God-for-us. Thus it would appear best to speak of the simultaneity of God's triunity and self-determination. Father, Son, and Spirit subsist eternally in the movement of this decision, and this decision is always concretely enacted in the relationships of Father, Son, and Spirit. Triunity and election, therefore, are each logically prerequisite for a proper understanding of the other: we cannot rightly understand God's determination to be with us apart from the triune identities who enact this determination, and we cannot rightly understand the triune identities apart from God's decision to be with us. According to this account, though McCormack is correct in suggesting that God's triunity cannot rightly be understood apart from God's self-determination, his assertion that self-determination *precedes* or *constitutes* God's triunity is unwarranted.[16]

16. We might set the difference between McCormack's position and Barth's in relief by relating each to the problem set by Kant's first *Critique*: the problem of knowing a thing-in-itself (or, in this case, God-in-Godself). It seems to me that McCormack overcomes this problem by identifying God's act (covenanting with humanity) as the in-itself-ness of God's being, such that to know this act is to know God-in-Godself. If God's *being* is contingent on God's *act*, then we can move more or less unproblematically from God's act (the economy of grace) to God's being (God's immanent triunity). Barth, on the other hand, overcomes this same problem by insisting that God's acts reveal God-in-Godself because God is *in* God's acts. Barth remarks that "God is who he is in his works . . . [but] he is not who he is only in his works. Yet he is not another than he is in his works. In light of what he is in his works it is no longer an open question what he is in himself" (*CD* II/1, p. 260). The breakthrough of *CD* II/2 is not (as some suggest) that Barth identifies God's inmost being with the act of election, but that Barth is now able to say that God's being has *eternally* been in the act of electing to be with humanity, such that we now have nonspeculative grounds (because God's act reveals

What, then, of McCormack's suggestion that Barth's doctrines of the Trinity and revelation must be revised in light of the doctrine of election? McCormack has said that "election must not be postponed until after the Trinity and certainly not until God's existence, nature and attributes . . . have been treated."[17] If God is eternally self-determined as God-for-us, there is no God prior to or abstracted from this self-determination. Accordingly, God's triunity, attributes, and existence must be explicated in its light. A revision of Barth's doctrine of the Trinity, therefore, might speak more carefully about the fact that the Father is eternally the one who would send the Son and Spirit; that the Son is eternally the one who would take humanity to himself; and that the Spirit is eternally the one who would unite humans with Christ, and so on. Though Barth's treatment includes these acts in the triune economy, he does not (and, at the time he wrote *CD* I/1, could not) recognize that the being of the triune identities is eternally a being-*for* these acts. Just as God's eternal self-determination and triunity are eternally simultaneous, so too, it would appear, must they be theologically simultaneous (in the ordering of dogmatic treatment). Election and triunity must be elaborated in each other's light.

McCormack has also suggested that "God is triune *for the sake of* his revelation," because God's triunity issues from God's self-determination to be God-with-us; God (eternally) chooses triunity for the sake of being-with-us, which includes the being-with of revelation.[18] If the preceding argument is correct, however, we cannot claim that God determines to be triune for the sake of revelation (or reconciliation, or redemption). However, we can (and perhaps must) say something close to this: God's triunity is eternally triunity-toward-revelation, toward-creation, toward-reconciliation, and toward-redemption. God's triunity never exists as abstracted from God's determination to be God-with-us, such that God's being is eternally being-for God's overture to humanity. While this conclusion would certainly be unacceptable to Molnar and many others, it seems that the logic of God's *eternal* self-determination presses it upon us: we can either side with Molnar and

God's being) for talking about God's eternal being. But McCormack's position does achieve something that Barth's cannot: it allows him to talk about the logical basis of God's self-constitution, whereas this must remain a mystery for Barth. For Barth, on the other hand, the question "Why does God constitute Godself triunely?" belongs in the same category as questions such as "Why does God elect to be God-with-us?" The answer is a mystery; yet this does not mean that we do not know who God is.

17. McCormack, "Grace and Being," p. 103.
18. McCormack, "Grace and Being," p. 101.

maintain God's absolute independence (at the expense of God's eternal self-determination), or we can side with McCormack and Barth and affirm God's eternal self-determination (at the expense of God's absolute independence). But we cannot have it both ways.

In conclusion, it appears that Barth's theology points (mostly) in McCormack's direction. Contrary to Molnar, Barth argues that God's freedom is not an abstract, absolute freedom, but is God's freedom *for* covenant with humanity; even God's freedom-from is, on this account, for the sake of this freedom-for. God has eternally determined to be God-with-us, such that (by God's *free* decision) God is not independent from us. Contrary to McCormack, however, this eternal decision takes place in the concrete relationships between Father, Son, and Spirit, so that we cannot posit the decision's logical priority over triunity. Yet, with McCormack, we must insist that God's immanent triunity is eternally for and toward God's economic triunity.

## Conclusion

Though McCormack and Molnar both attempt (a) to understand God's immanent triunity from the standpoint of God's economic triunity, and (b) to follow in Karl Barth's footsteps, their projects diverge in several respects. Whereas Molnar identifies God's immanent triunity as that which guarantees God's absolute freedom, McCormack contends that God's immanent triunity is that which guarantees that God is *God* in the economic Trinity. Molnar insists that the *Logos asarkos* is indeterminate, while McCormack argues that the *Logos asarkos* is an identity of the eternally self-determined God, which entails that the *Logos asarkos* is *Logos incarnandus*. In order to protect God's independence, Molnar ends up rejecting the eternality of God's self-determination, whereas McCormack goes so far as to suggest that this self-determination is logically prior to and constitutive of God's triunity.

As I have argued, Barth's theology appears to point away from Molnar in each of these disagreements and toward McCormack on all but the last. Indeed, God's immanent triunity, according to Barth, guarantees God's freedom, but not in an abstract sense: God's freedom is freedom-for-covenant. In God's economic triunity, then, God reveals God's *eternal* identity. Secondly, Barth maintains (though not without the occasional lapse) that God's being is eternally self-determined, so that there is no unknown, indeterminate "God" above or behind God-for-us. God's immanent triunity is accordingly triunity-for and triunity-toward the economy of grace, such that the *Logos asarkos* must be identified as the *Logos incarnandus*. Finally, though God's triunity is eternally for and toward us, Barth would likely reject the notion that God's decision so to dispose Godself precedes (even logically) God's triunity, because this decision takes shape in the concrete interaction of Father, Son, and Spirit. This being the case, we must speak of the *simultaneity* of election and triunity: Father, Son, and Spirit subsist eternally in the movement of this decision, but this decision subsists only in the relationship of Father, Son, and Spirit.

This simultaneity of God's triunity and determination to be God-with-us carries weighty implications, some of which are controversial. We might conclude, for instance, that creation is not only good (which Barth recognized as a necessary consequence of God's eternal self-determination), but is, in some sense, contingently necessary. That is to say, if God has eternally determined to be God-with-us, then God has freely *bound* Godself to creating the "us" with whom God would be. While Barth's doctrine of election has been widely heralded as among his most significant contributions to theology, it remains to be seen whether its devotees recognize its more radical implications. Could it be that Molnar is in the vanguard of those who see the direction in which Barth's doctrine of election points . . . and turn back?[19]

19. I am grateful to Bruce McCormack for his comments on this article. He helped me to specify the point of contention between us and pressed me to offer stronger arguments on behalf of my position.

## 2. The Trinity, Election, and God's Ontological Freedom: A Response to Kevin W. Hector

*Paul D. Molnar*

Kevin Hector has identified several crucial questions in an attempt to re-solve a disagreement between Bruce McCormack and me over how to con-ceptualize the relationship between the immanent and economic Trinity: (1) Can we say that God's determination to be with us is the basis of God's triunity? (2) Must we identify the Son's being as eternally toward-incarnation? (3) How does God's freedom relate to God's eternal decision to be God-with-humanity? Central to the discussion are the issues of just how to conceive of God's freedom and how exactly to conceive of the *Logos asarkos.*

In this response I hope to show that Kevin Hector does not properly interpret the concept of divine freedom that I offer in my book *Divine Freedom and the Doctrine of the Immanent Trinity;*[1] that he then incor-rectly equates triunity and election; that he mistakenly assumes that Barth's emphasis on God *for* us means that Barth no longer emphasizes God's freedom *from* us (whereas Barth always emphasizes both); and fi-nally, that he argues erroneously for the idea that creation is "contingently" necessary for God, an idea that Barth never accepted and never could ac-cept, given his conception of divine freedom.

Most notable, however, is the issue of which theologian's position is in continuity with Barth's own thought. Hector claims that his thinking and McCormack's are more in continuity with Barth's theology; but that is true only if Barth's thinking is revised in ways that they recommend. I never in-sist, as they do, that Barth must change his thinking so that my presenta-

---

1. Paul D. Molnar, *Divine Freedom and the Doctrine of the Immanent Trinity: In Dia-logue with Karl Barth and Contemporary Theology* (New York: T. & T. Clark, 2002).

tion of his views can be continuous with his. In my view, this is a telltale sign that their thinking is not at all in harmony with Barth's on this issue. Even more importantly, however, the very ideas that they think Barth needs to revise and reject are ideas that support Barth's emphasis on God-for-us (as the one who loves in freedom) so that he can distinguish between the immanent and economic Trinity in a way that McCormack and Hector cannot.

## Self-Determination and the Trinity

Is God's determination to be God with us the *basis* of his triunity, or is it an *expression* of it? In my book I argue that God's self-determination to be God for us in election and thus in the covenant of grace is an expression of his freedom. My point is simply this: since God exists eternally as Father, Son, and Holy Spirit, and would so have existed even if he never decided to create, save, and redeem the world, his decision to be God-for-us could neither be deduced from his nature nor could it be seen as necessitated by any external constraints. It certainly could not be seen as the basis of his triunity without implying that God needed us (or at least needed to choose us as covenant partners) in order to be the God he is. This, I argue, was important to acknowledge because any obscuring of God's freedom *in se* means undermining our human freedom, which finds its basis, meaning, and goal in God himself. It is extremely important to realize that, while Hector objects to Bruce McCormack's idea that "God's eternal self-determination *constitutes* God's triunity," as I do, he does so for a very different reason. He claims that "it is unlikely that Barth would agree with McCormack's suggestion" (p. 42 above). But he says that "this is not because of the problems it entails for God's 'freedom'; God's freedom is freedom-for-this-being-with, such that eternal self-determination poses no problems" (p. 42 above). He maintains that the problem is rather that McCormack makes God's self-determination into an abstraction, which is to say that it is not the triune God who is doing the determining in his thought, but rather the very idea of self-determination as a "thing-in-itself."

But that is precisely the point of my book. If Bruce McCormack's conception of God's self-determination can be seen as an abstraction in any sense at all, then the reality is that his thinking about the relationship between election and the Trinity is not at all dictated by the economic Trinitarian self-revelation, but rather by the *logical necessity* that he introduces into both the economic and immanent Trinity on the basis of this abstraction. One will remember that McCormack's argument against Barth is that Barth should have *logically* reversed the doctrines of election and the Trinity and thus that he should no longer accept his own (Barth's) view that God could have remained the triune God with or without creating, reconciling, and redeeming us.[2] While Hector criticizes McCormack's view that election *constitutes* God's triunity, his own thinking never escapes the logical necessity introduced by McCormack at the outset with the idea that "[i]f election is an eternal decision, then it has never not taken place."[3] Equating election with God's triunity is comparable to equating God's omnipotence with his omnicausality, something that Barth absolutely refused to do precisely because he recognized God's freedom.[4] That is why Barth insists that

> we must reject the idea that God's omnipotence and therefore His essence resolves itself in a sense into what God actually does, into His activity, and that it is to be identified with it. It is not the case that God is God and His omnipotence omnipotence only as He actually does what He does. Creation, reconciliation and redemption are the work, really

2. See Bruce McCormack, "Grace and Being: The Role of God's Gracious Election in Karl Barth's Theological Ontology," in *The Cambridge Companion to Karl Barth*, ed. John Webster (Cambridge: Cambridge University Press, 2000), pp. 103ff. McCormack makes a crucial error here. He assumes that the incarnation and outpouring of the Spirit are constitutive of the Trinity so that only "as a consequence of the primal decision in which God assigned to himself the being he would have throughout eternity (a being-for the human race) . . ." (p. 100) can God be seen as the triune God. But that is just the issue. For Barth, God is who he is from all eternity as the Father, Son, and Holy Spirit — he does not assign that being to himself. Rather he freely reaffirms himself as the God he is. This need to assign a being to himself is the nub of the difficulty in the rest of McCormack's position, particularly with his view that "[t]he *decision* for the covenant of grace is the ground of God's triunity and, therefore, of the eternal generation of the Son and of the eternal procession of the Holy Spirit from the Father and Son" (p. 103). But God is self-moved and self-limited and so he can freely determine to be God for us in his pre-temporal eternity and thus execute that decision in the incarnation and outpouring of the Spirit. Yet those actions *ad extra* are an expression of his freedom to exist as Father, Son, and Spirit from all eternity with or without us and are not in any sense constitutive of his triunity.

3. McCormack, "Grace and Being," p. 101.

4. See Karl Barth, *Church Dogmatics*, ed. G. W. Bromiley and T. F. Torrance (Edinburgh: T. & T. Clark, 1956-1975), II/1, pp. 526ff (hereafter, volume, part, and page references to the *CD* appear in parentheses in the text and footnotes).

the work of His omnipotence. He is omnipotent in this work. Loyally binding Himself to this work *He does not cease to be omnipotent in Himself as well as in this work.* He has not lost His omnipotence in this work. It has not changed into His omnicausality in this work . . . . It [God's love] has its power and its reality as love for us too in the fact that it continues to be free love, that God has bound and still binds Himself to us as the One who is able thus to bind Himself and whose self-binding is the grace and mercy and patience which helps us, because primarily He is not bound, because He is the Lord, because stooping down to us He does not cease to be the Lord, but actually stoops to us from on high where He is always Lord. He is wholly our God, but He is so in the fact that He is not our God only.[5]

Contrary to Hector's view that the idea that election *constitutes* God's triunity is not a matter of the divine freedom for Barth, but only a matter of "abstraction," I believe that it is indeed a matter of the divine freedom that God did not abandon but rather exercised in determining to be God for us and then acting within history on that eternal determination. There are, of course, two issues at stake in every aspect of this discussion: Have I properly conceptualized the divine freedom? And is my thought in continuity with Barth's own thought? As just noted, I think I have properly conceived of the divine freedom because I believe, with T. F. Torrance and Karl Barth, that what God is toward us in the economy he is eternally within himself, but that God's eternal being is not exhausted in his determination to be God for us and his actions *ad extra,* and therefore there are certain things that cannot be read back from the economy into the immanent Trinity without rationalizing the doctrine of the Trinity and without resolving God's essence into his activity *ad extra.* In addition, there remains a certain hiddenness and incomprehensibility or ineffability about God's eternal being as Father, Son, and Holy Spirit into which we cannot intrude because, as Torrance says, following Athanasius, "Thus far human knowledge goes. Here the cherubim spread the covering of their wings." And Torrance believes, quite properly I think, that he is following Barth here and argues that when we speak of Father, Son, and Holy Spirit, we refer to

5. *CD* II/1, p. 527 (emphasis added). Barth insists that "absolutely everything depends on whether we know God as the One who is omnipotent in Himself. . . . Absolutely everything depends on whether we distinguish His omnipotence from His omnicausality: not to the glory of an unknown omnipotent being who is beyond and behind His work; but to the glory of the omnipotent God who is present to us in His work . . ." (*CD* II/1, p. 528).

"ineffable relations" and "ineffable realities" which we know only in part through the incarnation and outpouring of the Holy Spirit. Here Torrance cites Barth's all-important point, which also plays a central role in my book, that "we can no more offer an account of the 'how' of these divine relations and actions than we can define the Father, the Son, and the Holy Spirit and delimit them from one another."[6] Any attempt to explain the *logical* relationship between election and the Trinity amounts to an attempt to explain the *how* of the Trinitarian relationships and of God's decision-making, something we are simply unable to do without falling into the error of insisting that because God *is* graciously free for us in his Word and Spirit, he *had to be* so from all eternity.

Certainly, God determined to be for us in his pre-temporal eternity. That he is so is the result of his primal decision. But his primal decision is an expression of the fact that God exists eternally as one who loves in freedom; therefore, while the *Logos asarkos* is indeed identical with the *Logos incarnandus,* the former cannot simply be reduced to the latter the way Hector and McCormack do, as we shall see in a moment. That is why I argue in my book that God remains the free subject of his actions within history in such a way that both creation and incarnation are *new* even for God, as Torrance repeatedly insists.[7] This is a critical point because once

---

6. Thomas F. Torrance, *The Christian Doctrine of God, One Being Three Persons* (Edinburgh: T. & T. Clark, 1996), p. 193 (the Barth reference is to *CD* I/1, p. 475f).

7. Hence Torrance writes: "The creation of the universe as reality 'external to God' was something new in the eternal Life of God. If the Son or Word of God by whom he created all things was not always incarnate, but became man in the fullness of time, then God's communication of *himself* to us in Jesus Christ who is of one and the same being and nature as the Father, is something new to the eternal being of God. Thus the incarnation and creation together, the latter interpreted in the light of the former, have quite breath-taking implications for our understanding of the nature of God. They tell us that he is free to do what he had never done before, and free to be other than he was eternally: to be the Almighty Creator, and even to become incarnate as a creature within his creation, while remaining eternally the God that he is." Thomas F. Torrance, *The Trinitarian Faith: The Evangelical Theology of the Ancient Catholic Church* (Edinburgh: T. & T. Clark, 1988), pp. 88-89. Torrance here makes the all-important point that, while God was and is always Father, he was not always Creator; and while he was always Son, he was not always incarnate. Hector and McCormack lose this crucial distinction by reducing the *Logos asarkos* to the *Logos incarnandus*. Of course, Torrance is not saying that God's nature as Father, Son, and Holy Spirit changes. God remains eternally who he was and is. Torrance is simply saying that God was not always creator and reconciler. In other words, the *Logos asarkos* is "eternally necessary" because it belongs to the Trinity by definition, while the *Logos incarnandus* is "eternally contingent" because it arises from a free decision of the triune God.

the relationship between the Trinity and election is thought to be explained logically rather than soteriologically, then we are forced to choose between God's independence and God's determination to be for us and his subsequent actions for us in history. Barth was adamant that God's actions for us within history, based of course on his primal decision to be for us in his pre-temporal eternity, must be seen against the background of God in himself, who was free and did not have to bind himself to us in covenant love.

> We know God's will apart from predestination only as the act in which from all eternity and in all eternity God affirms and confirms Himself. We must guard against disputing the eternal will of God which precedes even predestination. We must not allow God to be submerged in His relationship to the universe or think of Him as tied in Himself to the universe . . . in freedom (its affirmation and not its loss) God tied Himself to the universe. (*CD* II/2, p. 155)

As I noted in *Divine Freedom* (p. 148), Barth insists against Gogarten that "God for us" would not have its proper meaning "if it were not said against the background of 'God in Himself.'" Because God's love for us is "unmerited and free," it must always be discussed against the background of God in himself:

> [W]hat constitutes the mercy of its revelation, of its being spoken to us, is that it is spoken to us in virtue of the freedom in which God could be "God in Himself" and yet He does not will to be so and in fact is not so, but wills to be and actually is "God for us." (*CD* I/1, pp. 171-72)

A sharp distinction between the immanent and economic Trinity follows: "'God for us' does not arise as a matter of course out of the 'God in Himself' . . . it is true as an act of God, as a step which God takes towards man and by which man becomes the man that participates in His revelation." Our human becoming is conditioned by God, but God

> is not conditioned from without, by man. For this reason — and we agree with Gogarten here — theology cannot speak of man in himself, in isolation from God. But as in the strict doctrine of the Trinity as the presupposition of Christology, it must speak of God in Himself, in isolation from man. We know ourselves only as those addressed by God's Word, but precisely as those addressed by God's Word we must know

God as the One who addresses us in freedom, as the Lord, who does not exist only as He addresses us, but exists as the One who establishes and ratifies this relation and correlation, who is also God before it, in Himself, in His eternal history. (*CD* I/1, p. 172)

Any attempt to explain these or any Christian doctrines or their relations logically instead of exclusively soteriologically (on the basis only of God's free grace), as T. F. Torrance frequently notes, is a clear indication that one's thinking is not being dictated by the free revelation of God in Christ and the Spirit but rather by an abstraction — a logical necessity of thought on our part that is then imposed on the Trinity. This is what Barth was trying to guard against, and it is why he would not say the *Logos asarkos* is nothing but the *Logos incarnandus*. The latter refers to the beginning of God's ways and works *ad extra,* and that beginning must be seen against the background of God's freedom to have remained sufficient unto himself. He did indeed choose to be for us, but unless that is seen against his freedom to have existed without us, then a logical necessity is immediately introduced so that his freedom is reduced to his free decision to be for us. In other words McCormack and Hector are really claiming that God for us arises as a matter of course out of God in himself with the assertion that election and triunity must be identified or even reversed. While Hector disagrees with McCormack that "God determines to be triune for the sake of revelation," he himself believes that "God's triunity never exists so abstracted from God's determination to be God-with-us" (p. 44 above). And this in my view represents the collapse of the immanent into the economic Trinity that Barth himself was trying to avoid by refusing to say that the *Logos asarkos* is strictly identical with the *Logos incarnandus* without remainder. For Barth there is only one eternal *Logos* in these two different forms. But that does not mean that since both forms are eternal they must be strictly identical without remainder, as McCormack and Hector suggest.

## How to Conceptualize God's Self-Determination in Relation to God's Freedom

What about God's self-determination and freedom? How should we relate the two while doing justice to Barth's doctrine of election and to his doctrine of the Trinity? According to Hector, I not only reject McCormack's view of the connection between God's self-determination and his triunity, but I also reject "the *eternality* of this self-determination" (p. 38 above). This is simply not accurate. Of course, I agree that God determined himself to be God for us and actually lived that out as electing God and elected man in Jesus Christ. The fact that God's actions for us are actions of God himself gives them a power that is incontrovertible. That is why Barth insists that election is "the sum of the Gospel" (*CD* II/2, p. 24). That is the strength of Barth's idea of divine self-determination in his doctrine of election. But even in this doctrine Barth respects God's freedom in such a way as to be able to make a clear distinction between divine and human freedom and activity, between God's eternal being and act as Father, Son, and Holy Spirit, and his will to be God for us. He insists that even that self-determination — which, once made, God will not go back on — is still a free decision on God's part and does not arise as a matter of course out of God's nature as the triune God who loves in freedom. Hence, he can also say at crucial points things like this:

> How can we even understand this choice except as it is included in the choice by which God (obviously first) decides for Himself, i.e., for this self-ordination, this being under the name of Jesus, this being in Jesus Christ? The choice or election of God is basically and properly God's decision that as described in Jn. 1:1-2 the Word which is 'the same,' and is called Jesus, should really be in the beginning, with Himself, like Himself, one with Himself in His deity. And for this reason it is *per se* an election of grace. This is not, of course, self-evidently the case. God would not be God, He would not be free, if this had to be so. (*CD* II/2, p. 101)

And for Barth, all of this rests on the divine freedom: "When we say this, we say that in His decision all God's works, both 'inward' and 'outward,' rest upon His freedom" (*CD* II/2, p. 99). While Barth insists that God has determined himself from all eternity to be God for us in Jesus Christ and through the Holy Spirit, so that he is gracious to us in that way, he also insists that "He [Jesus] was not at the beginning of God, for God has indeed no beginning" (*CD* II/2, p. 102). Here Barth clearly indicates that in the doctrine of election, which is part of the doctrine of God, God's primal decision is the beginning of God's ways and works *ad extra* and is not *constitutive* of his divine being. And so Barth can argue that in the election of grace we are led beyond time, creation, and history "to the sphere where God is with Himself, the sphere of His free will and pleasure. And this sphere is His eternity, which gives to the world and time and all that is in them their origin, their direction and their destiny" (*CD* II/2, p. 100). God remains not only free with respect to us, but free with respect to his own eternal life. That is why Barth insists that God's

> inner union is marked off from the circular course of a natural process as His own free act . . . it is not subject to any necessity. The Father and the Son are not two prisoners. They are not two mutually conditioning factors in reciprocal operation. As the common source of the Spirit, who Himself is also God, they are the Lord of this occurrence. God is the free Lord of His inner union. (*CD* IV/2, pp. 344-45)

That is why it is important to Barth to emphasize both God's freedom from us and his freedom for us, and not undialectically focus on the one or the other.

## What Is the Proper Relationship between Election and Eternity?

McCormack and Hector argue that election and eternity are identical. Barth is saying, however, that God eternally exists as Father, Son, and Holy Spirit and could have so existed even without us and that, unless this is acknowledged, God will necessarily be related to us and the distinction between Creator and creature would be lost, and with it the strength of the Christian perception that God is really for us. So there is quite a lot at stake here. I admit that this is a difficult issue. But I think what needs to be said here is that, while God's self-determination to be for us is a decision made by God "from all eternity," as Barth says, that does not mean there is nothing more to God's eternity than that decision. One cannot simply equate eternity and election, as McCormack and Hector do, without implying that creation is in some sense necessary to God. McCormack is at pains to distinguish Barth's thinking from Hegel's on this subject in order to emphasize that creation, reconciliation, and redemption are not necessary to God in Barth's view as they are in Hegel's. And he insists on the distinction between the immanent and economic Trinity.[8] But when Hector concludes that creation "is, in some sense, contingently *necessary*" to God, and that "there is a sense in which humanity is necessary to God" (pp. 46, 30 above), his thinking betrays the fact that he never acknowledged God's

---

8. See McCormack, "Grace and Being," pp. 99ff.

freedom *in se* in the first instance. And when McCormack says election "has never not taken place," and that in some sense it *constitutes* God's trinity, he also fails to acknowledge God's freedom as Barth conceived it.[9]

What is more, Hector's conclusion (that humanity is necessary to God) follows his insistence (*contra* Barth) that because God really is for us in his covenant of grace, it is wrong to suggest that he ever could have been God-without-us. He puts it this way: "Molnar insists that God could have been God-without-us; but if God has eternally determined Godself to be God-with-us, such independence is ruled out — which leads Molnar to reject the eternality of God's self-determination" (p. 38 above).[10] This statement betrays the fact that Hector has introduced a *logical* necessity into the immanent Trinity because, as we have seen, Barth argues soteriologically and not logically that God-for-us must include our acknowledgment that he could have remained sufficient unto himself but did not. I emphasized both aspects of God's freedom in my book, as Barth did. So for Hector to say that I reject the eternality of God's self-determination is simply incorrect. What I reject is reducing God's eternity to the beginning of his ways and works *ad extra*. God always existed as Father, Son, and Holy Spirit, and thus the *Logos asarkos* must be seen as eternally necessary to this eternal being of God, while the *Logos incarnandus* must be seen as eternally contingent because it arises strictly from a free decision of the triune God.[11] God's Trinitarian being is neither self-caused nor self-chosen because God is who he is from and to all eternity as the one who loves in freedom. In that sense the Trinity is both logically and ontologically basic. If we did not make these distinctions, we would confuse the immanent and economic Trinity and resolve God's omnipotence into his omnicausality.

For Barth, then, creation might never have existed or could have existed differently according to God's own free wisdom and love, and God was un-

9. McCormack, "Grace and Being," pp. 101, 100, 103.

10. It is more than a little curious that Hector repeatedly refers to the triune God as "Godself." Robert Jenson has argued convincingly that such references inevitably have a Gnostic and polytheistic sense to them because "Godself" need not necessarily refer to the unique persons of the Trinity at all. See Robert W. Jenson, "The Father, He . . .," in *Speaking the Christian God: The Holy Trinity and the Challenge of Feminism*, ed. Alvin F. Kimel, Jr. (Grand Rapids: Eerdmans, 1992), pp. 95, 98ff.

11. I have adopted the terms "eternally necessary" and "eternally contingent" from George Hunsinger, who clearly recognizes both God's freedom from and freedom for us in the economy. See the latter's introduction to *For the Sake of the World: Karl Barth and the Future of Ecclesial Theology*, ed. George Hunsinger (Grand Rapids: Eerdmans, 2004), p. 16.

der no obligation to humanity. That conveys the true idea of contingence that, as T. F. Torrance frequently notes, is one of the most difficult ideas for philosophers and theologians to grasp.[12] Creation is utterly dependent on God, but God is not at all dependent on his creation. God may freely make himself dependent in the sense of expressing his love in Jesus Christ, who lived out his life for others as the Son of God incarnate, experiencing judgment in our place and representing us in his obedient life, death, and resurrection. But that is an expression of divine freedom and not a curtailment of it. When a theologian claims that creation or humanity are in any sense necessary to God, that claim is a sure sign that the true idea of contingency has been lost and a logical necessity has been introduced. And it is my contention that it is lost whenever a clear distinction between the immanent and economic Trinity is not made. Here the distinction between the immanent and economic Trinity — which McCormack, too, thinks is necessary, but which plays no conceptual role in his logical thought about election and the Trinity — is identical to the distinction between the *Logos asarkos* and the *Logos incarnandus,* and therefore between God freely existing and reaffirming himself as Father, Son, and Holy Spirit, as the one who loves in freedom and whose primal decision is to be for us.

## How to Conceptualize the Divine Freedom

Hector mistakenly assumes that I equate God's freedom with God's independence: "Molnar confuses God's freedom with an abstract account of freedom as absolute independence" (p. 41 above). "What McCormack identifies as inconsistencies in Barth's theology, Molnar sees as evidence that Barth was primarily concerned with affirming God's independence" (p. 35 above). I argued that, unless God's independent existence, which itself could only be seen and understood *from* God's actions in Jesus Christ himself and his Holy Spirit, is seen as the basis of his free actions *ad extra* on our behalf, then his positive freedom to be self-moved (the only self-moved being, according to *CD* II/1, p. 269) would be compromised and God's supposed actions *ad extra* would no longer be recognizable as distinctly divine (free) actions of God within history. This is why I emphasized Barth's positive point that "God has the freedom to be free without

---

12. See Torrance, *Trinitarian Faith,* pp. 102ff. For Torrance, as for Barth, God is related to the world neither arbitrarily nor necessarily (pp. 105ff.).

being limited by His freedom from external conditioning . . ." (*CD* II/1, p. 303), but that because of this he can also enter into communion with us and be conditioned "as an expression of his freedom" (*Divine Freedom*, p. 141). It is interesting that Hector offers that same quote, seemingly unaware that I used it in chapter 5 of my book to insist that God really is acting for us in the economy, enabling and upholding our true human freedom, though Hector presents it in distorted form because his citation substitutes the word "eternal" for the word "external." But clearly he has introduced just the necessity into the Godhead that Barth tried to avoid. He argues that "because God is the *God* of the covenant, God is free" (p. 40 above). That is exactly wrong.

For Barth, it is because God exists in and from himself in freedom and is not limited by that freedom that God can be and become and did become the God of the covenant. God is not God *because* he is the God of the covenant. He is God because he eternally loves in freedom as the Father, Son, and Holy Spirit. That truth is what is recognized through a properly conceived doctrine of the immanent Trinity. Certainly, God determined himself to be God for us. Certainly, this happened in eternity as the basis for what happened in time. But any notion whatsoever that this determination on God's part to be free for us made God to be the triune God or that he could not have done otherwise is utterly foreign to Barth's thinking, and precisely so because of the divine freedom that did not cease in God's self-determination to be God for us and in his activities for us within the economy. Hector is confused about the position for which I actually argued in my book. He claims that Barth's position that God can be free for us only because he is free in himself is the opposite of the position I have taken. Over against a "Molnarian account of freedom," therefore, Barth maintains that

> the freedom of God is primarily and fundamentally defined as God's freedom in Himself . . . . The absoluteness of God — that which makes it genuine absoluteness — does not derive primarily from the mode of His relationship to the world. For this very reason, He can enter into a real relationship with the latter. (*CD* II/1, p. 309)

> God is free *from* the world in order to be free-*for* it. (p. 41 above)

But for Barth, God is free because God alone loves in freedom and has his existence from himself alone. God is not free from the world *in order* to be free for it. Such an idea already introduces a logical necessity here. God is for the world because he chooses to love another outside himself in a free overflow of his love. In reality, I fully accepted this statement by Barth and made it my own. However, there is a major difference between Hector and me and it is this: since Hector, following Bruce McCormack, thinks that God's freedom means *only* his freedom for us, he claims that "because God's freedom is this freedom, freedom-for rather than freedom-from, there is no conceptual cleavage between God's freedom and eternal self-determination" (p. 41 above). Accordingly, Hector presents a wholly contrived dilemma that illustrates my point. He argues that "we can either side with Molnar and maintain God's absolute independence (at the expense of God's eternal self-determination), or we can side with McCormack and Barth and affirm God's eternal self-determination (at the expense of God's absolute independence). We cannot, however, have it both ways" (pp. 44-45 above).

Yet for Barth, as I have shown in my book and as we have seen above and shall see in a moment, it is precisely because God is and remains independently free that his self-determination to be God for us, and then his actions *ad extra* on our behalf, have divine weight and determination in the first instance. Barth does not play off God's independence against his self-determination to be for us; rather, he sees the one as the expression of the other. That is the nature of Barth's dialectical thinking: he holds both that God loves us with his eternal love and that God is free in that love both in himself and in his actions *ad extra*. That is why Barth can say God is who he is in his works but also who he is without them (*Divine Freedom*, p. 130). Here Hector has lost the emphasis of Barth's theology that he himself claimed was important: only if God is actually free from us can we recognize God's actions *ad extra* as God's actions and not the actions of some creature. That is why Barth would always stress that, even in his immanence within history, God remains free in himself:

> But God confronts all that is in supreme and utter independence, i.e., He would be no less and no different even if they all did not exist or existed differently. . . . If they all have their being and a specific nature, God in His freedom has conferred it upon them: not because He was obliged to do so, or because His purpose was influenced by their being and nature, but because their being and nature is conditioned by His being and nature. If they belong to Him and He to them, this dual relationship does not spring from any need of His eternal being. This would remain the same even if there were no such relationship. If there is a

connexion and relatedness between them and Him, God is who He is in independence of them even in this relatedness. . . . Even in His relationship and connexion with them, He remains who He is. (*CD* II/1, p. 311)

And Barth makes similar statements in *CD* II/2:

> From all eternity God could have excluded man from this covenant. He could have delivered him up to himself and allowed him to fall. He could have refused to will him at all. He could have avoided the compromising of His freedom by not willing to create him. He could have remained satisfied with Himself and with the impassible glory and blessedness of His own inner life. But He did not do so. He elected man as a covenant-partner. (*CD* II/2, p. 166)

For McCormack and Hector, Barth's abhorrent remark that God "could have remained satisfied with Himself" is not an isolated remark in the *Church Dogmatics,* and is the equivalent of his statement in *CD* IV that "[i]n Himself and as such He is not revealed to us [the *Logos asarkos*]. In Himself and as such He is not *Deus pro nobis,* either ontologically or epistemologically" (*CD* IV/1, p. 52). In McCormack's mind this thinking is completely unjustified, not only in the context of the doctrine of reconciliation but in any context — because it opens the door to an "unknown" God behind the God revealed in Jesus Christ. Yet Barth's concept of the *Logos asarkos* was not intended to advance an idea of an "unknown" God behind the God of revelation at all, as McCormack and Hector suppose, since even the *Logos asarkos* (the pre-incarnate Word who is not revealed to us) is precisely the eternal Son of the Father, and for Barth there is nothing higher or deeper to God than the fact that God eternally exists as Father, Son, and Spirit.[13]

And yet, for Barth, the *Logos asarkos* logically and ontologically precedes the *Logos incarnandus,* and the former could not be reduced to the latter. Therefore, he distinguishes between them for two reasons: (1) he was taking into account God's ineffability and therefore emphasizing the fact that we cannot explain the *how* of the mystery of the Trinity or of election

---

13. This is why Barth insists: "We cannot say anything higher or better of the 'inwardness of God' than that God is Father, Son and Holy Spirit, and therefore that He is love in Himself without and before loving us, and without being forced to love us. And we can say this only in the light of the 'outwardness' of God to us, the occurrence of His revelation" (*CD* I/2, p. 377).

or of God's salvific actions on our behalf in the economy; (2) he was emphasizing that the *Logos asarkos* had a relevant function in the strict doctrine of the Trinity and in Christology as the presupposition of creation, reconciliation, and redemption. The fact that we cannot know much about the *Logos asarkos* is simply a reflection of the fact that God did not exist before his primal decision as "another God," but as the triune God, and that we cannot know God as God knows himself. According to Hector and McCormack, unless we reduce the *Logos asarkos* to the *Logos incarnandus*, we would not be acknowledging the divine election of grace.[14] But Barth was actually arguing that the divine election of grace is precisely that because the *Logos incarnandus* is the beginning of God's ways and works *ad extra*. As such, it is an *opus internum ad extra*. For Barth, however, everything depends on the fact that the triune God eternally existed without beginning or end as Father, Son, and Holy Spirit and thus *freely* decided to determine himself to be for us in his pretemporal eternity.

That is why I reject McCormack's idea that, if God's election of us is an eternal decision, then it has never not taken place. Such a view simply does not respect God's freedom to have existed from all eternity without us and reduces the triune being of God to his decision to be for us (in other words, it collapses his omnipotence into his omnicausality). It fails to distinguish between what is *eternally necessary* to the being of the triune God, since God exists eternally as Father, Son, and Holy Spirit, and what is *eternally contingent*, since it arises from a free decision on God's part (to be God-for-us). Yes, his decision is a decision "from all eternity." Yes, his decision is a self-determination to be for us and an eternal one, since it is grounded in God's eternal being and act as Father, Son, and Spirit. But to think of it as constrained by his essence in the way suggested by McCormack and Hector is to project a logical necessity into the Godhead precisely in Hegel's manner, which McCormack so assiduously hopes to avoid.

A clear indication that McCormack and Hector have compromised

---

14. Hector claims that my characterization of McCormack's position as a "'thoroughgoing rejection of a *Logos asarkos*'" is simply inaccurate" (p. 32, n. 6 above). But in the context of the chapter in which I made that final assessment, I clearly indicated that McCormack intended to follow Barth, who maintained the distinction between the *Logos asarkos* and *Logos ensarkos*. Yet his reduction of the *Logos asarkos* to the *Logos incarnandus,* and his logical reversal of election and the Trinity, showed that his thinking was really dictated by a rejection of the *Logos asarkos* in Barth's sense. And his claim that Barth's acknowledgment of the *Logos asarkos* needs revision points in the same direction. So my judgment was not at all inaccurate.

God's freedom *in se* and *ad extra* is the idea, openly embraced by Hector, following the logic of McCormack's argument, that creation and humanity should be seen as contingently necessary to God. The explanations they offer to support their views of God's self-determination illustrate that, while they both recognize the need for a properly conceived doctrine of the immanent Trinity, as I do, their thinking actually undermines the doctrine. In the end they find themselves in conflict with Barth's own thought. Thus we see once again why a properly conceived doctrine of the immanent Trinity along the lines suggested by Barth himself is so vitally important for all aspects of Christian doctrine today.

## 3. Can the Electing God Be God Without Us? Some Implications of Bruce McCormack's Understanding of Barth's Doctrine of Election for the Doctrine of the Trinity

*Paul D. Molnar*

Bruce McCormack suggests in a recent article[1] that dialogue with him concerning the position he adopts in his *Cambridge Companion* essay[2] can take place only if Barth's view that Jesus Christ is the subject of election is taken into account in detail — so that the consequences McCormack thinks follow from that might be discussed. In this chapter I attempt to listen carefully to what McCormack has said, and again to what Barth has said, with a view toward genuine dialogue that will focus on the important matter of how to understand Jesus Christ as electing God and elected human being in the sense advanced by Barth, so that we can see once again that the doctrine of election really is the sum of the Gospel.

If I understand McCormack's thesis correctly, it is this: from *CD* II/2 onward, Barth finally became a full-fledged "post-metaphysical" theologian. And he did so by making Jesus Christ "rather than 'the eternal Logos'" the subject of election.[3] McCormack says that there is no dispute that, before *CD* II/2, Barth held the view that the doctrine of the Trinity logically preceded that of election. But after *CD* II/2 that was no longer the case. In effect, then, except for a few anticipatory elements found in *CD* II/1, Barth's views elaborated in the first volume, on the "Doctrine of

---

1. Bruce McCormack, "Seek God Where He May Be Found: A Response to Edwin Chr. Van Driel," *Scottish Journal of Theology* 60, no. 1 (2007): 62-79; also published in Bruce L. McCormack, *Orthodox and Modern: Studies in the Theology of Karl Barth* (Grand Rapids: Baker Academic, 2008). References here will be to the *Scottish Journal of Theology*.

2. Bruce McCormack, "Grace and Being: The Role of God's Gracious Election in Karl Barth's Theological Ontology," in *The Cambridge Companion to Karl Barth*, ed. John Webster (Cambridge: Cambridge University Press, 2000), pp. 92-110.

3. McCormack, "Seek God," p. 66.

God," tended to show evidence of "classical metaphysics," especially in parts of Barth's presentation of the divine perfections. Therefore, in McCormack's mind, any refutation of his position must appeal to *CD* II/2 and later or it is irrelevant. Let us grant this bracketing of the first three volumes of the *CD* just for the sake of argument, even though I am certain that Barth would not have wanted to discard what he says there. In support of this judgment, I would note that T. F. Torrance, for one, appropriately claims that *CD* II/1 and II/2 together should be seen as the high point of the *Church Dogmatics*.[4] Furthermore, he says that Barth himself agreed that this was the high point of the *Church Dogmatics*. And while there is much that is superb in the fourth volume, so that Torrance even says that it is "the most powerful work on the doctrine of atoning reconciliation ever written," Torrance's observation at least shows that it is important to see *CD* II/1 and II/2 together as expressing Barth's understanding of the doctrine of God.[5]

## I. Barth's Later Position on the Divine Freedom

Let me begin my analysis by observing that, in the years just before his death in 1968 and thus long after he had written *CD* II/2, Barth was asked about his depiction of the divine freedom in *CD* I/1 (recorded in George Hunsinger's summary of the second of two collections of nearly a thousand pages of recorded interviews and conversations with Barth).[6] An interviewer wondered whether Barth would "still endorse what he had written back in 1932 in the first volume of his dogmatics":

> God would not be any the less God if he had created no world and no human being. The existence of the world and our existence are in no sense necessary to God's essential being, not even as the object of his

4. See Thomas F. Torrance, *Karl Barth: Biblical and Evangelical Theologian* (Edinburgh: T. & T. Clark, 1990), p. 124: "I still hold the *Gotteslehre* of *CD* II/1 and 2 to be the high point of Barth's Dogmatics. . . . That second volume of *Church Dogmatics* surely ranks with Athanasius, *Contra Arianos*, Augustine, *De Trinitate*, St. Thomas, *Summa Theologiae*, and Calvin, *Institutio*, as a supremely great work of Christian theology."
5. Torrance, *Karl Barth*, p. 133.
6. Karl Barth, *Gespräche 1964-1968*, ed. Eberhard Busch (Zürich: Theologischer Verlag, 1997), cited in George Hunsinger, "Conversational Theology: The Wit and Wisdom of Karl Barth," *Toronto Journal of Theology* 17 (2001): 119-131.

love. . . . God is not at all lonely even without the world and us. His love has its object in himself.

Barth replied: "Splendid, isn't it!" (*Gespräche 1964-1968*, p. 286). According to Hunsinger, Barth distinguished the doctrines of reconciliation, election, and the Trinity "by ranking them."

Election, he stated, was always election to reconciliation — that is, to justification, sanctification, and vocation. Therefore, everything in the doctrine of reconciliation was but an explication of the doctrine of election. In turn, the doctrine of election was grounded in something beyond itself. "And behind the doctrine of election stands the doctrine of the Trinity. That is the order. The doctrine of the Trinity, election and then sanctification, etc." (*Gespräche 1964-1968*, p. 293)[7]

Here is a statement by Barth himself that clearly does not support the reading of *CD* II/2 offered by Bruce McCormack, namely, that Barth should have logically reversed the doctrines of election and the Trinity based on his presentation in *CD* II/2. Barth obviously did not think that he had or should have logically reversed the doctrines of election and the Trinity. Rather, it is apparent that he thought election was a free action of the God who is triune as one who loves in freedom from eternity to eternity. And the same thinking that is evident in *CD* I/1, where Barth says that God could have been God without us but chose not to, is embedded deep in *CD* IV/2, where he writes:

What is it that God wills when He loves us? He certainly does not will anything for Himself — for what have we to give Him? But He does not will Himself without us. In all the fullness of His Godhead, in *which He might well have been satisfied with Himself,* He wills Himself together with us. He wills Himself in fellowship with us. (*CD* IV/2, p. 777, emphasis added)[8]

---

7. See also Barth's important statement that "[t]he true and living God is gracious. He transcends Himself. He discloses Himself. *He does this first in Himself, and then and on this basis to man in His eternal election and its temporal and historical fulfilment.*" See Karl Barth, *Church Dogmatics*, 4 volumes in 13 parts, ed. G. W. Bromiley and T. F. Torrance (Edinburgh: T&T Clark, 1956-1975), IV/3.1, p. 81 (emphasis added). This statement clearly underscores the order mentioned here in this interview. (Hereafter, volume, part, and page references to the *CD* appear in parentheses in the text and footnotes.)

8. It should be noted against those who would appeal to Karl Barth, *The Humanity of*

This thinking also reiterates the point Barth makes in *CD* II/1, that God is who he is in revelation as the one who seeks and creates fellowship between himself and us: "But He is this loving God without us as Father, Son and Holy Spirit, in the freedom of the Lord, who has His life from Himself" (*CD* II/1, p. 257).

There is another important passage from *CD* IV/2, where Barth expresses exactly the position McCormack says he abandoned after writing *CD* II/2. It is this:

> *The triune life of God* which is free life in the fact that it is Spirit, *is the basis of His whole will and action* even *ad extra,* as the living act which He directs to us. It is the basis of his *decretum et opus ad extra,* of the relationship which He has determined and established with a reality which is distinct from Himself and endowed by Him with its own very different and creaturely being. It is the basis of the election of man to covenant with Himself; of the determination of the Son to become man, and therefore to fulfill this covenant; of creation; and, in conquest of the opposition and contradiction of the creature and to save it from perdition, of the atonement with its final goal of redemption to eternal life with Himself. (*CD* IV/2, p. 345, emphasis added)

Here it is evident that, for Barth, election is the free decision and action of the triune God and not the ground of his triunity. And Barth does not have to embrace classical metaphysics to make this assertion, because in his doctrine of God he never accepts the idea of "being," but only being as the being of the triune God. The fact that this thinking appears in *CD* IV/2 is significant, because it undercuts McCormack's thesis that Barth's understanding of God changed appreciably after *CD* II/2, so that he no longer maintained things he might have said before concerning the divine freedom, especially in volume IV. And this statement from *CD* IV/2 is fully in

---

*God,* trans. by Thomas Wieser and John Newton Thomas (Richmond, VA: John Knox Press, 1968) to say that Barth had changed his thinking and would no longer espouse this view of the divine freedom that Barth continues to say exactly the same thing: "God's deity is thus no prison in which He can exist only in and for Himself. It is rather His freedom to be in and for Himself but also with and for us . . ." (p. 49). Note well: Barth intends to emphasize both aspects of God's freedom and not one or the other. Further, Barth said: "Why should God not also be able, as eternal Love, to be sufficient unto Himself? In His life as Father, Son and Holy Spirit He would in truth be no lonesome, no egotistical God even without man, yes, even without the whole created universe" (p. 50). But of course he chose to be with us and for us in that freedom which is his alone.

accord with what Barth said in the interview cited above, which was recorded even later than he wrote the passage above, and was emphasized again in the passage cited from *CD* II/1.

Given these statements by Barth himself, then, it is fair to say that he believes that God's triune existence and his act of self-determination to be God-for-us are *two distinct acts* on the part of the triune God and cannot be conflated, as McCormack does when he argues that election and the act in which he believes God "gives to himself his own being as Father, Son and Holy Spirit" are not two acts but one.[9] Consequently, for Barth, in pretemporal eternity God the Father, Son, and Holy Spirit determined to be God for us in Jesus Christ. Election did not result in God becoming triune but rather expressed the free "eternal testament carried out between Father, Son and Spirit."[10] George Hunsinger rightly expresses it:

> God is who he is perfectly in his pretemporal mode of existence. For he is who he is before the world and without it. He is, that is to say, the Holy Trinity. . . . The Trinity is therefore the presupposition of creation, reconciliation and redemption. It is also the *presupposition of God's pretemporal decision of election.*[11]

And the fact that Barth can maintain this and yet not be thinking of an indeterminate deity even in *CD* II/1 is captured in Barth's own remark that God's pre-temporality is

> the pure time of the Father and the Son in the fellowship of the Holy Spirit. And in this pure divine time there took place the appointment of the eternal Son for the temporal world, there occurred the readiness of the Son to do the will of the eternal Father. (*CD* II/1, p. 622)

And the enactment of that pre-temporal election is what takes place in the history of the covenant. It is, Barth says, "an act which affects us, an act which occurs in the very midst of time no less than in that far distant pre-temporal eternity. It is the present secret, and in the history of salvation the revealed secret, of the whole history, encounter and decision between God and man" (*CD* II/2, pp. 185-86). This act of God to us and from us back to

9. McCormack, "Seek God," p. 66 (see above, n. 1).

10. Hunsinger, "Conversational Theology," citing *Gespräche 1964-1968*, p. 78.

11. George Hunsinger, *Disruptive Grace: Studies in the Theology of Karl Barth* (Grand Rapids: Eerdmans, 2000), p. 206 (emphasis added).

God is itself the movement of divine election in the face of which we cannot be spectators. Yet election cannot mean

> that God Himself is bound and imprisoned by it, not as though God's decree, the first step which He took, committed Him to take a corresponding second step, and the second a third. If it is true that the predestinating God not only is free but remains free, that He does not cease to make use of His freedom but continues to decide, then in the course of God's eternal deciding we have constantly to reckon with new decisions in time. . . . God continues always the Lord of all His works and ways. He is consistent with Himself. He is also consistent with the prearranged order of election and rejection. But He is always the living God. And since His life is the dynamic of that order, developments and alterations in it are always possible and do in fact take place. (*CD* II/2, pp. 186-87)

This statement in the heart of *CD* II/2 exemplifies a position Barth had already clearly stated in *CD* II/1. And this is not a position from which he departed in *CD* II/2 or anytime thereafter, as far as I am aware. It is this:

> When we ask questions about God's being, we cannot in fact leave the sphere of His action and working as it is revealed to us in His Word. God is who He is in His works. He is the same even in Himself, even before and after and over His works, and without them. They are bound to Him, but He is not bound to them. They are nothing without Him. But He is who He is without them. He is not, therefore, who He is only in His works. Yet in Himself He is not another than He is in His works. In light of what He is in His works it is no longer an open question what He is in Himself . . . there is no possibility of reckoning with the being of any other God, or with any other being of God, than that of the Father, the Son and the Holy Spirit as it is in God's revelation and in eternity. (*CD* II/1, pp. 260-61)

This is an extremely important statement because here Barth makes a number of very careful and crucial distinctions that are missing from McCormack's thinking.

First — and here both McCormack and I are in formal agreement — Barth insists that we can only know God's being in faith as we acknowledge his revelation to us in his Word and through his Spirit. In other words, we can only know the immanent Trinity on the basis of God's economic Trinitarian self-revelation. I say that we are only in formal agreement because, as we shall see later, McCormack ends up rejecting one of Barth's most important insights, an insight that strengthens Barth's assertion that God's election of us is an act of *free grace* and is neither necessitated by nor constitutive of his being as triune.

Second, Barth claims that God is none other than who he is from all eternity in his works *ad extra* as Creator, Reconciler, and Redeemer. Here, too, I think that McCormack and I would be in formal agreement. But Barth also insists that God is the same triune God "in Himself" and therefore "before and after and over his works," yet also "without them." Since election is the beginning of God's ways and works *ad extra*, Barth is clearly stating that God would be the same triune God he was and is with or without deciding to act outside of himself. McCormack certainly does not agree with this. In his depiction of God's pre-temporal existence, Barth emphasizes that God

> need not have done this [established fellowship with us]. For He could have done without it, because He is who He is before it and without it. For the very same reason, of course, He need not do without it, but can have it as a reality in His sight without owing it to us or to Himself. . . . He did in fact choose not to be without us. (*CD* II/1, pp. 621-22)

Third, Barth declares that God is freely bound to his works *ad extra*. His choice to act as Creator, Reconciler, and Redeemer does not constrain him but expresses his free love of another. As with the previous point, here McCormack and I begin to move in different directions because, while McCormack insists that God is free, he believes that election is an eternal decision in the sense that it has "never not taken place." No doubt he attempts to clarify what this means without seeming to imply that God in any sense needs the world and us. But, toward the end of this chapter, I hope to show that his very explanation demonstrates that Barth's concept of God's freedom as just expressed is methodically excluded from McCormack's proposal. The result is that McCormack does not in reality respect God's freedom as Barth understands it. We will come to this in due course; for now this statement will have to stand on its own — without further commentary.

Fourth, God is the triune God with or without his works *ad extra;* in no sense and at no time does God's triunity depend on his relationship with us. It is the other way around. We are completely dependent on him to have existence and life and indeed to have the eternal life promised to us in Christ himself. As I have already noted, while McCormack would certainly agree that God is never dependent on us in any way, he rejects the idea that God could be triune without election, since it is in election that God determines to be triune in the first place. We will explore this in more detail shortly. But here I will simply note that, if God's triunity is thought to result from his determination to be God for us, then it is my contention that the immanent Trinity has already been collapsed into the economic Trinity and God's freedom is in fact compromised.

Fifth, God is not someone or something other than the eternal Father, Son, and Holy Spirit who loves in freedom in his actions for us within history. Or, to put it another way, the economic Trinity is indeed the immanent Trinity — the economic and immanent Trinity being identical in content. Again, McCormack and I agree formally on this point. But materially, it is my contention that the immanent Trinity in reality would be reduced to the economic Trinity if election and the Trinity were to be logically reversed.

Sixth, in light of God's decision to elect us in his Son, Jesus Christ, as his covenant partners, Barth insists that it is not an open question who God is: he is who he is in eternity as Father, Son, and Spirit, and he is none other than this same triune God acting within history in his Word and Spirit. In eternity and in revelation God is not another God. And if we keep to the revelation of God in Jesus Christ, then we will see that any other God is not really God at all. In all six of these crucial points I think it is easy to see that Barth's thinking does not equate election and God's triunity in such a way that his choice to relate with us in his Son Jesus Christ makes him to be the triune God. Rather, it is his eternal free existence as the triune God that is the basis of his knowledge and will and thus his choice to create, reconcile, and redeem us in Jesus Christ and through his Holy Spirit.

## II. Consequences of McCormack's Proposal

In light of this discussion, and before elaborating on some specifics of Barth's doctrine of election and how it relates to the Trinity, let us pause to consider the five logical consequences that follow McCormack's proposal. As noted at the outset of this discussion, McCormack says, "Barth made *Jesus Christ* (rather than the 'eternal Logos') to be the electing God, i.e., the 'subject of election.'" Now, McCormack clearly would wish to eschew any hint of Nestorianism, as he makes plain when he says that he rejects the idea that suffering is to be predicated only of Christ's humanity. This is a notion that he rightly says follows from thinking that advances only God's impassibility. Nonetheless, the above remark has a Nestorian ring to it. In the relevant passages of *CD* II/2, Barth never thinks of Jesus Christ *rather than* the eternal Logos as the subject of election, but of Jesus Christ *as* the eternal Logos. Barth clearly expresses this himself in *CD* IV/2 when he writes: "The mystery of Jesus, the Son of Man, is that He is primarily the Son of God the Father, and as such Himself God and then, and as such, also the Son of Man" (*CD* IV/2, p. 347). McCormack first wants to say by this that there is no mode of being in the Trinity prior to or above "the eternal act of Self-determination in which God 'constitutes' Himself as 'God for us' . . . the Logos appears already in the immanent Trinity as the Logos *incarnandus.*" In other words, "the Father never had regard for the Son apart from the humanity 'to be assumed.'"[12]

Now, there is a difference between this way of putting the matter and what, for example, Barth actually says:

> In the beginning with God, i.e., in the resolve of God which precedes the existence, the possibility and the reality of all His creatures, the very first thing is the decree whose realisation means and is Jesus Christ. . . . It is the Son of God in His whole giving of Himself to the Son of Man, and the Son of Man in his utter oneness with the Son of God. This is the covenant of grace which is perfected and sealed in the power of God's free love . . . this decree is really the first of all things. It is the decision between God and the reality distinct from Himself. (*CD* II/2, p. 157)

With regard to McCormack's first point, I should note that Barth never thinks of Jesus Christ "*rather than* the eternal Logos," because for him predestination has a double reference: (1) to the elector and (2) to the elected, that is, to Jesus Christ as "very God and very man." For Barth, then, election refers to the fact that Jesus Christ "is the electing God and that He is also elected man" (*CD* II/2, p. 103). Barth claims that even as God, Jesus Christ is elected, though as Son he has no need of special election. Nonetheless, he is the Son of God who is elected in his oneness with us. Barth rejects Thomas Aquinas's restricting election to Christ's human nature, but nevertheless notes that, "[o]f course, the fact that Jesus Christ is the

12. McCormack, "Seek God," p. 66, 68.

Son of God does not rest on election" (*CD* II/2, p. 107). "Between the eternal Godhead of Christ which needs no election and His elected humanity" says Barth, "there is a third possibility which was overlooked by Thomas. And that is the being of Christ in the beginning with God . . . the covenant which God made with Himself and which is for that reason eternal, the oath which God swore by Himself in the interests of man" (*CD* II/2, p. 107).

This is an important point, because Barth is saying two things here: (1) election as the beginning of God's ways and works *ad extra* is first an eternal decision or oath the triune God made in himself in pre-temporal eternity; (2) Jesus Christ as God and as human was in the beginning because all that God was to do following his eternal "oath" he was to do in and through Jesus Christ himself, who was to become incarnate for the reconciliation and redemption of the world. So Barth insists that the Son of God, too, is an active subject of predestination *as* the Son of man — he himself, as Barth says, being the electing God. He is voluntarily obedient to the Father and in that way exists as the Son of man by fulfilling the will of God. If we were to follow Thomas, Barth says, we would only know about the election of the man Jesus; we would not know about the electing of the Son of God, "which precedes this election" (*CD* II/2, p. 107). Barth claims that this would detach election from the person of Jesus Christ. So it is crucial, in Barth's estimation, that when Jesus Christ is seen as the subject of predestination or election, he is seen as the divine/human person that he is. This enables Barth to uphold his assertion that God's election is free: "Without any obligation, God has put Himself under an obligation to man, willing that that should be so which according to Jn. 1:1-2 actually is so. It is grace that it is so, and it is grace that God willed it to be so" (*CD* II/ 2, p. 101).

### 1. Indeterminacy and Jesus Christ "in the Beginning"

What does Barth mean by "in the beginning"? Does he mean that God was indeterminate before deciding to relate to us in his incarnate Son Jesus Christ? Does he mean that God was not always — that is, from eternity to eternity — the triune God, the Father, Son, and Holy Spirit? He says that "in the beginning" describes God "before time and space as we know them, before creation, before there was any reality distinct from God which could be the object of the love of God" (*CD*, II/2, p. 101). This could reasonably be taken to refer to what Barth describes as God's pre-temporal eternity in *CD* II/1 (described above). Clearly, Barth is thinking all along the line here about how and what God determined with respect to his dealings with a reality distinct from himself. In other words, Barth is thinking of the beginning of God's ways and works *ad extra* and how that relates to what will be his historical existence as the incarnate Word in Jesus himself. So Barth writes: "God anticipated and determined within Himself (in the power of His love and freedom, of His knowing and willing) that the goal and meaning of all His dealings with the as yet non-existent universe should be the fact that in His Son He would be gracious towards man, uniting Himself with him" (*CD* II/2, p. 101). Quite obviously, Barth has in mind the fact that all of God's actions *ad extra* are based in and related to his determination to become incarnate in the man Jesus in order to found, maintain, and fulfill his covenant of grace. So Barth can say:

> In the beginning it was the resolve of the Holy Spirit that the unity of God, of Father and Son should not be disturbed or rent by this covenant with man, but that it should be made the more glorious, the deity of God, the divinity of His love and freedom, being confirmed and demonstrated by this offering of the Father and this self-offering of the Son. (*CD* II/2, pp. 101-2)

It is quite obvious that Barth is thinking of the knowing, willing, and loving of the eternal Father, Son, and Holy Spirit and not of some indeterminate "God." In fact, it is just at this point that Barth makes a crucial distinction that is missing from McCormack's proposal concerning Jesus Christ as the subject of election. Barth writes: "As the subject and object of this choice, Jesus Christ was at the beginning." But, importantly, he adds: "He was not at the beginning of God, for God has indeed no beginning." And he continues: "But He was at the beginning of all things, at the beginning of God's dealings with the reality which is distinct from Himself" (*CD* II/2, p. 102). Barth's thinking could not be clearer. He most certainly has not substituted for "God" some indeterminate reality at this point in the *Dogmatics*. He is thinking of the one who loves in freedom, the eternal Father, Son, and Holy Spirit — and none other. And he insists that this God, who has no beginning, decides at the beginning of his movement *ad extra* in love and freedom to be God for us. Hence Jesus Christ, truly divine and truly human, makes his appearance as the one in whom all subsequent divine-human relationships will have their basis, meaning, and goal.

What is perhaps most significant here is that Barth does not say that God's decision for the covenant is the "ground" of his triunity. So he does not say what McCormack takes to be the most significant point of asserting that Jesus Christ is the subject of election. Nor was the fact that Jesus Christ is the subject of election, for Barth, a warrant to assert that God's being before election was indeterminate or after to assert that God's free election of grace was the "ground" of his triunity. Rather, as is clearly evident in what he says here, Barth is declaring that the triune God, who has no beginning, freely decided to include us in fellowship with himself at the beginning of his ways and works *ad extra*. Indeed, this is an expression of his inner and outer freedom to be glorious as the God who loves freely by placing himself under an obligation to us. Far from having God's freedom lead back to a classical metaphysics, Barth clearly has in mind the fact that God incarnate would be the God who would suffer and die on our behalf in order to fulfill the covenant of grace out of love for us.

## 2. The Father and the Humanity of the Son

With regard to McCormack's second point, namely, that the Father never had regard to the Son apart from the humanity to be assumed, I believe there lurks an incipient tendency to collapse God's eternal being as Father, Son, and Spirit before creation (to which we are not privy, but which nonetheless existed) into his eternal oath to be God for us.[13] And this is the beginning of a collapse of the immanent into the economic Trinity. Barth himself very carefully notes the following:

> We must guard against disputing the eternal will of God which precedes even predestination. We must not allow God to be submerged in His relationship to the universe or think of Him as tied in Himself to the universe. Under the concept of predestination, or the election of grace, we say that in freedom (its affirmation and not its loss) God tied Himself to the universe. Under the concept of predestination we confess the eternal will of the God who is free in Himself, even in the sense

13. See, e.g., my discussion of the important point, emphasized by both Barth and T. F. Torrance, that we cannot explain *how* God is triune any more than we can delimit Father, Son, and Holy Spirit from one another, and how this features in Barth's understanding of God in relation to us, in my earlier essay in this volume, "The Trinity, Election and God's Ontological Freedom: A Response to Kevin W. Hector," pp. 50ff. above.

that originally and properly He wills and affirms and confirms himself. (*CD* II/2, p. 155)[14]

I cannot see how McCormack's thinking here allows for a will of God that precedes his predestination. And I think this is the nub of the issue between us. That does not make this a simple issue; nor does it mean that it can be solved simply. Nor does it make it an unimportant issue. I think this is an extremely significant concern because it is at this point that God's actual freedom must be seen and acknowledged, or else God will become little more than a function of his actions *ad extra*. Put another way, we have here the locus in the doctrine of God where the freedom of God is either seen and respected or overlooked and subverted.[15]

14. This thinking is completely consistent with Barth's earlier thinking when he wrote: "God is not swallowed up in the relation and attitude of Himself to the world and us as actualised in His revelation . . . while He reveals Himself in them [his works], He remains at the same time superior to them" (*CD* II/1, p. 260).

15. It may very well be that McCormack cannot and does not want to allow for a will of God that precedes his predestination just because he equated election and God's triunity by conflating them into a single act. This is certainly the erroneous picture offered by Matthias Gockel, *Barth and Schleiermacher on the Doctrine of Election: A Systematic-Theological Comparison* (New York: Oxford University Press, 2006), p. 180, n. 85, when he argues that Barth actually intended to say that God's actions *ad extra* should be seen (with McCormack) as the ground of the Trinitarian processions *ad intra*. He claims that neither he nor McCormack would disagree with my assertion that "election is a decision of the living God, and thus, while it is irreversible, once made, it still was freely made" (Paul D. Molnar, *Divine Freedom and the Doctrine of the Immanent Trinity: In Dialogue with Karl Barth and Contemporary Theology* [London: T. & T. Clark/Continuum, 2002], p. 64), but that when I say that "God's being is not the result of his will. Rather his will to elect expresses his freedom to be God in a new way as God for us. . . . But none of this is required by his essence" (*Divine Freedom*, p. 63). I have "separated triunity from election, God's being in Himself and God's being for us, which is the very opposite of what Barth intended" (Gockel, *Barth and Schleiermacher*, p. 180, n. 85). Here he has missed the point that I make in my book: that the immanent and economic Trinity could neither be confused nor separated in Barth's thinking. And clearly what I mean in the passage quoted here by Gockel is that one could not argue that God's will to be God for us (election) was the basis of his triunity, because God could indeed be the triune God without us but freely chose not to. God's eternal election does indeed belong to God's eternal essence, but as an act that is "eternally contingent" and not "eternally necessary," as I argue in my earlier essay in this volume; see pp. 51, 46, and 61 above. Neither Gockel nor McCormack is able to make the distinction between the immanent and economic Trinity for which Barth consistently argued at this very point in their thinking precisely because they directly equate election and God's triunity, *Logos asarkos* and *Logos incarnandus* in such a way that God's triunity is subsumed in election and collapsed into the *Logos incarnandus*. Strangely, Gockel claims that Barth wants to maintain "an odd distinc-

### 3. Logos asarkos *and* Logos incarnandus

Let me make this point another way by presenting what Barth says in *CD* IV/1. There Barth claims that who God is as the eternal Logos is not revealed to us. But it is my contention that this does not mean, as McCormack believes, that Barth is here advancing the idea of an indeterminate Godhead behind the God revealed in Jesus Christ and that his thinking is thus inconsistent with his position explicated in *CD* II/2. Here are Barth's words:

> In this context we must not refer to the second "person" of the Trinity as such, to the eternal Son or the eternal Word of God *in abstracto,* and therefore to the so-called λόγος ἄσαρκος. . . . The second "person" of the Godhead in Himself and as such is not God the Reconciler. In Himself and as such He is not revealed to us. In Himself and as such He is not *Deus pro nobis,* either ontologically or epistemologically. He is the content of a necessary and important concept in trinitarian doctrine when we have to understand the revelation and dealings of God in the light of their free basis in the inner being and essence of God. But since we are now concerned with the revelation and dealings of God, and particularly with the atonement, with the person and work of the Mediator, it is pointless, as it is impermissible, to return to the inner being and essence of God and especially to the second person of the Trinity as such, in such a way that we ascribe to this person another form than that which God Himself has given in willing to reveal Himself and to act outwards. (*CD* IV/1, p. 52)

---

tion in God's self-determination" (Gockel, *Barth and Schleiermacher,* p. 179) with his belief that God's will preceded his predestination. But it is not odd at all; it represents Barth's conceptual acknowledgment that God's decisions for us are free and not necessitated by his being or by any external constraints. Here Gockel and McCormack have concocted a conflict in Barth's thought where one does not really exist, if one makes a clear and sharp distinction between the immanent and economic Trinity (without separation), as Barth clearly wished to do here. If Gockel could make this conceptual distinction, he would see that my objection to McCormack's statement that "if election is an eternal decision, then it has never not taken place" is not a reference to the immanent Trinity as such but to an eternally contingent decision on the part of the immanent Trinity to act economically as God for us in his Word and Spirit. Therefore, my objection to what McCormack says could not equally well be applied to the patristic idea of an eternal generation or procession, as Gockel argues, unless one had already confused the immanent and economic Trinity (Gockel, *Barth and Schleiermacher,* p. 179, n. 81).

It is extremely noteworthy, I think, that McCormack finds Barth's claim completely unacceptable that there is any context at all in which it would be acceptable to refer to the second "person" of the Trinity as such, that is, to a *Logos asarkos* who is not already identical with the *Logos incarnandus* without remainder. In McCormack's words: "What context could there possibly be which would justify speaking in this way?" McCormack would have been willing to assume that Barth perhaps had suffered "a lapse in concentration" by referring to "this context" in which we must not return to the second person of the Trinity as such. But since Barth proceeds to declare that this concept is necessary and important in Trinitarian doctrine, McCormack concludes:

> Barth either did not fully realize the profound implications of his doctrine of election for the doctrine of the Trinity, or he shied away from drawing them for reasons known only to himself. Either way, in what follows I am going to register a critical correction against Barth, the goal of which will be to remove what I view as an inconsistency in Barth's thought.[16]

That is the question. Was Barth inconsistent here, or was he quite consistent in maintaining that God's actions *ad extra*, including the beginning of God's ways and works *ad extra*, were freely determined as actions of the triune God and not actions that "constituted" God's triunity? McCormack here insists that Barth's refusal to speculate on a "free floating" concept of the Son who is not already and always the *Logos incarnandus* requires us to "see the triunity of God logically as a function of divine election."[17] But why should that be the case when it is soteriology and not logic that should dictate our understanding here? When anyone wishes to explain the relationship between election and the Trinity logically, does that desire in itself and as such not mean that Barth's own warning has been violated? What is that warning? It is this. With regard to the error of Protestant orthodoxy that began its doctrine of God elsewhere than with the revelation of God in Jesus Christ, Barth warns: "[W]ith a surprisingly common thoughtlessness it was usual to begin by deducing the doctrine of the Trinity — theoretically maintained to be the basis of all theology — from the premises of formal logic" (*CD* II/1, p. 261). In other words, to think of the Trinity as constituted by God's decision to be for us in Jesus Christ is nothing less

16. McCormack, "Grace and Being," p. 102.
17. McCormack, "Grace and Being," p. 103.

than to deduce the Trinity from the logic that places election prior to Trinity or equates them as one and the same act.

If we analyze carefully what Barth actually says in the long statement (from *CD* IV/1, p. 52, just cited), it is clear that he is saying that God has his life as Father, Son, and Holy Spirit in such a way that it cannot be reduced to his decision to be God for us. He is who he is in that decision; therefore, we cannot go behind his decision to a *decretum absolutum,* because Jesus Christ himself is that decree.[18] But he also has a life and a will "before" predestination, according to Barth, as we have seen. And if we dispute that, as we must if we claim that God's triunity and election can or should be logically reversed, then, according to Barth, we run the risk of reducing God's eternal being as triune to a function of his decisions to act *ad extra* and his subsequent actions *ad extra.* Instead of firmly grounding God's actions for us in divine freedom, as Barth clearly wished to do, any such thinking would in reality make God a prisoner of his electing to be God-for-us. So it seems clear to me that when Barth says that in the context of the doctrine of reconciliation we must not return to a *Logos asarkos,* he means that we cannot go back behind the fact that God actually has decided to be God for us. This is a divinely established fact that cannot be ignored or contested without changing the whole meaning of reconciliation and redemption. And so a retreat to some God prior to this or behind this when we consider reconciliation and redemption actually amounts to the construction of a God other than the God revealed and active in the history of Jesus Christ. Of course, this is the positive point that McCormack wants to emphasize but that he actually undermines by arguing for a logical reversal of the doctrines.

When Barth says that the Son, in himself and as such, is not revealed to us and is not God for us either ontologically or epistemologically, that is exactly his attempt to distinguish between the immanent and economic Trinity — not materially, of course, since it is the triune God who exists in pre-temporal eternity and again for us in time and history and post-temporally. Rather he wishes to make a heuristic distinction.

---

18. This was one of Barth's key reasons for saying that Jesus Christ is the subject of election in *CD* II/2, pp. 100ff. Barth wanted to stress that God's determination to be God for us is the determination of the triune God and not some hidden determination of an indeterminate being decreeing absolutely the salvation of some and damnation of others abstractly and without reference to the name of Jesus Christ, in whom God is *for* us and not against us. What he is against is our sinful being only in order to free us to live as those created and sanctified for him in Jesus Christ, the incarnate Word.

We cannot, then, attribute to this whole distinction between God in Himself and God in His relation to the world an essential, but only a heuristic, significance. It does, of course, have this significance. That God is both knowable and unknowable to us, the One who loves and the One who is free, becomes actually clear to us in this distinction. Neither of the two aspects is self-explanatory. Neither can be simply assumed. Both must become clear to us. The truth of both becomes manifest in the event of revelation in which God makes the transition from there to here, from His being in Himself to His being in fellowship with us, thus disclosing the truth of both these aspects, not in the form of a separation but of a distinction, as the same thing in distinguishable forms. By this distinction in God of His being in Himself and for us, as it is brought out in the event of revelation, the distinction between His love and His freedom can and must become clear to us; His love in that God as He is in Himself wills also to be God for us, His freedom in that He will and can be for us no other than as He is in Himself. (*CD* II/1, pp. 345-46)

Barth's statement here is parallel to the statements about God's freedom and love he makes in *CD* I/1. Barth insisted, against Gogarten, that "God for us" would not have its proper meaning "if it were not said against the background of 'God in Himself.'" As "unmerited and free," God's love for us must always be discussed against the background of God in himself. In the same way,

the Word of God is properly understood only as a word which has truth and glory in itself and not just as spoken to us. *It would be no less God's eternal Word if it were not spoken to us,* and what constitutes the mercy of its revelation, of its being spoken to us, is that it is spoken to us in virtue of the freedom in which God could be "God in Himself" and yet He does not will to be so and in fact is not so, but wills to be and actually is "God for us." (*CD* I/1, pp. 171-72, emphasis added)

A sharp distinction between the immanent and economic Trinity follows: "'God for us' does not arise as a matter of course out of the 'God in Himself' . . . it is true as an act of God, as a step which God takes towards man and by which man becomes the man that participates in His revelation." Our human becoming is conditioned by God, but God

is not conditioned from without, by man. For this reason — and we agree with Gogarten here — theology cannot speak of man in himself, in isolation from God. But as in the strict doctrine of the Trinity as the presupposition of Christology, it must speak of God in Himself, in isolation from man. We know ourselves only as those addressed by God's Word, but precisely as those addressed by God's Word we must know God as the One who addresses us in freedom, as the Lord, *who does not exist only as He addresses us,* but exists as the One who establishes and ratifies this relation and correlation, *who is also God before it, in Himself, in His eternal history. (CD* I/1, p. 172, emphasis added)

Clearly, Barth is not arguing here for an indeterminate deity behind the God revealed in Jesus Christ. But he is not equating God's eternal triune existence with his decision to be God-for-us either. What he is saying is that the God who is for us has his life in himself and acts for us in freedom. That is the positive freedom in which he determines to be for us but is under no inner or outer constraints in loving us or even in continuing to love us.

In Barth's doctrine of election, then, we are speaking of God's electing himself and us and of the fact that our relationship with God in Christ is grounded indisputably within the very being and will of God; more precisely, our relationship with God is grounded in his knowledge and will together. We cannot get beyond this decision any more than we can or should get beyond the economic Trinity to understand the immanent Trinity. But that does not mean that Barth equates the whole of the Trinitarian being of God with election. Once again, that is why he insists that we must guard against disputing God's will before predestination.

### 4. Omnipotence/Omnicausality — Being and Will: Distinguishing God's Acts ad intra *and* ad extra

By comparison, McCormack argues that "the eternal act in which God gives to Himself His own being as Father, Son and Holy Spirit and the eternal act in which God chooses to be God in the covenant of grace with human beings is *one and the same act.* These are not two acts but one."[19] This statement quite obviously ignores Barth's own careful distinction when he says the following: "There is, for example, the distinction between His willing of Himself and His willing of the possibility and reality of His creation as distinct from Himself" (*CD* II/1, p. 590). This comes in the context of

19. McCormack, "Seek God," p. 66.

Barth's discussion of God's omnipotence, which he insists cannot be reduced to his omnicausality. I have discussed this in detail elsewhere.[20] Here I will only note that, for Barth, it was imperative that God's omnipotence not be reduced to his omnicausality, as it would be if we did not acknowledge that God remains free and independent of the world even as he is deeply involved in it in his Word and Spirit.

> Absolutely everything depends on whether we know God as the One who is omnipotent in Himself. . . . Absolutely everything depends on whether we distinguish His omnipotence from His omnicausality: not to the glory of an unknown omnipotent being who is beyond and behind His work; but to the glory of the omnipotent God who is present to us in His work . . . to the glory of His divinity, of the freedom of His love, without which His love would not be divine love or recognisable as such. (*CD* II/1, p. 528)

With regard to McCormack's assertion that God's decision to be triune and to be God for us is one and the same act, we may note the following. First, it is problematic to say that God gives himself his own being as Father, Son, and Holy Spirit. This statement suggests to me that God was in fact "indeterminate" as God and only then became triune by giving himself his being as triune as a result of an act of will. I believe that what McCormack is espousing is reminiscent of the position of Hermann Schell, which Barth rightly rejects in *CD* II/1. Barth insists, referring to Jerome's statement that *Deus est causa sui*, that God cannot be the cause of himself because he cannot be both *causa* and *causatum*, but only *causa*.

> Therefore "aseity" cannot in any sense be interpreted as God's act of self-realisation. . . . The God who takes His origin from Himself or is *constituted* by Himself is in a certain sense limited by the possibility of His non-being and therefore He is not the free God. (*CD* II/1, p. 305, emphasis added)[21]

20. Molnar, "The Trinity, Election and God's Ontological Freedom," pp. 49-50, 56, 61-62 above.

21. Barth clarifies his view of God's being and will by relying on Thomas: "Thomas Aquinas . . . borrowing from Hilary . . . then explains that the begetting of the Son is certainly to be understood as an act of divine will, but only as the act of will in which *Deus vult se esse Deum*, as the act of will in which God, in freedom of course, wills Himself and in virtue of this will of His is Himself. In this sense, identically indeed with God's being Himself, the begetting of the Son is also an ἔργον θελήσεως, for here θελήσεως and φύσις are one and

Barth, of course, notes Schell's positive intentions, which were to avoid thinking of God as the unmoved mover of Aristotle and to speak of God as active in his inner life and his actions *ad extra*. Barth is very cautious in his use of the expression "self-realization" with respect to God; he rejects it as applying to the Father and then to the processions if it implies that God takes his origin from himself. God's being does not need origination, "not even an origination from itself," Barth insists. And this is the key. He then concludes:

> The freedom in which God exists means that He does not need His own being in order to be who He is: because He already has His own being and is Himself . . . this being does not need any origination and *constitution*. He cannot 'need' His own being because He affirms it in being who He is. (*CD* II/1, p. 306, emphasis added)

This is the primary meaning of God's freedom, as I assert it in my book. McCormack does not seem to grasp this, since he claims I am maintaining God's freedom in the classical sense merely as God's independence of creation. This is incorrect. I am following Barth, who insists that God's independence of creation is not to be equated with God's freedom because God's freedom is his positive freedom to be self-moved; God is the only self-moved being (*CD* II/1, pp. 268f.). God's independence of everything that is not God is seen only in the exercise of his positive freedom. Therefore, the second meaning of God's freedom is freedom from conditioning from without. But I carefully follow Barth in insisting that, while "in every way He is independent of all other reality," that "does not in itself constitute God's freedom but its exercise" (*CD* II/1, p. 308). This is important, but it cannot come first, because God is first free in himself. Hence, in my book I do not drive a wedge between God's being and will, and I certainly

---

the same. But the begetting of the Son is not an act of the divine will to the degree that freedom to will this or that is expressed in the concept of will. God has this freedom in respect of creation — He is free to will it or not to will it — and creation is thus an ἔργον θελήσεως. But He does not have this freedom with respect to His being God. God cannot not be God. Therefore — and this is the same thing — He cannot not be Father and cannot be without the Son. His freedom or aseity with respect to Himself consists in His freedom, not determined by anything but Himself, to be God, and that means to be the Father of the Son. A freedom to be able not to be this would be an abrogation of His freedom. Thus the begetting of the Son is an ἔργον φύσεως. It could not not happen just as God could not not be God, whereas creation is an ἔργον θελήσεως in the sense that it could also not happen and yet God would not on that account be any the less God" (*CD* I/1, p. 434).

do not suggest, as McCormack does, that God's triunity is the result of his willing to be God-for-us, but insist that God is God as one who knows and wills *in se* and *ad extra*, but as the God who is not subject to any need, as Barth maintains (see *CD* II/1, pp. 306-7).

Because Barth refuses to collapse God's omnipotence and omnipresence into his omnicausality, he also insists — in a way that McCormack does not — that "God's will is in all things as His eternal living act, and it is wholly and utterly free in itself. In this it is true and genuine and proper will" (*CD* II/1, p. 587). Consequently, for Barth, "God is not compelled to do what He does. Nor is He forced to any of the apparent consequences of His action. On the contrary, He does what He does because He wills it. And when He does it again, again it is because he wills it" (*CD* II/1, pp. 588-89). Perhaps more importantly, Barth says: "God wills in a genuine and proper sense because He is what He is and therefore omnipotent in this differentiation" (*CD* II/1, p. 590). Note that there is no hint in Barth's thought that God's triunity results from his act of will. Rather, God's will, like his knowledge, is an act of the triune God that expresses the kind of God he is as one who loves in freedom. And it is also clear that, for Barth, God's willing himself and his willing us are *two distinct actions* of the one eternal God and cannot be equated, as McCormack does. This is so important that Barth's words bear repeating: "There is, for example, the distinction between His willing of Himself and His willing of the possibility and reality of His creation as distinct from Himself" (*CD* II/1, p. 590). This includes his decrees, according to Barth, and the latter claims that because God is one who knows and wills, "what God knows He wills, and what He wills He knows," so that "He is not conditioned in any of these spheres, but He Himself conditions" (*CD* II/1, p. 590). Here Barth makes the very distinction that I wish to make (and did make in my earlier article), adopting categories helpfully suggested by George Hunsinger about what is "eternally necessary" and what is "eternally contingent."

> It is natural or necessary for God to will Himself and in Himself the basis and standard of everything else. But He wills freely the possibility and reality of everything else. This distinction may be allowed to stand as an instructive one, provided we add that the will of God is free even in His necessity to will Himself, and necessary even in His freedom to will everything else, so that the *non posse non velle* is determined by His will and the *posse non velle* is rejected by His will. The distinction concerns the ontological side of the problem. It differentiates between God

as the sovereign Subject of all His works and God in the effecting of all these works of His. This differentiation is necessary if God's omnipotence is to be understood as the omnipotence of His will. (*CD* II/1, p. 591)

And, perhaps most importantly with regard to this discussion, Barth insists, in a way that McCormack does not, that God's will is a free decision:

It is the will of His own good-pleasure, His own will in His works, which as such and in itself cannot be the object of any other knowledge but its own. If this hidden nature is not true of it, it is not a true and genuine will. For there is will only where there is the mystery of freedom in which a subject decides on its act in a way that is known only to itself in the first instance, before the decision is actually carried out. Now while the mystery of creaturely freedom of will in our actions is no mystery to God, the divine freedom of will is always an absolute and quite impenetrable mystery for all knowledge which is distinct from God's knowledge, and therefore for all creaturely knowledge when it is face to face with the works of God. But this hidden will of God is revealed to us by Himself. . . . What man cannot know by himself, what he has not deserved to be able to know, what he has no claim on God to know, God did and does really permit him to know. He reveals to him His own will. . . . (*CD* II/1, p. 591)

While McCormack and I agree that God is the Lord over his being and essence, we do not agree about two crucial ideas. First, God's self-determination to be God for us is a distinct and new action on God's part as the beginning of his ways and works *ad extra*. Therefore, we have two acts of God here and not just one. Second, God's triunity is certainly not the result of his will to elect us. Nor is it the result of his will in the sense that he might have willed not to be triune. Rather, his will expresses who he is and who he wills to be as the eternal Father, Son, and Holy Spirit. This leads to a vital third logical implication of McCormack's position, namely, his idea that "the triunity of God is a function of the divine election." McCormack insists that neither precedes the other "chronologically"; still, "it is God's act of determining Himself to be God for us in Jesus Christ which constitutes God as triune."[22] This idea, understood logically and not chronologi-

---

22. McCormack, "Seek God," p. 67 (hereafter, page references to this essay appear in parentheses in the text).

cally, represents, as I have shown in this chapter, precisely the confusion of the immanent and economic Trinity that Barth sought to avoid by ordering the doctrines and placing the Trinity first and election second. What McCormack rightly wants to emphasize is that God is who he is in his actions *ad extra* and therefore in his actions for us within history.

In other words, there is a genuine divine supra-temporality, to use Barth's categories. There is no God hidden behind this God, who is for us in his love and freedom. But I believe it is a serious mistake to speak, as McCormack does, of the "'Father' as the subject who gives himself his own being in the act of election" (p. 67). From all that Barth says about the doctrine of election, it is clear that he does not mean to suggest that the Father gives himself his own being when he decides to act *ad extra*. As I have shown above, God already and always existed and exists as Father, Son, and Holy Spirit and decided to be God for us in his Word and Spirit. In reality, there would be no God to decide for us if God the Father had to give himself his own being in electing us. In addition, the very idea that the Father as subject gives himself his own being either within the immanent Trinity or in his economic activity has a modalistic and subordinationist tinge to it that is absent from Barth's thinking. For Barth, God is not first Father and then triune as a result of his acts of will. Rather, God is eternally and simultaneously Father, Son, and Spirit, who knows and wills himself in himself and for us. Furthermore, McCormack maintains that "there is no difference in content between the immanent and economic Trinity" (p. 67). As I have noted above, I agree completely with this. I also agree that "[t]he *Logos incarnandus* is both *asarkos* (because not yet embodied) and *ensarkos* (by way of anticipation, on the basis of God's self-determination in the act of electing); the *Logos incarnatus* is both *asarkos* (the so-called 'extra-Calvinisticum') and *ensarkos* (having become embodied)" (pp. 67-68). But I do not agree that the *Logos asarkos* can be equated with the *Logos incarnandus* without remainder, as I have explained above in detail. And that is the main point of McCormack's proposal.

## III. Indeterminacy and God's Triunity: Time and Eternity

Before closing, let me very briefly consider a point I raised earlier, which I have postponed until now. If God gives himself his being in the event in which he determines to be God for us, how exactly can God be free, that is, free in himself as the only self-moved being and free for us without being constrained to be for us by his need to become Father, Son, and Spirit by choosing to act *ad extra*? Moreover, how can one avoid implying that, before God determined to be triune, he was actually indeterminate? McCormack maintains that, classically, theologians always asserted God's freedom by holding that God existed independently as "pure being" and therefore in a "wholly timeless mode of existence" (p. 74). And he says that the doctrine of the Trinity was simply added to this. This leads to the idea that God's triunity was the triunity that existed in and for itself in eternity — "above all relation to the world." When God "steps out of this mode of 'pure being' and determines to be God in the covenant, this is an utterly free act because God was 'already' perfectly realized and fulfilled being" (p. 74). The price paid for this thinking, McCormack believes, is that God was conceived as impassible and thus removed from suffering.

As I have noted above, McCormack thinks I have adopted this classical view of the divine freedom in my book *Divine Freedom*, because I said that Barth believed God would exist as Father, Son, and Holy Spirit even if there had been no creation, reconciliation, or redemption (p. 76). But nothing could be further from the truth. I have repeatedly indicated, as I have in this article, that the freedom I have in mind is the freedom characterized by Barth in *CD* II/1, namely, that God is free in himself as the living God who loves in freedom and who is none other than the eternal Father, Son, and Holy Spirit. This God is the only self-moved being and thus one who is free irrespective of his relations *ad extra*. He is free, then, to place himself under an obligation to us by loving us without losing his freedom, but exercising it for our benefit as one who elects himself to suffering and judgment in our place. In other words, God's omnipotence cannot be reduced to his omnicausality. That is not the issue here at all. The problem is that McCormack has equated God's determination to "constitute" himself as triune with his decision for the covenant of grace. This represents the collapse of the immanent into the economic Trinity that Barth consistently attempted to avoid and did indeed, for the most part, avoid.

McCormack thinks that when I read his *Cambridge Companion* essay, in which he says, "If election is an eternal decision, then it has never not taken place" to mean that it has "always taken place," I made the mistake of reading this logically. This, he says, is not what he meant to say, even though the whole sense of his argument rests on the logical point that election and Trinity need to be reversed! McCormack claims that these two statements do not mean the same thing materially, because materially what he intended to say was that "the election of the human race (as the internal ground of creation) is, in fact, the act which *founds* time" (p. 75). But if election, as he understands it in its logical relation to God's triunity, is the act that *founds* time, then McCormack still has not escaped the Hegelian dilemma here, because election would have to have taken place with the same necessity with which God exists as triune. Hence God could not be triune without electing to create time and to relate with us in time. In reality, therefore, God would have no triune existence in himself without his relationship with us. That is precisely the thinking that Barth consistently and rightly rejected!

I am perfectly willing to admit that the covenant is the internal basis or ground of creation. What I reject is McCormack's belief that there could not be a "time" before the act in which God "founds" time (here, of course, it is clear that we are both speaking of created time and not of God's uniquely eternal "time"). McCormack insists that, if there is such a time, then we must conceive of God — with classical metaphysics — as "indeterminate." This is simply false, and it is based on a wholly contrived dilemma fabricated by McCormack to strengthen his misguided thesis. Barth insisted that God existed before created time and history in his pretemporal eternity, and also within time and after time, as we have already seen. That is why he could say, "Eternity is not, therefore, time, although time is certainly God's creation or, more correctly, a form of His creation" (*CD* II/1, p. 608). And Barth also says, perhaps somewhat ambiguously, "The God who does this [who creates and heals time] and therefore can do it is obviously in Himself both timeless and temporal" (*CD* II/1, p. 617). What he means, of course, is that God's unique time is his eternal existence as triune prior to our time, within our time, and after our time, since he has created it.

So Barth wants to emphasize that God is not timeless but has time in his own unique way, and yet God is not in any way conditioned by or subordinated to our time. And thus Barth could also say, "The Christian knowledge of eternity has to do directly and exclusively with God Himself, with Him as the beginning before all time, the turning point in time, and the end and goal after all time" (*CD* II/1, p. 639). Barth insists, therefore, that God's pre-temporality, supra-temporality, and post-temporality cannot be played off against each other any more than the persons of the Trinity can or should be played off against each other. Consequently, God is not bound to time as we are. While he freely binds himself to us, he remains the one who is both pre-temporal and post-temporal: "For ethics depends on its proclamation of the command of the supra-temporal God, and the only supra-temporal God is the One who is also pre-temporal and post-temporal, bound to no time, and therefore the Lord of all times" (*CD* II/1, p. 638).

McCormack mistakenly thinks that, for Barth, the relationship of eternity to time should be understood as "the relation of a founding 'moment' and all subsequent temporal moments" (pp. 75-76). But it is clear that this is not Barth's understanding at all. Eternity is God's being as simultaneously pre-temporal, supra-temporal, and post-temporal. God is the one who freely creates our time. If God's eternity is reduced to being the founding moment of all subsequent temporal moments, then God would be only the beginning of a series of moments and not the very condition of the possibility of the moments we are given as creatures. McCormack claims that because I reject his thinking here, I must accept the idea that God is timeless in the sense of "classical metaphysics." But my position is with Barth, as he expresses his here:

> God was in Himself. He was no less Himself, no less perfect, not subject to any lack, superabounding from the very first even without us and the world. This is God's eternity as pre-temporality. Always and everywhere and in every way God exists as the eternal One in the sense of this pre-temporality. (*CD* II/1, p. 621)

Yet this does not mean that God is confined to his pre-temporality. He can and does exist as God within time and after time, and we must not seek to overemphasize one or the other of these aspects of eternity any more than we should overemphasize any aspect of God's triunity, his being as Father, Son, and Holy Spirit. The positive point embedded in McCormack's proposal is that God really is God with us and before us. But McCormack has neglected this important aspect of God's eternity precisely because he directly equates election and the Trinity and thus confuses the immanent and economic Trinity.

There is one more point that needs to be made here, and it concerns the false dilemma McCormack has concocted, which suggests that either we must accept his thesis or think of God as timeless and unable to suffer for us in his Son, as did the classical theology he depicts. This is indeed ironic because, all of his protestations to the contrary notwithstanding, he is the one — and not I — who actually ends up adopting an indeterminate notion of God in order to preserve God's freedom.

The proof that McCormack himself has embraced "indeterminacy" can be seen quite clearly in his own remarks about God's freedom. He claims that a statement such as "'*God* would be God without us' is a true statement and one whose truth must be upheld at all costs if God's grace is to be truly gracious." But he then declares:

> If we were to go further and seek to specify precisely what God would be without us — as occurs, for example, when Molnar says that God would still be triune without us — then we would make ourselves guilty of the abstract metaphysical speculation which was the bane of early church theology. (p. 76)

Such speculation, McCormack insists, *must* always lead to a separation or disjunction between the immanent and economic Trinity. But here McCormack's own thinking demonstrates perfectly that he — and not I — is the one engaged in abstraction. Who else would God be but the triune God who is genuinely free in himself? McCormack claims we cannot, and must not, say who or what God is who could be God without us. And if we were to specify who this God is, we would be guilty of abstraction and of falling into the classical metaphysics he rejects. But Barth repeatedly identifies this God, as did Athanasius before him, with God who eternally exists as Father, Son, and Holy Spirit, as McCormack himself admits (p. 74, n. 32). What is more, any thinking about the being of the triune God that leaves this an open question is not only an abstraction but an open promotion of some kind of divine indeterminacy, the very thing McCormack claims to have overcome with his position on the logical relationship of election and the Trinity. Here McCormack's own thinking demonstrates that when God's freedom to be God for us is not seen against the background in which he could have been God without us but freely chose not to, it *necessarily* and *always* leads both to abstractive thinking about God's freedom and to the idea that God's choice of us is not a free choice but is necessitated either by his need for us, by the very nature of his being as triune, or by his need to become triune. That is to say, when God wills to become triune, it is only for the sake of his relationship with us.

Let me conclude this chapter where I began. I have attempted to listen carefully once more to what Bruce McCormack and Karl Barth intend to say when they state that Jesus Christ is the subject of election. And I have noted some very clear differences between the two. McCormack thinks those differences are due to an inconsistency in Barth's thought, whereas I have sought to show that Barth is not inconsistent but dialectical in emphasizing both God's love and his freedom. And I have also sought to show why I think McCormack's desire to logically reverse the doctrines of election and the Trinity is problematic from within any reasonable and thorough understanding of Barth's theology. McCormack is correct when he says that what is at stake in this debate is "the coherence of our affirmation of the full and complete deity of Jesus Christ" (p. 79). And it is toward that end that I have tried to show that the thesis of my book *Divine Freedom* was built on Barth's rejection of Ebionite and Docetic Christology, in the interest of affirming Christ's deity as "definitive, authentic and essential" (*CD* I/1, p. 400), solely on the basis of God's economic self-revelation.[23] Can Jesus' authentic deity be recognized and acknowledged if the Word of God is no longer seen as the free Word who has his life in himself irrespective of his relationship with us as Creator, Reconciler, and Redeemer? That is the question that Barth's theology poses for us all with a new urgency in this time when Hegel's thinking remains such an appealing temptation, as McCormack's thinking amply demonstrates.

23. See Molnar, *Divine Freedom*, pp. 32ff.

# 4. Election and the Trinity: Twenty-five Theses on the Theology of Karl Barth

*George Hunsinger*

How the Holy Trinity and election are related has become a hot topic in Barth studies. On the one side are the "traditionalists" (for lack of a better term), who contend that Karl Barth, throughout his *Church Dogmatics,* never changed his mind that the triune life of God was prior to the divine decision of election. On the other side is a growing tribe of "revisionists," who maintain that, for the later Barth, the situation was much the reverse in that God's pre-temporal decision of election actually gave rise to the Trinity.[1] The later Barth came to see pretemporal election as the Trinity's moment of eternal origination, according to the "revisionists," whereas the "traditionalists" argue that the Trinity remained what it had always been for Barth, namely, election's essential presupposition and ground.[2]

---

1. For the "revisionists," the driving force has been Bruce L. McCormack. In *Karl Barth's Critically Realistic Dialectical Theology* (Oxford: Clarendon, 1997), he first proposed that in 1942, Barth's doctrine of God underwent a sea change with the appearance of his doctrine of election (*Church Dogmatics,* vol. II, part 2 [Edinburgh: T. & T. Clark, 1957]). The full force of what McCormack had in mind did not start to emerge, however, until his essay "Grace and Being" appeared in *The Cambridge Companion to Karl Barth,* ed. John Webster (Cambridge: Cambridge University Press, 2000), pp. 92-110. Even so, matters still remained fairly cryptic until he stated his case more recently in "Seek God Where He May Be Found: A Response to Edwin Chr. van Driel," *Scottish Journal of Theology* 60 (2007): 62-79. The revisionist line now pops up in a growing number of younger scholars: see, e.g., Matthias Gockel, *Barth and Schleiermacher on the Doctrine of Election: A Systematic-Theological Comparison* (Oxford: Oxford University Press, 2006); see also Kevin W. Hector, "God's Triunity and Self-Determination: A Conversation with Karl Barth, Bruce McCormack and Paul Molnar," pp. 29-46 above (first published in *International Journal of Systematic Theology* 7 [2005]: 246-61).

2. Paul D. Molnar has objected vigorously to the revisionist position. In *Divine Freedom and the Doctrine of the Immanent Trinity* (Edinburgh: T. & T. Clark, 2005), he disputes what

At stake are not only some of Barth's most difficult dialectical moves, but also some of the most fundamental questions in contemporary theology. How time is related to eternity, for example, is a perennial subject that continues to divide Anselmians, Thomists, and other traditionalists — from Hegelians to process theologians to demythologizing existentialists. It is also a subject on which Barth's complex reflections are unique. A closely related matter — how God is related to the world — raises basic questions about God's sovereignty, God's aseity, and God's essential perfection. Can a God who needs the world in order to be God really be the Lord, at least as attested by Holy Scripture? Is the Trinity free to be the living God with or without the world? Similar perplexities emerge for Christology. In what sense, if any, does the incarnation presuppose the Son's eternal priority? Does the Son exist only "for us," or does he enjoy a more basic existence in the Trinity? When the Word became flesh in the incarnation, did the *Logos asarkos* disappear into the *Logos ensarkos,* or did it persist in some sense in its own right? These are questions in the debate that have a momentous bearing on every aspect of theological inquiry. Until recently, however, the revisionist proposal has not been easy to assess, because it has been long on assertion but short on details. Under pressure from the traditionalists, however, the reasoning behind the revisionists' claim has recently become more clear.

My defense of the traditionalist standpoint that follows falls into two parts. First, I argue that the passages that the revisionists appeal to do not support their case. I then suggest in part two that the revisionist proposal involves implications that fly in the face of some of Barth's most basic convictions. Since the debate is likely to continue, I have adopted a thesis format for the sake of clarity and ease of reference.

---

was then known of McCormack's view. Another important contribution was his essay "The Trinity, Election and God's Ontological Freedom: A Response to Kevin W. Hector," *International Journal of Systematic Theology* 8 (2006): 294-306. See also Molnar, "Can the Electing God Be God Without Us? Some Implications of Bruce McCormack's Understanding of Barth's Doctrine of Election for the Doctrine of the Trinity," pp. 63-90 above; and Edwin Chr. van Driel, "Karl Barth on the Eternal Existence of Jesus Christ," *Scottish Journal of Theology* 60 (2007): 45-61. In his book *The Image of the Immanent Trinity* (New York: Peter Lang, 2005), Fred Sanders suggests that the revisionist view of Barth represents a failure to think dialectically (pp. 153-54). Another theologian who would seem to belong to the "traditionalist" camp is John Webster. In *Confessing God: Essays in Christian Dogmatics II* (Edinburgh: T. & T. Clark, 2005), he maintains that God's being is Trinitarian and perfect in itself (the core traditionalist conviction). Therefore, God's relationship to the world is "not the first but a second movement" of God's being (p. 166).

## Part I

1. Barth nowhere says that God's being is *constituted* by God's act. He says only that God's being and act are inseparable. I read him to mean that act and being for God are each ontologically basic. For Barth, act is no more prior to or constitutive of God's being than the reverse. Barth does not teach — and nowhere states — that act is a consequence of being *(operari sequitur esse)*, or that being is a consequence of act *(esse sequitur operari)*. They are equally and primordially basic.[3]

2. Barth distinguishes between an act and a work. The term "work" applies only to God's relationship to the world. Creation, for example, is a work. "Act," however, is a term that pertains not only to God's relationship with the world but also to God's being in eternity in and for itself. God's being is in act — God is the living God — as Father, Son, and Holy Spirit to all eternity.

> The whole being and life of God is an activity, both in eternity and in worldly time, both in himself as Father, Son and Holy Spirit, and in his relation to the human being and all creation. (*CD* IV/1, p. 7 rev.)[4]

> There is no rigid or static being which is not also act. There is only the being of God as the Father and the Son with the Holy Spirit. . . . (*CD* IV/2, p. 345)

> . . . God as God is in himself the living God. . . . His eternal being of and by himself has not to be understood as a being which is inactive because of its pure deity, but as a being which is supremely active in a *positing* of itself which is eternally new [*in ewig neuer Setzung*]. . . . (*CD* IV/1, p. 561, emphasis added)

> The triune life of God . . . is the *basis* of his whole will and action also [*auch*] *ad extra*. . . . It is the *basis* [*ist begründet*] of his *decretum opus ad extra* . . . of the election of the human being to covenant with himself; of the determination [*Bestimmung*] of the Son to become human, and

3. I refer here (and throughout this essay) to the mature Barth, not to anything he may have written prior to 1932.

4. Karl Barth, *Church Dogmatics,* 4 vols. (Edinburgh: T. & T. Clark, 1936-1969) (hereafter, volume, part, and page references to the *CD* appear in parentheses in the text and footnotes; a revised translation is indicated by "rev.").

therefore to fulfill the covenant." (*KD* IV/2, p. 386; ET: p. 345 rev., emphasis added)[5]

Note that in this latter passage from *CD* IV/2 (i.e., the later Barth), Barth explicitly describes the Trinity as the ground of election.

3. Throughout II/2, Barth speaks of the Holy Trinity as being *determined* by God's free decision of election. I take this clearly to indicate that the Trinity is ontologically prior to and logically presupposed by the pretemporal act of election.[6] For Barth, something can be "determined" only if it already exists.

    a. It is not election that constitutes the Trinity, but the Trinity that constitutes election.

    b. Election is an act of the Holy Trinity in which God determines himself *ad intra* for the sake of his saving work *ad extra*.

    c. Election is a free and contingent act of divine self-determination (not self-constitution).[7]

    d. It is eternally necessary (true by definition) that God is the Holy Trinity, whereas the act of election is eternally contingent (not necessary to the definition of God's being).

4. Barth says repeatedly throughout his career that God would be the Holy Trinity whether the world had been created or not. There is nothing incon-

---

5. Barth, *Kirchliche Dogmatik*, 4 vols. (Zürich: Theologischer Verlag, 1932-67) (cited in the text as *KD*).

6. For backing, see, e.g., the representative passages cited below from *CD* II/2, pp. 101-2, 107, 155, 157.

7. The idea that "God gives himself being" (so some revisionists) seems unintelligible. Who or what is it that supposedly "gives being" to himself in the event of election? Did this very curious eternal entity (monad?) otherwise have no being? Or was the being that it enjoyed somehow deficient? How did this apparently needy entity give something to itself that it did not previously have? Would not this gift of self-enhancement have entailed an astonishing ontological change within the godhead? Would it not have made this entity radically dependent on the world? Whatever one makes of this idea (to say nothing about how it would supposedly be known), it has nothing to do with Karl Barth, who always maintained that "what can need existence, is not God Himself, or His reality" (*CD* II/1, 306). For the idea that God gives himself being, see McCormack, "Seek God," pp. 66-67 (n. 1 above). Against this idea, see the decisive discussion in *CD* II/1, pp. 305-7; see also *CD* III/2, pp. 218-19. Barth never departed from the important distinctions he made in I/1, p. 434 (see n. 20 below).

sistent in his saying this; in fact, he would have been inconsistent if he had
denied it.

a. Here is a statement from 1932:

> God would be no less God if He had created no world and no
> human being. The existence of the world and our own existence
> are in no sense vital to God, not even as the object of His love.
> The eternal generation of the Son by the Father tells us first and
> supremely that God is not at all lonely even without the world
> and us. His love has its object in Himself. (*CD* I/1, pp. 139-40 rev.)

b. Here is a relatively simple statement from 1938:

> . . . Father, Son and Holy Spirit would be none the less eternal
> God, if no world had been created. (*CD* I/2, p. 135)

c. Here is a more elaborate statement from 1940:

> As [*indem*] and before [*bevor*] God seeks and creates fellowship
> with us, he wills and completes [*vollbringt*] this fellowship in
> himself. In himself . . . he is Father, Son and Holy Spirit and
> therefore alive in his unique being with and for and in another
> [*in seinem eigensten Miteinander und Füreinander und In-
> einander*]. He does not exist in solitude but in fellowship. There-
> fore what he seeks and creates between himself and us is in fact
> nothing else but what he wills and completes and therefore is in
> himself. (*CD* II/1, p. 275)

d. A related passage dates from 1953:

> [N]othing would be lacking in his inward being as God in glory,
> as Father, Son and Holy Spirit, as the One who loves in freedom,
> if he did not show himself to the world, if he allowed it to com-
> plete its course to nothingness, just as nothing would be lacking
> to his glory if he had refrained from giving it being when he cre-
> ated it out of nothing. (*CD* IV/1, p. 213 rev.)

e. Finally, here is a remark from an interview in 1968, the year of his
death:

> Election means election to justification, to sanctification, to
> mission. All the particular things which I then try to develop in

the doctrine of reconciliation are explications of the doctrine of election. . . . And behind the doctrine of election stands the doctrine of the Trinity. That is the order [*Reihenfolge*]. The doctrine of the Trinity, election, and then sanctification, and so forth.[8]

The point of all these passages is that Barth, from 1932 onward, saw God in himself as the Holy Trinity, with or without the world. On this point the documentary record shows that his position did not change. When asked in the 1968 interview whether he still stood by the 1932 passage cited above, Barth replied: "Ist doch herrlich, nicht?" ("Splendid, isn't it?")[9]

5. When Barth declares that Jesus Christ is "the subject of election," he is not speaking without qualification *(simpliciter)* but only in a certain respect *(secundum quid)*.

    a. Consider the following case. If I say, "The Queen was born in 1819," I do not mean it without qualification. I don't mean that Victoria was literally the queen of England from the moment of her birth. I am speaking about the infant who would eventually be the queen. Though she was not yet the queen in 1819, she enjoyed coronation in due course. We might say that Victoria became what she was ordained to be. In that light one can say, retrospectively, "The Queen was born in 1819." No one familiar with ordinary conventions would take this statement literally as though it were without qualification.

    b. To some extent, though only roughly, this manner of speaking corresponds to Barth's discourse about the *incarnandus* status of the eternal Son.

      • The eternal Son and the incarnate Son are numerically the same, but different in their modes of existence.

      • Strictly speaking, however, only the Son *incarnatus* is identical with Jesus Christ.

      • The eternal Son qua eternal is not *incarnatus* but *incarnandus*.[10]

8. Karl Barth, *Gespräche 1964-1968* (Zurich: Theologische Verlag Zürich, 1997), p. 293.
9. Barth, *Gespräche 1964-1968*, p. 286.
10. The Son's identity as such can be known through and only through revelation (and not in any other way, such as natural theology). For Barth's alternative to natural theology (which preserves some of its concerns), see my essay "Secular Parables of the Truth," in

- The eternal Son qua Son, however, is not even *incarnandus*, because the Son qua Son is properly defined without reference to his being *incarnandus*.
- The eternal Son, by definition, is the second person of the Holy Trinity, generated eternally by the Father, and he would be such whether the world had been created or not. He is necessarily the eternal Son; he is only contingently *incarnandus*.
- We can, therefore, say that the second person of the Trinity is, by a free divine decision, *also* the one determined from all eternity to be *incarnandus*.

c. Jesus Christ *elects* to be *incarnandus* only in the sense that he is numerically the same as the eternal Son.
- Strictly speaking, it is the eternal Son, not the Son *incarnatus*, nor even the Son *incarnandus*, who is the subject of this decision.
- The eternal Son becomes *incarnandus* by virtue of his own free decision. He does not become *incarnandus* by being generated eternally by the Father. Becoming *incarnandus* is not a necessity that he passively undergoes. On the contrary, it is a matter of his own free decision in obedience to the Father's will.
- Nevertheless, because the eternal Son is not only eternal but also *incarnandus*, and because the Son *incarnandus* is numerically identical with the Son *incarnatus*, it is not illegitimate to say that in a certain respect *(secundum quid)* it is the Son *incarnatus*, or Jesus Christ, who is the subject of this decision. This statement cannot be made absolutely or without qualification *(simpliciter)*.

6. The statement "Jesus Christ is the subject of election," however, can be made in a stronger sense. What makes the stronger sense possible is a thesis in Barth about the Trinitarian shape of eternity as simultaneity-in-distinction and distinction-in-simultaneity. This difficult idea often seems presupposed as a background belief. Barth rarely makes it explicit, and even when he does, it is only in a more or less piecemeal fashion.[11]

---

George Hunsinger, *How to Read Karl Barth: The Shape of His Theology* (New York: Oxford University Press, 1991), pp. 234-80.

11. See Hunsinger, "*Mysterium Trinitatis:* Karl Barth's Conception of Eternity," in *Disruptive Grace: Studies in the Theology of Karl Barth* (Grand Rapids: Eerdmans, 2000), pp. 186-209.

7. From one point of view *(sub specie aeternitatis)*, for Barth, the cross of
Christ, the Last Judgment, and pre-temporal election are not three different events, but three different forms of one and the same event. The relationship of unity and distinction among these three forms is governed by
what might be called "the grammar of *perichoresis*."[12]

    a. It is not the substance but only the grammar of *perichoresis* that is
       at stake. Whereas the substance is sui generis, the grammar can be
       applied analogously across diverse cases.

    b. What Barth says in another connection would apply also to this
       case:

> It is not merely that these three forms are interconnected in the
> totality of the action presented in them all, or in each of them in
> its unity and totality, but that they are mutually related as forms
> of this one action by the fact that each of them also contains the
> other two by way of anticipation or recapitulation, so that, with-
> out losing their individuality or destroying that of the others,
> they participate and are active and revealed in them. (*CD* IV/3,
> p. 296)[13]

8. The cross in its unabridged historicity is in some sense really present to
God in the pre-temporal decision of election. The Lamb of God is slain
from the foundation of the world (Rev. 13:8; cf. *CD* II/2, p. 167).

    a. The temporal form of the event (the cross) participates in the
       pretemporal form (election) without ceasing to be temporal. The
       Son *incarnatus* subsists in the eternal Son without ceasing to be
       *incarnatus*.

    b. God the Son is not only numerically one in his various modes of
       existence, but these modes actually somehow coinhere with one an-
       other, and are really present to one another, without losing their
       real distinctiveness. They coexist simultaneously in and with each

---

12. See Hunsinger, *How to Read Karl Barth*, pp. 175-76, where I call this grammar the
"trinitarian pattern" of dialectical inclusion.

13. Although Barth first sets this grammar forth explicitly (and belatedly) in a discussion of Jesus Christ's "threefold parousia" (*CD* IV/3, p. 296), it is clear that he has been pre-
supposing it all along. It is the grammar that everywhere governs his understanding of Heb.
13:8: "Jesus Christ is the same, yesterday and today and for ever." This was a seminal verse for
Barth. He explicates it, e.g., just prior to his discussion of the threefold parousia. Most important, it is just this verse, understood according to precisely this perichoretic grammar,
that governs his entire discussion of "Jesus, Lord of Time" (*CD* III/2, pp. 437-511).

other. *Sub specie aeternitatis,* they form a unity-in-distinction and distinction-in-unity.

c. Because of this mutual indwelling, what obtains between the eternal Son and the Son *incarnatus* is a real, if mysterious, unity-in-distinction.

d. Because of this unity-in-distinction, or coinherence, it can be said (*secundum quid,* not *simpliciter*) that the Son *incarnatus,* or Jesus Christ, is the subject of election. The Son *incarnatus* is not external but internal to the preexisting eternal Son.

e. The temporal mode of existence is internal to the eternal mode of existence without ceasing to be temporal.

f. This unity is what makes it possible to describe Jesus Christ as the acting subject of election, while the distinction is what makes it necessary to understand what is meant *secundum quid.*

g. "In the free act of the election of grace, the Son of the Father is no longer *just* [*schon nicht mehr*] the eternal Logos, but as such [*als solcher*], as very God from all eternity, he is also [*zugleich schon*] the very God and the very human being he will become in time" (*CD* IV/1, p. 66, emphasis in the original German, though not in the translation).

h. "The Word is what he is even before and apart from [*auch bevor und ohne*] his being flesh" (*CD* I/2, p. 136).

i. "[W]ithout ceasing to be the Word, he nevertheless ceased to be only the Word" (*CD* I/2, p. 149).

9. Certain passages have been adduced as supporting the strange idea — contrary to what has just been argued — that for Barth, election is ontologically prior to the Trinity, so that the Trinity is a consequence of election.[14] I will take them up one by one.

a. "What God is as God . . . the *essentia* or 'essence' of God is something which we will encounter either at the place where God deals with us as Lord and Savior or not at all" (*CD* II/1, 261). Comments:
   • This passage, like the next two candidates to be considered, does not appear in Barth's doctrine of election, nor does it pertain to it.
   • What Barth says he is speaking about here is "the act of revela-

14. For an appeal to these passages, see McCormack, "Seek God," pp. 74, 78 (n. 1 above).

tion," not the act of election. He is saying that God has given us "no less than himself" in revelation (*CD* II/1, 261).

- He is also saying that we cannot know who God is apart from the place in history where God deals with us. Barth is not discussing pre-temporal election here at all.

b. "To its very depths God's Godhead consists in the fact that it is an event — not any event, not events in general, but the event of his action, in which we have a share in God's revelation." (*CD* II/1, p. 263)

Comments:

- Again, this statement says nothing about election. It says only that God's being is always in act, never prior to or apart from the event of his action.
- The act to which Barth is referring — the act in which God's being just is — is the act in which God to the very depths of his Godhead is the Holy Trinity.
- The context is entirely Trinitarian — "Father, Son and Holy Spirit" (*CD* II/1, 263) — and the point is that the action of the triune God cannot be transcended for a God who is not active.
- God the Holy Trinity enjoys no being that is not in act — not in eternity (the "very depths of God's Godhead"), and not in revelation.

c. "The fact that God's being is event, the event of God's act, necessarily . . . means that it is his own conscious, willed and executed decision. . . . No other being exists absolutely in its act. No other being is absolutely its own, conscious, willed and executed decision" (*CD* II/1, p. 271).

Comments:

- Not even here (supposedly a most compelling case) do we find Barth saying that God's will "constitutes" his own being. What he is saying is that God exists absolutely in his own act.
- The point is largely polemical: Barth is positioning himself over against Feuerbach, Kant, Hegel, Schleiermacher, and Ritschl.
- For Feuerbach, God's being is not his own; for Kant, it is not conscious; for Hegel, it is not absolutely free; for Schleiermacher, it is not alive as *actus purus et singularis;* for Ritschl, it is not unconditionally self-moved. Or so Barth interprets them (*CD* II/1, pp. 269-70).
- For Barth, by contrast, God's being is absolutely in act; therefore,

God's being is really his own, fully conscious, absolutely free, truly alive, unconditionally self-moved.

- To say that God's being is an "executed decision" is to say that there is no potentiality in God's being. As Father, Son, and Holy Spirit, God is necessarily who and what he is to all eternity. God eternally affirms and confirms himself, in an executed decision, as the Holy Trinity.
- God does not bring himself into being out of nothing, nor is he self-caused, nor does he constitute himself by eternal fiat out of some prior, non-Trinitarian state of being. Even less does God "constitute" himself by his decision to become incarnate in Jesus Christ.
- "[T]he divine being . . . is in need of no origination (not even an origination from itself) [*auch keiner Entstehung aus sich selbst*]" (*CD* II/1, 206).
- "As manifest and eternally actual [*in Ewigkeit wirklich*] in the relationship of Father, Son and Holy Spirit, God is the one who already has and is his own being. Therefore this being does not need any origination and constitution [*keines Entstehens und Bestehens bedarf*]" (*CD* II/1, p. 306 rev.).
- "God is the One who in himself is the Existent [*der in sich selber der Existierende ist*" (*CD* II/1, p. 306).
- "We know God's will *apart* from predestination [*abgesehen von der Praedestination*] only as the act [*nur als jenen Akt*] in which from all eternity and in all eternity God affirms and confirms himself [obviously as the Holy Trinity]" (*CD* II/2, p. 155; italics in the original German, though not in the translation).
- Jesus Christ has a beginning, but "God [the Holy Trinity] has no beginning" (*CD* II/2, 102).
- Yet Jesus Christ is "in the beginning" — "at the beginning of all things, at the beginning of God's dealings with the reality which is distinct from himself" (*CD* II/2, 102).
- He is at the beginning of all God's ways and works by virtue of his real coinherence with the eternal Son (not by his being identical *simpliciter* with the eternal Son).
- Jesus Christ is "the beginning of God before which there is no other beginning apart from that of God within himself [*außer dem Anfang, den Gott in sich selber ist*]" [i.e., as the Holy Trinity] (*CD* II/2, p. 94).

- "[A]s the Son of the Father he has no need of any special election (*als Sohn des Vaters einer besonderen Wahl nicht bedürftig ist*). . ." (*CD* II/2, p. 103).

d. "There can be no Christian truth which does not from the very first contain within itself as its basis the fact that from and to all eternity God is the electing God. There can be no tenet of Christian doctrine which, if it is to be a Christian tenet, does not reflect both in form and content this divine electing. . . . There is no height or depth in which God can be God in any other way" (*CD* II/2, p. 77).

Comments:

- This passage does appear in Barth's doctrine of election.
- The electing God of which it speaks is the Holy Trinity.
- In the same immediate context Barth states that the primal decision of election takes place "within his triune being" [*in seinem dreieinigen Wesen*] (*CD* II/2, p. 76).
- If Barth had wished to argue that God's triune being was a consequence of election, this would have been a place to do it.
- Instead, here as elsewhere, he takes it for granted that election presupposes the Trinity and is grounded in it.

e. "Jesus Christ is the electing God. We must not ask concerning any other but him. In no depth of Godhead shall we encounter any other but him. There is no such thing as Godhead in itself. Godhead is always the Godhead of the Father, Son and Holy Spirit" (*CD* II/2, p. 115).

Comments:

- This passage, also from the doctrine of election, means that there is no Godhead that is not Trinitarian. Like the turtles in another story, the being of God, for Barth, is Trinitarian "all the way down."
- It is only in and through Jesus Christ that we encounter God; and when we encounter God in this way, we encounter God as God truly is. We must not ask concerning any other than Jesus Christ, because the eternal Son has freely made himself one with him.
- Jesus Christ is therefore "the electing God," not *simpliciter* but *secundum quid*. For, *unlike* the eternal Son as such (with whom he is at once one and yet also distinct), he enjoys an eternal *determination* and a temporal *beginning*.
- The eternal Son, who is the electing God in this determination, is

thus logically and ontologically presupposed as the subject (and object) of election (*CD* II/2, p. 103).

10. Barth did not change his mind in 1942. In his volume on election he still clearly regarded the Trinity as ontologically prior to, and presupposed in, the pretemporal act of election. The following passages are representative.

a. "In the beginning it was the choice of the Son to be obedient to grace, and therefore to offer up himself and to become human in order that this covenant might be made a reality" (*CD* II/2, p. 101). The acting subject of this choice is, unmistakably, the eternal Son. It is an act of self-determination, not self-constitution.

b. "The subject of this decision is the triune God — the Son of God no less than the Father and the Holy Spirit" (*CD* II/2, p. 110). It would be hard to imagine a clearer statement that the Trinity precedes the decision of election.

c. God "might well have been satisfied with the inner glory of his *threefold being* [*dreieinigen Seins*], his freedom and his love" (*CD* II/2, p. 121, emphasis added). The inner glory of the Trinity is perfectly sufficient in itself apart from any relationship of God to the world.

d. "God's first thought and decree [*ad extra*] consists in the fact that in his Son he makes the being of this other his own being, that he allows the Son of Man Jesus to be called and actually to be his own Son" (*CD* II/2, p. 121). In the decision of election, the being of the human Jesus is made to be one with that of the ontologically preexistent eternal Son.

e. "The Son of God determined to give himself from all eternity. With the Father and the Holy Spirit he chose to unite himself with the lost Son of Man. The Son of Man was from all eternity the object of the election of Father, Son and Holy Spirit" (*CD* II/2, p. 158). The entire Trinity is the subject of this decision, and the lost Son of Man is its object. The Trinity is clearly presupposed, not generated, by this decision.

f. ". . . in all his willing and choosing, what God ultimately wills is himself. All God's willing is primarily a *determination* [*Bestimmung*] of the love of the Father and the Son in the fellowship of the Holy Spirit" (*CD* II/2, p. 169, emphasis added). The Trinity wills to be for humankind what it already is in itself.

g. "From all eternity [*schon in Gottes ewiger Vorherbestimmung*] God is within himself the living God. The fact that God is means that from all eternity [*von Ewigkeit her*] God is active in his *inner relationships* [*inneren Beziehungen*] as Father, Son and Holy Spirit, that he wills himself and knows of himself, that he loves, that he makes use of his sovereign freedom, and in doing so maintains and demonstrates himself" (*CD* II/2, p. 175, emphasis added). God does not become the living God only in relation to the world. God is already the living God in himself — as Father, Son, and Holy Spirit — from all eternity. This is what it means to say that God is.

h. "God does not, therefore, become the living God when he works or decides to work *ad extra* — in his being *ad extra* he is, of course, the living God in a different way. . ." (*CD* II/2, p. 175). The living God does not become the Holy Trinity by virtue of his decision of election, but in this pre-temporal act of self-determination, God becomes what he is as the Trinity in a different way. The tri-personal God becomes also for us what he is already in himself.

Already in his eternal self-determination prior to election (*seine ewige Vorherbestimmung*), God is Father, Son and Holy Spirit, the living God, in and for himself.

11. When Barth writes about the *Logos asarkos,* he always does so in a certain respect *(secundum quid).* He does not reject the idea absolutely. On the contrary, he affirms it as necessary in principle. What he rejects is the idea that, as a matter of contingent fact, we might still have access to a *Logos asarkos* above and beyond the *Logos ensarkos.* Pre-temporal election, which begins, strictly speaking, with the *Logos asarkos* and ends with the *Logos ensarkos,* or more precisely, which presupposes the *Logos asarkos* in union with Jesus as the subject and object of election, makes any human access to the *Logos asarkos* of no practical or theoretical consequence.[15]

> [The man Jesus] is to the created world, and therefore *ad extra,* what the Son of God as the eternal Logos is within the triune being of God. If the eternal Logos is the Word in which God speaks with himself, thinks himself and is conscious of himself, then in its identity with the man Jesus it is the Word in which God

15. For confirmation of these observations, see *CD* I/2, p. 170; IV/1, pp. 52, 66, 181; IV/2, pp. 33, 34. It would perhaps be tedious, at this point, to examine these passages in detail. They only underscore the line of interpretation already established. A few representative passages, however, are given in the text.

thinks the cosmos, speaks with the cosmos and imparts to the cosmos the consciousness of its God." (*CD* III/2, p. 147)

The following passage from *CD* IV/1 shows how the *Logos asarkos* functions for Barth:

> The second "person" of the Godhead in himself and as such is not God the Reconciler. In himself and as such he is not revealed to us. In himself and as such he is not *Deus pro nobis*, either on- tologically or epistemologically. (*CD* IV/1, 52)

While this statement may seem startling, Barth had important rea- sons for making it, and would have contradicted himself if he had denied it. The idea of the *Logos asarkos* is essential to the logic of his theology. It serves to make clear that God the Holy Trinity has a re- lationship in and for himself that cannot be collapsed into, or strictly identified with, God's relationship in and for the world.

> The content of the doctrine of the Trinity is not that God in his relation to the human being is Creator, Mediator and Redeemer, but that God in himself is eternally God the Father, Son and Holy Spirit. . . . [God himself] cannot be dissolved [*nicht aufgeht*] into his work and activity [for us]. (*CD* I/2, pp. 878-79)

The autonomy of God's eternal self-relationship is a necessary con- dition for the fulfillment of the covenant, since God's people and all things are to be taken up into it. The idea of the *Logos asarkos* means that the eternal Word in itself and as such is perfectly deter- minate without us (not indeterminate), just as the eternal Trinity in itself and as such is perfectly determinate (not indeterminate) without us. The Word and the Trinity do not first become determi- nate in relationship to the world. God's pretemporal act of election is a further determination of what is already perfectly determinate in itself and as such.

As the passage just cited from *CD* IV/1 suggests, there is and re- mains something incommunicable about God's being in itself and as such, just as there is also about the eternal *Logos* in itself and as such. The primordial *form* of God's eternal self-relationship is nec- essarily inaccessible to us, even though its *content* assumes a sec- ondary form for our sakes. *Deus pro nobis* would not be *God* if he were not perfectly and primordially *Deus extra nos*.

The one God who becomes completely accessible is the same God who remains completely inaccessible. God makes himself accessible in a secondary and contingent form while remaining inaccessible in the primordial form that he enjoys in and for himself. These two forms of the one indivisible God fall into a pattern of *totus/totus*: total communicability for our sakes in and with total incommunicability in the ineffable form that God enjoys in himself and as such. This is finally the dialectic of hiddenness and revealedness in God.

12. One last point. Barth may indeed have liked to do a little "Hegeling," especially throughout *Church Dogmatics*, volume IV.[16] But he always took special care to avoid making Hegel's mistakes. In particular, he would never allow pre-temporal election — or anything else — to make God's triune being depend on his relationship to the world.

> God confronts all that is in supreme and utter independence, i.e., he would be no less and no different even if they did not exist or existed differently. . . . If they belong to him and he to them, this dual relationship does not spring from any need of his eternal being. This would remain the same even if there were no such relationship. He would be who he is even without this connection. (*CD* II/1, pp. 311-12)

> We know God's will *apart* from predestination [*abgesehen von der Praedestination*] only as the act [*nur als jenem Akt*] in which from all eternity and in all eternity God affirms and confirms himself [as Father, Son and Holy Spirit]. We must guard against denying [*in Abrede zu stellen*] God's eternal will as it precedes even predestination [*der Praedestination vorangehende ewigen Willen Gottes*]. We must not allow God to be submerged [*aufgehen zu lassen*] in his relationship to the world or to think of him as tied to the world. (*CD* II/2, p. 155 rev.; emphasis in original German, though not in the translation)

The logical and ontological priority of the Holy Trinity, as eternally perfect and complete in itself, over against the primal decision of election, was essential to Barth's strategy for avoiding Hegel's errors while he indulged in a little "Hegeling."

---

16. Cf. McCormack, "Seek God," pp. 72, 79.

## Conclusion

For Barth, God is necessarily the Holy Trinity, but only contingently the God of election. As Father, Son, and Holy Spirit to all eternity, God is self-existent and self-sufficient as the living God in and for himself. He does not first become the Holy Trinity in relationship to the world. The pre-temporal act of election is not an act of Trinitarian self-origination. Rather, it is an act of Trinitarian self-determination. The God who would be the Holy Trinity whether the world was created or not is the same God who determines his triune being to be for the world in his primordial decision of election. For Barth, the logical and ontological priority of the eternal Son in the act of election is presupposed, rather than contradicted, by his (contingent) unity with the man Jesus. But because of that unity, it can indeed be said (*secundum quid,* not *simpliciter*) that Jesus Christ is himself the electing God.

## Part II

13. The eternal generation of the Son, as affirmed by the Nicene Creed, does not take place for the purpose of election or for the purposes established in election. This idea — that the Son's generation by the Father takes place merely for the sake of God's relationship to the world — seems to be required by the claim that the Holy Trinity is a function of God's pre-temporal decision of election. Nowhere in the *Church Dogmatics,* however, is this Barth's view, whether explicitly or by implication. My remaining theses are an attempt to explain why. (It goes without saying that these Nicene statements apply to the Trinitarian theology and to the Christology of the entire Christian Church and are not to be seen as restricted merely to Barth's theology.)

14. The Father is God, the Son is God and the Holy Spirit is God, and yet there are not three gods but one God. By the same token, the Father is infinite, the Son is infinite, and the Holy Spirit is infinite — and yet there are not three infinites but only one infinite deity.

15. The eternal Son is the *Logos asarkos.* And yet the Son is so infinite that he can (and does) become *ensarkos* without ceasing to be *asarkos.* The *Logos asarkos* represents the Son in his primary objectivity, the *Logos*

*ensarkos* in his secondary objectivity. The Son is always hidden from us in his first mode of being *(asarkos)*, but manifest to us in his second mode of being *(ensarkos)*. These two modes of being represent the "double structure" of the eternal Son.[17]

16. It is eternally necessary that the Son be *asarkos,* but eternally contingent that he also be *ensarkos.*
   a. To say that the Incarnation is "eternally contingent" means that it rests entirely in the free grace of God. "When it says that the Word became flesh, this becoming took place in the divine freedom of the Word. . . . [I]t does not rest upon any necessity in the divine nature or upon the relation between the Father, Son and Spirit, that God becomes human" (*CD* I/2, rev.).
   b. Barth's position on this matter did not change in his later theology. "In this free act of the election of grace, the Son of the Father is no longer *just* the eternal Logos, but *as such,* as very God *from all eternity,* he is *also* the very God and very man he will become in time" (*CD* IV/1, p. 66, emphasis added). Not to put too fine a point on it, this passage shows that, for the later Barth, as for the earlier one, the Son of the Father existed as the eternal Logos not merely in relation to the world, but independently and primordially *from all eternity.* Barth did not cease to maintain that the eternal Logos in its prior existence was presupposed in the act of election.[18]

17. The *koinonia* of the Holy Trinity occurs as an end in itself. It is also sufficient in itself. The being of God exists eternally in an act of perfect *koinonia,* love and freedom, joy and peace.
   a. The *koinonia* in which God has his being is his act of self-affirmation as Father, Son, and Holy Spirit.
   b. This self-affirmation is identical to the eternal generation of the Son by the Father and the Spirit's procession from the Father through the Son.[19]

   17. See n. 21 below.
   18. See the list of passages at the end of n. 20 below.
   19. I here follow the formula agreed on in the Reformed-Orthodox dialogue. Barth, of course, followed the traditional Western *filioque.* Which formulation is used makes no difference to my argument. See "Agreed Statement on the Holy Trinity," in *Theological Dialogue Between Orthodox and Reformed Churches,* vol. 2, ed. Thomas F. Torrance (Edinburgh: Scottish Academic Press, 1993), pp. 219-226, esp. p. 224.

18. The Father does not eternally generate the Son for the purpose of pre-temporal election. If election were the purpose of the Son's eternal generation by the Father, at least three consequences would follow, all of which would be intolerable. First, the Trinity would necessarily be dependent on the world; second, the Son would be subordinated to an external end; and third, the Son would be the object but not the subject of election. The next three theses spell out these consequences.

19. First, only the Father would be necessarily independent of the world. Both the "eternal" Son and the entire Trinitarian structure of the Godhead would be necessarily world-related. They would both necessarily be dependent on the world for their existence. For neither could be defined, neither would originate, and neither would exist, without necessary reference to the world. The tri-personal reality of God would not be sufficient in itself, but would necessarily (logically and ontologically) require the world in order to be. The Father alone would be independent, but the Trinity would be dependent on the world.

20. Second, both the Son and the Trinity would merely be instrumental to the Father's relationship to the world. The Son's generation would take place precisely for the sake of God's *koinonia* with the world. There would be no independent *koinonia* of the Holy Trinity in and for itself. Nor would the Trinity's eternal *koinonia* be sufficient in itself. The primary form of *koinonia* would be that of the Father with the world through the Son and in the Spirit. The *koinonia* of the Father with the Son in the Spirit would be a secondary function of the Father's preeminent end of *koinonia* with the world.
   a. God's self-relationship would necessarily be mediated through his world-relationship. God would have no self-relationship that was logically and ontologically prior to his world-relationship.
   b. Moreover, God would not necessarily be the Holy Trinity whether the world were created or not. Without the world to relate to, there would have been a "Father," but God might conceivably have been something other than the Holy Trinity.[20]

20. It is not clear what the idea of God as "Father" without the created order, and so without the Son, could possibly mean for the revisionists, since, for them, the Trinitarian structure of God's being is not necessary to God but is instead entirely discretionary and dependent on the decision of election (and therefore on the existence of the world). For Barth, however, throughout the *Church Dogmatics* from beginning to end, God is seen as free not

21. Third, if election were the purpose for which the Father generated the eternal Son, then the pre-temporal decision of election would rest entirely with the Father alone. It would not be an inner-Trinitarian decision. It would be a decision legislated autonomously by the Father. The role of the Son and the Spirit, who prior to the decision would not even exist, would be to implement a decision made without them. It would be merely to give their consent to the Father's fait accompli.

    a. Jesus Christ would not be the subject but merely the consenting object of the decision.

    b. The Trinitarian implications here are clearly subordinationist.

    c. Only if the Trinity is the presupposition of election rather than its consequence can Jesus Christ be a coequal partner in the pre-temporal divine decision.

    d. The correct view is that election presupposes the Trinity, not that the Trinity is the function of some prior, pre-temporal decision of election by the Father alone.

22. The Trinity that exists eternally in and for itself resolves *also* to exist for the sake of the world. The Trinity exists as the self-affirmation of God. Election originates as a self-*determination* of the Holy Trinity. The Trinity is not *constituted* for the sake of election by virtue of the Son's eternal generation by the Father. Neither the Son nor the Trinity can properly be *instrumentalized* in this way. Neither can be made subordinate to the purpose of election. They are not, in the first instance, the means to this end.

23. In short, the being of the Holy Trinity in the act of eternal *koinonia* in and for itself is the presupposition of election. In the inner-Trinitarian decision of election, the act in which the Trinity has its being is determined in a new and special way. This act of self-determination is not necessary but contingent. It is a free decision of grace. The Father, Son, and Holy Spirit would be entirely who and what they are without it. But they do not choose to be without the world. The one act of eternal *koinonia*, in which God has his being in and for himself, is freely determined to be *also* the act in which God has his being for the sake of the world.

---

to have created the world, but he is not seen as free not to be himself, and thus he is not seen as free not to be the Holy Trinity (to all eternity). Therefore, the Father is not free not to be the Father of the Son. See the explicit statement at I/1, p. 434. For the later Barth, see *CD* IV/1, pp. 66, 204, 213, 536, 561; IV/2, pp. 113, 341-47, 755, 757, 777; IV/3, pp. 79-80, 397; see also Barth, *The Christian Life* (Grand Rapids: Eerdmans, 1981), p. 155. See also n. 7 above.

24. The one act in which the tri-personal God has his being, therefore, sub-sists in two modes at the same time. These modes represent God's primary and secondary objectivity. The one mode is immanent, the other is eco-nomic; the one is primordial, the other derivative; the one is self-existent, the other is dependent on it; the one is necessary, the other contingent. The one would exist whether the world had been created or not; the other pre-supposes the creation and fall of the world.

  a. The world's creation is divinely willed; the fall into sin and death is not divinely willed, though it is divinely permitted.

  b. The creation is purely an act of sovereign grace and divine freedom. It is in no way necessary for God, not even "contingently" (what-ever that might mean).

  c. The idea that creation was "contingently necessary" for God has nothing to do with Barth, and would in any case be absurd, if it is meant in some pre-temporal way.

  d. It would be false to declare that Barth ceased to derive his view of the Trinity from the logic of revelation. For him, revelation and election were not — and could not possibly be — opposed.

  e. The historical Trinity is the appointed means by which the Trinity's independent, primordial reality is revealed in and to the world.

25. For Barth, therefore, the Holy Trinity enjoys a double structure and a double historicity.[21] It is a matter of one and the same Holy Trinity in two simultaneous modes of existence.[22] The relationship between them is gov-erned by the Chalcedonian pattern.[23] It is a matter of inseparable unity,

---

21. I here follow Eberhard Jüngel, *Gottes Sein Ist im Werden* (Tübingen: J. C. B. Mohr, 1965), pp. 85 ("Doppelstruktur des Sein Gottes in der Entsprechung") and 111 ("so wird man Gottes Sein wesentlich als doppelt relationales Sein zu verstehen"). ET: *God's Being Is in Be-coming*, trans. John Webster (Grand Rapids: Eerdmans, 2001), pp. 87, 114.

22. It would be false to assert that Barth later abandoned this double structure. In *CD* IV, the relationship between the immanent and the economic Trinity remained what it had always been, one of correspondence, not of dialectical identity. To suppose the opposite would be like looking at Barth's doctrine of the Trinity through a funhouse mirror, where the funhouse was owned and operated by a character named Hegel. For a representative pas-sage, see *KD* IV/2, pp. 385-87 (ET, pp. 345-47). Note Barth's important use of the terms "gulf" *(Abgrund),* "repetition" *(Wiederholung),* "correspondence" *(Entsprechung)* and "also" *(auch).*

23. For the Chalcedonian pattern, see Hunsinger, *How to Read Karl Barth,* pp. 185-88, 201-18, 272-73. Note that the pattern is merely a formal device, a kind of grammar by which selected terms may be related in a particular case.

abiding distinction, and irreversible asymmetry in the relationship of the Trinity's eternal mode of existence with its historical mode of existence.

    a. The first mode — eternal, immanent, primordial, self-existent, and necessary — is the *koinonia* of the Father with the Son as the *Logos asarkos* in the Holy Spirit. This mode, which remains forever hidden from us, represents the Holy Trinity in its primary objectivity.[24]

    b. The second mode — historical, economic, derivative, dependent, and contingent — is the *koinonia* of the Father with the Son as the *logos ensarkos* in the Holy Spirit. We have noetic access to the Holy Trinity only through this mode, which represents its secondary objectivity.

    c. The teleology of this relationship of double historicity is governed, in turn, by the Hegelian pattern.[25] Through the mediation of Christ at the end of all things, the historical mode will be sublated, with the world, into the eternal mode, while still remaining necessarily distinct from it.

    d. The Father, Son, and Holy Spirit enjoy a *koinonia* in and for themselves, which, though it is shared with the world, is not something in which the world can directly participate. Its participation is only indirect through being united to the life-giving *sarx* of the *Logos ensarkos*.

    e. The *Logos asarkos* is not eliminated upon becoming *ensarkos*. On the contrary, as intimated by the doctrine of the *extra Calvinisticum,* the Logos subsists in two modes (*asarkos* in eternity, *ensarkos* in history) simultaneously (through a pattern of unity-in-distinction). It is one

24. See, e.g., *CD* II/1, p. 16, where Barth, following Luther, distinguishes God's "clothed" from his "naked" objectivity. The latter is God's direct objectivity to himself in his eternal self-knowledge as the Holy Trinity. "Naked" means no mediation by any creaturely object, and therefore alludes to the *logos asarkos*. Despite assertions to the contrary, Barth never departed from this view, and no real evidence has been adduced that he did. Every piece of would-be evidence rests, without exception, on a tissue of tendentious inferences. The view that is unfortunately attributed to Barth has produced (and apparently can produce) no direct statement from him in support. This lack of clear, noninferential evidence stands as a prima facie indication that the claim cannot be sustained. It is also highly implausible that Barth would have so drastically revised his own views — and the entire Nicene tradition — without ever being conscious of it, and without ever once explaining it to his readers, as the theory rejected by this essay requires.

25. For the Hegelian pattern, see Hunsinger, *How to Read Karl Barth*, p. 98. Again, note that the pattern is a merely formal device that can be applied across a range of cases, and that substantively each case needs to be understood according to its own distinctiveness.

and the same unabridged Logos in two simultaneous modes of existence — *totus/totus,* primary and secondary objectivity. The *Logos asarkos* becomes the *Logos ensarkos* without ceasing to be the eternal *logos asarkos* in God's relationship in and for himself to all eternity.

## Conclusion

The mature Barth never collapsed the divine being into the divine act, nor did he turn "essence" into a verb. He spoke deliberately about God's "being in act." The preposition is important here, and should not be erased, because it indicates a complex relationship between God's "being" and God's "act" — a relationship that was not flattened out into an absolute or simple identification.[26] Moreover, Barth always maintains a crucial distinction between the idea of the divine self-constitution and that of the divine self-determination. God was constituted as the Holy Trinity, but determined by a free inner-Trinitarian decision to be the same God also with respect to us. It would be false (and unintelligible) to declare that such a secondary self-determination would necessarily entail a radical change in the divine being. It most certainly would not.

God is free, as Barth saw it, to reiterate himself in time precisely as the Holy Trinity he is in eternity — and always would be in eternity — in and for himself, even if time did not exist. I agree with Eberhard Jüngel that "God's 'being-already-ours-in-advance' . . . is grounded in the trinitarian 'being-for-itself'" ["das in trinitarischen 'Für-sich-Sein' begründete 'Schon-im-voraus-der-Unsrige-Sein' Gottes"].[27] In other words, God's being for himself is the *ground* of God's being-for-us. But God's being-for-us does not arise as a *necessary entailment* of God's being for himself as the Holy Trinity. God's-being-for us is not a necessary entailment, but a free inner-Trinitarian decision in which the prior and independent existence of the Holy Trinity is obviously and necessarily presupposed.[28]

26. Although, for Barth, there is no substance prior to the divine persons, it would be false to suppose that he flatly rejected the term "substance" or "being" in favor of "act." That move would leave God without a nature. But Barth states explicitly that God's acts occur only in the unity of spirit and nature (*CD* II/1, p. 267).

27. Jüngel, *Gottes Sein Ist im Werden,* p. 88; ET, p. 91.

28. The idea that God is "already ours in advance" (which Barth qualifies by saying "so to speak," indicating that he is speaking *secundum quid*) means that the Trinitarian structure of God's being in and for himself is *the condition for the possibility* of God's being the same

Barth's whole point in emphasizing that God would be the Holy Trinity without us was that God does not need the world to be God, nor, furthermore, does God need it to be constituted as the Holy Trinity, because God just is the Holy Trinity prior to and independently of the world. It would be hard to imagine a view more contrary to Barth than one that makes the Holy Trinity a mere function of God's relationship to the world. For Barth, God's act of pre-temporal election is a free self-determination of his prior existence as the Holy Trinity.

Whether or not one agrees with Barth's view, it must be admitted that it is internally coherent. That there is some supposed contradiction in Barth on this matter is easy to assert, but it has never been proven or even clearly set forth. Perhaps the claim is not that Barth was internally inconsistent, but that he would have been more consistent if he had adopted the view rejected by this essay. But even the claim of greater consistency is highly doubtful. Anyone who wishes to hold it is free to do so; but under no circumstances should it be attributed to Karl Barth.

Nor did Barth change his mind on this score over the course of writing his *Church Dogmatics* — another dubious claim that, though easy to assert, has not been proven. The notion that the eternal Son was constituted by pre-temporal election was something so bizarre — and obviously false — that Barth could see little point in pausing very long to refute it. He did, however, make at least this statement: "Daß Jesus Christus der Sohn Gottes i s t, das beruht freilich nicht auf Erwählung" (*KD* II/2, 114) ["Of course, the fact that Jesus Christ *is* the Son of God does not rest on election" (*CD* II/2, 107 rev.)]. Barth's "of course" (*freilich*) should have been sufficient in itself to make the argument of this essay unnecessary.[29]

---

Holy Trinity who is also for us in the act of pre-temporal election. As Jüngel understands very well, it does not mean that God's being for us is the *necessary consequence* of who God is in and for himself, nor does it mean that God's Trinitarian self-relationship is somehow radically and necessarily dependent on his world-relationship. It is in this independent and transcendental sense that Barth writes that as Father, Son, and Spirit, God is "sozusagen im voraus der unsrige" (*KD* I/1, p. 404). Cited by Jüngel, *Gottes Sein Ist im Werden*, p. 36; ET, p. 37.

29. I would like to thank my friends Paul Molnar, Keith Johnson, and Bruce McCormack for their kind comments on an earlier draft of this essay.

# 5. Election and the Trinity: Theses in Response to George Hunsinger

*Bruce L. McCormack*

In April 2008, George Hunsinger published twenty-five theses that were critical of my views on the logical relationship between the being of God as triune and the eternal act of election.[1] In what follows I am not going to try to match every Hunsinger thesis with a counterthesis of my own. Such a procedure would allow his polemic against my reading to frame the debate, leaving his own reading challenged only in the details and not in its underlying premises and commitments. Instead, I am going to allow my own convictions and concerns to provide the structure of my presentation. My answers to criticisms raised by Hunsinger will emerge quite naturally in the process. I will divide the material into three sets of theses: the first set of theses will critically engage Hunsinger's reading of Barth; the second set will set forth my own reading; the third set will describe (in outline form) my attempt to move beyond Barth.

Before turning to my own theses, I would like to make a preliminary observation that will help to provide a context for what I say in them. Hunsinger characterizes his own position on Barth's understanding of the relationship of the Trinity and election as "traditionalist"; he characterizes my position as "revisionist."[2] I would say that this characterization gets things exactly backwards where the historiography is concerned. If any position in this debate is "revisionist," it is Hunsinger's. My own reading has been amply prepared for in the German literature by Eberhard Jüngel and Wilfried Härle, and it has been stated explicitly by Hans-Theodore Goebel

---

1. George Hunsinger, "Election and the Trinity: Twenty-Five Theses on the Theology of Karl Barth," pp. 91-114 above (first published in *Modern Theology* 24, no. 2 [2008]: 179-98).

2. Hunsinger, "Election and the Trinity," p. 91 above.

and Thiess Gundlach.[3] In the English-speaking world, it has been stated explicitly by Rowan Williams and Paul M. Collins.[4] Hunsinger's take on the issues, by contrast, was constructed specifically with a view toward responding to a position I had already taken. It is, therefore, the newer of the two.

## Section I: The Return of the Neo-Orthodox Barth

Thesis 1: Hunsinger's reading of Barth's doctrine of God is fundamentally incoherent.

3. I have in mind here the following works: Eberhard Jüngel, *God's Being Is in Becoming: The Trinitarian Being of God in the Theology of Karl Barth,* trans. John Webster (Edinburgh: T. & T. Clark, 2001); Jüngel, " . . . keine Menschenlosigkeit Gottes: Zur Theologie Karl Barths zwischen Theismus und Atheismus," in *Barth-Studien* (Zürich-Köln and Gütersloh: Benziger Verlag and Gütersloher Verlagshaus Gerd Mohn, 1982), pp. 332-47; Wilfried Härle, *Sein und Gnade: die Ontologie in Karl Barths Kirchlicher Dogmatik* (Berlin/New York: Walter de Gruyter, 1975); Hans Theodor Goebel, "Trinitätslehre und Erwählungslehre bei Karl Barth," in *Wahrheit und Versöhnung: Theologische und Philosophische Beiträge zur Gotteslehre,* ed. Dietrich Korsch and Hartmut Ruddies (Gütersloh: Gütersloher Verlagshaus Gerd Mohn, 1989), pp. 147-66; Goebel, *Vom freien Wählen Gottes und des Menschen: Interpretationsübungen zur 'Analogie' nach Karl Barths Lehre der Erwählung und Bedenken ihrer Folgen für die Kirchliche Dogmatik* (Frankfurt am Main: Peter Lang, 1990); Thiess Gundlach, *Selbstbegrenzung Gottes und die Autonomie des Menschen: Karl Barths Kirchliche Dogmatik als Modernisierungsschritt evangelischer Theologie* (Frankfurt am Main: Peter Lang, 1992). I have described in detail the ways in which these works provide a genealogy of my own work in Bruce L. McCormack, "Karl Barth's Version of an 'Analogy of Being': A Dialectical No and Yes to Roman Catholicism," in *The Analogy of Being: Invention of the Antichrist or the Wisdom of God?* ed. Thomas Joseph White, O.P. (Grand Rapids: Eerdmans, 2010). A more detailed comparison of my views with Jüngel's may be found in "God *Is* His Decision: The Jüngel-Gollwitzer 'Debate' Revisited," in *Theology as Conversation: The Significance of Dialogue in Historical and Contemporary Theology; A Festschrift for Daniel L. Migliore,* ed. Bruce L. McCormack and Kimlyn J. Bender (Grand Rapids: Eerdmans, 2009), pp. 48-66.

4. See R.W. Williams, "Barth on the Triune God," in *Karl Barth — Studies of His Theological Methods,* ed. Stephen Sykes (Oxford: Clarendon Press, 1979), p. 178: "From all eternity, God's self-differentiation as Son or Word is directed towards the human and worldly object of election, Jesus of Nazareth." See also Paul Collins, *Trinitarian Theology West and East: Karl Barth, the Cappadocian Fathers, and John Zizioulas* (Oxford: Oxford University Press, 2001), pp. 84-85: "The divine intentional agency lies at the very heart of God's relationship with that which is other than himself, and also is that which is constitutive of the divine being, and thus of the divine relationality." Collins goes on to speak of "the decision to be the Trinity," and he concludes: "The divine intentionality is expressed in the decision to have being-in-act as the Holy Trinity."

*Explanation*

A. On the one hand, he says that "the Trinity is ontologically prior to and logically presupposed by the pre-temporal act of election" (thesis 3). Talk of an "ontological priority" must mean that *being precedes act* in precisely the same way it does on the human plane. The fact that Hunsinger stoutly maintains that being and act in God are "ontologically basic" and equally "primordial" (thesis 1) must not be allowed to obscure this point. For the "act" that he has in mind in saying that being and act are equally "primordial" is not an act in the ordinary sense of the word. For most of us, what counts as an act consists in a free exercise of the will. For Hunsinger, by contrast, the word "act" in the phrase "being-in-act" refers to the sheer actuality of a being that is complete in itself: the fact that there is no unrealized potentiality in God's being as such, without respect to the existence of the world (thesis 9, c, bullet point 5). God's being is, for him, "necessary" being (thesis 3, d), which God can only "affirm" (thesis 17). In any event, such a being precedes the contingent act in which God chooses to be God for us in Jesus Christ, which is why I say that, for him, being precedes act. Being precedes *this* act.

When thinking along these lines, Hunsinger's understanding of being in act of the triune God stands in close proximity to Thomas's understanding of God as *actus purus*. Like Thomas, Hunsinger makes necessary a distinction between the eternal processions (which belong to God's necessary being) and the eternal missions (a determination that God freely gives to himself). And like Thomas, he makes it difficult to understand how a God whose being is fully realized without respect to human beings can do anything. For surely a God who has no unrealized potentialities in himself, in his own being as such, could not move himself to do something new. And if he did, in fact, do something new, then surely there were unrealized potentialities in him after all.

B. On the other hand, Hunsinger holds that the act of self-determination that is election — an "act" that he does think of in the ordinary sense — is a determination of God's *being* as Father, Son, and Spirit. "In the inner-Trinitarian decision of election, the act in which the Trinity has its being is determined in a new and special way" (thesis 23).

C. It is precisely at this point, however, that Hunsinger's reading begins to lose coherence. For if the act of self-determination is indeed a determination of *being* — and the Son enjoyed another and different mode of being prior to this act of self-determination — then a determination of that prior mode of being would seem to entail change on the level of God's being (albeit a change that takes place in pre-temporal eternity). Such a change would occur when "[t]he eternal Son becomes *incarnandus* . . ." (thesis 5, c, bullet point 2). Of course, such a change would render any talk of necessary being nonsensical, since a necessary being, by definition, cannot change. There are two ways of avoiding this problem. The first would be to treat the eternal act of self-determination spoken of by Barth as a determination simply to *do* something, not to *be* something. We could then describe the eternal Son qua Son in terms of his one and only (necessary) mode of being and his act of revelation as a mode of *appearing*. This is, in fact, what the ancients believed, and Hunsinger's goal of bringing Barth into closer proximity to the fathers would be better served by this move. But Hunsinger cannot be completely satisfied with this. For he knows all too well that it is one of Barth's principal concerns to say that God is God precisely in his self-revelation in time. Barth will not allow revelation to be treated in terms of a mode of appearing (which in his view would be a mere theophany).

Still, this is the solution that is most compatible with Hunsinger's treatment of the divine being-in-act. The second way to avoid positing change in God as a consequence of his eternal self-determination would be to abandon all talk of "ontological priority" where the relationship of triunity to election is concerned (which is the move I make). If the Son had no "mode of being" above and prior to the eternal act of self-determination, then the construal of that act of determination as a determination of being would not introduce change into God. For according to this view, the act of self-determination would stand "at the beginning" of God himself — with nothing prior to it. If one were to view it in this light, one could continue to speak of a logical priority of Trinity over election, but all further talk of an ontological priority would have to be surrendered. But it is clear that Hunsinger will have nothing to do with this second option, since it would mean a concession to my own point of view. Hunsinger finds himself, then, on the horns of a dilemma that he fails to resolve. The result is incoherence.

Thesis 2: The incoherence of Hunsinger's reading is only deepened by his attempt to use Jüngel's interpretation of Barth to invest his own reading with authority.

*Explanation*

A. Jüngel certainly does grant a logical priority to Trinity over election, but *only* a logical priority.[5] Talk of an "ontological priority" of Trinity over election must inevitably result in an abstract, wholly metaphysical conception of the triune being of God that stands behind the event in which God chooses to be God "for us" in Jesus Christ: a metaphysical being that, by definition, has no history since there can be history in God only where there are a purpose and a goal. Jüngel will have nothing to do with this. His goal throughout is to show how it is possible to think of God's being in the act of revelation in time as corresponding to his being-in-act in eternity. He accomplishes this by positing the existence in God of a twofold "historicality": "[T]he historicality of the being of God . . . reiterates itself in the historicality of revelation."[6] What it means to speak of the eternal being of God in terms of "historicality" is made clear when Jüngel says, "Decision does not belong to the being of God as something supplementary to this being; rather, as event, God's being is His own decision. 'The fact that God's being is event, the event of God's act, necessarily . . .means that it is His own conscious, willed and executed decision'" (p. 81).[7] And so "God's being is constituted [*konstituiert*] through historicality" (p. 81). And if God's being is constituted through historicality, then there can be no higher or different state of being in God standing in back of what God is in election. That is why Jüngel can say, "[W]e have to understand God's primal decision as an event in the being of God which differentiates the modes of God's being [as Father, Son and Holy Spirit]" (p. 86).

Seen in this light, the "double structure" spoken of by Jüngel refers to the complete and perfect correspondence of the being of God as the subject of a historical life in time to his being in election. Again, there can be no question but that Jüngel understands triunity in God to have a logical precedence over election. In his view, God appears in the primal decision that inaugurates his primal and prevenient history as already triune. But the "already" here is strictly logical: it is an answer to the question, What should humans think of first in their efforts to think about the eternal being of God responsibly? But talk of an "ontological priority" of Trinity over

5. For a thorough investigation of Jüngel's book on Barth's doctrine of the Trinity, see McCormack, "God *Is* His Decision," pp. 48-66.

6. Jüngel, *God's Being Is in Becoming*, p. 83 (hereafter, page references to this work appear in parentheses in the text).

7. Here Jüngel is citing Barth, *CD* II/1, p. 271.

election (à la Hunsinger) would immediately open up a metaphysical gap between God's essence and his will. It is precisely this gap that Jüngel sought to overcome in the debate with Gollwitzer, which he carried out in this work. Jüngel's conclusion vis-à-vis Gollwitzer would surely have to be his conclusion vis-à-vis Hunsinger as well: "Gollwitzer's conception of God's being is . . .thoroughly in line with the classical concept of substance" (p. 106).

B. Hunsinger's use of Jüngel's phrase "double structure" has only the name in common with Jüngel's position. For Hunsinger, the "double structure" of the eternal Son consists in a *Logos asarkos/Logos ensarkos* distinction that so abstracts the former from any relationship to the man Jesus that any attempt to relate the latter to the former must finally end in defeat. "The Son is always hidden from us in his first mode of being *(asarkos)*, but manifest to us in his second mode of being *(ensarkos)*" (thesis 15). What we have before us here is the *classical* distinction of the immanent Trinity from the economic Trinity. The economy is said to "manifest" the immanent Trinity, but the degree of this manifestation is beyond knowing, since the *Logos asarkos* remains "forever" hidden from us (thesis 25, a).[8]

C. Hunsinger tries to rescue this situation by positing a simultaneity of the immanent and economic Trinities. "The one act in which the tri-personal God has his being . . . subsists in two modes at the same time. These modes represent God's primary and secondary objectivity. The one mode is immanent, the other is economic. The one is primordial; the other derivative. The one is self-existent; the other dependent on it" (thesis 25). No doubt, it is the epistemological problem created by the metaphysical gap he has opened up between the Son qua Son and the *Logos incarnandus* that leads Hunsinger to speak in this way. He is trying to overcome the consequences of that gap. But he cannot. For he holds that "[t]he eternal Son qua Son . . .

---

8. The "hiddenness" of God, for Hunsinger, has to do with the relationship of the *Logos asarkos* and the *Logos ensarkos:* the *Logos asarkos* is hidden behind the *Logos ensarkos*. For Barth, by contrast, it is a description of the ontological structure of the *Logos ensarkos*. That is why Jüngel says, "He [Barth] wanted as little to do with a *deus absconditus* lying in back of the *deus revelatus* . . . as he did with a Logos *asarkos* which was fundamentally distinguishable from the Logos *ensarkos*." See Jüngel, ". . . keine Menschenlosigkeit Gottes," p. 338; cf. p. 342: "According to Barth, every concept of God which treats the Godness of God only in terms of the absoluteness of His essence and not, at the same time, as a relatedness of this essence to humanity turns God into the Devil."

is not even *incarnandus,* because the Son as Son is properly defined without reference to his being *incarnandus*" (thesis 5, b, bullet point 4). And if that is the case, then there are *two* acts in pre-temporal eternity, not one. The first is a completely timeless act of self-affirmation that is said to be identical to the eternal generation of the Son and the eternal spiration of the Spirit, and the second is an act of self-determination that founds time. The problem this creates is this: a "simultaneity" of the being of God with moments in time can only be spoken of with respect to an eternal Son qua Son, not with respect to the *Logos incarnandus.* The reason for this has been well explained by Aquinas. In his view, the "eternity" of a timeless God stands in a relationship of immediate presence to every moment in time: every moment is immediately present to God in an eternal Now that admits of no past or future — hence "simultaneity." But Barth's concept of eternity does admit of past and future, and it does so because of his belief that what happens in the incarnation is that God becomes the subject of a human life and as this subject suffers and dies. "Eternity" conceived on this christological basis *must* embrace time; it must admit of past and future. But "eternity" so defined can only be a predicate of the *Logos incarnandus,* not of an eternal Son qua Son in Hunsinger's sense. And this also means that the relationship of the *Logos incarnandus* to the *Logos incarnatus* is not rightly described in terms of "simultaneity." It would be better to speak of anticipation and fulfillment as events that define the being of God: first an eternal event that founds time, and then a temporal event in which time is fulfilled.

D. Closely related to the preceding abortive effort to speak of the simultaneity of the modes of being of the *Logos* is Hunsinger's effort to give to Barth's claim that "Jesus Christ is the subject of election" a stronger sense than that found in his more basic reading of this statement as a figure of speech (thesis 5). The "stronger sense," which he describes in theses 6-8, finds its root in the claim that election, cross, and final judgment are "three different forms of one and the same event" (thesis 7). But such a claim only refers to the unity of God's works *ad extra* and says nothing at all about the relationship of his entirely abstract "eternal Son as such" to these works. Hunsinger's basic conviction remains intact: "Strictly speaking, it is the eternal Son, not the Son *incarnatus,* nor even the Son *incarnandus,* who is the subject of this decision [i.e., election]" (thesis 5, b, bullet point 2). Once he has made this statement, there can be no "stronger sense." At the end of the day, Barth's claim that "Jesus Christ is the subject of election" is, in

Hunsinger's hands, a figure of speech with no ontological significance whatsoever. It is a figure of speech and nothing more — such as when we say "Queen Victoria was born in 1819" (thesis 5, a).[9]

## Section II: My Own Reading of Barth

Thesis 3: If there is a constant in all the phases of Barth's development, from his student days on through to the end of his life, it lies in his protest against the introduction of metaphysics into the domain of Christian theology.

A. Essential to Barth's antimetaphysical outlook is his refusal to open up a metaphysical gap between the divine essence, on the one hand, and God's decision to be God in a redemptive relationship with sinful humanity, on the other. Consider the following.

1. "Everything *that* God is, He is insofar as *He* is. He is essence. He essences [*west*] as Person. He is Father, Son, Spirit, from eternity to eternity. As soon as we abstract from the speaking Person who *addresses* us, who addresses *us* — even if only for a moment — transposing the Godhead into a general truth or idea which is *not* Person, we would no longer be thinking God."[10]

The divine person of whom Barth speaks in this passage is the "speaking Person." There can be no abstracting from this person, for he is what he is in the event of his address to us — and in no mode of existence abstracted from it. That is why Barth replaces the noun form *Wesen* ("essence) with the verbal form *west* ("essences"). He wants to understand the divine "essence" in terms of willed activity directed toward the human creature.

2. On the basis of the kind of move we saw in the previously cited pas-

---

9. I am unable to attach any meaning to Hunsinger's claim in this context that "[t]he Son *incarnatus* subsists in the eternal Son without ceasing to be *incarnatus*" (thesis 8, a). A subsistence of the members of the Trinity in a divine essence that is itself understood against the background of substance metaphysics — that I can understand. A subsistence of the human nature of Christ in the "person" of the *Logos* (as Cyril had it) — that, too, I can understand. But a subsistence of the Son *in the Son?*

10. Karl Barth, *"Unterricht in der christlichen Religion": Zweiter Band; Die Lehre von Gott / Die Lehre vom Menschen, 1924/1925*, ed. Hinrich Stoevesandt (Zürich: TVZ, 1990), p. 70.

sage, Barth can say, "The relation of God to the human is not accidental; it is necessarily contained in and grounded in God's *essence*. . . . God would not be God if the relation to the human were not intrinsic to Him from the start."[11] To some extent, Barth's reach here exceeds his grasp. He has yet to revise the doctrine of election, which he put in place in his second *Romans*. And that means he has yet to ground the speaking activity of God in time in the eternal act of election. But here already he understands God's essence as constituted by means of an act in which God sets himself in relationship to the human.

3. What is added to the train of thought set forth in the previous two points by Barth's revised doctrine of election (in *CD* II/2) is the eternal ontological ground of the address of God in time. From this point on, Barth would speak of an act of self-*determination*, a word that, as we have seen, has its provenance in German idealism.[12] That Barth did not make use of the verbal form of "essence" in his mature thought does not mean that he has set aside the thought of a freely willed act of self-constitution. For once he makes the eternal act of self-determination that is election to be a determination *of the divine essence*, he has committed himself to the view that election *makes essential* to God that which is its content. This he clearly did in *CD* IV/1, at the latest.

4. The most significant body of material in this regard is to be found in *CD* IV/1 (pp.192-210), where Barth treats the "inner moment of the mystery of Christ's deity" as the mystery revealed to us that " . . . for God it is just as natural to be lowly as to be high."[13] The lowliness that is proper to God he then further explains in terms of "humility" and "obedience." "The humility in which He dwells and acts in Jesus Christ is not alien to Him, but proper to Him. His humility is a *novum mysterium* for us in whose favor he executes it when He makes use of His freedom for it. . . . But for Him this humility is no *novum mysterium* . . . . He is amongst us in humility, our God, God for us, as that which He is in Himself, in the most inward depth of His Godhead" (*CD* IV/1, p. 193).

Barth then continues on to the second point:

---

11. Barth, *"Unterricht in der christlichen Religion": Erster Band; Prolegomena, 1924,* ed. Hannelotte Reiffen (Zürich: TVZ, 1985), pp. 156-57.

12. See n. 10 above.

13. Karl Barth, *Church Dogmatics,* 4 volumes in 13 parts, ed. G. W. Bromiley and T. F. Torrance (Edinburgh: T. & T. Clark, 1956-1975), IV/1, p. 192 (hereafter, volume, part, and page references to this work appear in parentheses in the text and footnotes).

If the humility of Christ is not simply an attitude of the man Jesus, if it is the attitude of this man because . . . there is a humility grounded in the being of God, then something else is grounded in the being of God Himself. For, according to this New Testament, it is the case that the humility of this man is an act of obedience. . . . If, then, God is in Christ, if what the man Jesus does is God's own work, this aspect of the self-emptying and self-humbling of Jesus Christ as an act of obedience cannot be alien to God. But in this case we have to see here the other and inner side of the mystery of the divine nature of Christ and therefore of the nature of the one true God — that He Himself is also able and free to render obedience. (*CD* IV/1, 193)

So far, then, Barth has said that both humility and obedience are "natural" and "proper" to God in the sense that God is "free" for them. The difference between the two is the difference between an "attitude" (a disposition or basic posture) and a freely willed activity that can only, in the nature of the case, be described as purposeful. But this leads to a further question.

"Obedience as a possibility and actuality in God Himself seems at once to compromise the unity and then logically the equality of the divine being. Can the one God command and obey? Can the one God be above and below, the superior and the subordinate? If we speak of an obedience that takes place in God, do we not have to speak necessarily of two divine beings, and then of two beings who are not equally divine, the first and the commanding properly divine, the second and obeying only divine in an improper sense?"(*CD* IV/1, p. 195) Barth's answer to this question takes him on a brief detour through the tensions in early church consideration of the doctrine of the Trinity.

It belongs to his most brilliant insights that he recognized that subordinationism and modalism have a common root. Both are born from a refusal to see in the event of the cross "the truth of the humiliation, the lowliness and obedience of the one true God Himself. . ." (*CD* IV/1, p. 199). In other words, both are committed to upholding an abstract concept of divine impassibility, but they do this in differing ways: subordinationism by treating the obedient Christ as a "heavenly or earthly being distinct from God," modalism by treating the obedient Christ as a mere appearance of the one true God. Barth's solution is to affirm that it is "essential" [*wesentlich*] to the being of God "that there is in God Himself an above and a below, a *prius* and a *posterius,* a superiority and a subordination . . .

that it belongs to the inner life of God that there should take place within it obedience" (*CD* IV/1, pp. 199-200).

Taking a step back, we can say with confidence that Barth now believes that obedience is *essential* to God. That is to say, a willed activity whose purposive character can have to do only with the covenant of grace is essential to God. Now, if this is the case, then Barth leaves us with only two remaining options. Either you say, "That which God is, He is necessarily" — so that obedience is a necessary act (and with that affirmation, creation and redemption are made to be necessary to God). Or you say that divine "essence" is an activity whose purpose is rooted in the divine freedom. The first is the route of a good many of the theological followers of Hegel. The second is my own option.

B. Given that Barth has closed the metaphysical gap between the divine essence and the divine will, the only priority of the Trinity over election that he makes room for is a logical priority. Talk of an ontological priority would reopen that gap.

Thesis 4: That Barth was committed in a principled way to keeping metaphysics out of the domain of Christian dogmatics did not prevent him from reading appreciatively those theologians for whom metaphysical conceptions were basic to their understandings of God and the human, seeking to identify the theological values that came to expression in their metaphysical thought forms, and translating those values into a non-metaphysical scheme. During the years of what we might think of as his "apprenticeship" in dogmatic theology (stretching from the Göttingen Dogmatics on through *CD* II/1), however, his effort to "hear the voice of the Church and the Bible" absorbed his attention to such a degree that he had little time for the more constructive task of translation.[14] It was not

14. Karl Barth to Rudolf Bultmann, 12 June 1928, in *Karl Barth–Rudolf Bultmann: Letters, 1922-1966*, ed. Bernd Jaspert, trans. Geoffrey W. Bromiley (Grand Rapids: Eerdmans, 1981), pp. 41-42: "I will not defend in principle what you call my ignoring of philosophical work. . . . It is also a fact that the defect of older theology was never clear to me at the point where Harnack's *Dogmengeschichte* lays its finger, that the Platonism and Aristotelianism of the orthodox was not a hindrance to my (shall we say apparently) perceiving what was at issue and therefore to adopting the older terminology into my own vocabulary *without identifying myself with the underlying philosophy*. . . . My own concern is at any rate the voice of the Church and the Bible, and to let this voice be heard, even if in so doing, for want of anything better, I have to think somewhat in Aristotelian terms" (emphasis added).

until he developed his christologically grounded doctrine of election in *CD* II/2 that he was able to begin the work of elaborating a nonmetaphysical theological ontology capable of providing the basis for that constructive work.

Thesis 5: In his 1951 work on Barth, Hans Urs von Balthasar spoke of a final shift in Barth's thinking around 1938. He described it in formal terms as a shift from a theology of the Word to a truly Christocentric theology. I have tried to describe the same shift in material terms as a move from a more nearly pneumatocentric theology that had as its focus the "here and now" situation of the believer who is addressed by the Word to a theology that sought to ground all doctrinal reflection in the "there and then" of Jesus Christ, in the divine humiliation and the human exaltation that took place in him. The timing of this shift is something that cannot be pinned down with precision. Already in *CD* II/1, intimations of the coming change are present. The explanation for this lies in the fact that Barth had begun to rethink his doctrine of election as a consequence of hearing a lecture on the subject by Pierre Maury at the 1936 celebration of the 400th anniversary of the Reformation of Geneva. But the shift was completed only in the writing of *CD* II/2, where Barth made the astonishing claim that Jesus Christ is not only the object of election but also its subject (i.e., its author). This was not a claim made by Maury.[15]

Thesis 6: The meaning of the statement "Jesus Christ is the subject of election" is disputed. The most minimal understanding of it is that the event in which the eternal Son affirms the will of his Father that he should become incarnate is, at the same time, the event in which he is made to *be* (by way of anticipation) Jesus Christ. Thus is the man Jesus present at the very beginning of all of God's works *ad extra*. But I think Barth wanted to say more than this. I think he wanted to overcome the metaphysical gap introduced into theology in the West by the Thomistic distinction between the eternal processions (by which the being of God is constituted) and the eternal missions (by which God sets himself in relationship to human beings) by collapsing the processions and the missions into a single eternal event. However, the full implications of this move would not be made clear until Barth

---

15. On this point, see Matthias Gockel, *Barth and Schleiermacher on the Doctrine of Election: A Systematic-Theological Comparison* (Oxford: Oxford University Press, 2006), p. 162, n. 14.

had written his doctrine of reconciliation and directed his attention, specifically, to the problem of God's unchangeability in becoming incarnate.

*Explanation*

A. Barth's doctrine of the Trinity experienced a significant development between *CD* I/1 and *CD* IV/1. To be sure, the basic *structure* of Barth's earlier doctrine remained in place. There is in God but one subject in three "modes of being" (*CD* IV/1, pp. 204-5).[16] One subject: that means that "divine unity consists in the fact that in Himself He is both One who is obeyed and Another who obeys" (*CD* IV/1, p. 201). What has changed is that Barth no longer derives his doctrine of the Trinity from the *logic* of revelation (i.e. from the structure of the address of God to the believer) but from the *history* of Jesus Christ, the God-human who exists in the unity of humiliation and exaltation.[17] "As we look at Jesus Christ we cannot avoid the astounding conclusion of a divine obedience. Therefore we have to draw the no less astounding deduction that in equal Godhead the one God is, in fact, the One and also Another, that He is indeed a First and a Second, One who rules and commands in majesty and One who obeys in humility. The one God is both the one and the other. And, we continue, He is the one and the other without any cleft or differentiation but in perfect unity and equality because in the same perfect unity and equality He is also a Third, the One who affirms the one and equal Godhead through and by and in the two modes of being, the One who makes possible and maintains His fellowship with Himself as the one and the other. In virtue of this third mode of being, He is in the other two without division or contradiction, the whole God in each" (*CD* IV/1, p. 202).

16. "By Father, Son and Spirit we do not mean what is commonly suggested to us by the word 'persons.' This designation was accepted — not without opposition — on linguistic presuppositions which no longer obtain today. It was never intended to imply — at any rate in the mainstream of theological tradition — that there are in God three different personalities, three self-existent individuals with their own self-consciousness, cognition, volition, activity, effects, revelation and name. The one name of the one God is the threefold name of Father, Son and Holy Spirit. The one 'personality' of God, the one active and speaking divine Ego, is Father, Son and Holy Spirit. Otherwise we should obviously have to speak of three gods. . . . Christian faith and the Christian confession has one subject, not three. But He is the one God in self-repetition, in the repetition of His own and equal divine being, and therefore in three different modes of being." Cf. *CD* I/1, pp. 350, 353-68.

17. For the derivation of the doctrine of the Trinity from the grammar of revelation, see *CD* I/1, pp. 304-33.

Two things are made clear in this passage. First, Barth is seeking, with his doctrine of the Trinity, to describe the ontological conditions in God for his self-revelation in time. That his self-revelation in time takes place in obedience must mean that obedience is not alien to the innermost being of God. But now notice: Barth has identified the differentiation of Father and Son with the "commanding" and "obeying" that takes place in election. In so doing, he has described the ontological conditions for the possibility of a correspondence of the history of the incarnate God to what God is in eternity. There is no longer any room left here for an abstract doctrine of the Trinity. There is a triune being of God — only in the covenant of grace. Second, the unity of Father and Son is made to depend on the role played by the Spirit, in binding them together. It is not dependent on subsistence in a Godhead that has been interpreted along the lines of a substance metaphysics.

B. Barth's later doctrine of the Trinity thus entails a collapse of the eternal processions into the eternal missions. That much is clearly seen in the following passage.

> In humility as the Son who complies, He is the same as the Father is in majesty as the Father who disposes. He is the same in consequence (and obedience) as is the Father in origin. He is the same as the Son, i.e., as the self-posited God (the eternally begotten of the Father as the dogma has it) as is the Father as the self-positing God (the Father who eternally begets). Moreover, in His humility and compliance as Son, He has a supreme part in the majesty and disposing of the Father. The Father as the origin is never apart from Him as the consequence, the obedient One. The self-positing God is never apart from Him as the One who is posited as God by God. . . . The Father is not the Father and the Son is not the Son without a mutual affirmation and love in the Spirit. (*CD* IV/1, p. 209)

In this passage the command of the Father has been directly identified with the act of self-positing, and the obedience of the Son has been directly identified with being posited. We would not be stretching a point if we said that the "command" of the Father simply *is* the generation of the Son, the act in which God posits a mode of being in himself in which he can then "obey" (and the act in which God posits in himself a third mode of being to secure the unity of the other two).

128

C. Read in the light of the doctrine of the Trinity, which is implied by Barth's treatment of the incarnation, the statement "Jesus Christ is the subject of election" means that Jesus Christ, the eternal Son, elects his own election by means of the *same will* by which the Father elects him, and that this takes place in one and the *same eternal* event.[18] By the "same will": this means that the unity of the divine subject is not set aside by the "command" and "obedience" structure proper to the covenant of grace. What we have before us here is an eternal act of *self*-differentiation on the part of a single, unified subject. In "one and the same event": this means that there is no temporal gap between "command" and "obedience." As the act of the one divine subject in differentiating himself into modes of being, "command" and "obedience" take place simultaneously. But this also means that the one generated by the Father is already "joined" (on the level of his identity) to the human nature he would assume even *as* he responds in obedience. It is as joined to the human nature that he is the subject who obeys the command of the Father — that is, as Jesus Christ. Therefore, there is no "eternal Son qua Son," no abstract being of the Son in which he is not already Jesus Christ. The one who agrees with and affirms the will of the Father and who thereby makes himself the subject of election is Jesus Christ.

Thesis 7: Christology constitutes the theoretical basis for all other doctrinal constructs from *CD* II/2 to the end of Barth's life. But it was not until he had thoroughly "historicized" his Christology (beginning in *CD* IV/1) that he began to realize the *critical* potential of this epistemological starting point. For if this new Christology is now the epistemological basis for theology, then nothing may be said of God or the human that does not find its basis in *this* Christology. To express it another way: a doctrine of God built on the soil of this epistemological foundation may seek to find in God the ontological conditions for the possibility of this Christology

---

18. I take it that this is also what Gregory of Nyssa means when he says, "Rather does every operation which extends from God to creation and is designated according to our differing conceptions of it have its origin in the Father, proceed through the Son, and reach its completion in the Holy Spirit. . . . [T]here is one motion and disposition of the good will which proceeds from the Father, through the Son, to the Spirit." But that, then, is the same as saying that there is in God *one* mind, *one* will, and *one* energy of operation, which proceeds from the Father, through the Son, to the Holy Spirit. See Gregory of Nyssa, "An Answer to Ablabius: That We Should Not Think of Saying There Are Three Gods," in *Christology of the Later Fathers*, ed. Edward R. Hardy (Philadelphia: Westminster, 1954), p. 262.

*only.* Anything beyond that is unwarranted speculation that takes place on a different basis — and is thus to be excluded. Seen in this light, much in Barth's earlier doctrine of God can remain standing only if seen in a different light, and some things need to be rejected.

*Explanation*

A. The following statements are very good indeed:

1. "*Actus purus* is not sufficient as a description of God. To it there must be added at least '*et singularis*'" (*CD* II/1, p. 264). God's being and act is a being in a "particular event"(*CD* II/1, p. 264) in history; an event whose singularity consists in the fact that its basis is different from all other events. "No other being exists *absolutely* in its act. No other being is *absolutely* its own conscious, willed and executed decision" (*CD* II/1, p. 271, emphases added).[19] To speak of God as *actus purus et singularis* is to say that God has his being in the singularity of an event in history in which God simply *is* the mode of his self-revelation in time. That is why Barth can also say, "What God is as God, the divine individuality and characteristics, the *essentia* or 'essence' of God, is something which we shall encounter at the

---

19. With respect to this passage, Hunsinger makes a series of claims that merit close scrutiny. He holds, first, that this statement says nothing more than that "God exists absolutely in His own act" (thesis 9, c, bullet point 1). In reducing the act in question to his own version of a necessary act of self-affirmation, Hunsinger has made nonsense of the emphasis Barth places on the divine willing. He then says, second, that "the point is largely polemical" and that Barth is "positioning himself over against Feuerbach, Kant, Hegel, Schleiermacher, and Ritschl." This, too, is incorrect. The point is altogether a positive one. In the context in which this statement appears, Barth is explaining why it is that God defines what it means to be a "person" — not human beings. The polemic against Feuerbach et al. is intended to serve this greater point. Third, Hunsinger takes the phrase "executed decision" to mean that there is "no potentiality" in God's being. Where this claim is made to apply to the being-in-act of the necessary God, however, one winds up with the Scholastic concept of God that Saint Thomas taught. This cannot be Barth. Fourth, he tells us that "God does not bring himself into being out of nothing, . . . nor does he constitute himself by eternal fiat out of some prior, non-Trinitarian state of being" (p. 101 above). The first half of this statement is so obviously true that it leaves me to wonder why it has been said. Certainly, I have never said anything remotely like it. The second half of the statement is problematic because it speaks of a *prior* state of being; but it is precisely every thought of a prior state of being — whether of a non-Trinitarian or Trinitarian kind — that I have been seeking to erase. With the exception of bullet point 13 (which again speaks of a "coinherence of Jesus Christ in the eternal Son" [see n. 9 above]), the remainder of the bullet points under 9, c consist of quotations from Barth, whose meaning as implied by Hunsinger I do not dispute.

place where God deals with us as Lord and Savior or not at all" (*CD* II/1, p. 261). And " . . .God is who He is in the act of revelation" (*CD* II/1, p. 261).

2. "God is not *in abstracto* Father, Son and Holy Spirit. He is so with a definite purpose and reference . . ." (*CD* II/2, p. 79). Seen in context, the statement appears as a conclusion registered against the traditional "orthodox" account of the relationship between God's being in and for himself and God's being for us in his gracious act of election. According to the view held by "the Fathers and scholastics," the view that was "appropriated afresh by "the older Protestant orthodoxy,"

> God is everything in the way of aseity, simplicity, immutability, infinity, etc., but He is not the living God, that is to say, He is not the God who lives *in concrete decision*. God lives in this sense only figuratively. It is not something that belongs to *His proper and essential life, but only to His relation to the world*. Basically, then, it may only be 'ascribed' to Him, while it is believed that His true being and likewise His true Godhead are to be sought in the impassibility which is above and behind His living activity *within the universe*. . . . From the fact that God is the living God, that He is the living God inwardly as well as outwardly, a quality expressed and attested in concrete decision, they did not dare to deduce the further fact that God clearly does not exist otherwise, and that He does not will to be understood otherwise, than in the concreteness of life, in the determination of His will, which is as such a determination of His being. Strangely enough, they did not feel driven to make such a deduction even by their doctrine of the Trinity. They spoke of the three persons, of their inter-relationship, of the common work *ad extra*, without ever realizing the implication of the fact that this triune being does not exist and cannot be known *as a being which rests or moves purely within itself*. God is not *in abstracto* Father, Son and Holy Ghost, the triune God. He is so with a definite purpose and reference. . . . (*CD* II/2, p. 79)

Barth goes on to say that a triune being of God that rests or moves purely in itself has no existence. If it is ever appropriate to speak of a being of God "in and for Himself," it is so only with this qualification: the being of God in and for himself is a being of the God of electing grace in and for himself. There is, in other words, a relationship of identity in both content and form between the immanent Trinity in protology and the economic Trinity in time.

131

3. "There can be no Christian truth which does not, from the very first, contain within itself as its basis the fact that from and to all eternity God is the electing God. There can be no tenet of Christian doctrine which, if it is to be a Christian tenet, does not reflect both in form and content this divine electing. . . . There is no height or depth in which God can be God in any other way" (*CD* II/2, p. 77).[20]

B. The following statements can be retained only if seen in a different light from what surrounded their original articulation.

1. "To its very depths God's Godhead consists in the fact that it is an event — not any event, not events in general, but the event of his action, in which we have a share in God's revelation" (*CD* II/1, p. 263).[21]

2. "What God is as God . . . the *essentia* or 'essence' of God is something which we will encounter either at the place where God deals with us as Lord and Savior or not at all" (*CD* II/1, p. 261).

C. The following statements cannot be redeemed and should be rejected.

1. "As manifest and eternally actual in the relationship of Father, Son and Holy Spirit, God is the one who already has and is His own being. Therefore this being does not need any origination and constitution" (*CD* II/1, p. 306). This passage appears in the context of a treatment of God's "necessary existence." In this context, Barth considers the teaching of Hermann Schell, a modern Catholic theologian whose reflections on Jerome's claim that God is *causa sui* led him to posit that God's aseity consists in self-realization, self-constitution, and self-causation — "as though in a certain sense God arose out of Himself." This concept Barth rejects,

20. Hunsinger is much too cavalier in his handling of this text. He says simply that "[t]he electing God of which it speaks is the Holy Trinity" (thesis 9, d, bullet point 2). However true that may be, the force of this statement is to insist that even the triunity of God is *not* to be conceived in abstraction from election. One cannot open up a metaphysical gap between being triune and acting in election without violating the principle set forth in this statement.

21. Hunsinger holds that the "event" of which Barth speaks in this passage is not the event of his electing grace but an event that lies in back of that event, the event in which God is triune. Such a reading corresponds neatly to the Orthodox distinction of the divine essence and the divine energies. But if that were the case, Barth would then be saying that we humans have, in revelation, a share not just in the divine "energies" but in the divine "essence." This is not Orthodox; it is hyper-Orthodox. And I don't believe that Barth intended such an outcome, though an appropriate sense of the passage is more readily attainable when it is read in the light of Barth's mature Christology.

though the question must remain open as to whether his later Christology would allow him to continue to do so. In any event, it is important to see just how ambivalent Barth is, already at this early date. In spite of rejecting Schell's thesis, he thinks it important to find a way to honor Schell's "special concern," that is, to overcome "the scholastic equation of God with the unmoved Mover of Aristotle" (*CD* II/1, p. 305). And clearly, for Barth, the way to do this is to critically engage the medieval Catholic definition of God as the *ens necessarium*. What Barth seeks to avoid here is the logical necessity that attaches itself to a concept — as occurs in the following statement, whose source Barth does not identify: "It is an intrinsic impossibility that He should not be or should be other than He is" (*CD* II/1, p. 307). Over against this concept of "necessity," Barth places the lived actuality of God. "Of God we can say only that in the actuality of His being He is its affirmation, that in the actuality of His being His non-being or His being other than He is, is ontologically and noetically excluded, that it *becomes* an absolute impossibility, i.e., an impossibility which has no possibility as its background. As distinct from what is meant by these terms [i.e., *notwendig, necesse, necessarium, necessitas*], there is no need as a result of which God has to be. But if God is, it is the effect of His freedom, which knows no necessity, no inevitability" (*CD* II/1, p. 307). Barth comes very close here to the claim made by John Zizioulas that God is the being who is free not to exist but who chooses in fact to exist.[22] Had he not surrounded these claims with a rejection of the idea that "God takes His origin from Himself" (*CD* II/1, p. 306), had he allowed that this actuality of being ex-

---

22. See John Zizioulas, *Being as Communion: Studies in Personhood and the Church* (Crestwood, NY: St. Vladimir's Seminary Press, 1993), p. 41: "[T]he ontological 'principle' of God is traced back . . . to the person. Thus when we say that God 'is,' we do not bind the personal freedom of God — the being of God is not an 'ontological necessity' or a simple 'reality' for God — but we ascribe the being of God to His personal freedom. In a more analytical way this means that God, as Father and not as substance, perpetually confirms through 'being' His *free* will to exist. And it is precisely His trinitarian existence that constitutes this confirmation: the Father out of love — that is, freely, begets the Son and brings forth the Spirit." Cf. *Being as Communion*, p. 44: "The manner in which God exercises His ontological freedom, that precisely which makes Him ontologically free, is the way in which He transcends and abolishes the ontological necessity of the substance by being God as *Father*, that is, as He who 'begets' the Son and 'brings forth' the Spirit. This ecstatic character of God, the fact that His being is identical with an act of communion, ensures the transcendence of the ontological necessity which His substance would have demanded — if substance were the primary ontological predicate of God — and replaces this necessity with the free self-affirmation of divine existence."

presses a freedom-in-decision, he would have arrived at the same concept of divine freedom as Zizioulas did. As it is, the statement we began with must be rejected.

2. "Jesus Christ has a beginning, but God has no beginning" (*CD* II/2, p. 102).

3. "We know God's will *apart* from predestination only as the act in which, from all eternity and in all eternity, God affirms and confirms Himself" (*CD* II/2, p. 155). Once Barth makes his later Christology to be the epistemological basis for all that may be said of God, such an "apart from" becomes a complete impossibility.

## Section III: With Barth — and Beyond Barth

Thesis 8: The divine "decision" that is election is not to be understood in analogy to decision-making on the human plane. In truth, the relationship is exactly the opposite. Decision-making on the human plane is a pale reflection of the divine decision, since all human decisions only imperfectly express and realize the intentions that inform them. The divine decision, on the other hand, simply *is* the divine intentionality.

*Explanation*

A. Human decision-making is characterized by the following features: (1) Being precedes act on the human plane because humans must first receive their being from Another *before* acting. (2) Human decision-making involves deliberation, an attempt to think through the consequences of available alternatives *before* acting. The "before" in this statement reflects the fact that human decision-making is temporally structured. And again, that consideration leads us quite naturally to the conclusion that being must precede act on the human plane. (3) Human decision-making is fraught with peril. Humans cannot know either the alternatives available to them or the consequences that attend those alternatives perfectly. Nor can they know themselves so well that their true intentions are known or realized in any decision made.

B. The divine decision that is election differs from human decision-making at each of the foregoing points (taking them this time in the reverse order). (1) Traditional theism held that God knows all things in knowing himself, that God knows all "possibilities" available to him "before" acting. But if God truly knows all things, then he also knows, by an act of immediate intuition, what he *will do,* and thus what his "intention" is. Self-knowing and intentional behavior are one in him.[23] In this way, the idea of counterfactual possibilities is rendered *unreal* (i.e., lacking in reality). (2) It follows that God does not deliberate in coming to a decision. Any attempt to temporalize the divine decision through the imposition of a "before and after" structure is illegitimate. But that is precisely what happens whenever we think of God's being as ontologically anterior to the act of election. (3) Therefore, God must give himself being eternally in the act in which he sets himself in relationship to Jesus Christ and, in him, to the world. There is thus no metaphysical gap between God's being and his acting.

Thesis 9: As a description of the being of God in the act of election, the freedom of God is a freedom for self-determination and, indeed, self-*limitation* and suffering for the sake of human beings. It is God's lordship over all things, including his own being. In that God chooses to be God for us in Christ, he is giving himself the being he will have for all eternity.

*Explanation*

A. Such a conception of freedom includes more than the negations that the tradition typically associated with the concept of divine freedom. That God is free from external constraint or conditioning is certainly to be affirmed. That he is free as well from all internal lack or deficiency or need is also true. But God's freedom cannot be exhaustively described when the reference is only to such negations. Seen positively, God's freedom is the freedom of the love that God is to set itself in concrete relationship to that which is other than itself.

B. However, God's freedom does not consist in a choice between alternatives. Such a conception, however venerable it may be, is far too anthropomorphic. It requires "time" for deliberation in order to be meaningful. God's freedom, by contrast, is a freedom *for* time. It is not a freedom that presupposes time.

23. I owe this formulation to my daughter Catriona, a fine theologian in the making and an excellent conversation partner.

C. God's freedom is finally the freedom to exist — or not to exist. The opposite of the determination to be God in the covenant of grace is not a determination to be God in some other way; rather, it is the absence of such a determination, which would mean choosing not to exist.

Thesis 10: If God is what he is in the eternal decision of election and not in a state or mode of existence that is above or prior to that decision, then the question Who is the subject of this decision? constitutes a transgression of the boundaries set by the divine reality itself. For embedded in that question is another, that is, What would God have been had he not made this decision? Such a question can only be answered on a basis other than the one provided by Barth's later Christology. It is, inevitably, an exercise in natural theology.

Thesis 11: Where the logical relationship of election to triunity is concerned, the foregoing considerations would allow us to take either element as a starting point and to reflect on the other in its light. To take up election first has the considerable advantage of laying emphasis on the decision in which God has his being. It is quite true that such an understanding leans in the direction of making the Father the source of being of the other two members of the Godhead (the so-called *monarchia* of the Father). But such a conclusion was one also drawn by Basil of Caesarea, and it certainly entails no departure from Nicene orthodoxy.

*Explanation*

The suspicion that seems to animate Hunsinger is that my understanding of the logical relationship of election to the divine triunity constitutes a violation of the creedal formulation "begotten, not made": hence, Arianism would seem to be the worry. That what I have sketched here is not "Arian" rests on three considerations. First, the primary concern of Arius was to safeguard the impassibility of what he called the "high God." I do not believe that impassibility is a biblical doctrine; thus, at the very least, our motivations are quite different. Second, I do not believe that there was Spirit when the Son was not. The generation of the Son and the bringing forth of the Spirit is the event of God's self-origination. There is nothing "before" it. Third, and most important, I do not make the Son to be a different subject from the Father. The act wherein God constitutes himself as triune is an act of *self*-relating for the sake of self-giving. That this view comports nicely with Barth's basic structure — one subject in three modes of being — goes without saying.

## Conclusion

In the history of reflection on Barth's theological ontology, it is Eberhard Jüngel who set the gold standard. And to the extent that Kevin Hector wants to find in Barth a logical priority of Trinity over election *only*, it is he who carries Jüngel's banner in the current debate. My own work has used Barth as a resource (the *primary* resource) for my own constructive work. I make no apology for this. Karl Barth was the greatest theologian since the Reformation. But we do him no service if we simply repeat him. For his interest lay in the subject matter to which he bore witness. And it is to that subject matter that we must direct our attention, not to Karl Barth as an end in himself.

# 6. Obedience, Trinity, and Election: Thinking With and Beyond the *Church Dogmatics*

*Paul Dafydd Jones*

Many readers of this book will know that the study of Karl Barth has recently become a somewhat contentious affair. Some sharp exchanges about the immanent and economic Trinity, the *Logos asarkos/ensarkos* and *Logos incarnandus/incarnatus,* and the meaning of election have taken place. Interpretative stances have been established, refined, and (perhaps regrettably) entrenched. The immediate reasons for the controversy lie close to hand: the emergence of an array of scholars with the clarity of mind, patience, and analytical flair needed to read Barth well; a continued affection for Trinitarian thought that has been building on pioneering texts published in the 1980s and 1990s; ongoing debates — post-Derrida — about "being," "onto-theology," and the divine; and finally, a welcome (re)engagement with German-language scholarship about Barth's early and late work. Yet an even more fundamental factor animating current disputes pertains to Barth's *legacy,* a pressing issue for a field that, for the most part, has now freed itself from the unfortunate paradigm of neo-orthodoxy. Who *is* this theologian, and what does his work portend for Christian theology in the twenty-first century? An able defender of the immanent Trinity, whose writings might countermand our baneful descent into heterodoxy and heresy? A creative but misunderstood "traditionalist" who could invigorate churchly theological reflection and ecumenical dialogue? A postmetaphysical pioneer whose audacious treatment of election might help theologians rethink the doctrine of God and bridge the divide between evangelical and mainstream Protestants? To express it still more broadly: How should Barth's thought be received by scholars who have bid adieu (or perhaps auf Wiedersehen) to prominent twentieth-century schools of thought and who now work in an undefined and unsettled intellectual context?

Needless to say, what follows does not provide a definitive answer to questions such as these. My principal concern is Barth's views about the Trinity and election. Yet my hope is that this "local" contribution to ongoing discussions will do more than add to the interpretative options now available. Having outlined what I judge to be a fair (but certainly not incontestable) reading of key claims in the *Church Dogmatics,* I propose that recent debates should be viewed as an opportunity for scholars to embrace a new sensibility, characterized by interpretative open-mindedness and a keen concern to think constructively — with and beyond Barth.

The first and second sections of the essay examine Barth's claims about the being and action of God qua Son. I focus primarily on *Church Dogmatics* IV/1, § 59.[1] My thesis is that Barth's presentation of the relationship between the Father and the Son in this paragraph amounts to a Trinitarian clarification of earlier claims about election. The history of Jesus Christ is not only a revelation of the only-begotten Son as obedient to the Father (although it is indeed that). The Son's obedience is also an event in which God exercises and applies God's sovereign freedom in a way that has consequences for the being of God. It is an event of divine self-determination, of divine "being" in its "becoming" (Jüngel), that God applies to God's own life.[2] In propounding this argument, I hope to show how a postmetaphysical reading of Barth's doctrine of God — or, to use terminology recently favored by George Hunsinger, a "revisionist" approach to the *Dogmatics* — is able to affirm the importance of the immanent Trinity while neither backing away from nor diluting the claim that God's second way of being is qualified, and in a significant way defined, by the concrete history of Jesus Christ. In the third section of the essay, I argue that Barth's legacy is not something to be pinned down, but an array of possibilities to be opened up. The *Church Dogmatics* should not be bound

---

1. Karl Barth, *Church Dogmatics,* 31 part-volumes (London: T. & T. Clark, 2009). Although I am using the new edition of the *Dogmatics,* all page numbers refer to the standard translation of the text (hereafter, volume, part, and page references to the *CD* appear in parentheses in the text and footnotes; "rev." indicates my revised translation). The original text: Karl Barth, *Die Kirchliche Dogmatik,* 13 part-volumes (Zürich: TVZ, 1980).

2. Eberhard Jüngel, *God's Being Is in Becoming: The Trinitarian Being of God in the Theology of Karl Barth; A Paraphrase,* trans. John Webster (Edinburgh: T. & T. Clark, 2001). Although this essay uses Jüngel's interpretative idiom, what follows is certainly my own reading of Barth. With that said, I have numerous points of agreement with Jüngel's interpretative masterpiece and some of his briefer papers. See esp. Eberhard Jüngel, ". . . keine menschenlosigkeit Gottes . . . zur Theologie Karl Barths zwischen Theismus und Atheismus," in *Barth-studien* (Gütersloh: Gütersloher Verlaghaus Mohn, 1982), pp. 332-47.

to a particular theological program. Rather, scholars ought to delight in the fact that this text accommodates (in fact, *demands*) a diverse set of interpretations. I also experiment with the idea that, if God's "being is in becoming," then human life might be construed analogously. Scholars have vigorously debated Barth's understanding of the Trinity and election. What is needful now is an examination of the significance of this debate for theological anthropology, broadly understood.

# I

A central argument of § 59 is that Jesus Christ reveals the nature of the relationship between God's first and second ways of being. In accord with the belief of many Christians, past and present, Barth believes the Son to be consubstantial with the Father. As the Son incarnate, then, Jesus Christ shares fully in the divine essence. He is not an especially exalted creature, adopted by God for a salvific purpose: he is the second person of the Holy Trinity, the divine person who assumes to himself an individuated human essence. More innovatively, Barth contends that the history of Jesus Christ reveals something important about the eternal relationship between Father and Son. One defining feature of this relationship is the fact that the Father commands, which means concretely that the Father specifies the way Jesus Christ disposes himself as the agent of salvation. Another defining feature of this relationship is the fact that the Son obeys the Father's command, which means concretely that salvation is accomplished by way of Jesus Christ's life, death, and resurrection.

Three more particular points clarify Barth's meaning. The first identifies obedience as a term that complements traditional assertions about the Father begetting the Son; the second underscores the scriptural underpinnings of Barth's dogmatic innovation; the third emphasizes that, for Barth, God's self-revelation is an event of self-conveyance.

First, then, the word "obedience" *(Gehorsam)*. The most obvious function of the term is to underscore that God's economic self-presentation is an event consistent with God's immanent life. One must beware of supposing or implying disparity between the humble and obedient bearing of the *Logos incarnatus* and the way the Son relates to the Father eternally. God's self-revelation is not at odds with God's being; on the contrary, the way "God was in Christ, reconciling the world unto himself" (2 Cor. 5:19 [KJV]) is materially directive for claims about God's Trinitarian being as such. Precisely because Jesus Christ disposes himself as obedient to the Father, the Christian theologian must affirm obedience as characteristic of the relationship that obtains eternally between God's first and second ways of being. To use Barth's own words, the dogmatic obligation "to affirm and understand as essential to the being of God the offensive fact that there is in God Himself an above and a below, a *prius* and a *posterius*, a superiority and subordination" (*CD*, IV/1, pp. 200-201), and to declare that "in equal Godhead the one God is, in fact, the One and also Another . . . a First and a Second, One who rules and commands in majesty and One who obeys in humility" (*CD* IV/1, p. 202), follows directly from the distinctive character of God's reconciliatory and revelatory work. God's activity *ad extra* exhibits the order of God's intra-Trinitarian relating.[3]

Yet there is more at stake here than the claim that the shape of God's self-revelation must regulate the theologian's doctrine of the Trinity. Barth also wants to describe the relationships that pattern God's life in a maximally actualistic way. To put it more technically, he wants to specify what activities are to be appropriated to God's first and second ways of being, granted their perichoretic relationship.[4] On this reckoning, talk of the Son's obedience counterpoints the traditional claim that the Father begets the Son. It indicates that, in the unity of the Holy Spirit, the relationship of Father and Son entails a double giving and receiving, with the Father's giving and the Son's receiving complemented by the Son obediently giving himself back to, and being received by, the Father. So, while the *procession* of the Son is a one-way street (for the Father alone generates the Son), the *relationship* between Father and Son moves in two directions, with the Father's begetting and commanding coextensive with the Son's begottenness and vital act of obedience. Or, to put it in terms borrowed from Saint Thomas: since "real relation in God can be based

3. Wolfhart Pannenberg and others are probably right, incidentally, to highlight connections between Barth's understanding of divine self-revelation and the legacy of Hegelian idealism. Barth is a theologian steeped in the German philosophical tradition, even as he challenges it in various ways. Having said that, and granting that I cannot tackle the issue here, I am not persuaded that divine self-revelation is an improper way to interpret the scriptural witness. See Wolfhart Pannenberg, Rolf Rendtorff, Trutz Rendtorff, and Ulrich Wilkens, *Revelation as History*, ed. Wolfhart Pannenberg, trans. David Grankou (London: Macmillan, 1968).

4. Jüngel's analysis of the *perichoresis*/appropriation pairing (which Barth treats in *CD* I/1, pp. 370-75) is masterful; see *God's Being*, pp. 42-53. More recently, see Peter S. Oh, *Karl Barth's Trinitarian Theology: A Study in Karl Barth's Analogical Use of the Trinitarian Relation* (London: T. & T. Clark, 2006).

*only on action*,"[5] Barth understands (divine) paternity and (divine) filiation in terms of a dynamic and perichoretic play of distinction-in-unity that passes constantly between God's first and second ways of being. The Son proceeds from the Father "by way of [an] intelligible action" that is simultaneously a relationship and a command, and the Son obeys as he responds and relates himself to the Father.[6] Certainly, one may not forget that such relationships obtain within — or, more correctly, are constitutive of — a person characterized by unique unity. Reprising the rhetoric of *Church Dogmatics* I/1, Barth insists that God is "one Subject, not three . . . one God in self-repetition, in the repetition of His own and equal divine being."[7] Yet a balancing claim, prominent throughout § 59, is that divine unity means Trinitarian *uniting,* and that the vital and determinate obedience of the Son to the Father, manifested in the concrete life of Jesus Christ, forms an integral part of the divine unity.

Second, it is important to grasp why Barth comes to the "astonishing conclusion of divine obedience" and acclaims some manner of superordination and subordination in the divine life (*CD* IV/1, p. 202). Here Barth

---

5. Thomas Aquinas, *Summa Theologica*, 5 vols., trans. Fathers of the English Dominican Province (New York: Benziger Bros., 1948; reprint, Notre Dame, IN: Ave Maria Press/Christian Classics, 1981), I.28.4 (emphasis added).

6. Aquinas, *Summa Theologica*, I.27.2.

7. *CD* IV/1, p. 205; see also *CD* I/1, pp. 348-83. Alan Torrance's handling of the *Wiederholung* motif is useful: "The Trinity," in *The Cambridge Companion to Karl Barth,* ed. John Webster (Cambridge: Cambridge University Press, 2000), pp. 72-91. An obvious question is whether Barth's later reflections on the Trinity "improve" on the statement of *Church Dogmatics* I/1, given that many believe that this part-volume exhibits an "underdeveloped sense . . . of the relations between the divine persons, the fellowship or mutuality between Father, Son, and Spirit"; on this, see Jeffrey Hensley, "Trinity and Freedom: A Response to Molnar," *Scottish Journal of Theology* 60, no. 1 (2008): 92; see also the sophisticated essay by Rowan Williams, "Barth on the Triune God," in *Wrestling with Angels: Conversations in Modern Theology,* ed. Mike Higton (Grand Rapids: Eerdmans, 2007), pp. 106-49. I would probably answer the question in the negative. Granted its strong emphasis on God's unity, *CD* I/1 does show a keen awareness of God's Trinitarian life. Barth never imagines divine unity apart from the Trinitarian relationships that are constitutive of that unity; indeed, when he discusses God as Spirit, he states that "from eternity, in His absolute simplicity, God is orientated [*sic*] to the Other, does not will to be without the Other, will have Himself only as He has Himself with the Other and indeed in the Other," and claims that in God there is "fellowship in separateness and separateness in fellowship" (*CD* I/1, pp. 483, 484). Nevertheless, as will become clear, Barth's doctrine of election perhaps enabled him to offer more assured statements about God's Trinitarian being than those offered in I/1. So much is demonstrated early in *CD* III, when Barth pointedly affirms "plurality in the being of God" (*CD* III/1, p. 192).

subtly challenges the age-old habit of associating obedience and humility with Christ's humanity, but not Christ's divinity — a problematic sleight of hand that both impugns the unity of Christ's person (for it risks suggesting that Christ's divinity and humanity do not act in seamless accord and enact *one* history) and disjoins descriptions of the divine economy from descriptions of the divine life as such (for it supposes that the Son relates to the Father in a way that is alternate to that disclosed by Jesus Christ). More pointedly, Barth shows an unflinching commitment to the belief that Scripture alone functions as the source and norm of dogmatic reflection. If the concrete person of Jesus Christ reveals who God is, and if the New Testament writers consistently describe the concrete person of Jesus Christ as obedient to the Father, the dogmatician must follow suit. He or she must describe the being of God, as Son, in terms of humility and obedience rendered toward the Father. Thus Barth says:

> [T]he humility of Christ is not simply an attitude of the man Jesus [but] it is the attitude of this man because, according to what takes place in the atonement made in this man (according to the revelation of God in Him), there is humility grounded in the being of God. . . . If . . . God is in Christ, if what the man Jesus does is God's own work, this aspect of the self-emptying [*Selbstentäusserung*] and self-humbling [*Selbsterniedrigung*] of Jesus Christ as an act of obedience cannot be alien to God. (*CD* IV/1, p. 193)

One might well say that, for Barth, humility and obedience serve as categorical summaries of Christ's life. While Barth associates humility with the basal fact of incarnation (so Phil. 2), obedience functions as an overarching description of Christ's sanctifying and justifying comportment: it summarizes the arc of the Gospel narratives that recount Christ's enactment of the history to which he has been appointed.[8] As the Father directs, the Son follows; as the Father commands, the Son lives out an atoning history. Indeed, exactly because Christ's work is coextensive with his revelatory action, one can say that, as Christ *does*, in obedience to the Father, so the Son, eternally, *is* in his relationship to the Father. Should critics raise the specter of "subordinationism" here, one can quickly dispel that. This in no way disparages or denies the divinity of the Son; rather, it dogmatically clarifies the character of the Son's eternal relationship to the Father. And nothing less than fidelity

---

8. This phrasing owes much to Hans Frei, *The Identity of Jesus Christ: The Hermeneutical Bases of Dogmatic Theology* (Eugene, OR: Wipf and Stock, 1997).

to Scripture animates the claims that Barth puts forward. The Son's mission, described authoritatively by the New Testament writers, reveals something about the way God lives as one subject in three ways of being. The theologian must conform his or her thought to this fact.[9]

Third, let me make explicit a conviction that underpins § 59: Christ's obedience to God the Father is an event in which God conveys himself to humankind. The *kenōsis* of the Son can neither be understood in terms of the non-use of the attributes of divine majesty (*contra* certain Lutherans in the seventeenth century) nor, more radically, in terms of divine self-divestment (*contra* Gottfried Thomasius and other nineteenth-century kenoticists).[10] Even as the Son concedes the form of deity in his activity *ad extra*, he retains the "content" of his being; even as Christ's life exhibits the eternal obedience of the Son to the Father, it is an event in which God gives himself to humankind. Thus Barth: "[I]n the form of a servant, which is the form of His presence and action in Jesus Christ, we have to do with God Himself in His true deity. . . . It is His sovereign grace that He wills to be and is amongst us in humility, our God, God for us" (*CD* IV/1, p. 193).

On one level this means that God's self-revelation as Son cannot be reduced to a disclosure of information or an event of "unveiling" (though it certainly is that). It is something rather more startling: it is a *communication* of the being that God is, as Son, before the Father and with the Spirit. In this communication, the distinction between giver and gift is collapsed to the extent that we, as recipients, are denied the means to possess or control what is being given. (As Barth remarks, the Son "gives Himself, but He does not give Himself away" [*CD* IV/1, p. 185].[11]) On another level, God

---

9. Incidentally, it would be wrong to claim that Barth's treatment of the Son's relationship to the Father represents a more thoroughgoing application of the *sola scriptura* principle than was achieved by his orthodox forebears. Granted the innovative force of Barth's outlook, and notwithstanding the (rather tired) complaints about scholastic "rationalism," the dogmatic procedure Barth follows is quite in keeping with mainstream Protestant theology in the sixteenth, seventeenth, and eighteenth centuries: systematic and exegetical reflection are consistently integrated. See Richard A. Muller, *Post-Reformation Reformed Dogmatics: The Rise and Development of Reformed Orthodoxy, ca. 1520 to ca. 1725*, vol. 4, *The Triunity of God* (Grand Rapids: Baker Academic, 2003), esp. pp. 196-244.

10. See *CD* IV/1, pp. 181-83. Barth's understanding of *kenōsis*, it seems, was marred by the extravagances of certain nineteenth-century Lutherans; the term has a broader meaning than he realizes. For more on this, see Sarah Coakley, *Powers and Submissions: Spirituality, Philosophy, and Gender* (Oxford: Blackwell, 2002), pp. 3-39.

11. The German is even better: "Gott gibt sich hin, aber nicht weg und nicht auf, indem er Geschöpf, indem er Mensch wird"; see *KD* IV/1, p. 202.

being "with us" entails nothing less than God's *imposing* himself on us. As well as confounding all efforts to reduce God to a datum of experience, religion, moral upbuilding, and the like, the incarnation makes every attempt to exist in splendid isolation from God impossible. It renders humankind the *object* of God's gracious election. The obedience of the Son, as a loving act of "divine self-involvement," means the coexistence of God with humankind — whether we like it or not.[12]

## II

Thus far, my analysis has stuck close to *Church Dogmatics* IV/1. I have not attempted to consider other part-volumes; in particular, I have made no significant reference to *Church Dogmatics* I/1, the principal function of which is to affirm God's unconditioned freedom and the elemental importance of the doctrine of the Trinity. I would now add that my disregard for the first part-volume of the *Dogmatics* is wholly intentional. Why so? Well, the best way to position § 59 in the context of Barth's broader dogmatic proposal is not to return to his prolegomenal statement, but rather to focus on his doctrine of election. While *Church Dogmatics* I/1 has great significance for Barth's overall project, it is II/2 that endeavors to "carry forward and complete the definition and exposition of the Subject God" (*CD* II/2, p. 6), which establishes the foundation on which Barth's claims about intra-Trinitarian obedience rest.

Recall a point made in the previous section, namely, that with the term "obedience" Barth intends to move beyond the bare claim that the Father begets the Son. Obedience characterizes the Son's dynamic relationship with and toward the Father. It indicates that the Father's generative action is matched by an ecstatic "return," that the Son's receipt of being, for all eternity, is complemented by his observance and fulfillment of the Father's command. But, still more particularly, what does the Son's obedience entail? It entails a history of "being" and "becoming" such that the identity of God qua Son becomes unthinkable in isolation from, and is in fact ontologically inclusive of, the concrete life of Jesus Christ. A passage at the beginning of § 58.4 is illuminating here: there Barth considers what it means to declare that Christ is truly God.

---

12. Edwin Chr. van Driel, *Incarnation Anyway: Arguments for Supralapsarian Christology* (New York: Oxford University Press, 2008), p. 74.

No general idea of "Godhead" developed abstractly . . . must be allowed to intrude at this point. *How* the freedom of God is constituted [*beschaffen*], in *what* character He is the Creator and Lord of all things, distinct and superior from them, in short what is to be understood by "Godhead" is something which — watchful against all imported ideas, ready to correct them and perhaps to let them be reversed and renewed in the most astonishing way — we must always learn from *Jesus Christ.* He defines those concepts: they do not define Him. . . . Jesus Christ is Himself God as the *Son* of God the Father and with God the Father the source of the Holy Spirit, united in one essence with the Father by the Holy Spirit. That is how He is God. He is God as He takes part in the event which constitutes the divine being [*an diesem Geschehen teilnimmt, das göttliche Sein ausmacht*]. (*CD* IV/1, p. 129, emphasis in original)

With these words Barth does more than prepare the way for the "astonishing conclusion" of intra-Trinitarian obedience. The claim to which he adverts is that the Son's economic enactment of the Father's command is an act of obedience that has ontological consequences for God's own life. Specifically, the obedience of the Son means that he "put into effect the freedom of His divine love" (*CD* IV/1, p. 187) in such a way that conventional ideas about divine simplicity and unity — that is, that they are ascribable to a divine essence that does *not* include the actual history of the man Jesus, that such terms must be understood along the lines of "pure and unadulterated divinity," as opposed to being defined by God's decision to be God on God's terms, not ours — are overturned and corrected by the way God determines and manifests God's being. Certainly, Barth will still use the word "obedience" to underscore thoroughgoing correspondence between God's economic activity and God's immanent, Trinitarian life. Yet he also uses the term to indicate that the concrete reality of Jesus Christ is not held at a distance from the divine being. Obedience functions as an integral part of a theological ontology that does not differentiate sharply between claims about the Son as such, the Son as *Logos incarnandus,* and the Son as *Logos incarnatus,* but rather focuses attention on the Son's self-determination to become and be the concrete person of Jesus Christ for all eternity.

A useful way to conceptualize this event of self-determination is to think of the Son's life in terms of a beginning, a middle, and an end that, in a mysterious way, bears back on God's being, this being a narration of the divine life of the Son that follows Barth as he "follows the being of God."[13] The beginning of the narrative is God's immanent life as it happens "apart from" and "before" the concrete reality of God's elected creature. Here, divine relating means *self*-relating; coexistence means "the original and essential determination" (*CD* IV/1, p. 201) of God's communal being as Father, Son, and Holy Spirit; unity means what "is open and free and active in itself . . . a unity of the One with Another" (*CD* IV/1, p. 202).[14] In § 59, as in other sections of the *Dogmatics*, Barth continues to insist that God's triune being is ontologically anterior to God's economic action. At no point does he temper his insistence that God's economic action has as its condition of possibility God's prevenient, self-sufficient reality. But why does Barth not become more expansive, for example, by mounting a defense of the immanent Trinity or underscoring the importance of the *Logos asarkos*? And why are his remarks on God's immanent life found at the *end* of § 59.1, as opposed to the beginning? The answer is not that Barth has already offered a defense of the immanent Trinity in *Church Dogmatics* I/1, and need not repeat earlier claims in the context of a treatment of reconciliation. It would also be a mistake to say that Barth is a staunch defender of the *Logos asarkos*. His excursive remarks suggest real wariness about this concept, even though he does not reject it outright.[15] It is rather that what Barth does say

---

13. Jüngel, *God's Being*, p. 9. By describing the Son's history in terms of a beginning, middle, and an end, I do intend some connection with Barth's understanding of divine temporality — but only in a loose sense. One cannot equate the Son's beginning, middle, and end with divine pretemporality, supratemporality, and posttemporality, not least because the treatment of the divine perfections at the end of *CD* II/1 is not quite integrated with the treatment of election in II/2.

14. Notice that no "Augustinian" emphasis on divine unity constricts Barth's thinking at this point. Precisely because the divine life is a dynamic and communal affair, talk about intradivine obedience is dogmatically intelligible.

15. See, e.g., *CD* IV/1, pp. 52-53. Barth's reasoning is complex. He begins with the claim that "we must not refer to the second 'person' of the Trinity as such, to the eternal Son or the eternal Word *in abstracto*, and therefore to the so-called λόγος ἄσαρκος." He then admits, with a backward glance to *CD* I/1, that "He is the content of a necessary and important concept in trinitarian doctrine when we have to understand the revelation and dealings of God in the light of their free basis in the inner being and essence of God," thereby making a distinction between the concept's utility within different dogmatic loci. However, he then proceeds to challenge the concept to such a degree that one wonders what value it has in *any* dogmatic context. Indeed, how does one understand the "inner being" of God *apart* from God's reconciliatory work? Is there a revelation of God additional to the revelation of the God who saves, in and as Jesus Christ? Barth would obviously answer these questions in the negative, therefore rendering somewhat nugatory his passing affirmation of the *Logos asarkos*.

147

about God's interrelating and, more particularly, the intra-Trinitarian obedience of the Son has a limited function. Barth intends only (1) to indicate that God qua Son is not reducible to (i.e., exhausted by) his being the *Logos incarnatus,* or, to put it more positively, that the Son's life has a meaning in excess of the incarnation, which means that the *Logos asarkos* could, in principle, be accorded a modest role in dogmatic inquiry; and (2) to consider how the gratuitous fact of incarnation enables the Christian to reflect, in a controlled and constrained way, on the triune life that happens "before" and "apart from" the Son's enactment of his salvific mission. In other words, the gracious quality of God's revelatory and reconciliatory work reveals to the Christian that God's being is prior to, and in a certain and important respect independent of, God's relationship with humankind.

Yet this aspect of Barth's thought is hardly made prominent in § 59. At this point in the *Dogmatics,* what Barth is really interested in is the "middle" of the Son's history: a middle that defines the present of Christian existence, given that "the one true God . . . is the subject of the act of atonement in such a way that His presence and action as the Reconciler of the world coincide and are indeed identical [*identisch*] with the existence of the humiliated and lowly and obedient man Jesus of Nazareth" (*CD* IV/1, p. 199), a middle that reveals that "the inward divine relationship between the One who rules and commands in majesty and the One who obeys in humility is identical [*identisch*] with the very different relationship between God and one of His creatures, a man" (*CD* IV/1, p. 203). Most obviously, such claims make plain Barth's unwavering affirmation of Christ's divinity. There should be no hedging about the subject who defines Jesus Christ. That subject is the eternal Word of God; that subject is God in God's second way of being.

More profoundly, § 59 suggests that Christ's history, both in its particulars and in its broader movement toward Calvary, shows the specific way in which the Son implements and realizes the Father's command. Obedience describes the Son's willingness to become and be the concrete person in whom and through whom God distributes God's love, something anticipated by none other than Julian of Norwich, who writes that, having "stood in front of his Father like a servant," the Son "leapt forward eagerly at the Father's will and immediately . . . fell low into the Virgin's womb."[16]

16. Julian of Norwich, *Revelations of Divine Love,* trans. Elisabeth Spearing, intro. and notes by A. C. Spearing (London: Penguin, 1998), p. 122. The passage is from "The Long Text," chap. 51.

Obedience is thus poorly described as a deferential attitude of the incarnate Son toward God qua Father. Obedience, rightly understood, refers to the Son's free and eager uptake of a command, the fulfillment of which ensures that God's love for humankind is genuinely communicated. Indeed, on this reckoning, the Son's obedience is not comprehensible in terms of an intra-Trinitarian ranking, even though talk about a "second" or "below" (along with an unforgivable aside about the relationship of husband and wife) risks suggesting as much. Obedience must be understood in terms of the divine Son freely exercising God's love on our behalf, existing under the conditions of finitude and committing himself to a history in which he bears God's rejection of sin. Obediently, the Son *delivers* God's love to humankind in a way that would be unthinkable were it not for the actuality of Christ's birth, death, and resurrection; obediently, the Son lives and dies in a way that actualizes God's decision to exist in loving fellowship with humankind.

The "end" of the Son's history discloses one of the most audacious dimensions of Barth's theology, because it shows how Barth's doctrine of divine triunity intersects with his understanding of election as an ontologically significant event of divine self-determination. Why so? Well, what has been said thus far about the Son's "beginning" and "middle" does not necessarily entail the claim that God qualifies or constitutes God's being in terms of Jesus Christ. Avowals about the "identity" of the Son and the man Jesus could pertain only to the economic being and action of the Son; the narrative I am tracing could stop with the assertion that, in the person of Jesus Christ, the Son of God becomes unequivocally and fully present to creatures. The entire first section of this essay, in fact, could be read as evidence for Barth's concern to defend a certain construal of the immanent Trinity, one that affirms no ontologically significant interplay between God's reconciling and revealing work and God's eternal being. But Barth is rather more ambitious than this, as is evident in his startling claim that Jesus Christ is the *subject* of election. While holding open the prospect of a conventional (I use the term loosely) affirmation of the immanent Trinity and the *Logos asarkos,* the later Barth advances a metaphysically dizzying suggestion: Jesus Christ is the agent who enacts God's elective intention *and* the person whose concrete life, in all of its concrete, historical particularity, has ramifications for the eternal being of God qua Son.

To make the point more fully: for Barth, the incarnation of the Son is the one occasion — the *only* occasion, according to God's own unconditioned, free decree — where what happens economically has relevance for who God is immanently. As "the strangely logical final continuation of . . . the history in which He is God" (*CD* IV/1, p. 203), the incarnation does not only impinge upon our history. That would suggest that God's own life is unaffected by the incarnation. That would require one to forget that Barth has already declared that in "this free act of the election of grace there is already present, already anticipated, already assumed into unity with His own existence as God the existence of the man whom He intends and loves from the very first. . . . In this free act of the election of grace the Son of the Father is no longer *just* the eternal logos, but as such, as true God from all eternity He is also the true God *and* true man that He will become in time" (*CD* IV/1, p. 66 rev., emphasis added). No, as a continuation of *God's* history, God freely incorporates into his own being the history undertaken (and endured) by the *Logos incarnatus*. God makes the "middle" of the Son's life — his being the concrete person of Jesus Christ — the "end" of the Son's life to such an extent that it has relevance for God's own being. It is the destiny of the Son, it is the realization and actualization of the Son's free obedience to the Father, for him to become and be the *Logos ensarkos*, not just in terms of his living as the concrete person of Christ but also in terms of his becoming and being the concrete person of Jesus Christ for all eternity, such that "in no depth of the Godhead shall we encounter any other but Him" (*CD* II/2, p. 115). Indeed, when Barth talks about the Son's obedience in § 59, he aims to specify more clearly what God's elective decision means for the divine life as such. He aims to elaborate an earlier claim that, "when we ask concerning the actuality of divine election, what can we do but see the One who performs this act of obedience, *who is Himself wholly this act of obedience ("der selber ganz und gar dieser Gehorsamakt ist"), who is in Himself in the first instance the Subject of election*" (*CD* II/2, p. 106 rev., emphasis added). The free obedience that passes ecstatically from the Son to the Father always intends to lift the concrete reality of human life into the divine life. The *Logos asarkos* always intends to become and be the *Logos ensarkos*. And, as God realizes God's free and loving decision, this intention is realized. The Son's incarnate history is embraced by God to such a degree that it has an effect on God's own being. One might even say that talk about the Son's session at the Father's right hand is more important than many have suspected. It reckons with the identity that God assigns himself as Son; it takes with full seriousness the claim that *Jesus of Nazareth* is "exalted at the right hand of God" (Acts 2:33).[17] It indicates

---

17. See also Mark 16:19; Rom. 8:34; Eph. 1:20; Col. 3:1. Barth puts it this way: "Without

(and Barth's phrasing, which slips between a reference to the Father's generation of the Son and the inception of the Son's temporal mission, is telling) that in "the divine *act of predestination* there *preexists* Jesus Christ who, as the Son of the eternal Father and the son of the virgin Mary, will become and be the mediator of the covenant between God and humankind, the One who accomplishes the event of reconciliation" (*CD* IV/1, p. 66 rev. ).

Two additional points help to round out this section. The first has to do with the difficult question of development within the *Dogmatics*. If § 59 provides a Trinitarian elucidation of claims implied, but not reasoned out, in *Church Dogmatics* II/2, is it appropriate to suppose that Barth "revised" his initial sketch of the doctrine of God? Certainly, Barth talks in later volumes about the Trinity, and the divine Son, without spelling out the narrative of divine self-determination that I have outlined. As noted earlier, he even uses the rhetoric of I/1 to talk about God's immanent being: he allows that God's being, and particularly the divine Son, can be considered without direct reference to the incarnation. Moreover, at no point does he retract any of his earlier claims. Nonetheless, I do think that II/2 entails a shift in Barth's thinking, and I do believe that this shift is ontologically consequential for Barth's later understanding of God.[18] This part-volume, I would suggest, announces a revision and expansion of the perspective drafted in the early 1930s. By "expansion" I mean that, with his doctrine of election, Barth begins to develop a theological ontology that surpasses anything anticipated in *Church Dogmatics* I. In *CD* II/2 and thereafter, Barth typically coordinates descriptions of the Trinity with claims about God's *Gnadenwahl*. A bare acclamation of God's triunity is no longer dogmatically sufficient, since it does not make explicit that "God Himself does not will to be God, and is not God, except as the One who elects. There is

---

the Son sitting at the right hand of the Father, God would not be God. But the Son is not only very God. He is also called Jesus of Nazareth" (see *CD* II/2, p. 7).

18. Bruce McCormack's pioneering essays on Barth's theological ontology are collected in *Orthodox and Modern: Studies in the Theology of Karl Barth* (Grand Rapids: Baker Academic, 2008); see, esp., pp. 183-277. See also Hans Theodor Goebel, "*Trinitätslehre und Erwählungslehre bei Karl Barth: eine Problemanzeige*," in *Wahrheit und Versöhnung: Theologische und Philosophische Beiträge zur Gotteslehre* (Gütersloh: Gütersloher Verlaghaus Gerd Mohn, 1989), pp. 147-66; Goebel, *Vom freien Wählen Gottes und des Menschen. Interpretationsübungen zur 'Analogie' nach Karl Barths Lehre von der Erwählung und Bedenken ihrer Folgen für die Kirchliche Dogmatik* (Frankfurt: Peter Lang, 1990); and Paul Dafydd Jones, *The Humanity of Christ: Christology in Karl Barth's Church Dogmatics* (London: T. & T. Clark, 2008), pp. 60-116.

no height or depth in which God can be God in any other way. We have not perceived or understood aright the Subject of all Christian doctrine if in our doctrine of God there is lacking the moment which is the specific content of the doctrine of election" (*CD* II/2, p. 77). By "revision" I mean that, given Barth's enlarged theological ontology, certain early claims — for example, that the "Word is what he is even before and apart from his being flesh" (*CD* I/2, p. 136) — no longer have the same force after *Church Dogmatics* II/2 and sometimes chafe against Barth's concern to integrate reflection about God's triunity and God's elective self-determination. As such, while George Hunsinger is right to claim that, for Barth, "[t]he Son *incarnatus* subsists in the eternal Son" and that the "Son *incarnatus* is not external but internal to the preexisting eternal Son,"[19] he is wrong to temper these assertions by arguing that "the Son *qua* Son is *properly* defined without reference to his being *incarnandus*" and wrong to parse Barth's later reflections about Trinity and election via a *simpliciter/secundum quid* distinction that sharply differentiates the *Logos,* the *Logos incarnandus,* and the *Logos incarnatus.*[20] Given the dynamic way in which Barth connects the Trinity and election — or, more vividly, given the fact that "God . . . lives in concrete decision" (*CD* II/2, p. 79), drawing into God's own being the lived history of Jesus Christ — it is important to posit a thoroughgoing ontological coinherence of the *Logos,* the *Logos incarnandus,* and the *Logos incarnatus,* and to affirm that the Son's becoming human has ontological ramifications for God. That is, the force of a doctrine of election made internal to the doctrine of God. And that is what animates an understanding of divine obedience that disdains a hard-and-fast differentiation of the Son's immanent and economic being, given a divine history that passes from a beginning, to a middle, to an end. Who God is as Son, and what God does as Son, are ontologically intertwined. By dint of God's free self-disposing, the principal vehicle of which is the free obedience of God in God's second way of being, God's elective self-determination bears back on God's eternal being.

Second, a related question: does this reading of Barth conflict with his emphasis on divine freedom, particularly as it is construed in *Church Dogmatics* I, given that it risks suggesting that God's being is dependent on, even beholden to, creaturely reality? Does this reading imply that the di-

19. George Hunsinger, "Election and the Trinity: Twenty-Five Theses on the Theology of Karl Barth," p. 99 above.
20. Hunsinger, "Election and the Trinity," p. 97 above.

vine being is only "completed" — that is, rendered fully determinate and fully actualized — when God fulfills God's election of grace, drawing into God's own being the concrete person of Jesus Christ? It would certainly be wrong to claim that "God's pretemporal decision of election actually gave rise to the Trinity" or that "the Holy Trinity is a function of God's pretemporal decision of election."[21] It is not the case that God's elective action is *required* for God to be who God is, as Trinity; God does not stand under obligations of this kind.[22] It is important, too, to affirm God's anterior, self-sufficient triune reality, not least because the history of the Son has a beginning that, in a complex way, precedes his becoming. However, once again, it is important not to interpret Barth's later work in ways that hold claims about the Trinity and God's self-determinative *Gnadenwahl* too far apart. One must think more actualistically. Barth develops a theological ontology in which God's triune being and God's elective activity converge — so much so that God "opens" Godself as Son, and qualifies God's being in terms of the actual life, death, and resurrection of Jesus Christ. This does not mean that God is less than fully actualized "prior" to the incarnation, or that God's being depends on (i.e., requires supplement by) the concrete life of Jesus Christ. Nor does it mean that the identity of the Son is engulfed by (i.e., rendered crudely equivalent to) the mission definitive of the person who is the *Logos ensarkos*. What it means is that Barth has reconceived the immanent Trinity in a way fitted to his own post-metaphysical theology. God's love for humankind is such that God does not close off God's pretemporal, self-sufficient, determinate perfection, and that God does not *end* God's history with God's pretemporal, self-sufficient, determinate, intra-Trinitarian relating. Rather, God's triunity is

21. Hunsinger, "Election and the Trinity," pp. 91, 107 above.

22. As Rowan Williams observes, albeit in a different context: "God would not be God were he not the God who is such as to be the ground and 'form' of [the] encounter [between Jesus and the God of Israel]; but this is not the same as saying that God would not be God were it not for a set of contingent events in the first century of our era." See Williams, *On Christian Theology* (Malden, MA: Blackwell, 2000), p. 161. Williams's rather Balthasarian words are certainly a little tricky to apply to Barth. They verge on overstatement. One cannot say that, for Barth, the "form" of the incarnation is supplied by the divine Son, while the "content" of his incarnate life is held at a distance from the divine being. Barth's point is that God self-determines in such a way that the Son is always becoming and being, for all eternity, the concrete person of Jesus Christ. Nevertheless, Williams does capture something of Barth's perspective. The Son cannot be reduced to the *Logos incarnatus*. And while one must beware of speculation, it is appropriate to say that the Son's self-determination has its ground in the divine being who is complete in himself — "before" the incarnation.

distinguished, reaffirmed — perhaps even *intensified* — given the Son's self-determination to become and be the "electing God" and "elected human."[23] By way of an event that would be unthinkable, were it not for its actuality (for who can imagine a perfect being opening himself to *this* kind of self-interpretation?), God becomes more than God needs to be. God makes God's intra-Trinitarian distinction-in-unity inclusive of the concrete life lived by the Word.

## III

Much, much more could be said about Barth's treatment of the Trinity and election. On one level, it would be possible to evaluate the claims above by asking whether they cohere with other aspects of Barth's theology. For example, if this interpretation connects easily with Barth's mature thinking about atonement, does that provide indirect evidence of its viability, maybe even its legitimacy?[24] And if this interpretation does not mesh with other claims that Barth puts forward — about creation and the covenant, say — is it therefore less persuasive? On another level, it might be profitable to consider further how my perspective relates to work offered by other Barth scholars — not, I hasten to add, simply to perpetuate intramural debate, but rather to clarify the options for understanding Barth's theological ontology. Those familiar with the secondary literature, for instance, will discern substantive overlap between my interpretation and that of Bruce McCormack, even as I draw on insights offered by George Hunsinger, Paul Molnar, and others. Still, there are points of difference. These arise from my decision to describe the life of the Son in terms of a beginning, middle, and an end, an interpretative move that al-

23. The term "intensified" is risky; certainly, it stands at the farthest edges of interpretative propriety. Jüngel puts the matter somewhat differently in *God's Being:* "In Jesus Christ the *concreteness* of the divine being is also maintained to the end for humanity. . . . Only in the concrete determination of the God who elects and of elect humanity can the *doctrine* of election enable us for our part to maintain in thought the concreteness of God's being which he maintains to the end for humanity" (p. 89).

24. I deal with this issue in "Barth and Anselm: God, Christ, and the Atonement," *International Journal of Systematic Theology* 12, no. 3 (2010): 257-82. Given the focus of this book, I must also mention Eberhard Jüngel's brief essay *"Das Verhältnis von 'ökonomischer' und 'immanenter' Trinität,"* in *Entsprechungen: Gott-Wahrheit-Mensch: Theologische Erörterungen* (München: Chr. Kaiser Verlag, 1980), pp. 265-75.

lows for a modest — and dialectically framed — affirmation of the *Logos asarkos*. As such, I would not claim, as McCormack does, that election has logical priority over divine triunity, even granting that the eternal identity of the Son encompasses and, in a sense, is constituted by the concrete life of Jesus Christ. It seems preferable simply to say that, for Barth, God's tri-unity and God's elective action are ontologically coimplicated, and to say that the concept of obedience allows Barth to explore this coimplication in a dogmatically intriguing way.

Indeed, while I agree that Barth sometimes "gave expression to a resid-ual commitment to aspects of classical metaphysics" after *Church Dogmat-ics* II/2, I believe that occasional references to the immanent Trinity, con-ceived without direct reference to the Son's economic mission, can be squared with an ontologically daring interpretation of the claim that Jesus Christ is the Subject of election.[25] Finally, it would also be possible to broaden the scope of debate by engaging the fraught question of divine suffering. Granted that this is a complex issue (what, precisely, is the "*particula veri* in the teaching of the early Patripassians"?) (*CD* IV/2, p. 357), it is a fascinating point at which to access some of the most impor-tant claims in the *Dogmatics*, not least because Barth has been both ac-cused of undue tentativeness and applauded for an understanding of di-vine passibility that coheres with an affirmation of divine immutability.[26]

However, it is time to move beyond the specifics of interpretation. Now I want to consider what I initially identified as "Barth's legacy," an

---

25. See McCormack, *Orthodox and Modern*, pp. 183-277. The comment about "classical metaphysics" is taken from Bruce L. McCormack, "The Actuality of God: Karl Barth in Con-versation with Open Theism," in *Engaging the Doctrine of God: Contemporary Protestant Per-spectives*, ed. Bruce McCormack (Grand Rapids: Baker, 2008), p. 211.

26. An important critique of Barth's tentativeness can be found in Paul Fiddes, *The Creative Suffering of God* (Oxford: Oxford University Press, 1988), esp. pp. 112-23. Alan Lewis follows Fiddes's lead in his brilliant work *Between Cross and Resurrection: A Theology of Holy Saturday* (Grand Rapids: Eerdmans, 2001). Lewis believes that Barth allows the "distinction" between the immanent Trinity and economic Trinity "to grow into a wedge" (p. 211) — so much so that, even as Barth sometimes "delights to thrust the cross of Christ back into eter-nity" (p. 212), he still "hesitates, illogically, before the ontological implications of Christ's grave as signifying death for God" (p. 214). McCormack, on the other hand, suggests that Barth's later theology promotes "an understanding of divine immutability which is no lon-ger controlled by the . . . thought of possibility." Since the divine Son *is* Jesus of Nazareth, God qua Son is always undergoing suffering and death. Christ's concrete life, for all eternity, is "the content of the eternal decision in which God gives himself his being." See "The Actu-ality of God," in *Engaging the Doctrine of God*, p. 223.

awkward turn of phrase, without doubt, but one that enables discussion about the meaning of Barth's work for Christian theology in the present. Two specific questions frame this final section: Why has the *Church Dogmatics* generated, and been able to sustain, such an energetic debate about Trinity and election? And what are the implications of this debate for Barth studies and Christian thought more generally?

One might well offer a bland response to the first question, perhaps noting that this kind of classic constantly outwits its interpreters, given an excess of meaning (which, incidentally, is nicely illustrative of Barth's convictions about the immensity of the divine being and the inexhaustible richness of God's creative, reconciliatory, and redemptive activity). Yet such a response does not hit the mark. It does not underscore the crucial point that Barth's own approach to dogmatics inevitably provokes different, perhaps even conflicting, interpretations. By this I mean the following. For Barth, the subject matter of Christian theology — God's being, ways, and works, witnessed in Scripture and made known to those who comprise the church — can only be described from limited vantage points, each of which opens up to a slightly different view of the whole. Therefore, Barth continually casts and recasts, examines and reexamines doctrines throughout the *Dogmatics*. He enters, inhabits, and apprehends the "strange new world" of biblical faith in different ways; his exploration of this territory *necessarily* involves new perspectives and discoveries.[27]

None of this is to say, of course, that Barth's writing amounts to a mystifying tangle of unfounded contentions that are loosely tethered to time-honored dogmatic loci. That was not the case with Barth's work immediately subsequent to his break with "liberal" theology, and it is certainly not the case with respect to the *Dogmatics*. My point is rather that, for Barth, Christian theology is an effort of human understanding that constantly endeavors to catch up with — and, more precisely, hopes to be caught up by — God's being and action. Just as the Christian's "subjective appropriation of faith is a continuing venture," so too is any dogmatic apprehension of the subject known in faith.[28] And precisely because the dogmatician

27. See, of course, Karl Barth, "The Strange New World Within the Bible," in *The Word of God and the Word of Man*, trans. Douglas Horton (Gloucester, MA: Peter Smith, 1978), pp. 28-50. The actual title of this piece lacks an adjective that I retain: the original German is "Die neue Welt in der Bibel."

28. William Stacy Johnson, *The Mystery of God: Karl Barth and the Postmodern Foundations of Theology*, Columbia Series in Reformed Theology (Louisville: Westminster John Knox Press, 1997), p. 34.

pursues his or her task in a necessarily partial and dialectical way, making multiple excursions into the lively realm of God's self-knowledge from differing points of departure, the whole cannot but be accessed by way of the parts, and each part will yield a somewhat different perspective on the whole. The "strange new world" of the Bible is exactly that: while this world has its own coherence, it never ceases to be strange, and it never ceases to be anything but new.

As with Barth, so with those who would interpret him. The claims about Trinity and election found in the *Dogmatics* cannot be freeze-framed, much less subjected to conclusive exposition. Beyond a scholar's own facilitating (and not-so-facilitating) prejudices, the way one reads Barth will depend on whether one takes the doctrine of the Word of God, the doctrine of God, creation, reconciliation, or redemption as points of departure; thereafter, judgments will be affected by the way one coordinates claims tendered in discrete doctrinal spheres.[29] As such, even were one to suppose that the *Dogmatics* does not involve shifts of perspective, being consistent to a preternatural extent, its style of argument effectively guarantees diverse interpretative judgments. Different passages will be identified as pivotal; varied emphases, judgments, and logics will be discerned; the coherence of the work will be apprehended in divergent ways. The moral? Even as I advocate strenuously for my own reading of Barth, I must calmly admit that the *Church Dogmatics* is patient of multiple interpretations. Even as I stand in the so-called revisionist camp, I am obliged to admit the viability of "traditionalist" readings. The force of this obligation does not bespeak interpretive humility or charitableness on my part, nor is it symptomatic of poststructuralist convictions about textual indeterminacy. Quite the contrary: it is an obligation grounded in the belief that varied, even conflicting readings of Barth's magnum opus are a function of the *text itself*, are a consequence of Barth's distinctive approach to dogmatic work.

This claim leads nicely into my concern to reckon with the significance of debates about Trinity and election for Barth scholarship in particular, and for the academic study of Christian theology in general. Given the interpretive latitudinarianism I have commended, scholars should be

29. Barth himself was quite aware of this. Recall, for instance, an admission in the preface to the English translation of the second edition of *Der Römerbrief:* "[N]o one can . . . bring out the meaning of a text [*auslegen*], without at the same time adding something to it [*einlegen*]." See Barth, *The Epistle to the Romans*, trans. Edwyn C. Hoskyns (Oxford: Oxford University Press, 1968), p. ix.

wary of attempts to bind the *Church Dogmatics* to a single theological program. We will, of course, all read on our own terms and tender our own best interpretive judgments; equally, each will place in the foreground those aspects of Barth's thought that she or he believes particularly germane to the present moment. But there is little to be gained, and much to be lost, with the assumption that the *Dogmatics* cannot tolerate diverse interpretations. Having loosed ourselves from the strictures of neo-orthodoxy, we must beware of the temptation of repeating past errors. (More succinctly: a new breed of "Barthian" is the last thing we need.) The most suitable way the *Church Dogmatics* can be honored is a cheerful, even "liberal," sensibility that accepts and delights in the possibilities of interpretation. Such a sensibility does not shy away from the provocative nature of Barth's writings, nor does it limit itself to the (considerable) challenge of reading Barth fairly, accurately, and effectively. Rather, it strives to promote lines of reflection that do justice to the stirring ingenuity of Barth's thought by re-presenting, in various ways, his most valuable and intriguing claims. And, at its best, this sensibility admits that the most important treatments of Barth tend to be freighted with constructive significance. It raises the prospect of creative theological work that thinks with — and then *beyond* — Barth.

A concrete example seems appropriate at this point, not least to ensure that this chapter ends not with a platitudinous hermeneutical whimper, but with a constructive gesture. One way in which scholars might be usefully provoked by Barth would be to consider how current debates about Trinity and election, and this particular proposal about divine obedience and "being in becoming," might relate to theological anthropology. Consider, for instance, a principal contention running through Colin Gunton's *The Promise of Trinitarian Theology:* "[I]t is only through an understanding of the kind of being that God is that we can come to learn what kind of beings we are and what kind of world we inhabit. . . . In the light of the theology of the Trinity, everything looks different."[30] These words, written over two decades ago, were, of course, prescient. Even as scholars disagree about a "social" doctrine of the Trinity, few would now deny some connection between an acclamation of divine triunity (or tri-personality) and reflections about church, society, friendship, and the like. But what if one expands Gunton's claim, given the interpretation tendered above? If "everything looks differ-

---

30. Colin Gunton, *The Promise of Trinitarian Theology* (London: T. & T. Clark, 2004), pp. xi, 7.

ent" in light of the doctrine of the Holy Trinity, things look even *more* different when one understands the life of the Son in terms of "being" and "becoming," for it becomes possible to think about human life in loosely analogous terms.

On a particular level, there is here an opportunity for theologians to embrace the possibility of thinking about "identity without an essence,"[31] refusing false, debilitating, and ultimately idolatrous essentialisms that sinfully prejudge — or worse, presume to cramp — the eschatological reality toward which we are being moved. Since God's being is an outgoing and adventurous affair, particularly in terms of a divine history that graciously assumes and embraces what is qualitatively different, human being can be figured similarly. The theologian is freed up to approve and celebrate individual and communal forms of life that involve experimentation, fluid identities, and the open-ended possibilities of interpersonal, cultural, and social action, granted the proviso, of course, that just as the Son's history has a distinctive shape, perfectly conformed to and illustrative of God's justifying and sanctifying love, human "being" and "becoming" cannot be construed in terms of irresponsible libertinism.

It might even become possible to read Barth against himself, directly challenging some of the patriarchal and heterosexist aspects of the *Dogmatics* and forging a surprising but important alliance between Barth's work and theological projects that reenvision sexual difference and sexual identity, a striking example of which is the remarkable body of work bequeathed to us by the late Marcella Althaus-Reid.[32] Why not? Why shouldn't Barth's suggestion that God's elective activity "drives us forward" (*CD* II/2, p. 31) be turned against him and be reconceived as an affirmation of the startlingly diverse ways in which humans are graciously re-created, day by day, and enlivened to live into a future, the precise shape of which cannot be foretold, never mind peremptorily contained? Why not find *new* meaning in the younger Blumhardt's claim, surely known to Barth, that the "purpose" of faith is its proving, given that "[b]elieving means being . . . and being means becom-

---

31. So David Halperin, *Saint Foucault: Towards a Gay Hagiography* (New York: Oxford University Press, 1995), p. 62. Gerard Loughlin deftly deploys this phrase in his remarkable introductory essay, "The End of Sex," in his edited volume *Queer Theology: Rethinking the Western Body* (Oxford: Blackwell Publishing, 2007), pp. 1-34.

32. See, *inter alia*, Marcella Althaus-Reid, *Indecent Theology: Theological Perversions in Sex, Gender, and Politics* (London: Routledge, 2000); see also Althaus-Reid, *From Feminist Theology to Indecent Theology: Readings on Poverty, Sexual Identity, and God* (London: SCM Press, 2004).

ing"?[33] Barth's (incomplete) pneumatology could be engaged at this point, too, with the Spirit identified as the divine agent who, in lieu of a baptismal beginning that "is a take-off for the leap towards what is not yet present" (*CD* IV/4, p. 38), impels us toward a future that, gloriously heedless of political, cultural, or social convention, makes concrete the reality of friendship between God and God's children.[34]

More generally, there is here an opportunity to further lose the gap between Barth scholarship and political and public theology of a progressive kind. While recent scholars have done sterling work in elucidating Barth's insistence that there "is no dogmatics which is not also and necessarily ethics" (*CD* II/2, p. 12), it is also important to recall the various ways that the *Dogmatics* has animated theological projects that underscore a deep affinity between Christian faith and political movements that demand and enact human liberation.[35] Such an affiliation between Barth and progressive politics needs desperately to be renewed in the present, partly to ensure that the specter of neo-orthodoxy not return to haunt Barth scholarship, making it again marginal to the broader study of Christian thought, and partly as but one way in which scholars (and others) may pay homage to the trenchant political engagement that Barth understood to be essential to Christian faith. To make the point rather more baldly, if the recent

33. Vernard Eller (ed.), *Thy Kingdom Come: A Blumhardt Reader* (Grand Rapids: Eerdmans, 1980), p. 139. The passage is taken from an 1884 table talk, with the title "Who Forgives All Your Iniquity." The original text: *Christoph Blumhardt: Eine Auswahl aus seinen Predigten, Andachten und Schriften,* vol. 1, ed. R. Lejeune (Erlenbach-Zürich: Rotapfel Verlag, 1925-1937), pp. 103-8.

34. While he and I read Barth somewhat differently, William Stacy Johnson's presentation of Barth's pneumatology dovetails nicely with my suggestion about human "being in becoming"; see Johnson, *The Mystery of God,* esp. pp. 115-49. While I am less critical of Barth's pneumatology than is Eugene F. Rogers, Jr., he also pushes Barth in a promising direction; see his excellent piece entitled "The Eclipse of the Spirit in Karl Barth," in *Conversing with Barth,* ed. John C. McDowell and Mike Higton (Aldershot, UK: Ashgate, 2004), pp. 173-90. Finally, I need to mention Janet Martin Soskice's terrific collection of essays entitled *The Kindness of God: Metaphor, Gender, and Religious Language* (Oxford: Oxford University Press, 2008), in which her key concern is to reenvision human life — an inherently embodied, gendered, and relational affair — in light of God's eschatological purposes. Soskice's final chapter, notably, signals that "the Christian life is one in which the believer is 'born again,' not into static perfection, but into a new life which must be characterized by growth and transformation" (p. 181).

35. I must, of course, mention the early work of James Cone at this point. See esp. *Black Theology and Black Power* (Maryknoll, NY: Orbis, 1997) and *A Black Theology of Liberation* (Maryknoll, NY: Orbis, 1990).

contretemps over Trinity and election concludes with nothing more than a keener comprehension of Barth's theological accomplishment, we will have missed an opportunity. However, if the debate opens out into a broader series of reflections about Barth's thought as it relates to the myriad political struggles in the present day — something I have only been able to gesture toward in these concluding remarks — then there is surely a greater likelihood that the Barth renaissance in Anglo-American theology will move from strength to strength, influencing and directing Christian thought and action in ways that we cannot yet imagine.

# 7. Barth and the Election-Trinity Debate: A Pneumatological View

*Paul T. Nimmo*

[The Holy Spirit] is the power of Jesus Christ in which it becomes an event that there are [people] who can and must discover and recognise that He is theirs and that they are His: their own history is genuinely enclosed in His and His history is equally genuinely enclosed in theirs.

Karl Barth[1]

## Introduction

Much recent work on the theology of Karl Barth has been dominated by attention to the relationship between the Trinitarian constitution of God and the act of divine election in which God determines to be for humanity in Jesus Christ.[2] There are two fundamental questions and one feature of

1. Karl Barth, *Church Dogmatics,* 4 volumes in 13 parts, edited by G. W. Bromiley and T. F. Torrance (Edinburgh: T. & T. Clark, 1956-1975), IV/1, p. 648, translation altered (hereafter, volume, part, and page references to the *CD* appear in parentheses in the text and footnotes). Cf. Karl Barth, *Die Kirchliche Dogmatik,* 4 volumes in 13 parts, 5th ed. (Zürich: Evangelischer Verlag, 1947-1967), IV/1, p. 724 (hereafter *KD* in parentheses in the text): "Er [ist] die Macht Jesu Christi . . . in der es Ereignis wird, daß es Menschen gibt, die ihn als den Ihrigen, sich selbst als die Seinigen vorfinden und erkennen dürfen und müssen: ihre eigene Geschichte als real eingeschlossen in die seinige und seine Geschichte als eben so real eingeschlossen in ihre eigene Geschichte."

2. See Bruce L. McCormack, "Grace and Being: The Role of God's Gracious Election in Karl Barth's Theological Ontology," in *The Cambridge Companion to Karl Barth,* ed. John Webster (Cambridge: Cambridge University Press, 2000), pp. 92-110; Paul D. Molnar, *Divine Freedom and the Doctrine of the Immanent Trinity: In Dialogue with Karl Barth and Contem-*

the debate up to this point that should perhaps be identified at the outset; thereafter, I will give an indication as to the direction the remainder of this chapter will take.

First, we should recognize that one of the key theological questions underlying these discussions is a hermeneutical one: How did Barth himself conceive of the relationship between Trinity and election? This is a contentious question. For some, it is clear that Barth maintained throughout his work that the Trinity must precede election; for others, it is equally clear that Barth underwent something of a change of view in the process and aftermath of writing *Church Dogmatics* II/2, such that he came to the conclusion that election must precede Trinity. For convenience, in the course of this chapter I will refer to the first view as a "weak" reading of Barth and the second view as a "strong" reading of Barth.[3]

Second — and following from the hermeneutical question — there is a constructive question: How might theologians today conceive of this relationship between Trinity and election, thinking after Barth? Those who follow the "weak" reading of Barth tend to view his understanding here as very much in line with the tradition. However, for those who follow the "strong" reading, there seems to be much room for constructive work to be done, not only in terms of defending the scriptural justification and theological orthodoxy of this reading itself, but also in terms of sketching out its further implications and challenges, particularly as these arise out of the doctrines of Trinity and election.

Common to both these questions, and to the attempts to answer them up to this point, is their formal and material focus on the person of Jesus Christ: on the *christological* implications of Trinity and election and on the *christological* results of the "weak" and "strong" positions. In one sense, this is good and right and proper: at the center of not only election but also

---

*porary Theology* (London: T. & T. Clark, 2002), pp. 61-81; Edwin Chr. van Driel, "Karl Barth on the Eternal Existence of Jesus Christ," *Scottish Journal of Theology* 60, no.1 (2007): 45-61; Bruce McCormack, "Seek God Where He May Be Found: A Response to Edwin Chr. van Driel," *Scottish Journal of Theology* 60, no. 1 (2007): 62-79; Aaron T. Smith, "God's Self-specification: His Being Is His Electing," pp. 201-25 below; Paul T. Nimmo, "Barth and the Christian as Ethical Agent: An Ontological Study of the Shape of Christian Ethics," in *Commanding Grace: Studies in Karl Barth's Ethics,* ed. Daniel L. Migliore (Grand Rapids: Eerdmans, 2010), pp. 216-38.

3. This choice of terms should not in any way be taken to offer an assessment of the relative merits or demerits of either reading, but rather to indicate the relative perceived "radicality" of the respective readings.

of revelation and of salvation, there does indeed stand the person of Jesus Christ. Up to this point in the debate, however, it is noticeable that questions concerning the Holy Spirit and pneumatology, the answering of which might offer a different line of inquiry and response to both the hermeneutical and the constructive questions, have been rather overlooked. The question thus emerges: Might Barth's understanding of the Spirit *also* shed some light on the contemporary discussions?

To explore this possibility, I proceed in four sections in this chapter. First, I consider the role of the Spirit in the act of election, as this is expounded by Barth in *Church Dogmatics* II/2. Second, I turn to the relationship between the role of the Spirit in the eternal act of election and the role of the Spirit in the community of God in time. Third, by way of the *Church Dogmatics,* I offer a pneumatological view of the hermeneutical question of Trinity and election. Fourth, I seek to briefly conceptualize some of the constructive implications of a "strong" reading of this relationship from a pneumatological perspective. I conclude by indicating some potential scope for further exploration on these grounds.

## I. The Electing Spirit

Barth's work on the doctrine of election in *Church Dogmatics* II/2 opens with the following *Leitsatz:* "The doctrine of election is the sum of the Gospel because of all words that can be said or heard it is the best" (*CD* II/2, p. 3). What follows in the ensuing four sections of the *Church Dogmatics* is an attempt to unfold this "Gospel," the good news that God elects to be for humanity in Jesus Christ: first, with respect to the dogmatic orientation, foundation, and position of the doctrine of election (*CD* II/2, § 32); and second, with respect to its material implications for the Christian understanding of the election of Jesus Christ, the election of the community, and the election of the individual (*CD* II/2, §§ 33-35). The pivot around which the whole doctrine turns, of course, is the election of Jesus Christ: Jesus Christ is both electing God and elected human being (*CD* II/2, p. 103).[4] In

4. Barth also adds at this point that "[i]t is not that He does not also elect as man" and that "[i]t is true, of course, that even as God He is elected" (*CD* II/2, p. 103). In other words, in addition to the two determinations noted in the main text above, Jesus Christ is also "elected God" and "electing human being." However, Barth concludes, "[p]rimarily . . . electing is the divine determination of the existence of Jesus Christ, and election (being elected) the human" (*CD* II/2, p. 103).

this twofold election of Jesus Christ, the elections of both the community and the individual are enclosed, for "[b]efore Him and without Him and beside Him God does not . . . elect or will anything" (*CD* II/2, p. 94).

The election of God to be for humanity in Jesus Christ is eternal, an event that, Barth writes, "precedes absolutely all other being and happening" (*CD* II/2, p. 99). However, precisely here is where Barth recognizes a possible temptation: "to think of this sphere as at once empty and undetermined . . . to think of God the Father, Son and Holy Spirit merely as a Subject which can and does elect" (*CD* II/2, p. 100). For Barth, this line of thinking would lead to a God "absolutely unconditioned, or . . . conditioned only by the Subject in and for itself and as such" (*CD* II/2, p. 100). Famously, then, Barth rejects this understanding of election as positing a *decretum absolutum* (cf. *CD* II/2, pp. 100-101; *CD* II/2, pp. 103-4) and asserts that "[t]here is no such thing as Godhead in itself" (*CD* II/2, p. 115).

For Barth, the result is that God is Father, Son and Spirit, the triune God, not in *abstracto*, but "with a definite connection and resolution; in virtue of the love and freedom in which in the heart of His triune being He has disposed over Himself from and to all eternity [er im Schoße seines dreieinigen Wesens von Ewigkeit her und in die Ewigkeit hinein über sich selbst verfügt hat]" (*CD* II/2, p. 79, trans. altered; *KD* II/2, p. 85). More expansively, Barth declares:

> [I]n all His choosing and willing, what God originally and finally wills is Himself [daß Gott in allem seinem Wählen und Wollen ursprünglich und letztlich sich selber will]. All God's willing is primarily a determination of the love of the Father and the Son in the fellowship of the Holy Ghost. . . . [I]n this primal decision God certainly does not choose only Himself [Gott wählt ja nicht nur sich selbst in jener Urentscheidung]. In this choice of self He also chooses another, that other which is man. (*CD* II/2, p. 169, trans. altered; *KD* II/2, p. 184)

Here lies the heart of Barth's doctrine of election. In a primal, eternal act, God determines and disposes over not only the being of the covenant partner, but also the very essence of God itself. The two determinations are equally primal. It may be true — as I will acknowledge below — that Barth is not always fully consistent on this understanding of the self-constitution of the divine being in the act of election, either in *CD* II/2 or beyond. Nevertheless, it seems that, at the very least, these last two quotations in particular unequivocally support a "strong" reading of Barth at this point.

What is of relevance at this juncture, however, is not so much the evidence for a "weak" or "strong" interpretation of Barth on election, but Barth's insistence, however inexpansive and seminal, that the primal act of election is formally and materially *Trinitarian*. In this connection, Barth recognizes that the act of election involves the activity of all three modes of being of the Trinity. First, there is activity on the part of the Father: "In the beginning it was the choice of the Father Himself to establish this covenant with man by giving up His Son for him, that He Himself might become man in the fulfilment of His grace" (*CD* II/2, p. 101). Second, there is activity on the part of the Son: "In the beginning it was the choice of the Son to be obedient to grace, and therefore to offer up Himself and to become man in order that this covenant might be made a reality" (*CD* II/2, p. 101). And third, and of equal import, there is the activity of the Spirit:

> In the beginning it was the resolve of the Holy Spirit that the unity of God, of Father and Son should not be disturbed or rent by this covenant with man, but that it should be made the more glorious, the deity of God, the divinity of His love and freedom, being confirmed and demonstrated by this offering of the Father and this self-offering of the Son. (*CD* II/2, p. 102)

The clear implication of the Trinitarian nature of this act of election is that Jesus Christ "does not elect alone, but in company with the electing of the Father and of the Holy Spirit [in Gemeinschaft mit dem Wählen des Vaters und des Heiligen Geistes]" (*CD* II/2, p. 105; *KD* II/2, p. 112). All three modes of being of God are in some way actively involved in the eternal act of election. Indeed, for Barth, the fact that Jesus Christ is no less the original subject of this act of election than its original Object takes place precisely in "the harmony of the triune God [*in diesem Frieden des dreieinigen Gottes*]" (*CD* II/2, p. 105; *KD* II/2, p. 112). Jesus Christ is indeed "electing God," but so, too, are the Father and the Spirit.

Two issues deserve further comment at this point. First, a methodological point: as I have already mentioned, in this expansive chapter of the *Church Dogmatics* on election, as in the pursuant discussions in more recent literature, most of the attention falls on matters christological. There is little directly pneumatological material here, either in the material on the election of Jesus Christ or in the material on the election of the community and the individual in him. Certainly, Barth mentions the Spirit at pivotal moments, such as those indicated above; but there is really no sustained engagement with the pneumatological dimension of election. On the one hand, this is perhaps to be regretted; on the other hand, it presents at this point the challenge of thinking through the doctrine of election constructively after Barth precisely from a pneumatological perspective, regardless of how one answers the hermeneutical question.

Second, a material point: it has already been noted that Jesus Christ is not the "electing" God in isolation, but is only "electing God" together with the Father and the Spirit. The Spirit, similarly, is "electing God" together with the Father and the Son. However, Barth insists that Jesus Christ is not only the "electing God" but also the "elected God" (*CD* II/2, p. 103). In light of this, the question arises concerning whether or not Barth can write of the Spirit in the same way: can Barth say that the Spirit is also, in whatever sense, not only "electing God" but also "elected God"? Further consideration of this pneumatological question will lead deeper into the issues of Trinity and election and will provide the focus of the next section of this chapter.

## II. The Elected Spirit

Given the scarcity of pneumatological material in Barth's chapter on the doctrine of election, one way forward in the attempt to consider the legitimacy and the implications of construing the Spirit as "elected God" is to work in parallel with Barth's christological statements about Jesus Christ as "elected God." In this connection, there is immediate recourse to a negative statement and a positive statement in *Church Dogmatics* II/2.

The negative statement about referring to Jesus Christ as "elected God" occurs in the form of a qualification. Barth emphasizes that "as the Son of the Father [Jesus Christ] has no need of any special election" (*CD* II/2, p. 103). Given that the Son is begotten of the Father, then, it would be inappropriate to write of him as elected in any conventional way. In a similar fashion, then, a parallel pneumatological statement might be envisaged: "As the Spirit of the Father and of the Son, the Spirit has no need of any special election." While Barth himself does not avail himself of such a statement, it seems likely that he would offer his assent to it. The corresponding implication would be that the Spirit proceeds from the Father and from the Son, and is thus not elected in any conventional way. This is an important reminder that it is the event of election that must be allowed to define the terms involved in its description.

The positive statement about referring to Jesus Christ as "elected God" occurs where Barth affirms the accuracy of this insight insofar as he is "the Son of God elected in His oneness with man, and in fulfillment of God's covenant with man" (*CD* II/2, p. 103). This statement demonstrates that, for Barth, the primal act of election in which God wills Godself is an act in which God also wills another — the human being. In the first instance, the object of this willing is Jesus Christ, the God-human in divine-human unity; however, Jesus Christ is not elected in splendid isolation, but is rather "ordained and appointed Lord and Head of all others" (*CD* II/2, p. 116).[5] Elected in and with Him, then, is "the people called and united by Him, and only in that people individuals in general in their private relationships with God" (*CD* II/2, p. 43).[6] The purpose of the eternal election of Jesus Christ is thus in his divine-human unity to fulfill the covenant of God with humanity.

In a similar fashion, then, it would be possible to consider parallel pneumatological statements that refer to the role of the Spirit in the fulfillment of the covenant of God with humanity in Jesus Christ. On this matter, it is possible to draw on the statements of Barth himself at various points in the *Church Dogmatics*. I will consider the relevant material from three viewpoints: first, with respect to the temporal being in action of the Spirit; second, with respect to the relationship between this temporal being in action and the eternal decree of election; third, with respect to the relationship between this temporal being in action and the eternal being in action of the Spirit.

First, then, there is the work of the Spirit in history that provides the

5. For Barth, as I have noted above, the election of the community and of individuals is ontologically and epistemologically dependent not only on the fact that Jesus Christ is "elected," but also on the fact that Jesus Christ is "electing." Barth asks: "How can these others be elected 'in Him,' how can they see their election in Him the first of the elect, and how can they find in His election the assurance of their own, if He is only the object of election and not Himself its subject, if He is only an elect creature and not primarily and supremely the electing Creator?" (*CD* II/2, p. 116). Materially, then, Barth insists both that the election of the community is "included in Jesus Christ" (*CD* II/2, p. 195), such that there is "no independent election of the community" (*CD* II/2, p. 196), and that "the election of Jesus Christ relativizes the election of individuals" (*CD* II/2, p. 310), such that the latter "can be real or significant only when included in the election of Jesus Christ" (*CD* II/2, p. 310). For Barth, however, the *order* in which these "three" elections are treated "is not of fundamental importance" (*CD* II/2, p. 309).

6. While Barth posits that "[i]n the strict sense only He can be understood and described as 'elected' (and 'rejected')" (*CD* II/2, p. 43), nonetheless he affirms that "[i]f we listen to what Scripture says concerning man, then at the point where our attention and thoughts are allowed to rest there is revealed an elect man, *the* elect man, and united in Him and represented by Him an elect people" (*CD* II/2, p. 58).

epistemological starting point for any consideration of the term "elected Spirit." For Barth, the Spirit in history is nothing more and nothing less than the power of the risen Jesus Christ. Barth writes: "We cannot say more of the Holy Spirit and His work than that He is the power in which Jesus Christ . . . attests Himself effectively, creating in man response and obedience. We describe Him as His awakening power . . . as His quickening [power and as His] enlightening power" (*CD* IV/1, p. 648).[7] The mode of being of God that awakens and quickens and enlightens the human being as she responds to and obeys the Word of God is the Spirit. Relating this to the doctrine of election, then, Barth posits that "the work of the Holy Spirit is merely to 'realise subjectively' the election of Jesus Christ and His work as done and proclaimed in time, to reveal and bring it to men and women" (*CD* IV/1, p. 667).[8]

This covenant work of the Spirit in time is both an individual work and a corporate work. On the one hand, Barth summarizes this work of the Spirit under the rubric of "summoning," explaining that "the concrete form of the purpose of the gospel is its proclamation and faith in it, the work of the Holy Spirit in the summoning of the elect man, in which his whole determination to blessedness, thanksgiving and witness has its basis and origin" (*CD* II/2, p. 457). On the other hand, Barth emphasizes that the result of such summoning is the Christian community: "It is the work of the Holy Spirit that the Lord does do this in His mercy, that He shines on men to give them this knowledge of Jesus Christ and themselves. And in this knowledge, in and with Jesus Christ, His body is known as His community, His community as His body" (*CD* IV/1, p. 667).

Second, however, Barth posits that this temporal activity of the Spirit in the covenant history of God with humanity is the outworking of an eternal decree. Barth says: "By the work of the Holy Spirit the body of Christ, as it is by God's decree from all eternity and as it has become in virtue of His act in time, acquires in all its hiddenness historical dimensions. The Holy Spirit awakens the 'poor praise on earth' appropriate to that eternal-temporal occurrence" (*CD* IV/1, p. 667). However, just as the body

7. These key functions of the Spirit — to awaken, to quicken, and to enlighten — are used in the thesis statements at the head of §§ 62, 67, and 72, in *CD* IV/1, IV/2, and IV/3, respectively.

8. It is evident from this statement (a) how Barth never conceives of the being in action of the Spirit as in any way independent of the being in action of Jesus Christ — for which reason, above all, perhaps Barth retains the *filioque* (cf. *CD* I/1, pp. 473-87); and (b) how Barth never conceives of the being in action of the Spirit to add anything objective to the work of atonement accomplished in the cross of Jesus Christ (cf. *CD* IV/1, pp. 295-96).

of Christ is decreed from all eternity, so too this work of the Spirit must be similarly decreed from all eternity, as Barth later confirms:

> Th[e] will of God is done on earth as He makes possible and actual the existence of this people by the presence and action of the Holy Spirit. It is this will of God which is the background of that earthly history; the second and higher dimension of His being and operation which we have always to keep in mind when we think and speak of the Holy Spirit and His work. (*CD* IV/2, p. 334)

If, as we have seen above, the Spirit is "electing" God together with the Father and the Son in the primal event of election, then it can be concluded that the temporal activity of the Spirit is elected in eternity both *by* God in the mode of being as the Spirit (as *electing* Spirit) and *for* God in the mode of being of the Spirit (as *elected* Spirit). It is this eternal decree of the Trinitarian God, as disposed in the act of election, that elects the Spirit to the activities of gathering the community, upbuilding the community, and sending the community.[9] This is the temporal work of the covenant for which the Spirit is elected in eternity.

Third, Barth offers further specification at this point of the relationship between the temporal activity of the Spirit and the eternal activity of the Spirit. Concisely put, Barth posits that "the Holy Spirit . . . is not only the divine power mediating between Christ and Christianity but the mode of being of the one God which unites the Father and the Son [die den Vater und den Sohn verbindende Seinsweise des einen Gottes ist]" (*CD* IV/2, p. 339, trans. altered; *KD* IV/2, p. 379).[10] Thus there is a certain *analogia operationis* in existence between the work of the Spirit in eternity and the work of the Spirit in time. Barth explains that, in the mystery of the being and action of the Spirit on earth,

> there is repeated and represented and expressed what God is in Himself. In [the Spirit's] being and work as the mediator between Jesus and other men, in [the Spirit's] creating and establishing and maintaining of fel-

---

9. These terms/activities come from the headings of §§ 62, 67, and 72, in *CD* IV/1, IV/2, and IV/3, respectively.

10. Barth similarly says that "the divine power of the transition from Christ to Christendom [is] identical with God in the mode of being of the Holy Spirit . . . in the third and mediating factor of that history, as in the third and mediating mode of being of God, we have to do with the Holy Spirit, in the one case within the undivided *opus trinitatis ad extra* and in the other in His specific *opus ad intra*" (*CD* IV/2, pp. 338-39).

lowship between [Jesus] and us, God Himself is active and revealed among us men, i.e., the fellowship, the unity, the peace, the love, which there is in God, in which God was and is and will be from and to all eternity. . . . It is with the unity of God, and therefore with God Himself, that we have to do when we have to do with the Holy Spirit in the event of the transition, the communication, the mediation between Jesus and us. (*CD* IV/2, p. 341)

Barth posits that this transition — which is a singular and great mystery — takes place "so sovereignly, so freely [vollzieht er sich so souverän, so frei]" (*CD* IV/2, p. 341, trans. altered; *KD* IV/2, p. 381). It is an event, first, "in God Himself . . . in His essence and being and life" and then "falls straight down from above into the sphere of our essence and being and life" (*CD* IV/2, p. 341). The *temporal* work for which the Spirit is elected (in eternity), therefore, corresponds directly with the *eternal* work of the Spirit. In other words, there is a clear ontological connection between the mediating activity of the Spirit in the history of the covenant in time and the mediating activity of the Spirit between Father and Son in eternity.

Thus, with these three dimensions of the work of the Spirit in fulfilling the covenant in view, it is possible to posit a pneumatological parallel to the original christological statement that the Son of God is "elected in His oneness with man, and in fulfillment of God's covenant with man" (*CD* II/2, p. 103). The parallel might run this way: the Spirit of God is "elected" in eternity to mediate between the God-human Jesus Christ and the community of God, and in fulfillment of God's covenant with humanity. However, this parallel remains at the level of temporal activity, and the question remains as to the nature of the ontic relationship between the being in action of the Spirit in time and the being in action of the Spirit in eternity. It is here, then, that the hermeneutical question of Trinity and election recurs in a pneumatological frame.

## III. A Pneumatological View of the Hermeneutical Question

The fact that Barth intimately relates the mediating activity of the Spirit in time and space to the intra-Trinitarian mediating activity of the Spirit in eternity is itself uncontroversial. Yet this relationship could be read in one of two ways, corresponding to the "weak" and the "strong" readings of Barth in connection with his Christology. Restating the issue in the frame of reference of the Spirit, the question for Barth's interpreters becomes this: Is the Spirit an existing person within the immanent Trinity who is subsequently elected for this mediating activity in time — the "weak" reading — or is God's very mode of being as Spirit elected with this temporal activity in view — the "strong" reading?[11] Pushing this question ecclesiologically sharpens the issue further: Can there be, for Barth, in any sense an existence of the Spirit that does not have the existence of the community of God in view?

This hermeneutical question is not easily settled. On the one hand, there are passages in the *Church Dogmatics,* long after II/2 was written, in which Barth seems strongly to offer support to a "weak" reading of his theology of Trinity and election. For example, Barth writes that "[t]he triune life of God . . . is the basis of the election of man to covenant with Himself; of the determination of the Son to become man, and therefore to fulfill this covenant; of creation; and, in conquest of the opposition and contradiction of the creature and to save it from perdition, of the atonement with its final goal of redemption to eternal life with Himself" (*CD* IV/2, p. 345). There is no doubt that this text supports a "weak" reading of Barth, in which Trinity precedes election. Or again, a "weak" reading finds support in other Trinitarian texts of Barth, such as: "God's eternal election of grace, i.e., . . . the divine decision and action which are not preceded by any higher apart from the trinitarian happening of the life of God, but which all other divine decisions and actions follow, and to which they are subordinated" (*CD* IV/2, p. 31). To prefer a "strong" reading of Barth does not mean disputing either the existence of such "weak" texts or the need to account for them plausibly.

However, if a "strong" reading of Barth is nevertheless to be advocated, it is because at certain crucial moments Barth's theology seems to point in an altogether different direction from the two quotations immediately above. The case for a "strong" pneumatological reading is related, of course, to a "strong" christological reading of the relationship between Trinity and election. One of the key passages that support this "strong" reading is a text from *CD* IV/1, which, in its consideration of the question *Quo iure Deus homo?* deals directly with the relationship between Trinity and election (*CD* IV/1, § 69.1).[12] In this passage, Barth recognizes that in

11. I use of the word "subsequently" here in its logical rather than its chronological sense.

12. For what follows, see Paul T. Nimmo, "Barth and the Christian as Ethical Agent: An Ontological Study of the Shape of Christian Ethics," in Migliore, ed., *Commanding Grace,* pp. 216-38.

the obedient humility of the incarnate Jesus Christ, it is a matter of the being in action of God, and not of a *novum mysterium.* He writes: "[Jesus Christ] is amongst us in humility, our God, God for us, as that which He is in Himself, in the most inward depth of His Godness [in der innersten Tiefe seiner Gottheit]" (*CD* IV/1, p. 193, trans. altered; *KD* IV/1, p. 211).

However, this (relatively uncontroversial) understanding of the incarnate humility of Jesus Christ is, for Barth, only the second and outer moment of the mystery of the deity of Jesus Christ (*CD* IV/1, p. 192). Corresponding to this, there is a first and inner moment of the mystery of the deity of Jesus Christ, on the grounds that the incarnate aspect of the "self-emptying and self-humbling of Jesus Christ as an act of obedience cannot be alien to God" (*CD* IV/1, p. 193). Barth posits that "it belongs to the inner life of God that there should take place within it obedience" (*CD* IV/1, pp. 200-201). The result of this is that Barth posits the existence of obedience in the very being of the eternal God, between the mode of being of the Father and the mode of being of the Son.

Barth makes two particular comments about this ordering between the modes of being of God that are core to the "strong" reading at this point. The first is that in this obedience, God "does not make just any use of the possibilities of His divine nature, but He makes one definite use that is necessary on the basis and in fulfillment of His own decision. . . . What takes place is the divine fulfillment of a divine decree" (*CD* IV/1, pp. 194-95). The second is that "[w]e have not only not to deny but actually to affirm and understand as essential to the being of God the offensive fact that there is in God Himself an above and a below, a *prius* and a *posterius,* a superiority and a subordination . . . that it belongs to the inner life of God that there should take place within it obedience" (*CD* IV/1, pp. 200-201). Barth concludes that the result, once human ways of thinking about God are laid aside, is that "we cannot refuse to accept the humiliation and lowliness and supremely the obedience of Christ as the dominating moment in our conception of His *Godness* [den Gehorsam Christi als das geradezu beherrschende Moment in unsere Vorstellung von seiner Gottheit]" (*CD* IV/1, p. 199, trans. altered; *KD* IV/1, p. 218). And once obedience in a second mode of being of God is seen as being *both* the fulfillment of a decree and essential to the being of God, then the being of God itself in its Trinitarian modes of being is posited as being determined by the decree of election in which it is determined what God will be in time. In other words, election logically precedes the Trinity: the eternal act of election as an act of self-determination is primal and there is no triunity behind or without it.

While this, in short measure, is the christological case offered by this passage for the "strong reading" of the relationship between Trinity and election, the question remains as to the pneumatological content of this critical section of the *Church Dogmatics*. Parallel with what we saw above with respect to the Trinitarian dimension of the electing God, so here with the Trinitarian dimension of *Quo iure Deus homo?* Barth focuses largely on the relationship between the Father and the Son and spends little time explicitly reflecting on the role of the Spirit in particular. However, there are three important instances within this section of the *Church Dogmatics* where the Spirit is mentioned, and these deserve careful consideration.

The first instance is connected with Barth's view that in conceiving of the God of revelation, we must deduce that "[God] is indeed a First and a Second, One who rules and commands in majesty and One who obeys in humility" (*CD* IV/1, p. 202). He proceeds to clarify that:

> [God] is the one and the other without any cleft or differentiation but in perfect unity and equality because in the same perfect unity and equality He is also a Third, the One who affirms the one and equal Godhead through and by and in the two modes of being, the One who makes possible and maintains His fellowship with Himself as the one and the other. In virtue of this third mode of being He is in the other two without division or contradiction, the whole God in each. But again in virtue of this third mode of being He is in neither for itself and apart from the other, but in each in its relationship to the other, and therefore, in fact, in the totality, the connexion, the interplay, the history of these relationships. (*CD* IV/1, pp. 202-3)

This important passage affirms what I posited in the previous section about the mediating role of the Spirit between Father and Son and about the unity and peace that the Spirit is in the intra-Trinitarian divine life. However, this passage also makes clear that the Spirit performs this role precisely in the context of the Father and the Son as eternally determined as *prius* and *posterius*, as above and the below, that is, in the context of the being of God as it is self-determined in the primal and eternal decision of God to be the Trinitarian God of the covenant of grace. If this is the case, then the Spirit is not just the unity of the Father and the Son without further qualification, but also the unity of the Father, who has commanded the Son, and of the Son, who has obeyed the Father in eternity as well as in time. And this, in turn, would mean that as the eternal determination to incarnation is part of the determination of the eternal being of the Son, so the mediating activity of the Spirit in time between Jesus Christ and the community of God is part of the eternal determination of the Spirit. Indeed, Barth notes that the Spirit as the third mode of being of God is the one who enables and maintains the unity of the modes of being of Father and Son "in the totality . . . [and] the history of these relationships" (*CD* IV/1, p. 203). This last phrase similarly suggests that the temporal events of the covenant of grace in which the Spirit mediates between the Son and the community that is elect in him are as fundamental to the being in action of the Spirit as the mediating activity between the Father and the Son in the eternal life of the Trinity.

The second instance is linked to Barth's explication of the term "Son of God." Barth begins from his previous assertion that Jesus Christ is the one who reveals the lordship of God "in the determination which is native to Him, and therefore utterly natural, to go the way of the servant of God . . . to lowliness and finally to the cross" (*CD* IV/1, p. 208). On the basis of this starting point, Barth writes of the relationship between Father and Son as follows:

> The One who in such obedience is the perfect image of the ruling God is Himself . . . God by nature, God in His relationship to Himself, i.e., God in the mode of being of the Son in relation to God in the mode of being of the Father, One with Him and of the same essence. He fulfils in His mode — in the mode of the Son — the divine subordination, just as the latter in His mode — in the mode of the Father — fulfils the divine superiority. . . . The Father as origin is never without Him as the consequence, the obedient One. The self-positing God is never apart from Him as the One who is posited as God by God. The One who eternally begets is never apart from the One who is eternally begotten. Nor is the latter apart from the former. The Father is not the Father and the Son is not the Son without a mutual affirmation and love in the Holy Spirit. (*CD* IV/1, p. 209; *KD* IV/1, p. 229)

As before, there are two comments to make at this juncture. First, the Father and the Son once again affirm and love each other mutually in the Spirit, as Barth has declared throughout. Second, however, this mutual affirmation and love are posited clearly in the context of command and obedience, of the covenantal self-determination of the essence of God. Further evidence for this context is provided by the language of "self-positing" and "self-posited": at this juncture it is the Father who "self-posits" or begets, the Son who is "self-posited" or begotten, and the Spirit who is the mutual love and affirmation in which the "positing" and the "posited" both occur. Here Barth juxtaposes the language of the ancient creeds with this rather different language of positing and being posited; however, the latter is clearly a function of the will and thus in this context directly pertains to the divine act of self-determination in election.

The third and final instance also relates to Barth's understanding of the term "Son of God," and it pertains to the inadequacy of human language to refer accurately to the divine. He writes:

> [T]he term cannot bring out the ontological necessity in which this Father has this Son, and this Son this Father, the perfection in which this Father and this Son are one, i.e., are the different modes of being of one and the same personal God, the eternity of the fatherly begetting and of the being begotten of the Son, which is the basis of their relationship, their free but also necessary fellowship and love in the activity of the Holy Spirit as the third divine mode of being of the same kind, the self-evident fulfilment of that determination of a son to his father, the actual rendering of a perfect obedience, the ceaseless unity of the One who disposes and the One who complies, the actual oneness and agreement of that which they will and do. The history in which God is the living God in Himself can only be indicated but not conceived by our terms son and father and spirit. (*CD* IV/1, pp. 209-10)

While the quotation is once again focused on the relationship between the Father and the Son, it is noteworthy that explicit reference is made to the (activity of the) Spirit as the locus of their fellowship and love, and that implicit reference to the Spirit is found in the references to "unity . . . oneness . . . agreement." Moreover, the context once more indicates that the Spirit, precisely as the third mode of being of God, is intimately connected in the living history of God to the obedience of the Son in His elected covenant determination.[13]

These three passages that invoke the Spirit can be read to offer support

13. There is much more to be said here: an obvious lacuna in this chapter, which I cannot address further due to lack of space, is the mediating work of the Holy Spirit in the incarnation itself between the divine nature and the human nature of Jesus Christ. I hope to address this lacuna in a future article, with potential ramifications for the understanding of both the eternal and the temporal obedience of the Son.

to a "strong" reading of Barth on Trinity and election at this point. They all offer pneumatological backing to the view that, for Barth, the Trinitarian self-determination of God is a consequence of the primal divine decision of election in that they all refer to the eternal being of the Spirit in the direct context of the obedience of the Son. As such, they stand in something of a contrast to the passages noted above, which support a "weak" reading of Barth on this point.

The result of this juxtaposition of pneumatological ideas is perhaps to demonstrate that Barth's writing on the relationship between Trinity and election was less than entirely consistent in his later years. Against this background, the virtue of the "strong" reading is that it allows for an account of the gradual development of Barth's thought in the "strong" direction following the revision of his doctrine of election, in which development the full implications of his more radical work only penetrate his constructive work in an inconsistent and fragmentary way. The alternative position, which would be to continue to accept the "weak" reading of Barth on this point, is left with what seems to be the harder task of having to account for the radicality of Barth's language in texts such as those in the section cited above without interpreting, in a reductionist way, all his statements metaphorically. In either reading, however, while the Christological material may continue to be the most important evidence in assessing the "hermeneutical" question — simply by dint of its greater volume and prominence — we should no longer consider it sufficient to disregard the pneumatological evidence.

## IV. A Pneumatological View of the Constructive Implications

The potential implications for understanding the work of the Spirit in theology on the basis of the "strong" reading of the work of Barth are considerable. Each potential implication would, of course, need to be developed at greater length and with greater substance than is possible in this chapter; nevertheless, raising them in this context may offer some idea of the constructive theological import and potential of a "strong" pneumatological reading. In what follows I present two constructive consequences of thinking after Barth: both of them draw on existing christological statements with suggestive pneumatological outcomes.

First, Barth makes the following Christological claim: "We must not refer to the second 'person' of the Trinity as such, to the eternal Son or the eternal Word of God *in abstracto*, and therefore to the so-called [*Logos asarkos*]" (*CD* IV/1, p. 52). In a similar way, then, one could say that the Spirit without reference to the temporal activity of mediation between Jesus Christ and the community can only ever be a conceptual placeholder. In other words, there is simply no third person of the Trinity *in abstracto*, no Spirit to be considered either in time or in eternity without the mediating activity between Jesus Christ and the community of God in view. In turn, this would mean that the idea of a *pneuma anecclesion* (a Spirit without the community of God, a third person of the Trinity "as such") can only ever be a conceptual placeholder and cannot be the subject of independent inquiry.

Second, and further, Barth makes the following Christological claim: "[The] Lord Jesus Christ was elected from all eternity, not as the [*logos asarkos*], but as the *Verbum incarnandum*" (*CD* IV/3, p. 724). It is clear that, for Barth, the Son in eternity and prior to the incarnation, while certainly the *Logos asarkos*, is nevertheless always and also the *Logos incarnandus*, destined to be in the flesh. In a similar way, then, the Spirit in pretemporal eternity and prior to the gathering of the community of God, could be described as the *pneuma anecclesion*, the Spirit without the community. At the same time, however, the being in action of the Spirit is always determined by the eternal decree of election in the ways outlined above. Consequently, the eternal and temporal being in action of the Spirit is determined by its election to be the Spirit mediating between Jesus Christ and the community in time and thus, in the sense of a dynamic history, to be the "enchurched Spirit." In turn, this would mean that even the *pneuma anecclesion* in eternity, prior to the gathering of the community in time, is always the *pneuma inecclesiandus*, the Spirit destined to be "enchurched."

These two implications allow for a radical conclusion. Just as Barth declares that "[t]he concept of the true humanity of Jesus Christ is therefore primarily and finally basic — an absolutely necessary concept — in exactly the same and not a lesser sense than that of His true deity" (*CD* IV/2, p. 35), so too the concept of the actualistic enchurchment of the Spirit might also be considered primarily and finally basic to the ontology of the Spirit. To draw another pneumatological parallel from a christological base in Barth, one could say that neither in the case of Jesus Christ in the incarnation nor in the case of the Spirit in its activity in and for the community of God does one have to do "with what is noetically and logically an absolute paradox, with what is ontically the fact of a cleft or rift or gulf in God Himself" (*CD* IV/1, p. 184). To transfer another of Barth's christo-logical phrases, there can be no "ontic and inward divine paradox" be-tween the Spirit in eternity and the Spirit in time (*CD* IV/1, p. 188).

Precisely to be from eternity, the Spirit, who will be active in the com-munity, might thus correspond to the nature of the third mode of being of God. In this way, the following statement of Barth with respect to the in-carnation of Jesus Christ could be read equally well concerning the enchurchment of the Spirit: "His immutability does not stand in the way of this. It must not be denied, but this possibility is decided [*beschlossen*] in His unalterable being" (*CD* IV/1, p. 187, trans. altered; *KD* IV/1, p. 204). God retains the perfection of immutability even and precisely *within* the activity of the Spirit in the community of God. Nor need such a primal de-termination for covenantal activity in time compromise the freedom of the Spirit. Once again, the following statement by Barth with regard to the incarnation of Jesus Christ could be read just as well of the enchurchment of the Spirit: "It takes place in the freedom of God, but in the inner neces-sity of the freedom of God and not in the play of a sovereign *liberum arbitrium*. There is no possibility of something quite different happening" (*CD* IV/1, pp. 194-95). The self-determination of God for the history of the covenant does not jeopardize the divine freedom, but demonstrates that freedom precisely in its inner necessity. As Barth himself notes explicitly, "it is . . . an event in which Jesus Christ is a free subject and His Spirit moves where He wills when the apostolic community comes into being and exists as such" (*CD* IV/1, p. 718).

Perhaps the dominant reason for thinking after Barth in this way is to recognize that in the activity of the Spirit in the community of God one has to do with the very essence of God. Barth writes:

> In what takes place between the man Jesus and us when we may become and be Christians, God Himself lives. Nor does He live an alien life. He lives His own most proper life. . . . At the heart of this event we have to do unequivocally and unreservedly with God Himself. (*CD* IV/1, p. 342)

Therefore, as the *Leitsatz* of this chapter indicates, by the work of the Spirit the history of the community is genuinely enclosed in the history of the Spirit, and the history of the Spirit is equally genuinely enclosed in theirs (*CD* IV/1, p. 648).

PAUL T. NIMMO

## Conclusion

In this chapter I have explored the ways in which the Holy Spirit in Barth's theology could be described as both "electing God" and "elected God." It has indicated the relationship that Barth posits between the mediating work of the Spirit in time between Jesus Christ and the community, and the mediating work of the Spirit between Father and Son in eternity. I have attempted to demonstrate how a "strong" reading of this relationship does justice to some of the key passages in the later *Church Dogmatics,* while at the same time acknowledging the presence of other passages in the later *Church Dogmatics* that would offer support to the "weak" reading of Barth. Finally, I have pointed to some of the implications for constructive pneumatology of a "strong" reading of Barth.

The constructive pneumatological implications of reading Barth in this way have significant potential ramifications for other theological loci. In the present context I can indicate these ramifications only rather concisely, but there may be significant further theological work to be done in pursuing their trajectories.

First, the understanding after Barth of the work of the Spirit as one who is determined from all eternity to be *inecclesiandus* may offer a useful corrective to any contemporary notions of ecclesiology that posit and investigate the community of God as being determined by its own practices without profound accompanying theological reflection. While perhaps of much value sociologically and anthropologically, ultimately such construals can only be found theologically wanting. What is needed, precisely within valuable studies of the more practical or concrete dimensions and explorations of the being and activity of the community of God, is a consistent and enduring reemphasis on its pneumatological and thus Trinitarian foundations, foundations that are laid not only in time but also in eternity.

Second, an understanding after Barth of the work of the Spirit as one who is determined from all eternity to gather, upbuild, and send the community of God may offer a useful paradigm to missiologists who recognize the importance of rooting the mission of the community of God in an appropriate Trinitarian understanding of God. If we posit that the eternal foundations of this mission are rooted in the primal essence of the Spirit in itself, then it is clear that there is no alternative to the community of God being missionary and no future for a community of God that does not always look in its witness to the world beyond its walls. Given the constant attractiveness, particularly today, of ecclesiastical retrenchment in the face of secular opposition, such an awareness of the fundamental ecclesiological imperative of mission seems heuristic.

Taken together, these implications of a "strong" reading of the pneumatological dimension of Barth's theology of election and Trinity indicate not only the ongoing challenge to think after Barth, where Barth himself may have been silent, but also the significant potential of doing so and of pursuing further constructive theological work in these doctrines.

# 8. "A Specific Form of Relationship": On the Dogmatic Implications of Barth's Account of Election and Commandment for His Theological Ethics

*Christopher Holmes*

## I. Introduction

In this chapter I will describe the manifold ways in which Barth's doctrine of election makes theological space for a rich account of the command of God as the instrument whereby the risen Christ speaks and shapes a people who live in accordance with God's covenantal determination. Such description brings to the fore the *eschatological* character of Barth's ethics as well as its *concreteness*. It is well known that Barth was deeply suspicious of approaches to ethics founded on principles. This is because the reduction of ethics to principles obviates the need for repeatedly turning to the words of the apostles and prophets in favor of following ethical injunctions or guidelines for conduct mined from the Bible. Such approaches take seriously neither the exigencies of ethical decisions nor the way all of our pasts, presents, and futures are circumscribed by the living Word of God. Although Barth is often criticized for offering a voluntarist account of ethics that does not take into consideration "real world" concerns, I will show that Barth's focus on hearing the Word of God, specifically on our being addressed by the risen Jesus' command, is what gives his ethics its humane character and constitutes its concrete power to reshape human life today.[1]

In order to demonstrate the importance of the command of God in Barth's doctrine of election — the anthropological correlate of his doctrine

---

1. "Barth . . . was always preoccupied with the question of the truth of Christian faith and always seemed to Niebuhr to be insufficiently concerned with relevance." See Wallace M. Alston, Jr., introduction to *Ethics in a Christian Context*, by Paul L. Lehmann (Louisville: Westminster John Knox, 2006), p. xxiv.

— I will seek to do five things in this chapter. First, I will offer a synopsis of the most salient points that Barth raises in his account of "The Command of God" in Chapter 8 of *CD* II/2. Second, I will account for how his treatment of the command is further strengthened and developed in § 52 of *CD* III/4, "The Command of God our Creator." Third, I will comment on Barth's account of vocation in § 56.2 as that of our being responsible recipients of the command of God in the here and now. Fourth, I will reflect, via John Webster's recent work on aseity, on the ways in which Barth's account of the triune God brings itself to bear on his understanding of the command of God within the purview of the doctrine of election. Fifth, I will draw these strands together in a constructive reading of the concerns represented in the divergent readings of Barth on election by Bruce McCormack and Paul Molnar. I will do so by referring to Jüngel's language of "reiteration." Such language is salutary, I argue, as it does better justice to Barth's own concerns by framing the debate in terms of the freedom and love of God and the integrity of the corresponding creaturely freedom and love.

## II. Election and Command

God's election of humanity in Jesus Christ is, for Barth, election to a determination under God. It is God's eternal will that he be our God and we be his people. Regardless of the creature's degree of knowledge of or faith in this determination, this divine determination of creaturely freedom still stands. Indeed, the divine determination of election *is* the decision under which all people stand. This means that theological ethics has a very concrete and objective starting point. It lives and moves and has its being within this divine determination, without which Christian ethics would lack shape and substance. Accordingly, ethics becomes immanentized; it becomes a matter of the lone human or of ecclesiastical communities trying to figure out in an uncircumscribed space what is the most appropriate form of action in response to a given situation, rather than being a matter of all people learning to recognize that the space in which they act is a space delimited by the triune God's redemptive purposes — purposes that render the space intelligible and provide directives in relationship to it.

What this means is that ethics, for Barth, is never a formless or rootless or, for that matter, a secure undertaking. Rather, ethics has a determined character, for ethics involves the commandment of God, which is from grace and to grace, and which thus leads to life. This is important to note from the start, precisely because ethics, as Barth envisions it, is not a matter of us — of the individual or of the church — deciding what to do on the basis of what God has done. Such an account would be far too inattentive to the way the grace of God shapes and forms us in each temporal moment. Moreover, such an account presupposes a "dead" Christ rather than a resurrected Christ, a Christ who is confined to a static past and who as a result becomes reified into a set of principles that provide guidelines for how to live in the world today. Although such a Christology funds many contemporary approaches to ethics, it is by no means a Christology to which Barth is amenable. For Barth, ethics is a matter of the command *of God* in which God in Christ is present to us and speaks in the form of the commandment, which is permission and therefore freedom itself.[2]

That Barth equates the commandment with permission and considers it to be generative of freedom is itself highly significant. Most importantly, it helps us begin to see the extent to which Barth's doctrine of election is a doctrine that is formative of a peculiar people. It permits or licenses a certain kind of creaturely existence, one that is profoundly free in accordance with God's election in that it engenders freedom *from* bondage to self-will, self-determination, and self-rule, and thus freedom *for* the will of God and God's grace. In Nigel Biggar's words, "We should obey God's command, not out of spineless deference to the capricious wishes of an almighty despot, but out of regard for our own best good, which this gracious God alone truly understands and which he intends with all his heart."[3] Accordingly, the commandment of God frees us to live in accordance with God's election of us in his Son Jesus to be his people. To be sure, there is something deeply counterintuitive at work in Barth's account. Ethics, if it is to be truly *theological,* is about conforming to a set of affairs whose truthfulness is established in God and apart from us. Ethics, then, is not so much a constructive undertaking as a responsive undertaking. Indeed, it is responsive insofar as it is a matter of the hearing, the doing, and the obeying of the will of God. But the will of God is not formless and void. Rather, it

2. Karl Barth, *Church Dogmatics,* 4 volumes in 13 parts, ed. G. W. Bromiley and T. F. Torrance (Edinburgh: T. & T. Clark, 1956-1975), II/2, p. 743 (hereafter, volume, part, and page references to the *CD* appear in parentheses in the text and footnotes). As Paul T. Nimmo notes, Barth's ethics is "governed by a christological methodology [not] only in form, but also in content." Nimmo, "The Orders of Creation in the Theological Ethics of Karl Barth," *Scottish Journal of Theology* 60, no. 1 (2007): 35.

3. Nigel Biggar, "Barth's Trinitarian Ethics," in *The Cambridge Companion to Karl Barth,* ed. John Webster (Cambridge: Cambridge University Press, 2000), p. 215.

takes us to a very particular place: the revealed commandment of the revealed God in Jesus Christ.

A new kind of existence is thus assigned to us in our election, an existence that is pure gift. This new existence involves profound noetic and
ontic change in which all the tables for us have been overturned: the being
of humanity has been fundamentally reconstituted by the God who in his
Son elects to come among us and renew us in such a way that we may be
made fit participants in his rule. But this new existence, rooted as it is in
the gift of God's self-bestowal, includes a task. And that task is fulfilled to
the extent that we *reorder* our existence in accordance with God's determination of us in Christ, a determination that enables us to become in faith
and obedience what we are: God's children.[4] Simply put: "That God is gracious to us in Jesus Christ is the divine decision about our whole being,
what we do and do not do. This is the will of God for us" (*CD* II/2, p. 632).
God's will always remains *God's,* and so God's will to be gracious to us in
Christ is not something to be possessed or identified in any straightforward fashion with our own activity.

God's decision of grace, for Barth, is a decision that creates a response
for itself in the world. Indeed, God wills to be gracious to us in his Son and
wills, moreover, that we live in correspondence to such graciousness. Such
correspondence takes specific form via obedience to the commandment,
obedience that thereby creates a peculiar people. The commandment is
precisely what engenders obedience to the decision of God and enables us
to live responsibly in relation to it. "We come from pure responsibility. We
are caught up in responsibility. And we shall always be responsible" (*CD* II/
2, p. 642). The horizon of our responsibility *is* the commandment of God:
through it God creates and forms a people attentive to his mercies.

The essence of the responsible life, for Barth, is a life lived in obedience
to the commandment of God, the norm for what the Christian community does and does not do. But since God's will concerns a decision about
our whole being expressed in Jesus Christ, a decision in relationship to
which we are responsible, this must never be taken to mean that it is a decision that *we* can control or form. On the contrary, the commandment is of
God and always remains God's. It is, therefore, a command that we cannot

---

4. To be sure, our existence is only all too provisionally reordered on this side of the
*eschaton.* To put it differently, because sanctification is real and thus actual in Jesus Christ, it
is also as such an eschatological reality. The human's sanctification is indeed caught up in
and bound to Jesus Christ, he who *is* her sanctification (and justification, too).

domesticate, precisely because it is a command that controls us. Thus is the eschatological character of Barth's account evident: just as the decision is God's, so the form that the decision takes is also God's, even as it takes place through human agency. Yet the divine priority must always be continually acknowledged, for in so doing one notices the crucial role of the self-communicative presence of God that shapes so much of Barth's account. By emphasizing God's decision about our whole being, "[t]he question cannot [then] be whether He speaks, but whether we *hear*" (*CD* II/2, p. 670, emphasis added). God's speech is concrete speech that takes up space. And the task of the Christian community, if it is to be truly responsible, is to hear that speech in all of its mortifying and vivifying power.

It follows, then, that ethics that takes seriously the basic truth that God speaks is a disrupted ethics, disrupted insofar as an ethics concerned with hearing and therewith obeying is an ethics that takes the prophetic office of our Lord seriously. In the words of Wallace Alston, Jr., it is an ethic that is concerned with "what might an adequate response be to the contemporary presence and activity of God."[5] Therefore, theological ethics must indeed be preoccupied with the kind of hearing that leads to obedience in accordance with God's "contemporary presence and activity," precisely because there is only one whose Word is to be heard and accepted, namely, the risen Christ who speaks in the form of his Word and thus of commandment today. Just the same, theological ethics is bound to the commanding Son of God. Thus the one who commands cannot then be separated from what is commanded.[6] The one who commands is in his person — his very being — gracious, and so is his command. The grace of Christ takes up space, if you will, and it does so as command. By hearing God's command, argues Barth, the creature, the church, thus align themselves to God their Creator and the end for which they have been created. Inasmuch as they are in alignment with God's grace, they are shaped in accordance with the will of God, which is precisely God's chief desire for his people.

## III. Trinity, Election, and Commandment

Having revisited Barth's account of "The Command of God" in *CD* II/2 with a view to its relationship to Barth's doctrine of election, I propose

5. Alston, introduction to Lehmann, *Ethics in a Christian Context,* p. xxii.
6. See *CD* II/2, p. 679: "God actualises His covenant with man by giving him commands, and man experiences this actualisation by the acceptance of these commands."

now to turn our attention to § 52 of *CD* III/4 with a view toward further delimiting the contours of the account offered above. In order to do so, we must recognize from the start just how important in Barth's judgment it is to account for the commandment of God as the commandment of the tri-une God — Father, Son, and Holy Spirit: the "one whole command [is] of the one whole God" (*CD* III/4, p. 33). It is important to acknowledge this precisely because the command of God is as such the command of our *Creator*. To be sure, it is the command of our Redeemer and Sanctifier, too. But it is Barth's judgment that the command of God as the command of our Creator is important to consider — indeed, it "logically" precedes the others — precisely because such a consideration preserves the basic insight that our Creator really does *meet* us as such via his command: "His command already concerns man in his creaturely being," in particular as regards the sanctification of the human being (*CD* III/4, p. 33).[7]

In greater detail, as the commandment of God our Creator, the commandment is already "the sanctification . . . of man's creaturely action and abstention" (*CD* III/4, p. 38). This is important to note because, in so doing, one notices the extent to which Barth's account integrates the doctrine of creation with the doctrine of sanctification. That is, the commandment is said by Barth to be instrumental in the renewal of the human in accordance with his true end. For God not only turns to us in free grace, which is the very expression of his eternal determination to be our God, but God also turns *us* to himself, the very manifestation of his eternal determination that we be his people. That it is God and his command that do this work attests just how important it is for Barth that human ethical action be continually understood as that which is sanctified and moved in a direction without which it would be powerless to proceed. Human action is sanctified, then, via God's commandment, as the commandment enables the human to correspond to God's determination. But this is always only possible because, again, "God is the active Subject not only in reconciliation generally but also in the conversion of man to Himself" (*CD* IV/2, p. 500). The commandment of our Creator is that by which God gives us a share in his holiness and thereby claims us — the holiness we now participate in by virtue of the mercies of Jesus Christ. In Barth's words: "God

---

7. Biggar writes: "Logically, however, the command of God the Creator takes precedence, since the reconciliation of sinners to God (and their final redemption) presupposes that those reconciled sinners (awaiting final redemption) are already creatures." Biggar, "Barth's Trinitarian Ethics," p. 216.

claims this man and makes him willing and ready for His service" (*CD* IV/ 2, p. 503). The human corresponds to her sanctification inasmuch as she acknowledges — the noetic dimension — the implications for the entirety of her being that flow from her being created as a creature of God and continually claimed by God — the ontic dimension.

In Barth's account of the election and the commandment of God, the ontic is indeed always determinative of the noetic: what God eternally determines us to be — his children and covenant partners in Jesus Christ — is that from whence true self-knowledge originates. "The eternal decree of God which precedes creation and makes it possible and necessary is the gracious election of man in Jesus Christ" (*CD* III/4, p. 39). In other words, God's election of men and women in Christ to be his covenant partners is the basis for creation as a whole and the sanctification of the human person, fallen as she is, that she might live in accordance with the will of him who created her. Election underwrites the doctrine of creation: creation is to be understood within the purview of the doctrine of election.

In his account of "Ethics as a Task of the Doctrine of Creation" (§ 52), Barth is at pains to establish just how it is that God wills to eternally exist in relationship to us. That is, God wills that we exist in relationship to him precisely as the one who is our Creator. And the commandment of God is precisely what enables us to live in accordance with and in conformity to this determination, namely, that we have been created by and for the one who is Father, Son, and Spirit in himself and apart from us. Barth is so very insistent on this point because it is his way of keeping the account of the command of God as the command of our Creator *concrete*. According to Barth, "Our concern is not with a neutral but with a specific form of the relationship of God and man, with this form of divine grace and human gratitude" (*CD* III/4, p. 40). Stated somewhat differently, only when one appreciates the specific form of the relationship God elects for himself to take via his creature, can one appreciate the specific form that creaturely being is to take with respect to this determination. More specifically, obedience to the commandment of God — the form of grace — is demonstrative of gratitude on the human's part to the specific form of the relationship that God wills to have with the creature, which is a relationship of fellowship in his Son, Jesus Christ. Indeed, in the commandment — the "specific form of the relationship of God and man" — God addresses and speaks to us as friends who are recipients of his benefits and of his grace as our Creator.

As the command of God our Creator, the command concerns the

whole of our creaturely existence, so much so that even our knowledge of
ourselves and our being as creatures is derived from God's grace. But because of sin, pernicious as it is, we freely consent to forms of existence that
contradict our very selves not only on a noetic level but also on an ontic
level as well. We willingly and repeatedly refuse to live as creatures who are
addressed in the community via the Word, so that we are always all too
willing to view ourselves as the center of human existence and thus to look
to our own subjectivity to determine the shape and form of genuine ethical existence. But this, for Barth, is profoundly misguided, for the real human being is the one who regards himself as being in Jesus Christ and
therewith addressed by his Creator via the command. In an important passage, Barth observes:

> When we see the glory of God residing in Jesus Christ, then, in and with
> the most high God Himself, we also see man: humbled, accused and
> judged as a guilty and lost creature, and only as such, only in the fire of
> judgment, upheld and saved; but also exalted and glorified as the crea-
> ture elected and affirmed by God from all eternity. This is real man, man
> himself in the mirror of God's grace addressed to him in Jesus Christ.
> (*CD* III/4, p. 42)

Therefore, the "real man" for Barth is the judged and pardoned "man," the
humiliated and exalted "man" in Jesus Christ. Precisely as such the human
being is addressed by the command of God in Jesus Christ and thereby
judged, saved, and set upon the narrow path of renewal.

Barth's ethics is concrete, then, inasmuch as it is christological, for the
shape of true human being is found in one man, he who is the real man —
Jesus Christ. Ethics, therefore, is a matter of corresponding to a living person, the real person. Accordingly, for Barth, ethics is not so much a normative exercise as a responsive undertaking given in the dynamic relationship
of faith. It is not a question of asking, What is the right thing to do? Rather,
it is a matter of asking, Given that the right one, the real one — Jesus
Christ — has revealed himself, how then shall I (and the Christian community) live in a way that renders us most transparent and responsive to
the gracious address that we must always hear in life and in death? Simply
put, God's eternal election of us to fellowship with himself in his Son
through the mortifying and vivifying power of the Spirit means one thing
above all else, namely, that we as those who are elected should exist as such,
as the true *creatures* of God. Existing in this reality means, then, that we ex-

ist in a living person who can never be reduced to a set of principles or rules. This living person "excludes [and resists] all possibility of rational generalization into reliable ethical constants."[8] But because he ever always speaks and addresses us, obedience will never begin in a vacuum; rather, it will always start with a hearing, a hearing that is intent on listening to one who has spoken through the apostles and prophets and indeed continues to speak through those same apostles and prophets to form his people into those whom he has elected them to be — his people.

Barth's account of "The Command of God Our Creator" in *CD* III/4 is insistent on just this point: the command we must hear from our Creator is that we *are* his creatures. We are to exist as such and to hear in this new form of existence a summons. Indeed, election includes a summons, and that summons is one of being summoned to hear an address that proclaims to us that we *are* God's creatures — that our being starts and ends with the Word. The extent of our Creator's graciousness to us in Christ is evident, then, in the commandment that has as its aim and includes within itself the sanctification and liberation of the creaturely action. The command sanctifies and liberates inasmuch as it enables us to live as *addressed* men and women, which denotes the truest shape of human existence as creatures created by God for the hearing of the address of God. Thus Barth argues that "[t]he man to whom God is gracious in Jesus Christ stands before Him also as His creature and is to be sanctified and liberated by his command" (*CD* III/4, p. 45).

The person who recognizes herself as created by God indeed recognizes herself as sanctified and thereby liberated and turned to God *by God,* so that creation and sanctification (as well as justification) are intimately related to one another in Barth's account. The sanctification and liberation of the creature consists in the creature's standing before God in Christ *as* God's creature. The works that the Christian engages in — chiefly obedience — are works justified by God. In so doing, God effects the existence of a "royal and courageous people" (*CD* IV/2, p. 508). The works that the Christian cheerfully engages in are thus works that are always sanctified by God: the commandment *is* God's sanctification and the means by which he sanctifies. The commandment of God is thus addressed to creatures created by a God who wills that his creatures recognize themselves as such. Only inasmuch as a particular man or women confesses his or her createdness by the triune God — which is precisely the aim of the com-

8. Biggar, "Barth's Trinitarian Ethics," p. 217.

mand — can they be free and liberated persons and live in accordance with the will of their Creator.

It is my judgment that the counterintuitive character of Barth's account comes to the fore, once again, at points such as this. That we are created as the beings to whom God is gracious means just about everything for ethics, as ethics thus understood begins with the simple recognition that the person (or community) with whom it is dealing is not someone thrown into the cosmos, but rather is a creature whose being is circumscribed by a God who will stop at nothing — even the death of his beloved Son — to ensure that the creature be freed and thereby sanctified to live as a creature, a creature who does not write her own story about herself but rather submits to the story that God in Christ has given her, a story whose center is the simple yet profound declaration that the God who is gracious to her in Christ is her Creator, and that the command this God gives her is a command that effects her freedom to live precisely as such. To state the case somewhat differently, God's election of the creature — which discloses the eternal being of God — establishes human agency.[9] This agency is formed, shaped, and sustained by the command of God revealed in Christ. Hence this agency arises inasmuch as the creature and the Christian community reiterate in word and in deed this decision — this primal decision of God to be God for us.

## IV. Election and Vocation

It is necessary to turn to Barth's account of vocation in *CD* III/4 § 56.2 at this point because it further reminds us that his treatment of the command of God can never be reduced to a series of general principles, a program, or a matter of casuistry. The person — and therewith the Christian community — addressed by God in his command is wholly responsible to God alone. This is the human's and the church's *call:* to be responsible. That call is, of course, heard in a constellation of different contexts. But for Barth, it is never the context itself that generates the command or possesses some kind of imperative force; rather, the context is simply the place where a person (and the Christian community) finds himself as he hears himself addressed. As Barth puts it, the whole of life is the "place of responsibility," the place of address (*CD* III/4, p. 607).

9. John Webster, *Barth's Ethics of Reconciliation* (Cambridge: Cambridge University Press, 1995), p. 51.

In essence, this means that a person is responsible to God alone and that the vocation of the human being is to live responsibly before God as God's creature. Vocation, according to Barth, is not therefore continuous with the divine call or command, but is instead the *place* where a particular person and community take responsibility for receiving and hearing the divine command. Our vocations are thus truly our own to the extent that they are places where we freely receive God's commandment to be people of "the Now" (*CD* III/4, p. 615). To be a people of the now is to be an addressed people who view every moment as an opportunity for faith and obedience. Thus Barth writes that "[e]very special period of life can present only special opportunities for calling and discipleship" (*CD* III/4, p. 618).

One of Barth's chief concerns in his account of vocation is to relativize the claims of the situation or the manifold actualities in which one finds oneself in order that one may exist faithfully in relationship to them. Hence, one will be faithful to the situation to the extent that one allows oneself to be met and thus claimed and enabled by the command of God. In Barth's view, there is no other guarantor of faithfulness. Indeed, the concrete question of vocation is whether one "will achieve the freedom of obedience in this particular sphere and under all the other signs of his creaturely vocation" (*CD* III/4, p. 632). Our vocation is life-giving, then, to the extent that in it one answers God's call, God's address that comes to us in the form of the commandment, which not only reminds us of our creatureliness but also directs us to live as creatures elected by God for covenant fellowship with his Son. To be sure, obedience to God's commandment is hard work, but it is the work of our vocation. And to the extent that one engages in this work, one is deemed to be faithful to one's vocation.

The shape of faithfulness to the command, however, can never be captured. This denotes once again the strongly eschatological character of Barth's account of vocation: "Will he acquiesce in the fact that what seemed impossible yesterday has become possible to-day, and what seemed absolutely right yesterday is wrong to-day? . . . This is the most acute form of the question of the right existence of man in his sphere of operation" (*CD* III/4, p. 644). What Barth says can be easily misunderstood: one could read him as suggesting that humans are placed into a kind of void by the call and command of God, if one does not appreciate Barth's basic point that the address of the Creator God to his creature in the form of the command comes anew to the creature every morning.[10]

---

10. Biggar is not quite on the mark when he says that God's commands "do have certain

That is why the creature cannot simply assume that what was possible yesterday is possible today: to assume so would be to obviate the need for active listening and hearing the voice of the living God. Indeed, the address of God might involve any one of us changing our sphere(s) of operation.

In sum, a brief description of Barth's account of vocation is in order, for in it we see the extent to which the commandment of God can always only be heard and thus *not* discovered or identified somehow with the situation at hand. The vocation of the Christian and the Christian community is to simply hear and obey and thus to be disciples of the living, speaking Lord in their manifold spheres of operation, trusting that the will of God is the dynamic and permanent structure, for that will is a person who is at the same time his command.

## V. Election and Aseity

It might seem strange to briefly consider the dogmatic implications of an account of God's aseity in a piece devoted to a description of the theological work undertaken by the election and commandment of God in Barth's ethical vision. But such a step is necessary, even vital, if we are to have an adequate grasp of the relationship and correspondence between divine and human love and freedom. However, before I reflect on the importance of aseity for Barth's understanding, let me summarize the basic contours of a dogmatic account of aseity, via John Webster's extraordinary piece on that subject entitled "Life in and of Himself: Reflections on God's Aseity."[11]

Webster writes that an account of aseity must include two dimensions: "First, it indicates the glory and plentitude of the life of the Holy Trinity in its self-existent and self-moving originality, its underived fullness. In every respect, God is of himself God. Second, it indicates that God's originality

---

constant features" that are expressed "in the created structure of human nature." Such a reading ascribes to the orders of creation a kind of stability and possibly imperative force that does not adequately recognize that Barth, far from beating a voluntarist drum, simply wants to emphasize the necessity of hearing and never of mapping out in advance what those constant features might be. See Biggar, "Barth's Trinitarian Ethics," pp. 217, 218.

11. John Webster, "Life in and of Himself: Reflections on God's Aseity," in *Engaging the Doctrine of God: Protestant Perspectives,* ed. Bruce L. McCormack (Grand Rapids: Baker Academic, 2008), pp. 107-24 (hereafter, page references to this essay appear in parentheses in the text).

and fullness constitute the ground of his self-communication" (pp. 107-8). Simply put, Webster is arguing that on the basis of God's self-revelation in the history of Israel fulfilled in Christ, God reveals himself to be one who is utterly self-sufficient, one whose self-sufficiency grounds and make possible his communication of his very self to that which he has created: out of himself, he gives himself. Needless to say, such an account of aseity is not contrasting in character, because it is not dependent on or underwritten by "the contingency of the world" in any way (p. 110). Rather, it is underwritten by the doctrine of the Trinity. "To speak of God's aseity," Webster argues, "is thus to speak of the spontaneous, eternal, and unmoved movement of his being-in-relation as Father, Son, and Spirit" (p. 115). To speak of God's aseity is thus to speak of a God whose aseity "is his self-existence *in* these relations" as Father, Son, and Holy Spirit (p. 117). But of course we cannot speak of God's self-existence without following God's relationship to creatures, for God's own inner perfection and sufficiency "is not self-enclosed or self-revolving" (p. 119). Therefore, aseity cannot be equated with independence or distance; rather, it is — in the case of the person of the Son of God — "the presupposition of the Son's saving acts" (p. 122). Following Calvin, Webster notes that "the divine will is not simply to possess life as something 'hidden and as it were buried within himself' but rather to transfuse that life 'into his Son that it might flow to us.'"[12] It is Calvin's language of transfusion that is particularly instructive for our purposes, in that it demonstrates an important aspect of the anthropological payoff, or "practical aspect," of an account of aseity, namely, that the God who has life in himself freely gives of himself to creatures: "This life includes a self-willed movement of love" (pp. 122-23).

Tracing the dogmatic relationship between aseity and commandment proves helpful in an account of the relationship between election and commandment, precisely because it is one further way in which one teases out the implications of Barth's basic conviction regarding the unity of dogmatics and ethics and of the freedom of God in relationship to his creatures. More specifically, it is a way of demonstrating the extent to which identity descriptions of God shape human existence and elicit appropriate forms of creaturely correspondence.[13] Thus, when one reflects

12. John Calvin, *The Gospel according to St. John 1–10*, ed. and trans. T. H. L. Parker (Edinburgh: Oliver and Boyd, 1959), p. 131, quoted in Webster, "In and of Himself," p. 122.
13. "The attributes of God are conceptual glosses on God's name, indicators of God's identity." John Webster, *Holiness* (Grand Rapids: Eerdmans, 2003), p. 37.

on the nature of obedience to the commandment of God with a view to God's aseity, according to Webster, one recognizes the extent to which obedience and the commandment that calls for obedience are inconceivable "apart from its [the Trinity's] overflowing plenitude in giving itself to creatures" (p. 123). Accordingly, the commandment of God, dogmatically conceived, is a function of this overflowing plenitude that comes to us freely and abundantly because God has this abundance originally in his own being. We have the commandment before us precisely as a gift of the God whose self-will includes the most costly love for his wayward creature, a love that determines that this creature be subject to his life-giving will despite the creature's very strenuous objections to it.

Commandment relates to aseity, furthermore, in that we are quickened to life via the commandment of God by the God who is life *in se*. The commandment enables human beings to live in accordance with a certain state of affairs, namely, in accordance with the God whose very life makes alive. This God does not need our obedience in order to somehow be more God or to have his plans realized in the world. This God does not need a world in order to be perfect and complete in his triunity. On the contrary, the God of the Gospel has life *in se*. Discipleship to the commandment simply brings the church, and therewith the Christian, into fellowship with a God whose splendor is the only thing worthy of the unadulterated praise and obedience of his creatures.

Moreover, the commandment — as an instrument whereby God humanizes and gives shape to life in this world — is indicative of the extent to which the inner life of God creates a form of creaturely life commensurate *with himself,* in his own freedom and abundance. What is all the more miraculous is that God does so in a way that never compromises his freedom. The commandment does not enable us to claim God, but rather is what God uses to claim us and thus enable us to see that the God who gives life does so without reservation precisely because that is the kind of thing that the God who has life in and of himself does.

## VI. Reiteration and/or Anticipation?

In a collection of essays that concerns, among other things, the debate waged between Bruce McCormack and Paul Molnar on the doctrines of Trinity and election, it is important to consider how Barth's account of election and commandment bears on this debate. Therefore, in order to understand the relationship between election and commandment, I will begin with a brief rehearsal of the debate.

McCormack's important essay "Grace and Being" expresses well his reading of what is at stake in Barth's doctrine of God. In that essay McCormack argues that, for Barth, "election is the event in God's life in which he assigns to himself the being he will have for all eternity."[14] The implication is that "for him [i.e., God] 'essence' is given in the act of electing and is, in fact, constituted by that eternal act" (p. 99). Accordingly, the incarnation of the Son of God is regarded as an act *constitutive* of the being of God in eternity" (p. 99). Although alarm bells might certainly and justifiably go off at this point with respect to the implications of election thus conceived for the freedom of God in relationship to history, McCormack is quite careful in his account of what he means by "constitutive." In essence, what he is suggesting is that, for Barth, "God is already in pre-temporal eternity — *by way of anticipation* — that which he would become in time" (p. 100). God's being is thus, for Barth, "a being in the mode of anticipation" (p. 100). God's pre-temporal decision to be God for us in Jesus Christ is "by way of anticipation" constitutive of the life of God throughout eternity.

Such a reading of Barth strikes me as somewhat one-sided. By that I mean that there is a very important motif in Barth that is lacking in McCormack's reading, one that Jüngel succinctly brings to the fore in his remarkable work *God's Being Is in Becoming,* where he argues that the truth of theological statements is found in the extent to which they safeguard "the *freedom* of the subject of the revelation."[15] My concern with McCormack is that his reading of Barth on the divine being as "a being in the mode of anticipation" jettisons Barth's own very nuanced sense of God's being as not actualized in revelation but rather a being whose historicality, in Jüngel's words, "reiterates itself in the historicality of revelation" (p. 83).[16] No doubt

14. McCormack, "Grace and Being: The Role of God's Gracious Election in Karl Barth's Theological Ontology" in *The Cambridge Companion to Karl Barth,* ed. John Webster (Cambridge: Cambridge University Press, 2000), p. 98 (hereafter, page references to this essay appear in parentheses in the text).

15. Eberhard Jüngel, *God's Being Is in Becoming: The Trinitarian Being of God in the Theology of Karl Barth,* trans. John Webster (Grand Rapids: Eerdmans, 2001), p. 73, emphasis added (hereafter, page references to this work appear in parentheses in the text).

16. See also Jüngel, *God's Being,* pp. 73, 83, and *CD* I/1, p. 434, wherein Barth argues that "God would not on that account [i.e., in not creating] be any the less God." See also Paul D. Molnar, "Can the Electing God Be God for Us? Some Implications of Bruce McCormack's Understanding of Barth's Doctrine of Election for the Doctrine of the Trinity," pp. 63-90 above, esp. 81-82.

such an emphasis does not belie McCormack's reading of Barth on the election of grace, which, as Jüngel holds, is "God's primal decision in which *God* determines irrevocably his being-in-act" (pp. 73, 85). But what such an emphasis does is draw attention to an important motif in Barth that is eclipsed in McCormack, namely that Barth is — so as to avoid any taint of the charge of historicizing — quite concerned to think of and to account for God's freedom in terms of a freedom to exist, as Jüngel states, "in the historicality of revelation" (p. 83). This is to say that the eternal Son is never the Son without us, that the Son is in his very being existent as the one who is revealed in the fullness of time as the fulfillment of the covenant of grace. Barth not only eschews voluntarism in describing the Son's work — as if his work were accidental to his being — but also any sense that God does not freely will for all eternity to be this one: God with us.

Therefore, according to Jüngel's reading of Barth, revelation is *expressive*, not constitutive, of the self-movement of God's (historical) being. In this regard, God's being demands historical predicates: God wills to become in history what God already *is in himself as Father, Son, and Holy Spirit:* the triune God exists in time in the becoming of which he eternally is. Accordingly, there is not an ontic gap between the immanent and reiterated Trinity, but there is an asymmetrical order between them. The immanent Trinity remains identical with the economic Trinity without being exhausted by it. There is, in other words, no economic Trinity without the immanent, as that order is irreversible. God is always in advance of the one he is in time. For this reason, the immanent and economic Trinity can never be collapsed into one another. It would seem that such an emphasis overturns to an extent McCormack's reading, as it brings to the fore a very important consideration of Barth that is underdeveloped and overlooked in McCormack's account. Indeed, I wonder to what extent a description of God's being in terms of a being by way of "anticipation" is the best way to solve the theological problem at hand, namely, the obviation of the idea that there be space for an independent doctrine of the Trinity with respect to the covenant of grace. An account of God's freedom can be construed that does not suggest a gap, and the way of doing that is by using Jüngel's category of "reiteration." In other words, the covenant of grace is best described not as constitutive of God by way of *anticipation,* which suggests that God's being depends on the being of the world, but rather as a series of historical acts reiterative of the God who "*is,* in that he *sets himself in relation*" (p. 116). Put differently, God just *is* the God who sets himself in relationship as Father, Son, and Holy Spirit, who is both self-related in himself and to us in the outpouring of God's freedom and love.

Where this concerns the relationship between election and commandment becomes clear when one considers the account of human action that follows from what McCormack calls "covenantal ontology" (p. 107). McCormack writes, "Insofar as true humanity is realized only in the *act* of faith and obedience, 'covenantal ontology' is actualistic on the human side as well" (p. 108). Yet I wonder if it would not be better to describe true humanity as being reiterative humanity, that is, humanity is true humanity inasmuch as it reiterates in time what it is eternally determined to be. Stated differently, it is not so much a matter of true humanity being realized only in faith and obedience, but rather faith in and thus obedience to the commandment of God is the posture that most truly reiterates in the form of correspondence at the creaturely level of God's eternal election of us to covenant fellowship. Thus the shape of true human being is given us in advance, and so human acts of obedience to the commandment are acts wherein a determination is reiterated and not so much actualized.[17]

It follows, then, that I cannot affirm with McCormack the following: there is "an analogy [i.e., an 'analogy of being'] between an eternal act of Self-determination and a historical human act of self-determination and the 'being' (divine and human) which is constituted in each. Human being in the act of faith and obedience in response to the covenant of grace corresponds to the being of the gracious God; that is the shape of the analogy."[18]

17. Moreover, reiteration language, expressive as it is of a determination, must also be considered in terms of its ontic implications. That is, in the event in which we hear and obey the command of God and in which we elect God, we reiterate God's election of us. In this sense we determine our own being, but our determining is always *circumscribed* by God's eternal determination. This means, then, that we could talk of some sort of analogy between the divine self-determination and our self-determination in action. But I am nervous about doing so if the language of "actualize" is introduced, for such language not only suggests that human beings actualize their own being in response to the divine grace, but also — and more importantly — that God's being is actualized with respect to us. This would not only reduce God's being to God's work *ad extra*, thus collapsing the immanent and economic Trinity, but it also suggests that God's being is actualized and complete only with respect to creation, as McCormack's critics have vigorously charged. For this reason I prefer reiteration language, because in my judgment it better honors the *priority* of God's aseity and grace, such that grace is always what circumscribes our self-determining and indeed so renews the self in its determining that the one thing it desires is the one in whom its true self lies — Jesus Christ.

18. Jüngel, *God's Being*, p. 109.

Such an account would be rendered more acceptable if the language of constitution were removed and replaced equally strenuously with an account of — to draw on Jüngel's language — the "reiterative" character of human action in obedience to the commandment as action that does not "actualize" or "constitute" but rather is action that reiterates who we are determined to be and thus action that corresponds to our election by God to be his children.

Moreover, reiterative language, in my judgment, best preserves God's freedom, which "is the basis for human freedom and human self-determination."[19] Reiterative language honors God's freedom and ontological self-sufficiency and therefore truly establishes creaturely freedom and integrity. This is why I find Molnar's contribution important to this debate, for he writes forcefully, with respect to McCormack's conclusions, on the importance of maintaining that the Trinity exists in its own right, with this basic implication: "The covenant of grace is a covenant of *grace* because it expresses the free overflow of God's eternal love that takes place in pre-temporal eternity as the Father begets the Son in the unity of the Holy Spirit" (p. 63). The corollary, of course, is that God's being does not result from God's decision, God's will, as Barth himself insists (see *CD* I/1, p. 434). "Rather, his will to elect expresses his freedom to be God in a new way as God for us" (p. 63).

Molnar's point is an important point to draw together with an account of commandment, and it is expressive of Jüngel's deepest insights on this matter: men and women are not so much realized with regard to faith in and obedience to the commandment as much as they are freed or permitted to be creatures of this God who without compulsion or necessity elected them in his Son to be his creatures, and thereby chose to be God for them. Molnar is very concerned, as I am, about McCormack's account because it represents a compromise of God's freedom which leads in his judgment "to the dissolution of human freedom and ultimately the collapse of theology into anthropology" (p. 64).

In sum, I believe that Molnar is indeed correct in his insistence on maintaining the priority of God's freedom in relationship to human freedom, and this involves neither a separation of the economic from the immanent Trinity nor an abstract notion of divine freedom. I say "correct"

19. Paul D. Molnar, *Divine Freedom and the Doctrine of the Immanent Trinity: In Dialogue with Karl Barth and Contemporary Theology* (London: T. & T. Clark, 2002), p. 62 (hereafter, page references to this work appear in parentheses in the text).

because, as I read Barth on the crucial function played by commandment in his ethics, one encounters time after time an emphasis on the liberating character of the command, the command that frees us and in so doing sanctifies us in such a way that we might live in accordance with God's *free* and eternal decision to be our God and we to be his people. Obedience to the command, then, does not so much *actualize* our being, which would place the responsibility for our actualization in the fallen hands of human beings. On the contrary, it simply is the way that we as creatures of the tri-une God *reiterate* in our given sphere God's eternal decision to be God-for-us, a decision that reflects "the free overflow of God's eternal love" (p. 63).

## Conclusion

In this chapter I have sought, via an account of the relationship between election and commandment in Barth's theology, to demonstrate the extent to which Barth's account of election, located firmly within the doctrine of God, includes within itself a profound anthropological correlate. This correlate is brought home most concretely via Barth's account of the command of God as that which brings about creaturely conformity to the state of affairs established in the person and work of Jesus Christ. This state of affairs, namely reconciliation, effected by God the Father in Jesus Christ his Son and made effective through the Spirit whom they send, is, for Barth, profoundly dependent on the recognition that the God who does so stands under no compulsion to do so, save himself, and thus his utter propensity as the one he eternally is toward giving himself to what he freely creates as other than himself. The God of the gospel reiterates in time what he eternally is, and in so doing he calls the creature with whom he freely unites himself in Christ to live as a creature whose vocation it is, in whatever sphere she or the community she is part of finds herself, to do the one thing required of her, namely, to become what she is: God's covenant partner. She becomes this partner along with the Christian community inasmuch as she understands herself to be one addressed in the command that summons her to freedom from bondage to decay and for loving service to God and neighbor.

# 9. God's Self-Specification: His Being Is His Electing

*Aaron T. Smith*

The significance of Karl Barth's formulation of election is appreciated in part by the depths to which it penetrates vis-à-vis reflection on God's being, and by the intensity of disagreement it engenders relative to discourse about grace and being — in other words, by the extent of its ontological and theological provocation. The claims and debate it has provoked to date are substantive, and they are encapsulated in a group of publications by Bruce McCormack and Paul Molnar.[1] Affirming the ongoing impor-

---

1. See Bruce McCormack, "Grace and Being: The Role of God's Gracious Election in Karl Barth's Theological Ontology," in *The Cambridge Companion to Karl Barth,* ed. John Webster (Cambridge: Cambridge University Press, 2000), pp. 92-110; Paul Molnar, *Divine Freedom and the Doctrine of the Immanent Trinity: In Dialogue with Karl Barth and Contemporary Theology* (London: T. & T. Clark, 2002), pp. 61-81. For further elucidation of McCormack's position, see *Karl Barth's Critically Realistic Dialectical Theology: Its Genesis and Development 1909-1936* (Oxford: Oxford University Press, 1995), pp. 371-74, 455-62. For further background on Molnar's position on the place of the doctrine of the immanent Trinity for preserving divine freedom, see Paul Molnar, "The Function of the Immanent Trinity in the Theology of Karl Barth: Implications for Today," *Scottish Journal of Theology* 42, no. 3 (1989): 367-99.

Several publications have directly and indirectly taken up the subject matter of those essays, but most have not altered the discourse in any substantive way. An exception is an exchange between McCormack and Edwin Chr. van Driel: see van Driel, "Karl Barth on the Eternal Existence of Jesus Christ," and McCormack, "Seek God Where He May Be Found: A Response to Edwin Chr. van Driel," both essays published in *Scottish Journal of Theology* 60, no. 1 (2007): 45-61 and 62-79, respectively. Van Driel appeals to classical Christology in order to differentiate between the human identity of Christ and the eternal essence of God. But the main gain, for me, is on McCormack's side, and it is twofold. First, McCormack thematically addresses the issue of time/eternity, especially as this bears on the ontology of God's *ad extra* activity (pp. 75-76), a matter I have raised with McCormack and Molnar (and which I

tance of this discussion, I will reconsider here Barth's doctrine of election by attending to the constitutive claims made in these pieces, arguing finally that God's gracious act of electing represents the specification of divine being. I understand this position as a compulsory next step; I am basically in agreement with McCormack (the will of God in some sense participates in the constitutive nature of God's being, and this from all eternity), but I am appreciative of the corrective trajectory of Molnar's position (with God there is no conceptual priority of will to being).

I argue this, first, by offering a brief exposition of the salient features of Barth's construal of election. Next, I summarize the positions of McCormack and Molnar, particularly as they relate to Barth's understanding of the *Logos ensarkos* and of time and eternity. I draw attention to the strengths of each argument, which, when seen together, highlight an apparent contradiction in Barth's thinking, or at least a reliance on two seemingly contradictory ontological suppositions. Finally, as a way forward, I demonstrate the possibility of understanding Jesus Christ, the subject and object of election, as the statement (rather than the realization) of God's being for humankind, or the specification (rather than the effective determination) of divine being. As electing and elected God, Jesus Christ is simultaneously God's will and being.[2]

---

address below). Second, he concretely situates Barth's actualism relative to Hegelian history, allowing for God to be understood in terms of his temporal decision, not in general, but in the specific history of Jesus Christ.

2. Another voice should be acknowledged here. Kevin Hector, "God's Triunity and Self-Determination," pp. 29-46 above, argues a negative thesis that places him between McCormack and Molnar: contra McCormack, he argues that God's triunity logically precedes his gracious determination for the human; contra Molnar, he says that this does not entail the possibility of an unknown God or a species of freedom in which God remains apart from humankind. Both positions fail to sufficiently grasp the simultaneity of God's election and triunity. Inasmuch as we appreciate something of the respective cases at hand, and affirm the need for further emphasis on the simultaneity of God's essence and act, Hector and I work on parallel tracks. But there are two defining matters on which we disagree. First, in this initial offering, Hector does not recognize the difference between McCormack's and Molnar's conceptions of time and eternity. Indeed, he critiques Molnar (p. 38 above) for denying the eternality of God's self-determination. In fact, Molnar does not deny it if, as I show below, we acknowledge that he (with Barth) takes "eternity" to connote "divine sphere of existence" and not, à la McCormack, "infinite time." This distinction bears directly on our understanding of key components of Barth's Trinitarianism. Second, Hector adjudicates between our two expositors on the basis of their fidelity to Barth. Materially, I think he errs by suggesting that "Barth's theology points mostly in McCormack's direction" (p. 42 above). Ultimately, this is accurate only insofar as McCormack is truer to Barth's intentions than

## Barth's Doctrine of Election

Barth's contribution to the Reformed doctrine of predestination,[3] that is, the insight that distinguishes his thought from the classic Calvinist position as well as from that of the larger Christian tradition (save for a few perceptive individuals), is that the principal referent of God's elective grace is Jesus Christ.[4] His departure from the traditional position is twofold. In the first place, Barth rejects the teaching that in a moment of abstract decision-making the Creator predetermined the fate of his creatures according to an unfathomable will. In the second place, he disallows the possibility that the immediate object of God's elective decision was indistinct humankind (divided into two camps of elect and reprobate). Against both these notions Barth asserts the specificity of Jesus Christ:

> Our thesis is that God's eternal will is the election of Jesus Christ. At this point we part company with all previous interpretations of the doctrine of predestination. In these the Subject and object of predestination (the electing God and elected man) are determined ultimately by the fact that both are treated as unknown. We may say that the electing God is a supreme being who disposes freely according to His own omnipotence,

---

Barth himself is, which I think he is. Nevertheless, in terms of his stated position, it is Molnar who holds the "party line" and McCormack who offers the "critical correction." Formally, then, a preferable aim (i.e., preferable to judging McCormack and Molnar in light of Barth) would be to reconsider Barth in light of McCormack's suggestion and Molnar's critique. This would show the merits and demerits of each position more clearly in their own right.

3. Barth treats election in §§ 32-35 of *Church Dogmatics* II/2, pp. 3-506. Since my concern is principally with the person of Christ, I focus here on § 33, "The Election of Jesus Christ." *CD* II/2, pp. 94-194, § 32 introduces the discussion of election, including its importance to dogmatics broadly and its centrality to the doctrine of God. §§ 34 and 35 consider the second (but simultaneous) moment in election: God elects not only Jesus Christ, but also in him humanity, as the community of God (§ 34), and as individual members of that community (§ 35). Citations are from Karl Barth, *Church Dogmatics*, trans. G. W. Bromiley, J. C. Campbell et al., ed. G. W. Bromiley and T. F. Torrance (London and New York: T. & T. Clark, 2004). (Volume, part, and page references to the *CD* appear in parentheses in the text.) For a helpful summary of Barth's doctrine of election and its place in his larger theological program, see Colin Gunton, "Karl Barth's Doctrine of Election as Part of His Doctrine of God," *Journal of Theological Studies* 25 (1974): 381-92.

4. Those "few perceptive individuals" include, specifically, Augustine and Coccejus (*CD* II/2, pp. 106-16). For a helpful review of how Barth himself came to this position, see McCormack, *Karl Barth's Critically Realistic Dialectical Theology*, pp. 456-57.

righteousness and mercy. . . . But when we say that, then ultimately and
fundamentally the electing God is an unknown quantity. On the other
hand, we may say that the elected man is the man who has come under
the eternal good-pleasure of God. . . . But when we say that, then ultimately and fundamentally elected man is also an unknown quantity. . . .
In the sharpest contrast to this view our thesis that the eternal will of
God is the election of Jesus Christ means that we deny the existence of
any such twofold mystery. (*CD* II/2, p. 146)

God's will for his creation is mysterious, but it is a *known* will. His elective
grace is no hidden disposition, no volitional card yet to be played. It is a
*disclosed* truth. It is Jesus Christ. God's decision is not the judgment of a re-
mote Supreme Being, who in this act remains in obscurity as someone
about whom and about whose character the judged can only conjecture.
Nor is the elect nondescript humanity, unspecified "man" who, for reasons
to be known only on the far side of glory, receives this being's favor. Rather,
on both sides — electing and elected — stands the specific person Jesus
Christ.

Revelation is integral to Barth's formulation of election vis-à-vis the
agency of Christ: the doctrine should be explicated in a way that erases the
mystery of the dual "who." Historically, conceptions of predestination la-
bored without this accent and were thus characterized by darkness and obscurity, states that effectively became ends in themselves.

The history of the dogma is shot through with a great struggle for the
affirmation of the fact that in the mystery of election we have to do with
light and not darkness. . . . But this affirmation could not and cannot be
made . . . as long as it is not admitted that in the eternal predestination
of God we have to do on both sides with only one name and one person,
the same name and the same person, Jesus Christ. Unless this is done . . .
the assertion of the obscurity itself becomes the last and decisive word
on the whole subject. (*CD* II/2, p. 146)

The doctrine of election is intended to be at least moderately illuminating, to make plain the divide between saved and condemned and to
show how that divide honors a benevolent and just deity. But the record of
this dogma, so far as Barth sees it, presents a contrasting picture. Without
being clear as to who it is that judges and is judged, the most decisive statement of the doctrine is one of ignorance and darkness. Failing to recognize
the centrality of Jesus Christ to this dogma, we are left with an incompre-

hensible God, a God behind or above his works, and with no objective identification of the elect — with no option, therefore, but to make obscurity the defining mode of elective reflection.

The cause of historical obfuscation is hermeneutical. The hidden deity of traditional expositions of election derives from an exegetical willingness to predicate things of God not explicitly revealed in Jesus Christ. "When [older theologians] came across passages in the Bible which treat expressly of the electing God," Barth observes, "there in some inexplicable way seemed to open up before them the vista of heights and depths beyond and behind the Word" (*CD* II/2, p. 151). Traditional construals interpreted passages such as Romans 8 and Ephesians 1 without immediate recourse to Jesus Christ. They all too readily spoke of concepts such as foreknowledge and foreordination in terms of pre-temporal reality, as the decrees of a God who "before all time" purposed this particular world structure. But when considering the who of such decreeing, this move left them only with the Almighty, the transcendent one, the God whose ways are not our own, the God behind Romans and Ephesians — but not the God of these passages.[5]

For Barth, by contrast, if Scripture says that God elects, then it is Jesus Christ that elects, for he is the God of Scripture, the only God we know. In a formulation that encapsulates so much of Barth's thinking, he writes of election:

> In [the Word] is the fulness of all the information that we either need or desire concerning God and man, and the relationship between them, and the ordering of that relationship. At no point then, and on no pre-

---

5. Barth suggests that the "older theologians" may have deviated from an exegetical procedure that they themselves taught and otherwise practiced because of the decisive nature of the question asked in the sphere of predestination. "The question was not merely an incidental question, as the older theologians knew only too well. It was the question of the beginning of all things. . . . It was the question of the specific order of the kingdom or rule of God, with all that that means for the existence, the preservation, the history and the destiny of man. The question was in fact the actual and burning question: What is to become of us at the hand of God?" (*CD* II/2, pp. 151-52). In light of the ultimate nature of the question of divine determination, it may seem natural to appeal to ultimate mystery, an unsearchable corner of divine existence reserved for the particularly weighty and difficult matters of the God-world relationship. But this is not a path open to the exegetically responsible theologian, one who takes seriously the fact that "the Word of God [Jesus Christ] is the content of the whole Bible" (*CD* II/2, p. 152). If we keep our hermeneutical lens correctly focused and understand that there is no God of Scripture independent of Jesus Christ, then we must begin and end our discussion of even this most decisive issue with him.

text, can we afford either to dispense with, or to be turned aside from, the knowledge of Jesus Christ. (*CD* II/2, pp. 152-53)

If theology is to speak of God's elective grace, it must do so as it speaks of all other doctrines, in terms of Jesus Christ. It must recognize that all the information the Bible gives concerning God and humanity and their relationship it gives in Jesus Christ. Making his own hermeneutical suppositions plain, Barth rhetorically asks, "As presented to us in the Bible, what can the election be at all . . . if it is divorced from the name and person to which the whole content of the Bible relates as to the exhaustive self-revelation of God?" (*CD* II/2, p. 153). The God of Scripture is a revealed and thus known God. Predicating election of this God cannot mean speaking of absolute mystery, transcendent disposition, a volitional trump card yet to be played, because the revelation of this God is exhaustive. There is no part of God waiting to be revealed apart from Jesus Christ. There is no pre-temporal elective moment independent of Jesus Christ. If there were such a moment we would have no knowledge of it. The only electing God we know is the only God we know: Jesus Christ. The God to whom the entire Bible refers is this God and no other; hence, to speak of election, we must speak of this God and no other.

So to rescue the doctrine from its own obscurity, Barth reminds theology that Jesus Christ is the subject and object of election.[6] Now, Barth has

6. This is not to say that, for Barth, the mystery of election is solved. In removing the mystery of the who of election, Barth does not claim that election is now a doctrine laid bare, before which we no longer need be humble and adoring. He does not intend that, by making elector and elected known, he is somehow pulling back a curtain and exposing the inner workings of grace. What he is doing is putting the mystery of predestination on a surer footing, making it definite and thereby protecting it from any kind of mere speculation. "The mystery must have a definite character," Barth writes, "[which provokes] an equally definite silence and humility and admiration. Otherwise, it is inevitable that we ourselves should try to fill in the gap" (*CD* II/2, p. 147). The subject and object of election must be given, not so that inscrutability is eliminated, but so our admiration for God's elective operations may be properly focused; so that, in other words, we do not set the parameters of the mystery ourselves and then revere it. For Barth, if we are to think rightly of the mystery, we must recognize it as something revealed to us and not as something of God that is not revealed. We affirm that Jesus Christ is the subject and object of election precisely "so that we may know before whom and what we must be silent and humble ourselves and adore," and thus avoid a "self-projected image" of a hidden deity (*CD* II/2, p. 147). Such precision is helpful, not only to protect the integrity of our doctrinal formulation and the character of our piety, but also to buttress our sense of assurance in light of God's decision. Throughout § 33, Barth consistently attacks the well-known *decretum absolutum* (see esp. pp. 100-115, 134-

more to say about this reality than I can handle here.[7] However, what I must make a bit clearer before proceeding is the first of this two-part assertion: that Jesus Christ is the electing God.

Barth begins his discussion of election with an exegesis of John 1:1-2, wherein he considers two important issues: the nature of the phrase "in the beginning" and the fact that Jesus Christ is the Word. Each of these merits a brief restatement.

First, the Word was *in the beginning*. Barth understands this phrase in view of created reality. He takes the beginning, at which the Word was, to be the genesis of creation. "The Word," he writes, "is above and before all created realities. It stands completely outside the series of created things. It precedes all being and all time" (*CD* II/2, p. 95). The beginning is that realm of existence prior to all things that are (except God) and prior to all time. It exists in "eternity." "Within the sphere of creation," he continues, "there is . . . no time which is not enclosed by the eternity of this Word, no

---

45, 158-60). He does so because to speak effectively of any kind of absolute, unconditioned decree of elect and rejected relegates God's decision not to a gracious act of overflowing love, but to an incomprehensible, fixed principle (see also *CD* II/2, p. 333). But such a principle is hardly revealed. It is a deduction, a capitulation on the part of humanity to our own uncertainty and doubt. Barth acknowledges that there might be a kind of ironic comfort in such a move (abandoning ourselves in an "[unsearchable] idea of God and man is no doubt very mysterious and exciting and in its own way consoling" (p. 158), but it is a move we must resist and reject. All pastoral consolation founded on mystery and not revelation, on unknown and not known, cannot but prove unsatisfying. "All the earnest statements concerning the majesty and mystery of God, all the well-meaning protestations of His fatherly loving-kindness, cannot in any way alter the fact that we necessarily remain anxious in respect of our election" (p. 111). Our own assurance of election rests entirely on the fact that we know that God is not "electing elsewhere and in some other way" (p. 111). Barth wants to define the mystery of God's election not only so that we might not "fill in the gaps" ourselves, but also so that we can be assured. Therefore, against any *decretum absolutum*, against the possibility of losing ourselves in nonknowledge rather than knowledge of God, Barth forcefully concludes: "When we are called upon to define and name the first and decisive decision which transcends and includes all others, it is definitely not in order to answer with a mysterious shrug of the shoulders. . . . There is no such thing as a *decretum absolutum*. There is no such thing as a will of God apart from the will of Jesus Christ" (pp. 104, 115).

7. On the implications of this construal for human election and the grounds of human freedom, see *CD* II/2, pp. 115-27, 175-80. For a discussion of the repercussions of Barth's formulation of the doctrine for the double nature of predestination (that in Christ, God has ascribed to humanity salvation and to himself death), see *CD* II/2, pp. 161-75. This decision is, for Barth, a living decree and not a static outcome, in which God remains free to continue to decide for his creature, and therefore election is actualistic, something continually dependent on God's grace and realized in an ongoing way (see *CD* II/2, pp. 185-94).

space which does not have its origin in its omnipresence" (CD II/2, p. 95). There is no created time or thing that is not encompassed by the eternity of the Word. Again, I must emphasize that Barth resolutely defines this eternity in terms of creation and not in terms of divine existence. The eternity of the Word is not the primordial sphere of God *in se*, but the beginning of his ways and works *ad extra*. But can this hold? Can there be any other eternity besides the one in which God determines his own being? Why is "the beginning" the origin of "all that which, being created by Him, is distinct from God," and not the realm of existence wherein all that which, being uncreated, is God (*CD* II/2, p. 95)? In fact, this issue is at the heart of the aforementioned debate and is thus better considered below — after I have reviewed the parameters of disagreement. For now, suffice it to note that Barth understands the Word's eternity to be pre-temporal reality at the origin of creation and time, and not necessarily the eternity in which God assigns himself his being.

After establishing that this Word, which was in the beginning with God, is in fact God a second time — that is, "the mode of being, and being, of a second 'He' [which] is identified with the mode of being with and being of the first 'He,' God" (*CD* II/2, p. 96) — Barth considers, secondly, the identity of the Word. He understands that this Word is none other than Jesus Christ. In a quintessentially Barthian moment of elegant dismissiveness, he takes John's lack of specificity as to the referent of the *Logos* (Greek philosophy? Jewish/mystic name traditions?) not as presenting an unknown to be overcome by historical-critical research, but as an indication of John's unique appropriation of the term.

> It will probably always be a waste of time to look for that unknown quantity, the source used by the writer of the Fourth Gospel. . . . What is certain is that he had no intention of honouring Jesus by investing Him with the title of Logos, but rather that he honoured the title itself by applying it . . . as a predicate of Jesus. He offered no other exegesis of the concept apart from that in which he made this predication. (*CD* II/2, pp. 96-97)

Barth takes John's exegetical scantiness to indicate that his intention was to reinterpret the term by ascribing it to Jesus Christ. Beyond this, it is of little value (a waste of time even!) to try to determine the context of usage on which John was drawing in using the title. What is important is to note that in the Fourth Gospel the *Logos* is honored, it obtains its value, its content, from Jesus Christ and not the other way around. While this is a seemingly subtle move, the significance of the observation should not be overlooked. Barth is here contending that the Word of God, which is God, the God who elects "in the beginning," is Jesus Christ and not some abstract *logos*-concept. John does not invest Jesus Christ with the philosophical (epistemological or metaphysical) content of *"logos,"* but invests the title with the incarnate deity. The electing God is not the Word of the realm of divine Ideas, but none other than the concrete person Jesus Christ. Jesus Christ — not some abstract *logos* — is the subject of election. It is in this context that the debate between McCormack and Molnar finds its center.

## McCormack and Molnar on the *Logos asarkos* and the Being of God

The claim that Jesus Christ is the subject of election has profound implications for Barth's comprehension of the second person of the Trinity and the being of God. Once again, Barth's assertion is that the divine *Logos* is not only the object of a primordial decision for incarnation, but also participates in that decision as incarnational subject — that is, as Jesus Christ. In other words, it is not as though, in the first place, the *Logos* is a passive recipient of divine decree; rather, he actively takes part in decreeing. Nor is it, in the second place, that the decreeing *Logos* is an abstract modality; rather, he is none other than the God-man.

McCormack works from this basic structure of Barth's thought to draw two interrelated conclusions about God and his Word. First, he qualifies the need for a pre-enfleshed *Logos*. McCormack observes that, while the *Logos asarkos* is a necessary concept in Barth's program, its place is at the same time necessarily secondary, and its character must not be taken as indeterminate and wholly independent. Regarding its necessity, one must acknowledge the existence of the *Logos asarkos* and distinguish between it and the *Logos ensarkos* because, "after all, the human nature (body and soul) of Jesus only came into existence at a particular point in time, in history. It was not eternal; the Logos did not bring it with him, so to speak."[8] Barth ultimately did not wish to collapse history into eternity and read the human body and soul of Jesus of Nazareth into the Godhead. The *Logos* is eternally incarnational, not incarnate, and thus it is finally obligatory to af-

---

8. McCormack, "Grace and Being," p. 96 (hereafter, page references to this essay appear in parentheses in the text).

firm the reality of the *Logos asarkos,* which at a point in time took on flesh. However, having said that, I must immediately add that this *Logos asarkos* is not an independent agent existing for itself, not an abstract "being" awaiting action, but a concrete reality actively postured toward *ensarkos,* enfleshment. The subject of election is, again, not an indeterminate *logos* but the particular person Jesus Christ, God determined to be for the world and humanity, which means that the *Logos asarkos* does not exist as an unconditioned reality. According to McCormack,

> If now Barth wishes to speak of Jesus Christ (and not an abstractly conceived Logos *asarkos*) as the Subject of election, he must deny to the Logos a mode or state of being above and prior to the decision to be incarnate in time. . . . To say that "Jesus Christ" is the Subject of election is to say that there is no Logos *asarkos* in the absolute sense of a mode of existence in the second "person" of the Trinity which is independent of the determination for incarnation; no "eternal Son" if that Son is seen in abstraction from the gracious election in which God determined and determines never to be God apart from the human race. (pp. 95, 100)[9]

For McCormack (and for Barth), affirming the reality of a *Logos asarkos* is necessary to preserve the distinction between time and eternity, but it should not be taken in an absolute sense to indicate an existence in God apart from the temporal existence of Jesus Christ. There is no abstract Son prior to his inner triune decision to be God for humankind.

How can this be so? How can the eternally existing Son be only relatively and not absolutely distinct from Jesus of Nazareth? How, in other words, can the person of Christ be constitutive of divine determination without reading human nature (body and soul) back into eternal divinity? McCormack answers with the modality of anticipation. "God," he writes, "is already in pre-temporal eternity — *by way of anticipation* — that which he would become in time. . . . The being of God in eternity, as a consequence of the primal decision of election, is a being which looks forward.

---

9. In Barth's own words, "If it is true that God became man, then in this we have to recognize and respect His eternal will and purpose and resolve . . . behind which we do not have to reckon with any Son of God in Himself, with any *logos asarkos,* with any other Word of God than that which was made flesh. According to the free and gracious will of God the eternal Son of God is Jesus Christ as He lived and died and rose again in time, and none other. . . . We must not ignore [God's free decision] and imagine a 'Logos in itself' which does not have this content and form [Jesus Christ]" (*CD* IV/1, p. 52).

It is a being in the mode of anticipation" (p. 100, emphasis in original). In a primordial choice, God elects not to be God other than as looking forward, other than as by nature anticipative. The Son in and for himself, as subject of this pre-temporal, eternal decision (i.e., there never was a time when this decision did not exist), wills not to be other than incarnational, which is to say that he wills not to be in and for himself at all, but always in and for humankind. In this way the pre-incarnate *Logos* does not exist in abstract independence, but in his being he anticipates incarnation. By way of anticipation, he already is — in his eternal being — what he would become in time: Jesus Christ.[10]

This brings us to a second conclusion McCormack draws from Barth's doctrine of election: God's triunity logically follows his elective will. If we say that there is no *Logos asarkos* in any abstract sense, and that the Son is Jesus Christ and not some pre-Christian, speculative "being" operating in strict independence, then we must also say that the being of the God who chooses not to be other than this way obtains his existence as such as a logical consequence of his gracious choice:

> The denial of the existence of a Logos *asarkos* in any other sense than the concrete one of a being of the Logos as *incarnandus,* the affirmation that Jesus Christ is the second "person" of the Trinity and the concomitant rejection of free-floating talk of the "eternal Son" as a mythological abstraction — these commitments require that we see the triunity of God logically as a function of divine election. Expressed more exactly, the eternal act of Self-differentiation . . . is *given* in the eternal act in which God elects himself for the human race. The *decision* for the covenant of grace is the ground of God's triunity. (p. 103, emphasis in original)

God is as he is because of his gracious decision. He wills to be this way, for humanity in Christ (and Spirit) and not any other way. If the Son is Jesus Christ, then the Son obtains his existence as a consequence of the divine decision to be in time, for humanity.

McCormack acknowledges that this argument clearly stretches temporally conditioned, human cognition to its breaking point. "How can the second 'person' of the Trinity," he wonders, "participate in the decision which gives him his own distinctive mode of origination?" (p. 104) It

---

10. Specifically, the modality of anticipation allows McCormack to understand God's determination to be for the human in the concrete person of Jesus Christ, without making the Hegelian move of collapsing divine existence into human history (see pp. 99-100).

would seem impossible to assert that God's elective decision is prior to his triunity, while at the same time insisting that a result of that decision, the second person, participated in it. He must exist before he could will himself into existence. Even to conceive of the possibility that divine election determines divine being requires McCormack to emphasize that this relationship is *logical* and not temporally sequential. Again, God's decree and being are eternal:

> We are not asking here about a chronological relation. Election is an eternal decision and as such resists our attempts to temporalize it: i.e., to think of it in such a way that a "before" and an "after" are introduced into the being of God in pre-temporal eternity. . . . The triunity of God cannot follow this decision in some kind of temporal sequence of events. The two things belong together because God is a Subject insofar as he gives himself (by an eternal act) his own being. (pp. 101, 104)

It is necessary to consider election before being in light of Barth's claim that Jesus Christ is electing subject. Nevertheless, this ordering is of a conceptual and not chronological character. The concepts that the Son is not other than incarnational and that God's being is anticipative demand that election be given priority of treatment: God's being did not exist first for itself and then for humanity, but eternally for humanity, which means God's decision to be for his creature determined his mode of being. Still, we must remain clear that this priority of treatment is logical, that it does not suggest a temporal sequence. God's will and being are necessarily simultaneous, existing as they do among the same eternal subject.

This developed conclusion — that divine will logically precedes being — is again McCormack's and not Barth's. Barth himself never carried through the implications of his doctrine of election to this extent. "He should have," McCormack argues, "but he did not," and so McCormack sees his own work on this score as a "critical correction" to Barth's inconsistent — or at least incomplete — thinking (pp. 101, 102).

It is here that Molnar begins his defense of Barth's stated position. Molnar takes his point of departure from the recognition that Barth never corrected his way of speaking about God as self-existent prior to election, nor did he ever reverse his treatments of the doctrines of God and election. For Molnar, this is exactly so for the good reason that the existing content and structure of Barth's insights preserve divine freedom. "The order between election and triunity cannot be logically reversed," Molnar says, "without in fact making creation, reconciliation and redemption necessary to God." The fact that Barth does not alter his understanding or treatment of God in light of his mature doctrine of election is no oversight or shyness of expression. Barth intentionally checked his understanding of election against his overriding concern to preserve God's freedom to be other than he is as Creator, Reconciler, and Redeemer. "The reason Barth never changed his view," Molnar concludes explicitly, "is because he consistently recognized and maintained God's freedom, without which the doctrine of the Trinity becomes nothing more than a description of our relations among ourselves."[11] To speak of Trinitarian relationships without affirming the priority of divine being to divine will is, for Molnar, to speak of human relationships in a Schleiermacher-like loud voice — that is, not to speak of God at all. God is as he is over, apart from, and without need of the human.

> Barth insisted that the Trinity exists eternally in its own right and thus even the electing God is not subject to any necessities, especially a necessity that would suggest that the ground of his triunity is the covenant of grace. It is exactly the other way around. The covenant of grace is a covenant of grace because it expresses the free overflow of God's eternal love . . . as the Father begets the Son in the unity of the Holy Spirit. . . . God's being is not the result of his will. Rather, his will to elect expresses his freedom to be God in a new way for us.[12]

God is God *in se* primally, and this in triunity, and for the human consequently as a gratuitous act of overflowing love, as it is expressed in the eternal procession of the Son. God's triune existence is not a conceptual outcome of his elective affinity. Contra McCormack, Molnar shows that God's gracious decision to be for the human in Jesus Christ does not precede, even logically, the free being of God to be as he would with or without the human. There is no necessity to his being. God's gracious choice *expresses* his free, triune existence. It does not constitute that existence.

Molnar understands that the *Logos asarkos* plays a significant — albeit minor — role in Barth's Trinitarianism and Christology. What critics of this concept fail to perceive is that this doctrine functions as a necessary safeguard.[13] Affirming the *Logos asarkos* preserves the possibility that, logically

---

11. Molnar, *Divine Freedom*, pp. 63-64.

12. Molnar, *Divine Freedom*, p. 63.

13. Besides McCormack, Molnar also takes issue with Douglas Farrow, *Ascension and Ecclesia: On the Significance of the Doctrine of the Ascension for Ecclesiology and Christian*

speaking, there might never have been a *Logos ensarkos:* that is, as a doctrine the *Logos asarkos* allows God to remain free from us, and not just free for us.

> [Barth] believed [that the *Logos asarkos*] was necessary because God acting for us must be seen against the background of God in himself who could have existed in isolation from us but freely chose not to. He rejected a *logos asarkos* in his doctrine of creation if it implied a "formless Christ" or "a Christ-principle"; ... he rejected it in connection with reconciliation if it meant a retreat to an idea of God behind the God revealed in Christ; but he still insisted it had a proper role to play in the doctrine of the Trinity and in Christology.[14]

Molnar acknowledges that Barth was not unqualified in his inclusion of the doctrine of the pre-enfleshed Word in his dogmatic program. Nevertheless, Molnar grants it a more central place in Barth's thought than does McCormack. Recognizing the *Logos asarkos* not only staves off the deduction that the flesh of Christ inhabited pre-temporal divinity, but, more importantly, this doctrine affirms that the being of God exists as triune apart from anticipation of the creature's redemption. The Creator's being is in no way contingent on human need, even anticipatorily, because the second person of the Trinity exists free from enfleshment as well as free for it.[15]

---

*Cosmology* (Edinburgh: T. & T. Clark, 1999), and with Robert Jenson, *The Triune Identity: God According to the Gospel* (Philadelphia: Fortress, 1982), and *Systematic Theology*, vol. 1, *The Triune God* (New York: Oxford University Press, 1997). See Molnar, *Divine Freedom*, pp. 64-81. As Molnar sees it, both of these latter figures represent a radicalized position on the *Logos asarkos*, dismissing it entirely. It is for this reason that I chose to investigate Molnar's debate with McCormack, who, despite Molnar's conclusion to the contrary (*Divine Freedom*, p. 81), does not dispense with the *Logos asarkos* entirely. He allows the doctrine a place in Barth's thought, albeit a secondary or insignificant place. The greater proximity of McCormack's thought to Molnar's makes the disagreement between these two the more fruitful to explore, as it touches the heart of the matter: not simply whether one acknowledges the existence of the *Logos asarkos*, but the minimum conceptual and functional role that it must be granted in our doctrine of God in order to think rightly about (the order of) election and triunity. In other words, setting Molnar against Farrow or Jenson could give the impression of a false dichotomy, as though in discussing the topic of the God-world relationship, one either includes the *Logos asarkos* or does not.

14. Molnar, *Divine Freedom*, p. 71.

15. One might charge that Molnar's position is open to critique insofar as he seems to hold to a particularly modernist (Western post-Enlightenment) understanding of freedom, which is influenced by the notion of autonomous existence. Hector suggests something along these lines (see "God's Triunity," pp. 40-41 above). To Molnar, freedom and contin-

## Adjudicating the Debate: The Specification of Divine Being

What are we to make of this debate, and on what grounds might we suggest a way forward? Our first move must be to note the somewhat different concerns of our two Barthian expositors, and then to reconsider election in the light of their gains. McCormack's principal goal is to think through the implications of Barth's doctrine of election, a process that results in, among other things, a revised understanding of divine freedom. Molnar's principal aim is to defend the "accepted" position on Barth's construal of God's freedom. The focus of Molnar's critique, therefore, is primarily on a consequence of McCormack's argument, and only secondarily on the argument itself.

Molnar's thesis is more corrective than constructive. Along the lines of conciliar statements, it does not offer a case for understanding the relationship between God's being and choice in light of Barth's mature Christology, but sets boundaries around any such proposal. What this means is that Molnar does not really engage the core of McCormack's argument. He identifies what he knows is not an acceptable conclusion to it — that the being of God is in any way conditioned by human existence — but he does

------

gency seem antithetically opposed, and as such God is not free unless in his essence he is utterly free from external relationship in some primordial moment of selfhood. But how well does this accord with the biblical notion of freedom in self-deference to the other? Is it not the point of Genesis 3 that humankind fell by failing to grasp freedom-in-obedience, and instead opted for an "ideal" of unconditioned autonomy, a free-from existence? Barth, of course, when not read as McCormack does, is accused of the same kind of modernist impulse. And, of course, this question raises the corollary as to whether freedom-as-essential-unbridled-autonomy is not really more Scholastic than modern. (Does substantialist ontology not trade upon the same concept?) Nonetheless, it is instructive to consider whether Molnar and Barth are indeed concerned for divine freedom or for an abstract notion of divine freedom. However, we must at least honor Barth's intention, which is not to oppose freedom and contingency, but to contend for a kind of freedom that transcends this polarity, and in doing this grant a sympathetic reading to Molnar as following Barth here. God is indeed free of contingency, unrestrained by anything that is not him. But God is not free because he is independent. Rather, he is independent because he is free. His freedom is in essence threefold (this is my language, not Barth's): God is free from contingency, he is free for contingency, and he is free for relationship that is genuine yet not contingent. This last is the ultimate sense in which God is free: he is able to be in communion that finds its basis and fulfillment in nothing but himself. It is indeed genuine communion, genuine love, precisely because it is God's love. "It is His freedom not merely to be in the differentiation of His being from [created] being, but to be in Himself the One who can have and hold communion with this reality (as in fact He does) in spite of His utter distinction from it" (*CD* II/1, p. 304).

not address the full force of McCormack's concern: How can Jesus Christ, *not an abstract logos,* be the *eternal subject* of divine election without implying that God's being is in some measure determined by his will for humankind? If, as I made clear above, Barth understands, not some philosophical *logos,* but the God-man Jesus Christ to be God "in the beginning," then how can he simultaneously contend that God is primordially free from his creature? Molnar's response is less concerned with working this out for Barth than with asserting its necessity — though not entirely so.

Peppered throughout Molnar's efforts are the seeds of a counterargument, divergent suppositions that together form a rebuttal and that bring into relief exactly what is at stake in his disagreement with McCormack. Foremost, we note that McCormack and Molnar operate with different understandings of "eternity."[16] McCormack, I have already stated, takes "eternal" to mean never not taking place, such that, being an eternal choice, there never was a time when God did not elect the human. According to this definition, Molnar's position is strained: God could not remain free from humankind if there never was a time he did not elect himself for humanity, if God's election in Jesus Christ always was: free for, yes; free from, no. Not surprisingly, Molnar takes Barth's concept of eternity differently. "I don't think [Barth] means what [McCormack] takes him to mean," he acknowledges, "namely, that if it is an eternal decision, then it has never not taken place. By eternal in that context Barth simply wishes to distinguish God's unique existence from ours and from his works *ad extra.*"[17] Molnar under-

---

16. This difference has not been sufficiently addressed by either McCormack or Molnar. Molnar indicates that he finds McCormack's definition of "eternal" problematic. See *Divine Freedom,* p. 62. Critiquing McCormack's position, he says that "if God's election has always taken place, how then can it be construed as a decision; does it not then become a necessity?" Apart from this rhetorical observation, though, Molnar offers no alternative definition.

17. Paul Molnar, e-mail message to the author, March 28, 2005. As noted, McCormack does take on the relationship between time and eternity more directly in his 2007 response to van Driel, where he contends that Molnar errs in his understanding of McCormack's position: while God's election is eternal, it is not timeless, meaning that there was a "time" in God when it had not taken place. It seems to me that McCormack's earlier and less-nuanced argument was the stronger. Yet the problem is not with McCormack, but Barth. Barth's three-tiered concept of time/eternity is biblically awkward and philosophically deficient. If God's being is in the act of electing from all eternity, and he overcomes the discontinuity between time and eternity in Christ (all the while sustaining the distinction between his being and ours in the anenhypostatic dialectic), then it is correct to say that election has never not taken place, or positively, that is has always happened. But that implies necessity in God only to the extent that we bail out of the actualism underlying this observation. If God's being is and has always been act,

stands "eternal" in the context of divine election existentially (i.e., as concerned with the character of existence), connoting the distinction between the realms of divine and human existing. God's decision to elect humankind is eternal, but here that means that it takes place outside (free *from*) the reality of human affairs and prior to the way God works in those affairs (his operations *ad extra*).

In his definition, Molnar points to what appears in Barth's thought to be a three-tiered understanding of time and eternity, which we began to notice above in the observations about Barth's exegesis of John 1. First, there is that eternity in which God is in himself, as he exists in triune seclusion, utterly free and not contingent, able to assign himself his being with recourse to none but himself, happily alone in unfettered autonomy and perfect contentment apart from all that is not he.[18] Second, there is a kind of eternity between eternity and time, "in the beginning," at the origin of all God's "ways and works," at the genesis of the "theater" distinct from himself in which he interacts with humankind, at which point stands Jesus Christ (*CD* II/2, p. 94).[19] Finally, there is that sequential state of existence in which humanity carries on, what we might call earthly time, which is not God's realm but in which God nevertheless elects to participate, creating a "history" between himself and humanity (*CD* II/2, p. 175).

In Trinitarian terms, Barth understands God primally as Father, Son (*Logos asarkos*), and Spirit, who wills to be for humankind as Creator, Mediator (*Logos ensarkos*), and Redeemer.[20] In this, he follows a long-

---

then Christ's electing is nothing more than the specification of a subject that is already self-determining in perpetuity, by the objective content of that determination.

18. It is in this inward manner of being that God is pre-eminently "Lord" of his life, and from which he acts as Lord a second time, out of which his love "overflows" in a sovereign choice to be for humankind (*CD* II/2, pp. 99-101, 121, 176).

19. That Barth does in fact conceptually distinguish between God's *in se* eternity and that of Jesus Christ is made clear by the following assertion: "As the subject and object of [election], Jesus Christ was at the beginning. He was not at the beginning of God, for God has indeed no beginning. But He was at the beginning of all things, at the beginning of God's dealings with the reality which is distinct from Himself" (*CD* II/2, p. 102). In the sphere of God's primordial nonbeginning, Jesus Christ was not; but he was in the eternity at which God begins to deal with all that is not God, reality distinct from himself.

20. See *CD* I/2, pp. 878-89: "The content of the doctrine of the Trinity which the Church has formulated . . . is not that God in His relation to man is Creator, Mediator and Redeemer, but that God in Himself is eternally Father, Son and Holy Spirit. . . . This Subject God Himself cannot be dissolved into His work and activity, but wills to be known and recognized as this Subject in His work and activity."

standing tradition, operative at least since Aquinas, that distinguishes conceptually between the economic and immanent Trinity.[21] Furthermore, between God *in se* and the earthly, sequential realization of his operations *ad extra,* Barth places the sphere of Jesus Christ, "in the beginning," at the genesis of the overflow of God's love, and in so doing he introduces a second distinction. Now, between God a first time and the reality distinct from him stands Christ (*Logos ensarkos* anticipatorily), the electing God, God a second time. Jesus Christ is not in the beginning with God because God has no beginning (distinction one, between the Word for humanity and the nonbeginning of God [see n. 19 above]), nor as Elector is he in time, but "precedes all being and time" (distinction two, between the Word and the reality distinct from God [see the first section of this article]). Therefore, Molnar could argue, against McCormack, that in Barth's Trinitarianism the fact that Jesus Christ is electing God does not determine God's triunity, because it is the triune God, Father, Son, and Spirit, who chose to be a second time Creator, Mediator, and Redeemer. Jesus Christ is still the subject of election from all eternity, because the eternity in which he is for humanity is not that of God *in se,* but what is above and before earthly time. God remains the autonomous Lord of his inner life, yet Jesus Christ is the subject and not simply the object of election; standing in the beginning, he is the eternal (i.e., pre-temporal) electing God.[22] God's

21. On this issue, Barth's thinking reflects basic Thomistic Trinitarianism. Thomas, for the very reason Molnar identifies — the preservation of an absolute species of divine freedom — insists on a logical (not material) distinction between God's operations *ad extra* and his inner triune existence (see *Summa Theologica,* I.39). This distinction has resurfaced as a hotly debated topic in contemporary theology since Karl Rahner's highly interpretable, axiomatic identification of the immanent and economic Trinity (see Rahner, *The Trinity,* trans. Joseph Donceel [New York: Crossroad, 1997], p. 21). Molnar's assessment of how Barth would have replied to Rahner is by now predictable: Barth would affirm that in reality the immanent Trinity is the economic, but insist on a conceptual distinction with respect to the vice versa of this reality, in order to preserve divine freedom (see Molnar, *Divine Freedom;* see also Molnar, "The Function of the Immanent Trinity," pp. 397-98). For a more recent study, which also understands Barth's thought as ultimately anchored in this freedom-preserving logical distinction, see Fred Sanders, *The Image of the Immanent Trinity: Rahner's Rule and the Theological Interpretation of Scripture,* Issues in Systematic Theology 12 (New York: Peter Lang, 2005), pp. 142-58.

22. This is my own construal of some challenging material in *CD* I/2, II/2, and IV/1 relative to the *Logos* and the Trinity. Once again, I have brought together Barth's comments with respect to these themes as follows: God *in se* is Father, Son, and Holy Spirit, the Son being the *Logos asarkos.* God *ad extra* is Creator, Mediator, and Redeemer, the Mediator being the *Logos ensarkos.* However, because there is a beginning of God *ad extra* above and beyond

choice to be a second time as God for us *confirms* his being, it does not constitute it; the *Logos ensarkos* is not constitutive of the *Logos asarkos,* but authenticating.

Having said this, I must emphasize that the above distinctions are conceptual and not real. For Barth — and here we perceive the dialectical moment in his christological and Trinitarian reflections — the Son is the Word is Jesus Christ.[23] We distinguish conceptually between God *in se* and *ad extra,* between stages of the *Logos,* because not to do so would make the Creator dependent for his being on his creation. Nevertheless, because God is one and has revealed himself in an exhaustive way, we dialectically affirm that, though God could have been otherwise, he is in fact — in the very core of his being and not simply — none other than for us in Jesus Christ. God *in se* is God *ad extra;* the Son is Jesus Christ, the *Logos asarkos* is the *Logos ensarkos.* As Father, Son, and Spirit, God could have remained in and for himself (conceptual distinction), but he has chosen not to so remain, that the Son should be the Word should be Jesus Christ, and this from all eternity (no real distinction).

---

temporal reality and being, the "in the beginning" of John 1, there is a "time" when the second person of the Trinity is *Logos* for humanity yet pre-enfleshment, what I (not Barth) have called the *Logos ensarkos* anticipatorily. We might also call this "contingent *Logos asarkos*." The designation is not altogether important, so long as it is clear that the *Logos,* at this stage, is utterly for humanity, which is not the case at the stage of the autonomy of the Son.

This is not, however, the only way to understand Barth's comments with regard to the *Logos* and God's triune existence. If we take his exegesis of John 1 (*CD* II/2, pp. 95-99) programmatically, then we would be forced to hold a conceptual distinction between the Son and the Word, so that the eternity of the Word (not that of the Son) is the *Logos asarkos,* and its temporal fulfillment is the *Logos ensarkos.* The reasons I have not chosen this particular interpretation of Barth's work are (1) in *CD* IV/1 he associates the Son with the *Logos asarkos* (p. 52), and (2) that Molnar's argument is nonsensical in this structure. If there is no *logos* with God in his *in se* primordiality, then it can have nothing whatsoever to do with the preservation of divine freedom. The restriction of the divine persons' relationality to each other would be the only argument for maintaining divine autonomy from us, as the *Logos asarkos* would not participate in this reality. See also *CD* II/2, p. 79. Barth here commends a simple distinction — between the internal and external operations of God — and is critical of any notion of God *in se* if it implies an abstract Trinity without definite direction and reference. God is always directed out of himself, in the realm beyond time and in time. Again, though, this singular differentiation is difficult to reconcile with prior and succeeding claims about the pre-enfleshed *Logos* and the autonomous being of God, which, if it does not suggest an abstract deity, at least implies that God could have remained apart from his works, internal or external.

23. Cf. *CD* II/2, p. 99: "God Himself in all His ways and works willed wholly and utterly to bear this name, and actually does bear it: the Father of our Lord Jesus Christ, the Son of the Father, the Holy Spirit of the Father and the Son."

However, by affirming this, have we not come back to the very point of our debate's origin? Have we not fought ourselves full circle and returned to the crux of the whole matter, McCormack's first question: How can Barth maintain that Jesus Christ is the electing God and not revise his Trinitarian thought in such a way as to reflect the unity of Son and Word enfleshed, of God *in se* and *ad extra?* McCormack believes that Barth's doctrine of election forces him to hold together two contradictory assertions. On the one hand, as the Son, there never was a time in God's existence in which Jesus Christ did not participate in the decision in which God assigns himself his being, and as such there never was a time when God was not for us; yet, on the other hand, Barth continues to insist that in his essence God exists apart from humanity in isolated autonomy. Would it not be better for Barth to have rethought his commitment to the distinction between the *Logos asarkos* and *ensarkos,* between God in unfettered autonomy and God-for-humanity, and to have brought this into line with his insight about the agency of Christ in election? In light of the fact that Jesus Christ is electing God, should Barth not have abandoned his commitment to an abstract notion of God's potential freedom from humanity, and recognizing that God is God-for-us, collapsed the distinction between the sphere of God's *in se* existence and that "in the beginning," creating a more accurate division between a single eternity and time, between (strictly) the *Logos* enfleshed and the *Logos* anticipating enfleshment?

Indeed, we are back at the beginning of our disagreement; but, having circled its track, we may better understand its character, perceiving exactly what is at stake and thus being able to point a way forward. We now see that the axis on which the McCormack-Molnar debate turns is the dialectic between unity and distinction in Barth's comments on Trinity and eternity. McCormack works from the perspective of unity, the supposition that in God, Jesus Christ always was, that in reality he is the Word is the Son. As electing God, Jesus Christ stands at the most primordial moment of divine being, and thus we must conclude that God's gracious choice is in some measure constitutive of that being. In contrast, Molnar emphasizes distinction, that in order to preserve divine freedom, we distinguish between the eternity of Jesus Christ and the nonbeginning of God *in se.* Thus we do not say that God, being "eternal," never had a time when he did not decide for humanity, but that in pre-temporal existence God became God a second time, now not in isolated freedom from the realm distinct from himself, but free for it.

At every point along this axis we encounter the relationship of being and time/eternity. Once again, an understanding of time and eternity is integral to each interlocutor's conception of divine being. McCormack perceives congruence between eternity and time, taking the former almost as an infinite extension of the latter backward and forward; hence, to say that Jesus Christ is the eternal, electing God is to say that there never was a "time" when he was not (or will be). I say "almost" an extension of time because McCormack does not deny a pre-temporal eternity, but he effectively understands this as the beginningless period of God's existence before the created, temporal world, a world that not always was and thus came to be at a point in God's eternity. Molnar, as I have already mentioned, conceives of eternity differently, in terms of existence, or sphere and state of being, as in the divine realm and manner of existing (eternity) versus the human (time-bound). For him, to say that Jesus Christ is eternal as God's election means that he exists prior to creation, though not necessarily always in the same way of being.

In other words, each of these eminent students of Barth's work has discovered therein his own grounds for an ontology, both of which stand opposed as corollaries of the dialectical moments of unity and distinction in Barth's Trinitarianism, which suppose alternative understandings of time and eternity. McCormack sees Barth on his way to a pure actualism. Supposing congruence between the times of Jesus Christ — eternity and earthly time — McCormack perceives the integral nature of God's decision-making to his being: never being without Jesus Christ, God's being is determined by his gracious act of election. Again, this must be because Jesus Christ is one God now and forever, *ad extra* and *in se*, *ensarkos* and *asarkos*. Molnar, on the other hand, argues for a qualified essentialism.[24] Supposing distinction between the sphere of God in himself and his eternity in Jesus Christ, Molnar perceives the integral nature of God's being to his decision-making: recognizing that God could have been without Jesus Christ, God's gracious act is determined by his being. Again, this must be because in his essence God is triune, the sphere of time is not the sphere of this essence, that (conceptually) *ad extra* is not *in se*, and *ensarkos* is not *asarkos*.

Acknowledging these relationships — between Trinitarian unity, tem-

---

24. "Qualified" because Molnar does reserve a place for God's decision to determine his being; he simply insists that God makes this decision free from the human and thus as he is in himself. His inner life, then, is what makes him God (constitutes his being) and grounds his decision for humanity (and not vice versa).

poral congruence, and actualism, and between Trinitarian distinction, temporal divergence, and essentialism — we may at last reconsider Barth's doctrine of election and further the discussion begun by McCormack and Molnar. To begin (and the scope of this project will allow me to do little more than make a start), we must not allow the breadth of analysis thus far to obscure a most fundamental point: Barth's objective in considering Jesus Christ to be the subject of election was to assert that this act is *revelatory*.

By insisting on the centrality of Jesus Christ to the election event, Barth likewise insists that God himself is revealed in this event. What happens principally in election is not that humanity becomes grouped, but foremost that the truth of the being of God is disclosed. God reveals that he is the kind of being who elects. We know this because we know the one who does the electing, Jesus Christ, and we know that this one is God "in the beginning." In Jesus Christ, we have a revelation of the being of God, namely, that God is gracious-being.

In this disclosure, though, we learn another truth of the being of God, which is related to the first. In saying, as Barth does, that the Word of God obtains its content from Jesus Christ and not the other way around, we also affirm that God is a disclosing being. God is the kind of being who reveals who he is. We know this because we know the revealer, Jesus Christ, and this one (and not some unrevealed abstract *logos*) is God "in the beginning." This latter truth is related to the former in that both reveal the being of God as being open. God is a disclosing being in two senses: it is his essence to manifest himself, and as such it is equally his essence not to be closed but open. He is ready to show himself to and be in relationship with (elect) humankind.

These observations favor McCormack's argument. In the end, it appears that McCormack's position is the more tenable because, as I have indicated, he deals more directly with the implications of Barth's construal of election than does Molnar — or even Barth himself. If Jesus Christ is the revelatory subject of election, there is no closed deity, no God in himself free from the revealed contingencies of his own existence, no sphere of being in which God could have been other than ready. Molnar and Barth may want to assert a contrary conviction that derives from an abstract God-world distinction in Trinitarian thought and notions of temporality; but the character of what takes place in election, as Barth himself insists on it, prevents such a move. McCormack is right to correct the more abstract components of Barth's Trinitarianism in light of the concrete specificity of his doctrine of election. Barth's revelatory concerns in his explication of this doctrine carry implications for the kind of being who elects, and it is no aloof deity potentially free from his creation.

But in siding with McCormack, I must immediately point out that Molnar's instinct is correct. We must not give the impression that in saying Jesus Christ is the electing God, God cannot be apart from his creation. It is in order to recognize this important point that I offer the following, concluding remarks.

More attention must be given to the term "determination." To determine suggests both to decide and to establish, so what is implied in McCormack's claim is that, in the eternal act of grace, God both chooses and instates his being as a being this way, in and as Jesus Christ: the being of God a second time is effectively "determined" by its elective content. To put it another way, Barth's doctrine of election suggests both the agency of choosing and the fact of its accomplishment, such that in Jesus Christ, God simultaneously and eternally decides and realizes himself.[25] Molnar's difficulty is located principally in the latter aspect of this dual claim. He certainly would acknowledge that God is lord over his existence, meaning he retains the freedom to decide and assign himself his being. But for Molnar, that decision can only give expression to the primordial being that God already is. There can be no possibility, even logically, of content outside of God (human being) determining his being in the sense of realizing who God is; the being of God a second time is strictly the expression of God's relational being *in se*.

Affirming the basic verity of McCormack's insight while acknowledging the import of Molnar's counterclaim, I suggest we understand that what takes place in God's elective act, as Barth presents it, is not the determination of divine being but its *specification*. I have chosen this particular term because it communicates that in a revelation-orientated doctrine of election, God states rather than instates his being. The event in which God decides his essence does not make him to be, ontologically, something other than what and as he was: God was, is, and will be disclosing, open, God-for.[26] God subsequent to grace is not in any way other than God be-

---

25. He elects, and is elected, with ontological connotations.

26. I am not certain McCormack has completely carried through the implications of his own insight. If there never was a time that God was not in the decisive act of his being (i.e., deciding for humanity), then there is no *logical* possibility of ever speaking of the will of God prior to his being, and vice versa. McCormack is correct to devote serious attention to the subject matter or content of election as Barth construes it, and on this level we might with him speak of the constitutive or determinative character of God's will: in a primal and ontological way God calls humanity to himself. But just as we are prepared to affirm the log-

fore grace (logically or chronologically).[27] In election God states that he is eternally in the posture of openness toward his creature (or, as we see in this decisive happening, there never was a time when God was not for humanity). This is McCormack's account, but putting it thus more thematically situates it relative to Molnar's check.

As the specification of divine being, Jesus Christ is the event in which God identifies humankind as the substance of his openness.[28] In this event he engages in the moment-by-moment activity of identifying his very self with humankind, an event and act that is not a consequence of will but the iteration of his primordial and eternal existence. Here is the critical point. The logic of Barth's doctrine of election runs counter to the distinction between being and will that he held even up to his reflections in *CD* § 28. What Barth shows us in election is that the will of God *is* the being of God *is* Jesus Christ. There is no abstract willing or being in God, but Jesus Christ is both in total, so there is no possibility of any kind of conceptual priority of the one over the other. What Barth tried to hold on to as late as *CD* § 28, and spottily thereafter, was a dialectical notion of divine existence, grounded in a "time" of God's internal being, in which God retained

---

ical priority of divine will to being, we must retreat from speaking thus, because the formal significance of Barth's position — *as McCormack puts it,* there never was a time when this being-as-calling was not — refuses sequential statement and urges in its place the formulation of eternal reciprocity. There is no place conceptually prior to God's being for his will to inhabit, and the same is true the other way around, if there never was a time God was not being in the act of his decision.

27. Those of a Scholastic mindset find that this dictum cheapens what takes place in the act of grace. It would seem the very nature of grace qua grace to involve the (abstractly conceived) self-determination of a free individual to give what he otherwise does not have to, and so to set himself relative to another in a way that he could otherwise not; to be in this way and not that. But this is to fix the meaning of grace in advance and then apply it to God. Grace is not the state of being-for rather than being-not-for, reflexively considered and named. That would be nothing more than the hypostatizing of a desirable human dynamic, the altruistic decision not to be free-from but free-for writ infinite. Grace is not being-for; grace is *God*-for. To say grace is not to say "this state of being rather than that." To say "grace" is to say "God," and Barth understood this perhaps better than any theologian before him, despite the fact that he seems occasionally to forget it.

28. "Substance" is a term I use carefully. I am aware of its ontic implications, and, in fact, it is in light of these that I use it here (rather than, say, "content"). I am convinced that the trajectory of Barth's thought is not satisfied if we stop short of confirming that in election God affirms humanity in the very "stuff," however conceived, of his existence. My conviction, further, is that Barth's actualism pushes us to understand this stuff and being in postmetaphysical terms, but that is a subject for another essay.

autonomy while being in covenantal relationship. But what Barth unfolds in *CD* §§ 32-33 runs counter to this unique paradox of freedom, inasmuch as the reality that Jesus Christ is the subject of election precludes the possibility of the first pole, eternal autonomy, since in this event, as this event, a nonautonomous deity is fully revealed.

This does not necessarily mean that God's being is conditioned. It could mean this if we make a distinction between will and being. But because the one Jesus Christ is the primordial, eternal specification of the being of God as the will of God for humanity, there is no priority of volition to ontology, no option of conceiving consequentially of God's being relative to humanity; there is only the singular identification of Godself from all eternity. Ironically, this addresses Molnar's concern. He perceives the problem in McCormack's articulation precisely in that predicating divine being upon will seems to make God's essence subject to his own subjectivity in the elective act: that is, in this act God's essential being is established as a condition of his choice for humanity. Yet at the same time Molnar would not solve the problem (of conditionality) by admitting the unity of will and being, because for him, once more, a necessary distinction obtains here in order that the ground of God's decision should remain his triune being. Nonetheless, if we allow the profundity of Barth's insight vis-à-vis election to settle, unity is our only solution, and the language of consequence, to which McCormack's observation leads, vanishes.

Apprehending the deity in and as Jesus Christ means that there is no point at which God abstained from his self-iteration, that from all eternity God freely states his being as in the act of will, decision. *Specifically,* in election we observe that God's decision is for humankind. Election declares that the being of God reaches back to the same nonbeginning as the grace of God and vice versa, which means that one cannot be grounded in the other.[29] Before the electing God Jesus Christ, we must be content humbly to say that, as such and from all eternity, God is.[30]

---

29. Thus stated, this is a protological conclusion. Eschatologically, I affirm the converse: election reveals that the being of God reaches forward to the same nonending as the grace of God, and vice versa.

30. I am grateful to McCormack, Molnar, and Hector for the pleasure of several conversations and written correspondences that have helped me consolidate my understanding of the issues at hand, as well as their respective positions. Additionally, I owe a word of gratitude to John Webster and Ralph Del Colle, who read and commented on this article in an earlier draft. The work took shape during a seminar on Christology with Del Colle at Marquette University.

# II. Roman Catholic Perspectives

# 10. Karl Barth, German-Language Theology, and the Catholic Tradition

*Nicholas M. Healy*

Other contributors to this volume have rehearsed the main issues in the debate to which it is devoted, so I will not do so here. Everyone agrees that Barth shifted his thinking in various areas and directions in the course of writing the *Church Dogmatics*. I, for one, am convinced that, in John Webster's words, "the *Dogmatics* is, for all its detours, reconsiderations, and occasional retractions, a massively consistent argument, each part of which builds upon and helps interpret the other parts."[1] Bruce McCormack cites texts from *CD* II/2 and subsequent volumes to support his case for a less consistent Barth or, to put it more accurately perhaps, for a Barth who found the basic doctrine for which his theology was searching (and to which it was implicitly pointing) only after 1942 or so. McCormack willingly concedes that some other texts of the same later period conflict with his thesis, and he explains them not unreasonably as "a kind of limit-concept whose purpose is to point to the importance of the divine freedom."[2] However, I share the view of others that the shift is too radical for Barth not to have reflected explicitly on it, if only by a brief remark or two, as he did about other reconsiderations. Additionally, some late passages seem to me to be sufficiently clear in ruling out the doctrine of God that McCormack proposes.

I could attempt to support my view by discussing such texts. But the only good reason for adding my exegetical efforts to those of others who are far better Barth scholars than I would be to perform the kind of sophis-

---

1. John Webster, *Barth's Ethics of Reconciliation* (Cambridge: Cambridge University, 1995), p. 13.

2. Bruce L. McCormack, *Orthodox and Modern: Studies in the Theology of Karl Barth* (Grand Rapids: Baker Academic, 2008), p. 212. Throughout this chapter, page references to this work will appear in parentheses in the text.

ticated reading Webster exemplifies in the book from which I just quoted, where he displays the deep consistency of Barth's thinking. In the case at issue here, I cannot see any hope of doing that exegetically in a manner that would convince McCormack and those who agree with him. This is not merely because of my lack of expertise. Despite sharing much common ground, it is evident that Barth's readers may have diverse and often somewhat competing understandings of Christianity and, more specifically, the Christian theological tradition and its place and function vis-à-vis the broader cultural tradition. Their various beliefs bear upon their interpretation of Barth's texts.[3]

The beliefs expressed in McCormack's *Orthodox and Modern* go considerably beyond the specific issues at hand. First, while he might have some questions about certain aspects of Barth's project, it is clear that McCormack believes Karl Barth's response to the Enlightenment is by far the most promising way forward for Christian theological inquiry. Second, he considers one specific tradition of Barth studies to offer the best way to interpret Barth and his response to the Enlightenment, while others misinterpret him to a greater or lesser extent. And third, he seems to suggest — or so I think it reasonable to infer since he mentions no other tradition favorably — that the Protestant German-language tradition of modern theology after Barth is the only form of contemporary theological inquiry that adequately grapples with the consequences of the Enlightenment.[4]

I will address the first item only indirectly, partly because our response to it will depend on how favorably we respond to the second and third. And rather than engage in "plodding exegesis" (to borrow a nicely truculent phrase of the Radical Orthodox people),[5] I will bring the premodern theological tradition into the discussion, taking Thomas Aquinas as its exemplar, for I think McCormack may misunderstand and too readily dis-

---

3. This is not to say that Barth interpreters intentionally distort Barth in order to serve their particular theological interests. Nor do I think Barth's texts are so indeterminate that they can be made to support a wide diversity of interpretations.

4. These kinds of beliefs are not unreasonable. Anyone who is an advocate for a particular interpretation of an authority such as Barth is likely to maintain something along such lines. In McCormack's case — and to the benefit of the debate — he maintains these beliefs clearly and forcefully.

5. The accusation is made against "Barthianism" that "it can tend to the ploddingly exegetical" by John Milbank, Graham Ward, and Catherine Pickstock in their introduction to their edited volume, *Radical Orthodoxy* (London and New York: Routledge, 1999), p. 2. My point, should it be misunderstood, is meant ironically, as will become clearer below.

miss it. This will bring into clearer focus some of the background factors involved and throw some light on the main issue.

## A Typology of Realisms

In the introduction to *Orthodox and Modern*, which he rightly notes is important for understanding the book as a whole, as well as its proposal about Barth's new development in the early 1940s, McCormack sets up some distinctions among contemporary readers of Barth that he discusses in detail in several of the subsequent essays. He tells us that he learned to read Barth within the German-speaking tradition of Barth interpretation. From that viewpoint, and in contrast to it, he contends that "Barth's theology has been poorly understood in America and Great Britain," in large part because of its failure to acknowledge development within the CD (p. 113). English-language interpretation has tended toward one or the other of two wrong directions: attempting to make Barth into either a neo-orthodox or a postmodern theologian.

The fundamental problem with the "neo-orthodox position" is its failure to grapple with the legacy of Kant and its challenge to theological realism. The neo-orthodox continue to present Christian doctrine using language governed by the ontology that Kant and later modern philosophers rendered obsolete, an ontology McCormack calls "classical metaphysics." Reading Barth as a neo-orthodox theologian renders him liable to Bonhoeffer's charge of "revelational positivism" (p. 133). That is, his theological realism is preserved but at the cost of rendering it naive, since it fails adequately to address the Kantian critique of knowledge of God. On the other hand, postmodern readings of Barth accept Kant's critique but give up theological realism. They are merely a "variant of romanticism," but one that, unlike the original romantic movement, is characterized by "its lack of historical awareness" (p. 14).[6] McCormack's analysis of some

6. McCormack remarks that postmodern interpretation of Barth is "rather easily explained" on sociocultural grounds: "A well-developed historical consciousness never took root here" (p. 15) — "here" being the United States. This seems to suggest that the Anglo-American postmodern Barthians are by and large American, which seems unlikely. Nor does this explanation address the rise of postmodernism amongst the French intellectuals, to which much postmodernism in the United States is indebted. Postmodern French intellectuals have a well-developed historical consciousness, albeit different in significant respects from that of German intellectuals.

postmodern readings of Barth indicates their inadequate acknowledgment of Barth's insistence that noetic *ratio* follows and is dependent on ontic *ratio*. They do not follow Barth's methodological rule that doctrine must be based on the reality of God known in God's self-communication in Jesus Christ. Postmodern readings of Barth thus make his theology more or less nonrealist (p. 145).

McCormack devotes an essay to treating these two mistaken ways of interpreting Barth, during the course of which he offers interesting and, I think, somewhat revealing analyses of work on Barth by Hans Frei and George Lindbeck. McCormack praises Frei's work in general, but finds that it does not sufficiently emphasize Barth's theological realism (p. 123). Frei's typology is inadequate, too, in not considering "Barth's most basic problem (the knowledge of God)" (p. 127). With these lapses, Frei "opened the door to an understanding of Barth in which questions of reality-reference will be suppressed in favor of a concentration on the internal logic of theological statements" (p. 123). This is what happened with Lindbeck's "intratextual" reading of Barth's exegetical practice.[7] By refusing to "address questions of revelation and ontology," and turning instead towards Scripture alone, Lindbeck's reading "had the unintended effect of perpetuating the myth of the neoorthodox Barth" (pp. 133, 135). He suggests, accordingly, that "Lindbeck's [postliberal] program is best understood as an expression of American neoorthodoxy reinventing itself in a changed situation" and in "an evangelical-Catholic form" (pp. 134, 136).

## McCormack's Third Way

It is difficult to read McCormack without agreeing with him that neoorthodoxy and postmodernism, so described, are incorrect ways to interpret Barth and, more generally, are not the best way forward for theological inquiry. McCormack's own third way is impressive, and he carefully lays it out in a series of arguments that draw upon many resources besides Barth's texts. In brief: Barth accepted as true the Kantian critique of human knowledge and its forms and attempted to re-present "orthodox" Christian doctrine *"under the conditions of modernity"* (p. 17, emphasis in original). Accordingly, Barth's concept of theological knowledge is best described as "critical realist." It is "critical" in reference to "the fact that Barth

---

7. George A. Lindbeck, "Barth and Textuality," *Theology Today* 43 (1986): 361-76.

used Kant's critical attempt to establish the limits of human knowing in order to 'locate' the being of God beyond the reach of human knowing." It is "realist" in that the doctrine of God so located is "not a construct of the human imagination" in Kant's or any other sense. Rather "the being of God is something complete, whole and entire in itself, apart from and prior to all human knowledge of it" (p. 159).

For McCormack, then, "the nineteenth century is still with us" (p. 89; cf. p. 39). Barth continues the modern theological program of mediating Christian doctrine in a post-Kantian world without falling into postmodernism. Given that the old, pre-Kantian, "Aristotelian-biblical cosmology" is no longer acceptable, Barth sees "the necessity of constructing doctrines of creation and providence which find their ground in more modern theological and/or philosophical resources" (p. 11). He acknowledges, too, that "all human thinking is conditioned by historical (and cultural) location" (p. 10). Accordingly, he can be located within the same tradition of mediating theology to which Schleiermacher belongs (p. 37). Unlike Schleiermacher, however, he does not rely on a religious a priori but directly on the action of God in self-revelation, using Kant's limitation of "the grasp of human knowing in order to make room for divine action in revelation" (p. 84). It is only "by an act of God" that our language can "genuinely describe God" (p. 174). God is not simply there, as it were, to be discovered by us. God can be known only in "the revelation-relation, in the correspondence established in that relation between God and the creature, a correspondence which depends for its existence on an always-to-be-renewed act of graciousness" (p. 177).

In sum, Barth offers us "a nonmetaphysical, actualistic (divine and human) ontology which took the place of the classical metaphysics of being and the modern metaphysics of the religious a priori and which completed this language and made it meaningful in a new and different way" (p. 133). This has little or nothing to do with the nonfoundationalist enterprise, but is rather a "postmetaphysical outlook" (p. 303).

For McCormack, then, there are three kinds of Barth interpretation, operating with three different concepts of the force of Christian doctrine: naive realism, nonrealism, and critical-theological realism. They overlap to some degree with the often-used diachronic scheme of premodern, modern, and postmodern, which McCormack also uses. When he does so, however, the terms imply a judgment, as we have seen with regard to "postmodern" and "modern." The word "premodern" labels something outdated, the "older trains of thought" that are "no longer considered viable by the vast majority of European theologians" (p. 9). When used of a contemporary, it is pejorative, as for example, John Webster's Barth is accused of being "a bit too 'premodern'" (p. 164).

## A Fourth Way?

I will not attempt to defend Frei and Lindbeck's reading of Barth, but it is worth pausing here to offer a different account of what they were trying to do. The theologies of both Frei and Lindbeck are, in my view, neither naive realist nor nonrealist, but are attempts — rather different from one another — to recover aspects of premodern theology. Frei's historical work is part of an effort to reappropriate earlier ways of reading Scripture that had been lost. He is not naive about theological knowledge and is clear about the limits of theological inquiry, but the limits are based on the nature of the subject and how it can be known, rather more than on Kant.[8]

Something similar can be said with regard to George Lindbeck. I admire the boldness of McCormack's double-barreled attempt to charge him with both neo-orthodoxy and postmodernism. But it is an implausible account when one recalls how much Lindbeck's understanding of Christianity is informed by medieval Catholicism and by Luther, whom he reads as a reformer within the church catholic. Finding Barth's exegetical practice congenial to this understanding, Lindbeck attempted to display its consonance with his own understanding of premodern exegesis. In doing so he felt it necessary to reject Barth's post-Kantian doctrine of revelation set out in *CD* I, for at least three possible reasons.[9] First, Barth's tendency to emphasize knowledge might have appeared reductive and inadequate compared with the complexity and diversity of ways the Holy Spirit has traditionally been understood to bring humanity into relationship with

---

8. At least that is my view of his work. See, e.g., his remarks about the theology of the resurrection, in Hans W. Frei, *The Identity of Jesus Christ* (Eugene, OR: Wipf and Stock, 1997), p. 59. I recall an evening seminar with him, probably in 1987, during which he spoke with unaccustomed seriousness and depth of emotion of the problematic nature of speaking about Jesus Christ in an objective way. I say this not to reassure myself that Frei believed Christ is truly and really the Son of God; that was obvious. Rather, I understood him to be pointing to the mystery that is God, and in that light, the inadequacy of the modern Christologies we were examining and, indeed, our own work that evening.

9. This is my own view, gleaned from his written work. I have not talked to George Lindbeck about this article since 1987.

God in Christ.[10] Second, Barth's doctrine of revelation may have struck Lindbeck as less than sufficiently compatible with the traditional Catholic view that the Christian community is the primary locus of revelation and the reading of Scripture, and could be misused to support the contemporary church-less, individualistic Christianity. Finally, the doctrine may strike some as insufficiently critical, from both traditional and contemporary perspectives, as well as on philosophical, social scientific, and scriptural grounds, in that in some hands it operates rather too much like a deus ex machina that resolves the Kantian problem and permits us to go on largely as before. No doubt, Barthians can readily address such concerns. My point, though, is that Lindbeck was attempting to draw attention to what he considered the premodern qualities of Barth's exegetical practice. That is the focus of his article, not epistemology.

With these remarks on Frei and Lindbeck, I mean only to begin to suggest that, whether or not they were successful in their reading of Barth or in constructing their own theologies, their perspectives were different from any one or combination of the three interpretations set out by McCormack. The postliberal "research project" described by Lindbeck in a later work is, as it was then, an attempt to recover premodern ways of reading Scripture, together with methods of doing theology congenial to that kind of reading.[11]

McCormack's typology and background beliefs rule out such a project. One reason for this may be the narrative structure with which he approaches contemporary interpreters of Barth. At times McCormack seems to be laying out something like the grand narratives of enlightened modernity and liberal theology, where "liberal" means keeping up with the modern cultural changes that have rendered the older way of thinking impossible. If one reads McCormack and some within the German-language tradition he favors — and, not incidentally, many Anglo-American corelationists — the task of theology seems to be to respond to the Enlightenment, which got its critique of premodernity largely right. My response is to take the form of a reconsideration of all Christian doctrine in light of the new and better ontology, anthropology, and, correlatively, the new and better doctrine of God.[12]

10. Lindbeck did not have the benefit of John Webster's book that I cited in the opening paragraph above.

11. See James J. Buckley, ed., *The Church in a Postliberal Age* (Grand Rapids: Eerdmans, 2002).

12. On p. 230, McCormack contends that "much English-language theology," both

## Classical Metaphysics

In order to put this narrative into question, we should look a bit more closely at what is wrong with premodern theology, according to McCormack. Premodern theology is, of course, realist. But since it is bound up with classical metaphysics, its realism is based on a false ontology, the substantialism of which mistakenly understands action as subsequent to being. On this basis, theologians make use of the *analogia entis,* by which one moves from what one knows of created being to make statements about the being of God. McCormack puts the issue *in nuce:* they believe that in order to talk about God, one must talk about something else first (p. 293). That is, "the more traditional procedure" begins "with an 'abstract' concept of God (which is to say, one that has been *completely* fleshed out without reference to God's Self-revelation in Christ) and only then turning to that revelation to find in it confirmation of what was already attributed to God without it" (p. 58, emphasis added).

In the course of his book, McCormack discusses three closely linked mistakes among those who use the *analogia entis* and accept the metaphysics on which it is based. First, to repeat, they think true knowledge of God can be had without being informed and governed by revelation in Jesus Christ. Second, their method ignores or rejects our evident need for God to act in order for us to know God, since God alone — and not we ourselves — brings our language into correspondence with God. And third — the crux of this particular debate — they assert not only the possibility of knowledge of God apart from Christ and apart from prevenient grace, they postulate a mistaken *kind* of knowledge: knowledge of God as God is in himself, in distinction from how he is and acts toward us. In one of his more recent reviews of the debate, McCormack remarks that the main issue is not (*pace* Paul Molnar and others) whether he maintains the freedom of God. He does, he insists, whether or not they think his way of doing so is appropriate. Rather, what he "question[s] is the capacity of any human being to know what God would have been without us, to know, in fact, how the divine being would have been structured had God not determined to be God for us in Jesus Christ" (p. 299). This is Molnar's error, in

"conservative" and that found among "disaffected liberals," is "antimodern." These terms reflect his grand narrative rather than the variety and significance of what is actually going on, whether Protestant or Catholic, especially — but not only — among those outside the direct influence of Barth.

McCormack's view, for he opens up a "gap" between the immanent and economic trinity (pp. 297, 274).[13]

These three forms of the analogical method, either singly or in combination, are forms of speculation, the "bane of early-church theology," and frequent among contemporaries, too (p. 274). Speculation can be found in von Balthasar's theology and is a problem for the Roman Catholic theological tradition more broadly (p. 200). For, according to McCormack, "Barth's conflict with the Roman Catholic version [of the *analogia entis*] was and always remained a conflict between his own covenant ontology and the essentialist ontology presupposed by the Catholic tradition, which von Balthasar's thought continued to embody" (p. 200).

## A Premodern (and Catholic) Reply

Whether or not von Balthasar engages in speculation — and I think he does, but in a somewhat different form from that described by McCormack — I have no wish to defend him or any other "speculative" contemporaries, Protestant or Catholic.[14] However, I do want to question whether the premodern Catholic tradition engaged in any of these three forms of speculation.[15]

We can begin with the first form: moving from knowledge of created being to knowledge of God by the "analogy of being." In the discussion of the *analogia entis* in his book *God as the Mystery of the World*, Eberhard Jüngel takes to task the Protestant polemic against what he (ironically)

13. I disagree with McCormack's characterization of Molnar's position. Molnar clearly rejects the *analogia entis* and the possibility of any kind of knowledge of God apart from what we know of God in Christ. We know that God is perfectly God "without us," and thus there is a conceptual distinction (only that at most, not a real distinction) between the immanent and economic Trinity. But we know this and make the distinction solely on the grounds of God's actions *ad extra*. I agree. However Molnar's arguments are far more consistent with Barth's position than with the "premodern" and "Catholic tradition" position I develop below.

14. Most obviously, his gender metaphysics. Augustine makes a link between Gen 1:27 ("male and female") and Christ and the church, but that is as far as he goes. The link is noted, but not developed, for reasons that will be evident below.

15. For the fathers, see Lewis Ayers's account of what he calls "pro-Nicene" theology and its differences from contemporary Trinitarian theology in his *Nicaea and Its Legacy: An Approach to Fourth-Century Trinitarian Theology* (Oxford: Oxford University Press, 2004). As I have noted above, I take Thomas Aquinas's theology as my premodern example.

calls this "horrible phantom" of "grasping after God."[16] He notes how these polemicists presuppose belief in a metaphysics of absolute distinction and difference between God and humanity, a belief shared by Kant. This leads them to misunderstand Barth's remark, made in the introduction to the first volume of the *CD*, that the *analogia entis* is "the invention of the anti-Christ," which is why one could not become a Catholic. Jüngel argues that the Catholic tradition did not use the analogy in the way they were accused of doing. He appeals to the work of Erich Przywara, who clearly upheld the doctrine of the greater dissimilarity of all analogical language applied to God that was defined at the Fourth Lateran Council.[17]

That is well and good, as far as it goes, but one can readily understand why it would satisfy neither Jüngel nor premodern theologians. For one thing, Przywara thought of analogy as a theory that justified realistic claims about God. That is, he was engaged with the same problematic — centered on the epistemological question about knowledge of God — that so exercises the modern German-language theological tradition. For that tradition, represented by McCormack and Jüngel, Przywara's theory is inadequate in that it makes the third mistake noted above. He and the Catholic tradition fail to come to terms with what "the Bible calls *revelation*," namely, that "*event* in which God becomes accessible as God in language."[18]

In reply, we should begin by noting that the epistemological question was not anywhere near so central for the premodern Catholic tradition. The primary source for the modern theory of analogy found in Przywara is Thomas Aquinas, but Aquinas does not *ground* his theological language on a theory of analogy as a prolegomenon. When he talks about the possibility of knowledge of God in the *Summa Theologiae* (*ST* I.12 and I.13), it is after he has already been developing his doctrine of God.[19] Analogy is not the condition of possibility for such talk, but rather a "fitting" way of mak-

16. Eberhard Jüngel, *God as the Mystery of the World*, trans. D. L. Guder (Grand Rapids: Eerdmans, 1983), p. 282.

17. Jüngel, *God as Mystery*, p. 283.

18. Jüngel, *God as Mystery*, p. 288 (emphases in original). I do not address the issue of God being static here, partly because there is insufficient space, partly because enough (surely?) has been written on the matter to lay this canard to rest. For a vigorous defense of the traditional Catholic understanding of God as *actus purus* yet unchanging, see Thomas G. Weinandy, OFM Cap, *Does God Change?* (Petersham, UK: St Bede's, 1985); see also Weinandy, *Does God Suffer?* (Edinburgh: T. & T. Clark, 2000). For a briefer treatment — and more to the point at issue here — see Brian Davies, *The Thought of Thomas Aquinas* (Oxford: Clarendon, 1992), pp. 146-49.

19. See Davies, *Thought of Thomas Aquinas*, p. 73.

ing sense of what we already know: that God makes it possible for us to say true things about God in faith.[20]

For Thomas, knowledge of God comes in two forms, as it did for the premoderns generally: one through revelation, the other apart from it or (perhaps) more exactly, apart from direct revelation in Jesus Christ. He admits the latter because he finds grounds for it in Scripture and thus cannot deny it. However, the theology of Aquinas, as a Christian theologian, is governed by the scriptural witness to Jesus Christ. Any use of concepts drawn from other possible knowledge about God must conform to revealed knowledge and made to serve the presentation of Christian doctrine. There have been many arguments about what he is doing in the first part of his exposition of the doctrine of God in the *ST* (I.2-26). But it would certainly be a naive mistake to read Thomas as if he were a philosophical thinker engaged in a kind of deduction of God's being and attributes from principles generally available. If we read Thomas aside from Neo-Scholasticism and Protestant polemics, we can see that he is working within the context of faith, and developing language about God that will be useful for the life and work of the church. That language will help him construct a true presentation of Christian doctrine in such a way as to "tend to the instruction of beginners" — his overriding purpose as he states in the prologue. Thus, for example, his talk of God's simplicity (*ST* I.3) serves to ensure the correct understanding of the doctrine of the Trinity, purging our language of errors — the same function that the concept served for earlier theologians.

When Thomas moves to the doctrine of the Trinity as such in question 27 of the *Prima Pars*, he inquires more explicitly into what can be known of God through revelation (since he believes the Trinity cannot be known otherwise). Here is where we may begin to address more directly Jüngel's theological critique of the Catholic theory of analogy and McCormack's criticism of the second form of speculation. While it is true that the notion of "revelation as event" cannot be found in the premoderns, it is clearly the case that knowledge of God — true, salvific knowledge[21] — comes only by giving oneself up to a new way of life, the life of faith. Faith is not only something we do: believing or trusting in God. Faith is something that God does to us, "infusing" it in us and thereby drawing us up into a rela-

---

20. For a detailed account of Thomas's "fittingness" arguments, see Gilbert Narcisse, OP, *Les Raisons de Dieu* (Fribourg: Éditions Universitaires, 1997).

21. While there may be other ways to know something of God, they are inadequate, misleading, or much worse unless governed by the knowledge of faith brought to life by charity.

tionship with God that lies completely beyond our capacities. In faith, God works in us "inwardly by grace" (*ST* II-II.6.2) and then perfects us by the grace of charity (*ST* I.7.2). Faith and its knowledge are thus entirely dependent on prevenient grace, as are the gifts of understanding and wisdom. Grace moves us beyond the Przywarian limitation of the always "still greater distance" of analogous language to the strong affirmations Jüngel demands — rightly — on the basis of 2 Corinthians 1:18-21.[22] God's gracious action is *always* Christoform, because grace is the action of Christ, as Thomas indicates in his discussion of "capital grace" (*ST* III.8). Moreover, grace is *always* needed in order for us to know and love truly, for it is the action of the Holy Spirit who, "together with the Father and the Son, moves and protects us" (*ST* I-II.109.9 *ad* 2).[23]

## Transcendental Arguments

The third form of speculation, according to McCormack, is to talk about God as such, beyond what can be known from his creative and redemptive action. Thomas does indeed do this, in common with the premodern tradition generally. Yet he does not do it quite as McCormack describes. To see the difference, we need to examine the logical force and direction of material theological arguments within the doctrine of God. These usually take the form of transcendental arguments, arguments that move from $x$, where $x$ is known with some certainty and in sufficient detail, to $y$, where $y$ is/are the condition(s) for $x$. McCormack himself lays out the basic form: "On the basis of this Self-revelation . . . what must God be like if he can do what he has in fact done?" That is, given the scriptural witness to God's acts in Jesus Christ, what can or must we say about God? McCormack then lays out the specific form of the question he focuses on: "What is the condition of the possibility in eternity for the incarnation, death, and resurrection of the Son of God in time?" (*Orthodox and Modern*, p. 58).

---

22. Jüngel, *God as Mystery*, pp. 285-87.

23. Thomas would say that these two ways of describing the gracious agent follow from Scripture. But they are, of course, one action, on the principle that all God's actions *ad extra* are indivisible, a principle encapsulated in his doctrine of God's simplicity. Obviously, there is much more to say here about Thomas's complex understanding of grace. At the least, I would need to discuss his distinctions between operative and cooperative, habitual and the "second movement" of the Holy Spirit. I give a brief account in my book *Thomas Aquinas: Theologian of the Christian Life* (Aldershot, UK: Ashgate, 2003), pp. 107-31.

Thomas does something formally much the same throughout his discussion of the doctrine of God (*ST* I.2-43). His exposition, to repeat, is a presentation of the faith, moving from some elements faith shares with the nonrevealed knowledge of God (*ST* I.2-26), through God as known only in faith, as triune (*ST* I.27-43). In the latter section, Thomas concentrates mostly on the immanent Trinity, since he shares the traditional Catholic belief (believed to be based on Scripture) that God is God, and so was and is always perfectly the same triune God irrespective of his actions as Creator and Savior. The "transcendental arguments" Thomas presents as he lays out his understanding of the immanent Trinity (and in the earlier questions, too) do not claim anything about God as such that cannot be supported by Scripture.[24] Thus he argues that the second person is fittingly named the Word and the Image of God because he finds these terms there. The third person is fittingly named Love and Gift, due to the same source. We know these things of God's immanent life simply because Scripture tells us so. Anything that goes beyond Scripture has no force of itself, for what Thomas says with regard to the Holy Spirit applies generally: "We ought not to say about God anything which is not found in Holy Scripture either explicitly or implicitly" (*ST* I.36.2 *ad* 1). To be sure, he discusses processions, essence, attribution, persons, and other such nonscriptural concepts, but this is by way of offering explanatory hypotheses about God's triune life that make God's actions in Jesus Christ reasonable to faith. The truth of faith does not at all depend on such hypotheses, nor can they be permitted to guide our interpretation of Scripture except insofar as they display what it says more clearly. In this, Thomas exemplifies the "epistemological reserve" with regard to the doctrine of God that Lewis Ayres has noted is characteristic of orthodox premoderns.[25] Theological principles that limit human knowing prevent him from pushing further into the doctrine of God than Scripture will support.

Thomas's arguments, then, are transcendental, but they do not have the force of modern transcendental deductions, which usually claim necessity. Kant believed that the conditions of the possibility for human knowledge are necessarily and uniquely those he laid out in his critique. His account of human knowing is proposed as the right one and as such

---

24. At least that is his expressed intent. Of course, we invariably import something from elsewhere. How could we not?

25. "The shaping of Trinitarian theology one sees here has noticeably moved away from the epistemological reserve intrinsic to pro-Nicene thought." See Ayers, *Nicaea*, p. 409.

should govern and structure all subsequent developments in the relevant areas of philosophy and related fields, including theology.[26]

McCormack's transcendental argument for his doctrine of God appears to claim to have the force of a necessary deduction rather than an explanatory hypothesis. This would seem to follow from his confidence that the doctrine is secure enough that he can then *reverse* the argument's direction and make the doctrine fundamental. Having found the condition of the possibility for revelation in Jesus Christ within God's eternal decision for election, McCormack proposes we now reconstruct our account of the economy of salvation on this basis.

From a premodern point of view, McCormack's doctrine of election, so described, would appear speculative and uncritical. The error is twofold. First, the proposed doctrine of election is grounded not on Scripture but on a transcendental deduction, and thus on logic rather than revelation. Without the "plodding exegesis" that would demonstrate how Scripture requires or permits the doctrine (or the move more formally), it is a form of inference that a theological critique would suggest is invalid. The error is then compounded when the doctrine is said to require a reconstruction of Christian doctrine on its basis, rather than on Scripture. For a premodern Catholic, both these moves would be mistakes.[27] They transgress the limits of human knowledge of God, limits appropriate to the subject of theology rather than derived from philosophy.

In setting up his arguments, McCormack seems to reflect a way of thinking about theological inquiry that is specific to modernity. He notes how "the problem of knowing God, the problem of revelation" is the central concern of Barth (pp. 162-63). This is what makes Barth a modern theologian, for it is Kant's critique of the classical metaphysics that has set up the problem that he sought to solve. The notion of "problem solving" seems to be a characteristic of the style of modern theology, not least within the German-language tradition. Theological matters are to be sorted out scientifically by means of rigorous logic.[28] For a mediating the-

---

26. The validity of necessary transcendental arguments has become more doubtful within philosophical inquiry. See, e.g., S. Körner, "The Impossibility of Transcendental Deductions," *The Monist* 51 (1967): 317-31; see also Roderick M. Chisholm, *The Foundations of Knowing* (Minneapolis: University of Minnesota Press, 1982), pp. 95-99.

27. In my view, von Balthasar makes the same formal mistakes, which are more significant than anything that derives from his use of the *analogia entis*.

28. Consider, e.g., the opening pages of Wolfhart Pannenberg, *Systematic Theology*, vol. 1 (Grand Rapids: Eerdmans, 1988), where his express concern is to "maintain the preci-

ology in a world where the human is conceived as the center and arbiter of all, the problem becomes one of finding ways to have God make sense to humanity and bring God within our purview. I do not mean to suggest that McCormack necessarily intends to do this, and certainly not so flat-footedly. But this way of understanding theological inquiry is reflected in even so profound a theologian as Jüngel, in his dictum that "God is thinkable as one who speaks because and to the extent that he is human in and of himself."[29] While this statement may not be wrong, it would, I think, appear far too blunt to a premodern or a traditional Catholic. The emphasis on the knowledge question seems to overwhelm the doctrine of God.[30]

As a Scholastic, Aquinas certainly differs from the church fathers in his greater attention to making logical distinctions and similar clarifications. But he shares the premodern view that theology is not about the business of solving problems, least of all the problem of the knowledge of God. God gives of his endless goodness and love and truth in overflow; God *is* Gift, both giver and what is given. God is never a problem. As such, God is mystery, and it is the function of theology to do all it can to bring to light the mystery that is God, not to penetrate it or resolve it as if it were a mystery in the contemporary sense, but so that we may more reverently contemplate it and live in truer relationship to it. This is speculative only when it sets up a necessary formal or material principle that is not derived from Scripture.

As I understand Barth, he thought of speculation as the attempt to by-pass or go beyond the witness of Scripture. I think that the best of the premoderns would agree and did not do so any more than Barth did. As a traditional Catholic reader and admirer of Barth, I hope and believe that his doctrine of God is not, after all, speculative and uncritical.

---

sion, discrimination, and objectivity that are desirable and attainable in scientific investigation" (p. x), and address "the myriad problems inherent in the traditional language of Christian doctrine" (p. xi).

29. Jüngel, *God as Mystery*, p. 289.

30. An insightful analysis of the distinction between post-Enlightenment and premodern theology can be found in Andrew Louth, *Discerning the Mystery: An Essay on the Nature of Theology* (Oxford: Clarendon, 1983).

# 11. Christ, the Trinity, and Predestination: McCormack and Aquinas

*Matthew Levering*

Bruce McCormack argues that Karl Barth considers Jesus Christ to be the "subject" of election.[1] The key question among Barth scholars is whether Barth actually held the views that McCormack attributes to him.[2] But

---

1. Bruce McCormack, "Seek God Where He May Be Found: A Response to Edwin Chr. van Driel," *Scottish Journal of Theology* 60 (2007): 62-79 (hereafter, page references to this essay appear in parentheses in the text). McCormack's essay builds on his earlier "Grace and Being: The Role of God's Gracious Election in Karl Barth's Theological Ontology," in *The Cambridge Companion to Karl Barth,* ed. John Webster (Cambridge: Cambridge University Press, 2000), pp. 92-110. McCormack is responding to Edwin Chr. van Driel, "Karl Barth on the Eternal Existence of Jesus Christ," *Scottish Journal of Theology* 60 (2007): 45-61, as well as to Paul D. Molnar, *Divine Freedom and the Doctrine of the Immanent Trinity: In Dialogue with Karl Barth and Contemporary Theology* (New York: T. & T. Clark, 2002), pp. 61-64, 81.

2. See George Hunsinger, "Election and the Trinity: Twenty-five Theses on the Theology of Karl Barth," pp. 91-114 above; see also Kevin W. Hector, "God's Triunity and Self-Determination: A Conversation with Karl Barth, Bruce McCormack and Paul Molnar," pp. 29-46 above. Speaking as a dogmatic theologian rather than a Barth scholar, I agree with the view that Hunsinger defends as Barth's: "The mature Barth never collapsed the divine being into the divine act, nor did he turn 'essence' into a verb. He spoke deliberately about God's 'being in act.' The preposition is important here, and should not be erased, because it indicates a complex relationship between God's 'being' and God's 'act' — a relationship that was not flattened out into an absolute or simple identification. Moreover, Barth always maintained a crucial distinction between the idea of the divine self-constitution and that of the divine self-determination. God was constituted as the Holy Trinity, but determined by a free inner-Trinitarian decision to be the same God also in relation to us. It would be false (and unintelligible) to assert that such a secondary self-determination would necessarily entail a radical change in the divine being. It most certainly would not." Hunsinger, "Election and the Trinity," p. 113 above. In my view, the distinctions that Hunsinger makes are fundamental to true speech about the triune God.

when one reads McCormack's arguments from the perspective of dogmatic theology rather than Barthian exegesis, his position invites a constructive dialogue among theologians who seek to appreciate divine election (or predestination) within a fully christological and Trinitarian framework.

In this essay, therefore, I undertake two tasks. First, without entering into the intra-Barthian exegetical debate (beyond noting the concerns to which McCormack responds), I briefly summarize McCormack's interpretation of Barth on Christ, election, and the Trinity. Second, in dialogue with McCormack's views, I explore Thomas Aquinas's exposition of these topics. While disagreeing with McCormack on some key points, I welcome his arguments as an opportunity for exploring, theologically and metaphysically, the role of Christ and the Trinity in the doctrine of predestination.

## I. Bruce McCormack on Christ, Election, and the Trinity

In his 2007 essay "Seek God Where He May Be Found," McCormack attributes five claims to Karl Barth: (1) God's eternal act is his act of determining himself as "God for us," and so Jesus Christ names the Word of God even *asarkos;* (2) God's eternal act, which determines *how* he is as Father, Son, and Holy Spirit, is not less free than God's act of election (the same act), and so God "is Lord even over his being and essence"; (3) "it is God's act of determining himself to be God for us in Jesus Christ which constitutes God as triune" (although this must not be understood chronologically); (4) God's identity as "subject" is determined in the Father's act of "giving himself his own being in the act of election," that is, in begetting the Son and spirating the Holy Spirit; (5) since the Word is always both *asarkos* and *ensarkos,* the Word in the immanent Trinity "has a name and his name is 'Jesus Christ' (the God-human in his divine-human unity" (pp. 66-68).

In setting forth these five points, McCormack aims especially to safeguard Barth's critique of the traditional metaphysical doctrine of God. Responding to Edwin van Driel's concern that McCormack's interpretation means that the act of creation would no longer be a free act of God, but rather would become constitutive of God's being (God could not be God without it), McCormack explains that Barth's aim is to undercut all abstract thinking about God. As McCormack puts it, "the point of making election to be constitutive of the divine being is that no act can be called 'essential' in van Driel's completely traditional (abstract) sense of the word" (p. 69). Concretely, the divine "essence" is what God, in his eternal act, freely determines himself to be: having determined to create and elect in Jesus Christ, the Father begets his Son and spirates the Holy Spirit. The Son is the "subject" of election not "prior" to Jesus Christ, but eternally, because the Father's begetting (the "being begotten" who is the Son Jesus Christ) is not separate from the free divine determination to create and elect all things in the Son Jesus Christ.

But if the divine "essence" includes constitutively the free act of creation and election, does it then follow that creatures "constitute," in some sense, the very being or essence of God? This is van Driel's concern, and McCormack responds by emphasizing that God freely constitutes his triune being so that creation and election are contained in the Son Jesus Christ, without making it necessary that we who "participate" in Christ also are constitutive of God's triune being. In this respect, McCormack compares Barth's approach to Hegel's: "Hegel makes God's relation to Jesus a function of his relation to human beings generally, a relation (mind you) in which the ontological distinction between God and humankind is set aside. I follow Barth in making God's relation to human beings a function of his relation to Jesus, a relation in which the ontological distinction between God and the human is never set aside" (p. 70). God the Father relates to his Son Jesus Christ in the eternal free act in which he begets, and McCormack observes that this act is always "for us." As McCormack says, interpreting Barth, "[b]ecause God's being is a being *in* the act of electing, the identity of the one divine subject as 'Father' is something he gives to himself precisely in this decision — and, therefore, in the one eternal event in which the Son is begotten and the Holy Spirit is spirated" (p. 67). The "identity" (or being or "essence") of God is constituted by the Father's begetting of the Son and spirating the Holy Spirit "for us."[3]

Therefore, the Son is eternally the Son Jesus Christ who is (in his God-human identity) the "subject" and not merely the "object" of creation and election. But the Son Jesus Christ can only be understood to be the eternal "subject" of election insofar as there remains an "ontological distinction between Jesus and the rest of us" (p. 70). Far from agreeing with Hegel that

---

3. I argue against this derivation of the essence from the persons in my book *Scripture and Metaphysics: Aquinas and the Renewal of Trinitarian Theology* (Oxford: Blackwell, 2004). See also Gilles Emery's seminal "Essentialism or Personalism in the Treatise on God in St. Thomas Aquinas?" in *Trinity in Aquinas* (Ypsilanti, MI: Sapientia Press, 2003), pp. 165-208.

Jesus Christ manifests the divine-human unity that belongs to every human being, McCormack identifies Jesus Christ as the "subject" of election on the grounds of the radical uniqueness of Jesus Christ, who is the Son incarnate. Even if all human beings are eternally elect in the Son Jesus Christ — in accord with the Father's free determination to beget the Son and spirate the Spirit as being eternally "for us" — this does not mean that all human beings thus have the same relationship to the Father as does Jesus Christ in his humanity. McCormack underscores that, for Barth, "what is 'essential' to God is only what takes place in Jesus himself and not what takes place in us. It goes without saying that creation generally cannot be viewed as 'essential' to God on this basis" (p. 70).

Can the created humanity of Jesus Christ, however, be viewed as "essential" to God? In this regard van Driel suggests that McCormack's statement "Jesus Christ is the subject of election" is the same as saying that "Jesus Christ elects to be Jesus Christ." In other words, for van Driel, McCormack's reading of Barth places Barth in the position of advocating a position that can be shown to be false through *reductio ad absurdum*. McCormack responds by pointing out Barth's desire to overcome classical metaphysics while at the same time appropriating the "theological values" of "the ancient trinitarian and Christological formulae" (p. 71, n. 23). In his mature thought, according to McCormack, Barth retains his understanding of the Trinity as "a *single* divine subject in three modes of being" (p. 72), but interprets this Trinitarian doctrine in terms of the doctrine of election: "Where before [earlier in Barth's thought] election had been understood as an altogether this-worldly, historical activity on the part of God, it now became part of the doctrine of God itself — with some very obvious ontological implications" (p. 72). To conceive of divine being or essence requires recognizing the divine "subject" who freely elects: God *is* in this way, as electing. Since divine electing cannot be separated from the humanity of the God-man, the Son Jesus Christ, the created humanity of Jesus Christ cannot be separated from our understanding of the divine being or essence. The divine "subject" of election is the Son Jesus Christ, because the Son is Jesus Christ precisely in being begotten by the Father as being "for us."

Is the created humanity of the Son Jesus Christ therefore constitutive of the divine essence, so as to mingle the divine essence with what is not God (i.e., with a created humanity)? McCormack refuses to allow the validity, for Barth, of such an abstract view of the "divine essence." McCormack says:

> [I]f all that the Father is, he gives to the Son, then when we know God in his mode as "Son" (i.e. as the self-posited God, Jesus Christ), then of course we also know God as "Father" (as the self-positing God). For God in both modes of being is one and the same subject. There is no unknown mode of God here, and no being of God which is not constituted in the eternal act of self-determination to be God in Jesus Christ. (p. 73)

The eternal act of God the Father is the "eternal act of self-determination to be God in Jesus Christ." This eternal act is the triune divine being, and it contains the incarnation of the Son. McCormack says: "The eternal trinity of God is . . . a being which God gives to himself in the event in which he determines to be God 'for us' in Jesus Christ" (p. 74). In other words, we should not begin with a notion of God and then make arguments about what can or cannot be included in this notion; instead, we should begin with Jesus Christ, in whom we are elected, and on this basis alone draw conclusions about the freely determined being of the Father, Son, and Holy Spirit. From this latter perspective, we can see how election (God-for-us) eternally belongs to the free act by which the Father begets the Son, Jesus Christ. We can then develop a Trinitarian theology that recognizes the distinction between God and creatures (and therefore between *asarkos* and *ensarkos*), but that refuses to conceive of God (or the Son) without conceiving of him as "for us" in Jesus Christ.

But if this is the case, how does McCormack avoid the charge that his reading of Barth means that Jesus Christ elects Jesus Christ? McCormack seeks to avoid this charge by highlighting the Trinitarian pattern of the electing God. Jesus Christ does not elect Jesus Christ, because "in the strictest sense, it is the 'Father' who is the subject of election — and because that is so, 'Jesus Christ' can only be the subject of election because the subject that the 'Father' is, is the same subject that 'Jesus Christ' is" (p. 73). Jesus Christ and the Father are not two subjects who both, independently, will to elect; rather, the Father and Jesus Christ are one subject who wills to elect, and Jesus Christ receives this will from the Father — and indeed the Son is who he is as Son (that is, Jesus Christ) because of this will.[4] This eternal will to elect is free; God could have determined his being otherwise, but as it is, God eternally and freely wills that the Son begotten

---

4. For the opposite view, see Thomas Aquinas, *Summa Theologica*, 5 vols., trans. Fathers of the English Dominican Province (New York: Benziger Bros., 1948; reprint, Notre Dame, IN: Ave Maria Press/Christian Classics, 1981), I.41.2 (hereafter, references to the *ST* appear in parentheses in the text and footnotes).

of the Father be "for us," Jesus Christ. The divine determination, which has its origin in the Father, does not divide the divine subject: "'Before' and 'after' the decision, there is but one divine subject, identical with himself, albeit in differing 'modes'" (p. 73).

McCormack can thus affirm that his account of Barth's view that Jesus Christ is the "subject" of election does not reduce to absurdity and does not inscribe creation and election within God in a manner that either negates God's freedom or overlooks the Creator-creature distinction. God *freely* wills to create and elect in the Son Jesus Christ; the fact that the Son Jesus Christ (created as regards his humanity) is the "subject" of election does not constitute a metaphysical claim in the sense of classical metaphysics, but rather overcomes classical metaphysics by approaching the Son Jesus Christ from the perspective of election: God eternally wills that the Son be "for us," and this means that God's essence is determined in the act of election in Jesus Christ. Thus does McCormack avoid the abstract starting point of starting with an undetermined divine being or essence and then asking how Jesus Christ, as created, can belong to this divine being or essence. Rather, Jesus Christ is the Son posited by the Father as being "for us." His divine being or essence is determined: it is being *for us,* and hence the insistence on the inclusion of his created humanity within the electing subject (God) is not out of place. In McCormack's view, this insistence most definitely does not deny "that the immanent Trinity is 'complete' in pre-temporal eternity, above and prior to creation" (p. 79).

For the sake of clarity, we might ask what is gained by Barth's position as McCormack understands it. In a nutshell, what is gained is the God who has revealed himself in history as the electing God. Barth succeeds in recovering the God of Abraham, Isaac, and Jacob for a church that had been in thrall, in some degree, to the God of the philosophers. In this regard McCormack quotes a passage from *Church Dogmatics* II/2:

> There can be no Christian truth which does not from the very first contain within itself as its basis the fact that from and to all eternity God is the electing God. There can be no tenet of Christian doctrine which, if it is to be a Christian tenet, does not necessarily reflect both in form and content this divine electing. . . . There is no height or depth in which God can be God in any other way. (p. 78)[5]

---

5. Here McCormack cites Karl Barth, *Church Dogmatics,* 4 volumes in 13 parts, ed. G. W. Bromiley and T. F. Torrance (Edinburgh: T&T Clark, 1956-1975), II/2, p. 7 (hereafter,

Thus, for McCormack, the problem with conceiving of God as "God in any other way" is that by prescinding from God's free election in Jesus Christ, we arrive at an abstract God.

Moreover, McCormack argues that Van Driel's position cannot avoid conceiving of two eternal acts in God, thereby dividing the one God: "[F]irst, the event in which God is naturally and necessarily triune (the works of God *ad intra*) and, second, the event in which God chooses to be God 'for us' in Jesus Christ (the first of God's works *ad extra*)" (p. 76). Such a distinction would require supposing that the first event is atemporal, and McCormack suggests that this is incompatible with Barth's rejection of divine impassibility. Given Barth's "actualistic ontology," God's eternity must be characterized by free action and free decision, as indicated by the Father's begetting the Son and spirating the Spirit "for us," and so there is no need to hold to an "unchanging" metaphysical God. Likewise, McCormack criticizes Paul Molnar for arguing not simply that "God would be God without us" but also that we know *what* God would be in this hypothetical case — that is, triune (p. 76). God's triunity, the Father's begetting of the Son and spirating of the Spirit, does not manifest itself except as he determines to be "for us," and we have no grounds on which to speculate about God outside of this actual event.

At this stage, however, another concern arises. If God is free to act in various ways and to determine his being in this particular way ("for us"), does this not require that God possess attributes at least in some sense prior to election, if only the power and will to elect if he so chooses? Would not these attributes then constitute the divine being or essence "prior" to election? Van Driel raises this concern, and McCormack replies that the way it is phrased precludes an answer from the perspective of Barth's mature thought (beginning with *CD* II/2). McCormack quotes Barth: "'May it not be that it is as the electing God that he is the Almighty, and not *vice*

---

volume, part, and page references to the *CD* appear in parentheses in the text and footnotes). Among numerous passages, cf. *CD* II/2, p. 115, quoted by McCormack on p. 74: "Jesus Christ is the electing God. We must not ask concerning any other but him. In no depth of the Godhead shall we encounter any other but him. There is no such thing as Godhead in itself. Godhead is always the Godhead of the Father, Son and Holy Spirit." See also the passages that McCormack quotes on p. 74 from *Church Dogmatics* II/1, which in McCormack's view prepares for Barth's mature position in II/2. For example, Barth states: "The fact that God's being is event, the event of God's act, necessarily . . . means that it is his own conscious, willed and executed decision. . . . No other being exists absolutely in its act. No other being is absolutely its own, conscious, willed and executed decision" (*CD* II/1, p. 271).

*versa?'"* (p. 77) In other words, there are no foundations for the abstract speculation. To say that God is almighty and therefore can elect requires that one know God as almighty outside God's electing, and this is not possible. We know that the electing God is almighty, but we do not know the attributes of the nonelecting God, because we do not know this abstract God at all; there is no such "God" to know, because God freely is who he is. McCormack says, "Any attempt to look away from the God of electing grace revealed in Jesus Christ in an effort to find a ground of the possibility of election must inevitably open the door to natural theology. That is a door I chose not to open. What God in fact *does* is clearly possible for him; more than that I cannot say" (p. 77). What God is, is what God wills to be. According to McCormack, for Barth, "God's being is *absolutely* his willed decision; not additionally, not subsequent to a being above and prior to that decision, but *absolutely* his willed decision" (p. 74).

But if God's actions in the economy of creation and salvation are determinative for God-in-himself, then it seems that God would be chained to the progression of time in which election unfolds. Molnar especially challenges McCormack's reading of Barth on this point. For Molnar, the danger is that lacking the affirmation of a "prior" divine freedom in the immanent Trinity, election (having "always taken place") becomes a "logical necessity" for the self-determination and constitution of God's being, so that God would not be triune apart from the world.[6]

In reply, McCormack suggests that Molnar appears to be accepting the traditional metaphysical opposition between the "timeless" immanent Trinity — in whom "election has always taken place" — and the economic Trinity, who acts freely in history. By contrast, McCormack observes, Barth rejects both this metaphysical notion of God and its historicized Hegelian inverse. According to McCormack, Barth instead envisions "eternity as defined by the being of a God who freely determined himself for a covenant relation with creatures who exist in time — which makes the relation of eternity to time to be the relation of a founding 'moment' to all subsequent temporal moments" (pp. 75-76). By refusing to admit that God is either unchanging being or historicized process, Barth provides for a third way, in which God's election, which manifests God's freedom and determines him as who he is, is neither alien to nor reducible to created temporality: "The event which founds time [i.e., election] *comprehends* time, encloses and embraces it and takes it up (ineffably) into itself." The difficulty in un-

6. Molnar, *Divine Freedom*, p. 62, cited in McCormack, "Seek God," p. 75.

derstanding this ineffable embrace is not unexpected, as McCormack notes, "given that the event in which God constitutes himself as triune is also the event in which he determines himself for the covenant of grace and, therefore, for the human experience of suffering and dying *in time*" (p. 75). The paschal mystery's embrace of all human history provides a glimpse into the relationship between human temporality and divine event.

## II. Aquinas on Christ, Predestination, and the Trinity

I leave to Barth experts the task of evaluating the accuracy of McCormack's interpretation of Barth. Instead, my goal is to receive McCormack's interpretation as a challenge to Thomistic theology. As McCormack notes, many of his claims conflict with those of the fathers and medieval theologians. For example, McCormack's view that "[t]he eternal triunity of God is . . . a being which God gives to himself in the event in which he determines to be God 'for us' in Jesus Christ" (p. 74) requires, I think, God to be his own product. Arguing explicitly against Arius and drawing on the patristic discussion, Aquinas makes clear that the Father's will is not the source of the Son, for this would imply subordinationism (*ST* I.4. 2; cf. *ST* I.42. 2). Indeed, if God determined his own triune being, then the Father could have willed not to be a Father, and thus "God" would precede "Father" — an essentialism that precludes a fully Trinitarian account of God.[7] Likewise, McCormack suggests that classical metaphysics locks God into an ahistorical stasis, whereas the patristic and medieval use of metaphysics has the very opposite aim, namely that of upholding (successfully in my view) a dynamic transcendence without which God could not be radically immanent.[8]

Such disagreements, however, diverge from McCormack's central concern, which is to affirm as strongly as possible the doctrine of election. This effort to elucidate more clearly the place of the election in the theology of the triune God (and vice versa) strikes me as helpful. Can McCormack help non-Barthian theologians see more clearly the relationship of the doctrine of election to the doctrine of the triune God? I wish to

7. For a discussion of this, see esp. Emery, *Trinity in Aquinas*.
8. See Thomas Weinandy, OFM Cap, *Does God Suffer?* (Notre Dame, IN: University of Notre Dame Press, 2000).

ask this question by examining, in light of McCormack's position, Aquinas's theology of predestination as it relates to Christ and the Trinity.

## Trinitarian Creation and Trinitarian Missions

Aquinas defines predestination as "a certain divine preordination from eternity of those things which are to be done in time by the grace of God" (*ST* III.24.1). Predestination, then, has to do with the mission of the Son and the Holy Spirit. Those who enjoy "the indwelling of grace" or who receive "a certain renewal by grace" do so by the invisible missions of the Son and the Holy Spirit (*ST* I.43.6).[9] Both renewal and indwelling signify not just any movement of grace, but the sanctifying grace by which the human being comes to enjoy God beyond the natural mode according to which "God is in all things by His essence, power, and presence" (*ST* I.43.3). By the invisible mission that is sanctifying grace, the Holy Spirit elevates and perfects the human being so that he or she "can freely use not only the created gift itself, but enjoy also the divine person Himself" (*ST* I.43. 3 *ad* 1). When the Trinity draws the human being into supernatural communion of knowledge and love with the persons of the Trinity, this establishes in the human being a new relationship to the persons of the Trinity. For such a change to be possible, the Father, Son, and Holy Spirit need not become different from what and who they are; rather, the new relationship arises through a change in the human being. The change in the human being draws the human into the eternal divine life, rather than making requisite the historicizing of the divine life.

God's acting upon the human being through the invisible mission that is sanctifying grace, therefore, is an eternal action that manifests itself in the historical change that the human being undergoes. Because God acts upon the human being without ceasing to be eternal, God's action in forming a communion of partakers in the divine life is properly conceived as a predestining action, so as to emphasize that God's perfecting of the human creature does not take place as though God were one agent among others in the linear temporal continuum. God is entirely "outside" this continuum, and it is precisely this transcendence that enables him to be so

9. For a masterful exposition of Aquinas's theology of Trinitarian missions, see Gilles Emery, OP, "Missions invisibles et missions visibles: le Christ et son Esprit," *Revue Thomiste* 106 (2006): 51-99.

perfectly immanent in his work of "predestination." As Aquinas observess, "That a divine person be possessed by any creature, or exist in it in a new mode, is temporal" (*ST* I.43.2). Are the Son and Holy Spirit, then, paradoxically not active in their invisible missions? On the contrary, the Son and Holy Spirit are active in the invisible mission both in causing the creature to receive a temporal participation in the eternal procession, and insofar as the eternal procession itself is the active cause of every temporal effect.

How are the eternal processions — as subsisting relations, the very Persons of the Trinity — causal with respect to temporal effects? After all, Aquinas holds against Arius that there is absolutely no temporal change involved in the procession of the divine persons (*ST* I.27.1). By contrast, there is much change in temporal creatures. Does God, then, have no real activity in history? In other words, does history perhaps align itself to God while God stands aloof, eternally preoccupied by his own divine act?

This is far from the case. Aquinas observes, "The processions of the divine Persons are the cause of creation" (*ST* I.45.6 *ad* 1).[10] In this regard he compares the Trinity to a craftsman who causes things to be by knowledge and will: "Hence also God the Father made the creature through His Word, which is His Son; and through His Love, which is the Holy Spirit" (*ST* I.45.6). Does this mean that the Son and Holy Spirit are the instruments of the Father, whom the Father relies upon to accomplish his purpose? Aquinas explains that power in God pertains to the divine essence, what is common to the persons. Thus the Father does not need to rely on the Son and Holy Spirit as mere instruments; rather, Father, Son, and Holy Spirit act in concert, through the divine essence, to accomplish an effect. But "power implies a notion of a principle putting into execution what the will commands, and what knowledge directs" (*ST* I.25.1 *ad* 4), and so it would be a mistake to imagine God's causal power as separate from the order of Trinitarian procession.[11] The generation of the Son and the spiration of the

10. For further discussion, see Gilles Emery, OP, "The Personal Mode of Trinitarian Action in St. Thomas Aquinas," in *Trinity, Church, and the Human Person: Thomistic Essays* (Naples, FL: Sapientia Press, 2007), pp. 115-53. See also Emery, "Trinity and Creation: The Trinitarian Principle of the Creation in the Commentaries of Albert the Great, Bonaventure, and Thomas Aquinas on the *Sentences*," in *Trinity in Aquinas*, pp. 33-70. In "Trinity and Creation," Emery summarizes the results of his *La Trinité créatrice: Trinité et création dans les commentaires aux Sentences de Thomas d'Aquin et de ses précurseurs Albert le Grand et Bonaventure* (Paris: Vrin, 1995).

11. On God's power, see John F. Boyle, "St. Thomas and the Analogy of *Potentia Generandi*," *The Thomist* 64 (2000): 581-92.

Holy Spirit cause created effects, even though they do so through the divine essence, because the power to create is not a distinguishing property of one of the three persons.

In seeking the root of every temporal effect, therefore, Aquinas turns to the persons of the Trinity. As the Word of God, the Son expresses not only the entirety of God the Trinity, but also all creatures. The Son contains every created effect caused by God. Aquinas notes that "because God by one act understands Himself and all things, His one only Word is expressive not only of the Father, but of all creatures" (*ST* I.34.3). Furthermore the Son is not only "expressive" but also "operative" of creatures, "because in the Word is implied the operative idea of what God makes" (*ST* I.34.3). In knowing himself, God knows all the finite modes in which he can be participated. Likewise, God "loves Himself and every creature by the Holy Spirit, inasmuch as the Holy Spirit proceeds as the love of the primal goodness whereby the Father loves Himself and every creature" (*ST* I.37. 2 *ad* 3). If the Son expresses every created effect of God, then the procession of the Son includes, eternally and by God's free will, the humanity of Jesus Christ as an effect that God wills in time. For McCormack, this means that election belongs within the very divine procession, so that election is constitutive of the Trinity. Aquinas could agree that "in the one eternal event in which the Son is begotten and the Holy Spirit is spirated," the Father knows the Son as Jesus Christ. Does this mean that for Aquinas, too, "it is God's act of determining himself to be God for us in Jesus Christ which constitutes God as triune"? ("Seek God," p. 67).

In order to see why Aquinas rejects this possibility, let us return to predestination. Aquinas explains: "Predestination presupposes election in the order of reason; and election presupposes love" (*ST* I.23.4). What is the source and goal of the election and love that moves God to draw rational creatures to share in the divine life, something impossible for human beings solely on the basis of their natural resources? The source and goal, Aquinas says, is "the goodness of God . . . towards which the whole effect of predestination is directed as to an end; and from which it proceeds, as from its first moving principle" (*ST* I.23.5). This special providential communication of the divine goodness, as we have seen, takes place through the invisible missions of the Son and Holy Spirit that bestow the gift of sanctifying grace on human beings. Sanctifying grace provides the human being with a participation in the divine person, a participation in time in the eternal coming forth of the divine person from his principle. Aquinas attends here to Romans 5:5: "God's love has been poured into our hearts through the Holy Spirit who has been given to us" (*ST* I.43.3 *ad* 2). The Father gives us the Holy Spirit "through our Lord Jesus Christ, through whom we have now received our reconciliation" (Rom. 5:11).

Aquinas's distinction between procession and mission distinguishes his position from that of McCormack. Not only does God not will his own triunity, but also the procession of the Son from the Father is distinct from the mission of the Son. The creature's participation in the divine procession has the divine procession as its cause, and in this sense belongs to the divine procession; but the creature's participation is not constitutive of the divine procession. Yet, were we to end there, we would not have done justice to Aquinas's position. As we have seen, Aquinas argues that the divine processions are themselves causal as regards created effects, and most profoundly so as regards the effects of grace. A human being (like an angel) can and does become a "partaker of the divine Word and of the Love proceeding, so as freely to know God truly and to love God rightly. Hence the rational creature alone can possess the divine person" (*ST* I.38.1). Only God can cause this effect, and Aquinas emphasizes that this causality has a Trinitarian pattern: "Thus a divine person can *be given,* and can be a *gift*" (*ST* I.38.1), both in the eternal procession and in the temporal mission by which a rational creature shares in the gift.

This unity of procession and mission as divine gifting indicates the relationship of the Trinitarian procession to the predestination (election and love) of the human being. The mission could not be divine gifting if the procession were not divine gifting; the communication of divine goodness that characterizes the Trinitarian processions also characterizes the communication of divine goodness in God's special election and love of the human being. In this light, one can sympathize with the intention of McCormack's argument that "God's being is a being *in* the act of electing." In the divine processions, God communicates his goodness in a manner mirrored by his "act of electing." If by "Jesus Christ" one means the divine gifting or communication of divine goodness, then one sees why McCormack emphasizes not separating the Son from Jesus Christ. McCormack's affirmation that the Son is eternally the electing Son Jesus Christ makes clear that the communication of divine goodness is what the Son, as the Word of the Father, actually expresses.

Yet, while the Son is the intradivine communication of the divine goodness (since the Father begets the Son by communicating the very divine essence), we must make a distinction between this intradivine communication — which, *pace* McCormack, is not "free," because it belongs to who God is by nature rather than to who God has willed to be — and the free extradivine communication of divine goodness that reaches its height in the incarnation of the Son Jesus Christ. The aspect that McCormack wishes to stress is that the gifting of God in the processions is eternally inclusive of the gifting of God in the missions, and that we know the processions only through the missions. Although this is true, Aquinas makes an important distinction regarding the "term" of the procession and of the mission. With regard to the eternal procession of the Son, Aquinas denies that it can be understood as "an effect proceeding from its cause" or as "the cause proceeding to the effect" (*ST* I.27.1). Aquinas argues that "[c]areful examination shows that both of these opinions take procession as meaning an outward act; hence neither of them affirms procession as existing in God Himself" (*ST* I.27.1).

Why is it important to insist on procession as strictly an intradivine act? The answer is that only in this way can we retain the absolute equality of begetter and begotten, Father and Son. The only kind of procession that remains entirely within itself is an intelligible procession (of knowing or of loving), which fits with the truth that "God is spirit" (John 4:24) and that "the Word was God" (John 1:1) (*ST* I.27.1).[12] But do not all created things proceed from the Father in the Word, so that what proceeds is in fact eternally the Son Jesus Christ? As we have seen, Aquinas affirms that all created things proceed in the eternal Word: "[T]he Word of God is only expressive of what is in God the Father, but is both expressive and operative of creatures; and therefore it is said (Ps. xxxii[33].9): 'He spake, and they were made.'" (*ST* I.34.3). Even so, Aquinas also insists that there must be a difference between the eternal procession — in which God the Son proceeds from God the Father — and the procession of creatures in God the Son. The reason is that the "term" of the procession of creatures, even though it is (freely) inscribed in the eternal procession, is temporal rather than eternal. Only the Son is the eternal "term" of the Father's begetting.

---

12. Cf. *ST* I.31. 2, which insists on caution when describing the distinction between Father and Son. Aquinas says that "to avoid the error of Arius we must shun the use of the terms *diversity* and *difference* in God, lest we take away the unity of essence: we may, however, use the term *distinction* on account of the relative opposition. Hence, whenever we find terms of *diversity* or *difference* of persons used in an authentic work, these terms of *diversity* or *difference* are taken to mean *distinction*. But lest the simplicity and singleness of the divine essence be taken away, the terms *separation* and *division*, which belong to the parts of a whole, are to be avoided: and lest equality be taken away, we avoid the use of the term *disparity*: and lest we remove similitude, we avoid the terms *alien* and *discrepant*."

This does not mean, as McCormack at times suggests, that the Son is separated in a Nestorian fashion from his humanity in Christ Jesus. (Recall McCormack's concluding point: "For me, what is at stake in this debate is the coherence of our affirmation of the full and complete deity of Jesus Christ" (p. 79). Rather, the point is that the created humanity of the Son is a temporal "term" of the eternal procession. As Aquinas says, "The processions of the divine Persons are the cause of creation" (*ST* I.45. 6 *ad* 1), but creatures are not the eternal terms of the eternal processions; only the Son and Holy Spirit are such. Describing the mission of the Son and Holy Spirit, Aquinas makes a crucial point: "The procession may be called a twin procession, eternal and temporal, not that there is a double relation to the principle, but a double term, temporal and eternal" (*ST* I.43.2 *ad* 3). This is the appropriate response to McCormack's claim that the logic of van Driel leads to two eternal acts (thereby dividing the unity of God): "First, the event in which God is naturally and necessarily triune (the works of God *ad intra*) and, second, the event in which God chooses to be God 'for us' in Jesus Christ (the first of God's works *ad extra*)" (p. 76).

Although McCormack argues that this two-event model requires supposing a "timeless" first event, so that the first event is not temporally prior to the second, Aquinas shows that the unity of the two "events" can be upheld in the divine processions themselves. The difference is not in God, as if the first "event" were timeless and the second temporal. Rather, the procession is eternal, but it has diverse "terms" with respect to the principle of the procession. Only the Son is equal to the Father in divinity; only the Son is the Word and the Image. As Aquinas points out, therefore, among "the words that express the origin of the divine persons," some words express the eternal term with respect to its principle, whereas "[o]thers express the temporal term with the relation to the principle" (*ST* I.43.2). The temporal term is the created effect.

### Divine Image, Human Image

Nonetheless, does this distinction so separate the eternal image of the Father from the created image of God that an implicit Nestorianism inevitably results? How do the two "terms" of the divine processions retain their bond? If the eternal term is the Son, how is the unity of the eternal term and the temporal term (the Son Jesus Christ) to be conceived?

In his discussion of the Son as the divine image in the *Summa Theo-*

*logiae,* Aquinas undertakes his interpretation in light of Colossians 1:15: "He is the image of the invisible God, the first-born of all creation" (*ST* I.35.2). This biblical text is the first clause of a lengthy Pauline profession of faith, which continues:

> [F]or in him all things were created, in heaven and on earth, visible or invisible, whether thrones or dominions or principalities or authorities — all things were created through him and for him. He is before all things, and in him all things hold together. He is the head of the body, the church; he is the beginning, the firstborn from the dead, that in everything he might be preeminent. For in him all the fullness of God was pleased to dwell, and through him to reconcile to himself all things, whether on earth or in heaven, making peace by the blood of his cross. (Col. 1:16-20)

Interpreting this passage, N. T. Wright argues that "[t]he poem refers to the exalted man [Jesus], but identifies him with the pre-existent Lord."[13] For Wright, "there is therefore no suggestion that Jesus pre-existed in human form: merely that it was utterly appropriate for him, as the pre-existent one, to become man" (p. 69). This "pre-existent" one differs from God the Father, but yet is fully divine: "Paul regarded Jesus as identical with the one who was, and always had been, fully divine, and yet who could be distinguished in thought from the Father" (p. 69). But what about Paul's claim that "the image of the invisible God" is also "the first-born of all creation" (Col. 1:15)? Wright answers: "From all eternity Jesus had, in his very nature, been the 'image of God,' reflecting perfectly the character and life of the Father. It was thus appropriate for him to be the 'image of God' as man: from all eternity he had held the same relation to the Father that humanity, from its creation, had been intended to bear" (p. 70). In God's covenantal relationship with Israel, God reveals that humanity, in and through Israel, is called to share in the Son's relationship with the Father as the "image of God." This sharing will be fulfilled through what later Chris-

---

13. N. T. Wright, *Colossians and Philemon* (Grand Rapids: Eerdmans, 1986), p. 69 (hereafter, page references to this work appear in parentheses in the text). Wright holds that the author of Colossians is, in fact, Paul; see also Marianne Meye Thompson, *Colossians and Philemon* (Grand Rapids: Eerdmans, 2005), pp. 27ff. Thompson reads Colossians 1:15-20 as aimed at identifying Christ as the one who reveals the invisible God: "[T]o say that Christ is the *image* of God means that, in some way, the unseen or invisible God becomes visible, moves into our sphere of sense perception, in the life of this human being" (p. 28).

tians call the "Incarnation." Wright observes: "Paul's way of expressing the doctrine is to say, poetically, that the man Jesus fulfils the purposes which God had marked out *both* for himself *and* for humanity. Upon Jesus Christ, then, has come the role marked out for humanity, and hence for Israel: Christ is *the firstborn over all creation*" (pp. 70-71).

Does this mean that the man Jesus, who is the "image of the invisible God," is this image as the first creature? Wright does not think so. Instead, he argues that Paul means that in Jesus, God fulfills Israel's purposes from within: Jesus, "*in virtue of* this eternal pre-existence" (p. 71), can draw humanity into the divine intimacy (the perfection of the image of God) that God, through his promises to Israel, revealed to be the goal of creation. Wright says: "That this is the correct way to read verse 15 is immediately confirmed: *for by him all things were created*. He is not simply part of the created world itself" (p. 71, emphasis in original).[14]

For his part, Aquinas approaches Colossians 1:15 by asking what it means to be an "image": "The notion of an image includes three things. First, an image must be a likeness; second, it must be derived or drawn from the thing of which it is a likeness; and third, it must be derived with respect to something that pertains to the species or to a sign of the species." All three elements are important, but the third deserves further comment here. The point that Aquinas is making is that being an image requires more than simply sharing some characteristics; the image must be like what it images by sharing characteristics that are *specific* to the kind of thing that is being imaged. As Aquinas puts it, "Thus, a man has many accidents, such as color, size, and so on; but they are not the reason for calling something an image of a man. But if something has the shape or figure of a man, then it can be called an image, because this shape is a sign of the species."[15] What then would enable something to be the "image of the invisible God"?

Before giving his own answer, Aquinas recalls Arius's answer to this question. Arius answers that for Christ Jesus to be the "image of the invisible God," what is needed is that Jesus image the Father's goodness. For Aquinas, however, this is not enough. To be uniquely the "image of the invisible God," one needs to possess a characteristic that is specific to God, a

14. See Simon Gathercole's debate with Robert Jenson in Gathercole, *The Pre-existent Son: Recovering the Christologies of Matthew, Mark, and Luke* (Grand Rapids: Eerdmans, 2006), pp. 288ff.

15. Thomas Aquinas, *Commentary on Colossians*, trans. Fabian Larcher, OP, ed. Daniel A. Keating (Naples, FL: Sapientia Press, 2006), ch. 1, lect. 4, § 31, p. 18.

characteristic that most clearly identifies God. An "image" of the invisible God must itself be invisible, because God is spirit. What would it mean to say that Christ Jesus is "image" as himself "invisible"? Aquinas quotes Hebrews 1:3: "He [the Son] reflects the glory of God and bears the very stamp of his nature, upholding the universe by his word of power. When he had made purification for sins, he sat down at the right hand of the Majesty on high."[16] Christ Jesus, Aquinas concludes, shares the invisible divine nature and the divine power.

If the Son is invisible, however, how is the Son also Jesus Christ in whom we have our election? Does Aquinas conceive of a divine Son who then has a relationship with creatures as "Jesus Christ"? No. For Aquinas, as we have seen, the divine Son is never unrelated to creatures. Concerning Colossians 1, Aquinas teaches that "inasmuch as the Son is begotten, he is seen as a word representing every creature, and he is the principle of every creature. For if he were not begotten in that way, the Word of the Father would be the first-born of the Father only, and not of creatures."[17] Aquinas thus underscores that the Word of the Father is not the first-born only of the Father, as if creation and election came later. As McCormack emphasizes, the Word of the Father is the first-born of all creatures. But how so, since the Word is not a creature? First, the divine Word is the first-born of creatures as being their "principle" or cause with respect to creation ("in him all things were created" [Col. 1:16]), with respect to the diversity of creatures ("in heaven and on earth" [Col. 1:16]), and with respect to the preservation of creatures ("in him all things hold together" [Col. 1:17]).

Second, Aquinas argues that the Word is the first-born of creatures according to the incarnation. The human nature of the Word, which is never a human nature separate from the Word, is a temporal effect of the divine Trinity: "The whole Trinity effected the conception of Christ's body" (*ST* III.32.1). God brought this human nature into being and at that very instant assumed this human nature into unity (a created unity) with the divine nature in the person of the Word. In other words, God the Trinity creates the human nature of the Son, Jesus Christ. As Aquinas explains, "A man is called Creator and is God because of the union, inasmuch as it is terminated in the Divine hypostasis; yet it does not follow that the union

MATTHEW LEVERING

itself is the Creator or God, because that a thing is said to be created regards its being rather than its relation" (*ST* III.2.7 *ad* 3). If Christ's human nature is created, is the incarnation simply the effect of grace in the same way that others receive grace? Aquinas answers no: God the Trinity makes this human nature, at the instant of its conception, to be the Word's human nature, united to God not merely by operation but "by personal being" (*ST* III.2.10). Christ, therefore, is the "first-born" because "he is the beginning" (Col. 1:18), in Aquinas's words "the beginning or source of justification and grace in the entire Church."[18] Christ is first-born because he is the principle not only in the order of creation, but also in the order of grace. As Aquinas puts it, "all Christ's actions and sufferings operate instrumentally in virtue of His Godhead for the salvation of men" (*ST* III.48.6).

But if God the Trinity creates the flesh of the Son of God, and God works instrumentally through this flesh, does election really have any fundamental connection to the Son who takes on flesh? Like Athanasius, Aquinas suggests that the fundamental connection has to do with the relationship of the Image to the image: the Son "has a particular agreement with human nature, since the Word is a concept of the eternal Wisdom, from Whom all man's wisdom is derived. And hence man is perfected in wisdom (which is his proper perfection, as he is rational) by participating in the Word of God" (*ST* III.3.8). The incarnation of the Image in the image has as its goal, Aquinas notes, the raising of human nature to its perfection. As the Word incarnate, the Image-image "is the efficient cause of the perfection of human nature, according to John i.16: *Of His fulness we have all received*" (*ST* III.1.6). The perfection of the created image of God is the perfection of wisdom and love, since the divine Image is not "any sort of word, but one who breathes forth love" (*ST* I.43.5 *ad* 2).[19]

Not only the name Image, but also the name Son gives us insight into why it is the eternal Son, in particular, who is Jesus Christ. The two names come together in Romans 8:29: "For those whom he [God] foreknew he also predestined to be conformed to the image of his Son, in order that he might be the first-born among many brethren." The eternal Son is connected to divine election because of the Father's will to be the Father of

18. Aquinas, *Commentary on Colossians*, § 48, p. 29.
19. For Athanasius's emphasis on the healing and perfecting of the image by the Image, see St. Athanasius, *On the Incarnation*, trans. and ed. by a Religious of C.S.M.V. (1944; reprint, Crestwood, NY: St. Vladimir's Theological Seminary Press, 1993). On the spiration of the Holy Spirit, see *ST* I.36.2 and elsewhere; on the perfected image of God, see *ST* I.93.8.

human beings. Divine fatherhood of human beings means that we possess the triune God as our "Father" both as creatures and as adopted sons, but we receive this relationship by being adopted in the Son by the Father through the Holy Spirit. Aquinas points out that in naming God "Father," one conveys both the Father's relationship to the Son and God's paternal relationship to human beings. The Father's relationship to the Son has priority: "[C]ommon terms which import relation to the creature come after proper terms which import personal relations; because the Person proceeding in God proceeds as the principle of the production of creatures"(*ST* I.33.3 *ad* 1). Note that the relationship to the creature is not absent from divine procession, though it is secondary because of the twofold "term" of the procession, in which the eternal "term" has priority. The temporal "term" is the election of adopted sons in the Son, Jesus Christ.

Why does election not have priority in our understanding of the Son? Aquinas explains that "as the word conceived in the mind of the artist is first understood to proceed from the artist before the thing designed, which is produced in likeness to the word conceived in the artist's mind, so the Son proceeds from the Father before the creature" (*ST* I.33.3 *ad* 1). Thus the Son differs from creatures in a way that is comparable to how an artist's conception of his works differs from his works. For this reason, Aquinas points out, the Son is not simply the "first-born of all creation" (Col. 1:15), but also is "the only Son" who alone "is in the bosom of the Father" (John 1:18) (*ST* I.33.3 *ad* 2). This eternal "term" of the Father's begetting has priority over any temporal "term" that the divine Trinity, like a "craftsman" working "through the word conceived in his mind and through the love of his will regarding some object" (*ST* I.45.6) freely creates/elects. But election and creation, as we have emphasized, are not on this account extrinsic to the divine processions, even though they are secondary. Rather, it is in knowing his wisdom and loving his goodness — in begetting the Son and spirating the Holy Spirit — that the Father, with the Son and Holy Spirit, wills to communicate the divine wisdom and goodness to others, and thereby creates and elects.

In so doing, God does not "act for the acquisition of some end; He intends only to communicate His perfection, which is His goodness" (*ST* I.43.4; see also *ST* I.19.5). Aquinas comments in this regard that God "alone is the most perfectly liberal giver" (*ST* I.43.4 *ad* 1). We might imagine that God is such because, in the fullness of his eternal processions, God has all he needs and does not mind sharing; but such a view distorts the reality of God. It is because God is so good that he is supremely self-diffusive both in himself (in the divine processions) and "for us." As Aquinas says, "It pertains, therefore, to the nature of the will to communicate as far as possible to others the good possessed. . . . Hence, if natural things, in so far as they are perfect, communicate their good to others, much more does it appertain to the divine will to communicate by likeness its own good to others as much as possible"(*ST* I.19.2). God's infinite goodness manifests itself both in the divine self-communication, and in his communication of finite participation in himself; and these are not two "events" or acts (*pace* McCormack's misunderstanding of the traditional position represented by Aquinas[20]), but one act united by its end or goal, namely the divine goodness. In this one act, which is necessary with respect to God's being and free with respect to creaturely being, God "wills both Himself to be, and other things to be; but Himself as the end, and other things as ordained to that end; inasmuch as it befits the divine goodness that other things should be partakers therein" (*ST* I.19.2).[21]

God's overflowing goodness constitutes the reason not only for creation, but also for the incarnation of Jesus Christ. In the very first question of the *Tertium Pars,* on the fittingness of the incarnation, Aquinas recalls his principle that "the very nature of God is goodness," from which he concludes: "Hence, what belongs to the essence of goodness befits God.

20. According to McCormack, "Traditionally, of course, it was believed that the works of God *ad intra* precede and make possible the works of God *ad extra* — so that the eternal generation of the Son and the eternal procession of the Holy Spirit constitute an activity that is natural and necessary for God and, therefore, precedes and grounds all activity that is willed and contingent (which is what election was understood to be). To the extent that God also wills to be what he is naturally and necessarily, this is an act of self-affirmation (rather than an act of self-determination) and, as such, must be kept clearly distinct from any subsequent act of self-determination. To insist as I do, however, that both the works of God *ad intra* and the first of God's works *ad extra* take place *simultaneously,* in one and the same eternal event, would set aside this traditional understanding" (McCormack, "Seek God," p. 67). On the contrary, Aquinas — representative of the classical tradition on this point — holds that "the works of God *ad intra* and the first [and indeed all] of God's works *ad extra* take place *simultaneously,* in one and the same eternal event." Having misunderstood the traditional position, McCormack thus poses a false alternative between his position and the "two-event" model, neither of which is adequate to the transcendence and immanence of God.

21. In *ad* 3 of this article, Aquinas notes, "From the fact that His own goodness suffices the divine will, it does not follow that it wills nothing apart from itself, but rather that it wills nothing except by reason of its goodness. Thus, too, the divine intellect, though its perfection consists in the very knowledge of the divine essence, yet in that essence knows other things." For necessity and freedom in God's willing, see *ST* I.19.3.

But it belongs to the essence of goodness to communicate itself to others, as is plain from Dionysius (*Div. Nom.* iv). Hence it belongs to the essence of the highest good to communicate itself in the highest manner to the creature" (*ST* III.1.1). Thus the self-communication of God the Father in the begetting of the Son and spirating of the Holy Spirit cannot be disjoined from election/creation, in which God's self-communicating goodness freely overflows to creatures. Even if, as Aquinas rightly says, "the Son proceeds from the Father before the creature" (*ST* I.33.3 *ad* 1), nonetheless this priority does not separate Trinitarian theology from the doctrine of election.

In reflecting on the divine paternity, filiation, and procession, Aquinas always keeps election at the heart of his reflection. The Trinitarian (and biblical) names "Father," "Son," "Word," "Image," "Love," and "Gift" each express something proper to the divine Persons, but each contain also a "relation to creatures" (*ST* I.34.3) that has at its core the election of rational creatures in Christ Jesus. In the case of the relation paternity-filiation, which distinguishes the Father and the Son, Aquinas observes that the election of rational creatures "participates in the likeness of the Son, as is clear from the words of Rom. viii.29: *Whom He foreknew and predestined to be made conformable to the image of His Son*" (*ST* I.33.3 *ad* 1). Reflection on election thus leads Aquinas into Trinitarian theology, as befits the contemplation of the mysteries of salvation. Indeed, this is why Aquinas insists that "in *sacra doctrina* all things are treated of under the aspect of God; either because they are God Himself; or because they refer to God as their beginning and end" (*ST* I.1.7). To fail to contemplate election in a Trinitarian manner, or to contemplate the triune God only in and through the doctrine of election, would be to fail in *sacra doctrina*.

### The Predestination of Christ

In this light, Aquinas's attention to Romans 8:29 deserves further notice as a key to his Trinitarian Christology. In Aquinas's view, Romans 8:29 "speaks of that predestination by which we are predestinated to be adopted sons" (*ST* III.24.1 *ad* 1), and thereby provides insight into how Christ is "the first-born of many brethren" (Rom. 8:29). God's election of creatures must include, in a preeminent fashion, the election of Christ in his human nature. Aquinas says that "just as Christ in a singular manner above all others is the natural Son of God, so in a singular manner is He predestinated" (*ST* III.24

*ad* 1). In making this affirmation, however, Aquinas relies on a faulty Latin version of Romans 1:4: his text reads that Christ was "predestinated the Son of God in power" rather than "designated Son of God in power" (RSV) (*ST* III.24.1 *sed contra, ad* 2 and *ad* 3).²² Moreover, it seems that this connection of Christology with predestination/election causes difficulties. As we have seen, Aquinas defines predestination as "a certain divine preordination from eternity of those things which are to be done in time by the grace of God" (*ST* III.24.1). If predestination refers to the effects of the grace of the Holy Spirit in time, it would seem that a divine person cannot be predestined. But Christ is a divine person, and Aquinas teaches not only that Christ is predestined but also that predestination applies to the person (rather than, in a Nestorian fashion, to the nature).

Recall McCormack's observation that "what is at stake in this debate is the coherence of our affirmation of the full and complete deity of Jesus Christ" ("Seek God," p. 79). By insisting that Christ is predestined, has Aquinas joined election and Trinitarian theology in a way that approximates McCormack's key claim that "there is no mode of being or existence in the triune life of God above and prior to the eternal act of self-determination in which God 'constitutes' himself as 'God for us' and, therefore, there is no such thing as an 'eternal Logos' in the abstract" (p. 66)? I have already noted that, for Aquinas, "there is no such thing as an 'eternal Logos' in the abstract," at least in the sense that the name Word always imports relation to creatures. Because for Aquinas "[t]he processions of the divine Persons are the cause of creation" (*ST* I.45.6 *ad* 1), it would be a mistake to imagine the divine Word as *first* generated and *then* related to creatures.²³ In the eternal generation of the Word, the Word is related to all

22. Aquinas is aware of Origen's reading: "Origen commenting on Rom. i.4 says that the true reading of this passage of the Apostle is: *Who was destined to be the Son of God in power;* so that no antecedence is implied" (*ad* 3). Aquinas goes on to say: "Others refer the antecedence implied in the participle *predestinated,* not to the fact of being the Son of God, but to the manifestation thereof, according to the customary way of speaking in Holy Scripture, by which things are said to take place when they are made known; so that the sense would be — *Christ was predestinated to be made known as the Son of God*" (*ad* 3). Those who argue for this sense, Aquinas points out, do not understand the meaning of the word "predestination." Rather than indicating that something will be made known, predestination means "being directed to the end of beatitude" (*ad* 3).

23. McCormack seems to suppose that the acts of God in his unity, in the traditional account, exclude the Trinitarian processions: as McCormack says, "the point of making election to be constitutive of the divine being is that no act can be called 'essential' in van Driel's completely traditional (abstract) sense of the word" (McCormack, "Seek God,"

creatures as the one in whom the Father knows all creatures. The Father and Son freely know and love creatures into existence in spirating the Holy Spirit: "God the Father made the creature through His Word, which is His Son; and through His Love, which is the Holy Spirit" (*ST* I.45.6). The Word is indeed, as McCormack reminds us, always "God for us." In this sense, McCormack's emphasis on the relationship of election to Trinitarian theology serves to bring out the importance of Aquinas's affirmation that "we must attribute predestination to the Person of Christ" (*ST* III.24.1 *ad* 2). The very Person of Christ is predestined; Christ Jesus is not a mere add-on to the eternal person of the Word.

But by not appreciating the fact that the one divine act — which is none other than the divine generation and spiration — has a twofold term (eternal and temporal), McCormack does not make the distinctions that Aquinas recognizes to be necessary for speaking about the incarnation. After all, the incarnation is an event in time, and consists in the assumption of a human nature, at the instant of its conception, to union with the divine nature in the person of the Word. The act who is the Word, divine filiation, does not take on a new divine relationship, as though he were now characterized not only by his divine relationship of origin but also by a new divine relationship to this human nature. In short, the incarnation does not require the Word to change; the change — a radical and unfathomable change indeed — occurs on the side of the creature. Otherwise, it would not be an incarnation of the Word, because the Word would become something different and thereby would no longer be the Word. He is eternally the fullness of who he is, and it is for this reason that the incarna-

---

p. 69). McCormack would appear to have misunderstood the point of the distinction between essential and notional acts in God. The former are not somehow detached from Father, Son, and Holy Spirit. See also McCormack's comment that "[c]lassically, theologians always secured the freedom of God by means of a concept of ontological independence which was controlled by the thought of 'pure being,' an abstract, wholly timeless mode of existence. The doctrine of the Trinity was simply added on to this prior conception — which led to the supposition that God is triune in and for himself, in a timeless realm above all relationship to the world (or even to Jesus Christ as the embodied existence of God in the world). On the basis of this conception, securing divine freedom came quite easily. God's freedom, on this account, is a function of God's timeless triunity 'in and for itself.' When God steps out of this mode of 'pure being' and determines to be God in the covenant, this is an utterly free act because God was 'already' a perfectly realized and fulfilled being" (p. 74). What this misses is that God as "pure being" is "God in the covenant"; transcendence and the fullness of actuality serve, rather than negate, immanence and the covenantal relationship. See Weinandy, *Does God Suffer?*

tion is so exciting: Christ Jesus is none other than the Word, true God made man.

The key distinction that Aquinas makes, therefore, is that the person of the Word is predestined "not, indeed, in Himself or as subsisting in the divine nature, but as subsisting in the human nature" (*ST* III.24.1 *ad* 2). What does this mean for the relationship of election to Trinitarian theology? What is the difference between the Word "as subsisting in the divine nature" and the Word "as subsisting in the human nature" of Christ? On the one hand, the Word that subsists in the divine nature is not a different Word from the one that subsists in the human nature: Christ Jesus is the very Word who subsists in the divine nature. In this regard, McCormack's insistence that Christ Jesus is not only predestined (the "object" of election) but also the one who predestines (the "subject" of election) rightly emphasizes that Christ Jesus, after all, is the Word. As we have seen, God's superabundant communication of his goodness is at the heart of the Trinitarian processions, creation, and election. The Word, divine filiation, contains within himself the pouring out of goodness in creation that reaches its pinnacle in the incarnation.

Therefore, when McCormack says that "Christ Jesus" is the "subject" of election, he underscores the truth that divine filiation and divine election (adoptive filiation) cannot be separated — even if one holds with Aquinas, as I do, that the latter differs from the former in being a freely willed temporal "term" of the divine causality in the eternal processions. That the *Son* becomes incarnate has for Aquinas a profound "fittingness." He finds this fittingness in the intrinsic relationship of the two filiations, divine and human. As he points out, the incarnation of the Son includes the election or "the fulfilling of predestination" promised by Romans 8:17: ". . . if children, then heirs, heirs of God and fellow heirs with Christ" (*ST* III.3.8). Quoting Romans 8:29, "for those whom he foreknew he also predestined to be conformed to the image of his Son," Aquinas further highlights this bond of election (adoptive sonship) and divine Sonship: "Hence it was fitting that by Him who is the natural Son, men should share this likeness of sonship by adoption" (*ST* III.3.8). Election (new creation) constitutes the purpose of creation, and both should be seen in terms of the Word Christ Jesus. In this sense, the Word Christ Jesus is not merely the passive "object" of election. Rather, the incarnation of the Word ensures that Creator is the Redeemer. Aquinas declares: "The first creation of things was made by the power of God the Father through the Word; hence the second creation ought to have been brought about through the Word, by the power of God the Father, in order that restoration should correspond to creation" (*ST* III.3.8 *ad* 2). In affirming the unity of the Word's creating and electing action, Aquinas understands himself to be following Paul's teaching that "God was in Christ reconciling the world to himself" (2 Cor. 5:19).

### Union in the Subsisting Word

On the other hand, we must carefully distinguish the two modes of the Word's subsisting. Aquinas points out that "it is natural to that Person [the Word], considered in Himself, to be the Son of God in power, yet this is not natural to Him, considered in the human nature, in respect of which this befits Him according to the grace of union" (*ST* III.3.8 *ad* 2). McCormack suggests that this distinction cannot be easily made. The danger is that the Son Jesus Christ (the Word "considered in the human nature") might no longer clearly appear as caught up in the eternal filiation of the Son; in other words, the incarnation would become only accidental to the Son, so that one could not affirm that the human nature's very subsistence (personhood) is that of the Son of God. McCormack therefore insists that the Son is begotten in God's will to be "for us," so that the Son is eternally constituted as "Jesus Christ": "The *Logos incarnandus* is both *asarkos* (because not embodied) and *ensarkos* (by way of anticipation, on the basis of God's self-determination in the act of electing)" (pp. 67-68). As I have argued throughout this essay, McCormack finds himself in this position in part because he imagines the traditional position to be that "the works of God *ad intra* precede and make possible the works of God *ad extra*," so that there are two divine acts rather than one (p. 66). In fact, the divine act is one but has two "terms," and this distinction is what allows for my affirmation of McCormack's claim that "the Father never had regard for the Son apart from the humanity 'to be assumed'" while denying that this means that to be Word is, in some constitutive sense, to be human. For McCormack, God's decision to become incarnate for us (election) brings about the divine processions. This position stems, I think, from an apparent lack of any other way to account adequately for the unity of the divine act (in which are the divine processions) and the fact that election is never separate from this one divine act.

McCormack warns that any distinction between the two "terms" of the divine act entails a Nestorian separation between divine and human

MATTHEW LEVERING

nature in Christ Jesus. He comments that "the net effect of this classical line of thought was to assign suffering to the human nature alone. The classical commitment to interpreting immutability in terms of impassibility always had, as its consequence, a separation of the natures which could only serve the interests of Nestorianism in the long run" (p. 68). But the divinity and humanity are obviously quite different, a point that McCormack would hardly deny. By suggesting that their unity in Christ can be found in the passibility of both, their shared suffering, McCormack seems to suggest that the union ultimately must be sought, in some sense, in the natures (Eutychianism).

At stake here is ultimately the transcendence of God. In this regard, Aquinas follows John of Damascus: "As Damascene says, the divine nature is said to be incarnate because it is united to flesh personally, and not that it is changed into flesh. So likewise the flesh is said to be deified, as he also says, not by change, but by union with the Word, its natural properties still remaining" (*ST* III.2.2 *ad* 3). I suspect that McCormack fundamentally does not disagree with this, although it remains somewhat unclear what he means when he affirms "the ontological distinction between Jesus and ourselves" (p. 69). My point, however, is that in his concern about Nestorianism, he downplays the significance of the fact that the divine nature "is united to flesh personally," that is, in the person of the Word.

In seeking the principle of the unity of Christ Jesus, we need to look not to a common trait shared in some sense by God and humanity, but to the personal subsistence of the Word. Aquinas notes that "to the hypostasis [person] alone are attributed the operations and the natural properties, and whatever belongs to nature in the concrete" (*ST* III.2.3). Jesus Christ is the divine Word because "whatever belongs to nature in the concrete" belongs, in Christ, to the Word. The Word is the person to whom we attribute the words and actions of Jesus Christ in the flesh. Because the Word is God, the Word incarnate subsists in two natures, divine and human. The unity of the two natures depends on the unity of the one subsistence, the Word himself. Aquinas observes, "The unity of the divine Person is greater than numerical unity, which is the principle of number. For the unity of a divine Person is an uncreated and self-subsisting unity" (*ST* III.2.9 *ad* 1). When the Word assumes a human nature to himself, he is the principle of the unity of the two natures, because both natures are his. Yet the difference between divinity and humanity makes it necessary to continue to distinguish the two natures: Christ, in his human nature, is created in time and receives the grace of the Holy Spirit. In his human nature, Jesus Christ is not the Word or the "subject" of election, but rather is caused by "the processions of the divine Persons" as a temporal effect (*ST* I.45.6). Does this make Jesus Christ any less the Word (Nestorianism)? No. The union is in the person of the Word, and thus is a supremely perfect unity. Jesus Christ's words and deeds in the flesh are the Word's. But these words and deeds — the fruit and fulfillment of election — are still created effects, and thus to be distinguished (not separated) from the eternal "term" of the divine procession, which is the Word in his divinity.

By grounding this distinction in the divine processions, Aquinas is able to affirm more strongly than McCormack can the falsity of the statement "the human nature is the Son of God," while affirming with McCormack the truth that "it was predestinated that the human nature should be united to the Son of God in the Person" (*ST* III.24.1 *ad* 2). Aquinas and McCormack agree that, in Aquinas's words, "human nature was not always united to the Word; and by grace bestowed on it was it united in Person to the Son of God" (*ST* III.24.2). It is this graced human nature that, as the human nature in which the Word subsists, God predestines in the order of creation and election to be the graced human nature of the Word. Predestination/election has to do with created effects, and the Word himself is obviously not a created effect. Thus Christ Jesus is predestined insofar as he, in his human nature, is a created effect of the Word; but Christ Jesus in his divine nature is indeed the "subject" of predestination/ election who wills, in the divine processions, to create and assume a human nature. Can this be the same Christ Jesus, or have we now fallen into Nestorianism? The answer is again the unity of the subsisting Word, who subsists in two natures.

### Election, Predestination, Providence

By means of this emphasis on the bond between election and Christology/ Trinitarian theology, what can we say, finally, about election? McCormack observes that "[a]ll human beings are, for Barth, elect in Jesus Christ," and he draws out the implications of this election: "[A]ll that takes place in him (as a consequence of the divine humiliation and the exaltation of the royal human) is effective for them in that it takes place: justification, sanctification, vocation" (p. 69). While Aquinas does not move in a universalist direction, he similarly insists on the centrality of Jesus Christ in God's predestination/election. The one divine act, in which God freely knows and loves creatures into existence, includes predestination/election: as Aquinas says, "[I]n the same way and by the same eternal act God predestinated us and Christ" (*ST* III.24.3). The Word's subsisting in human nature, however, is predestined in a unique manner. This is so in two ways. First, Christ is the "exemplar" of predestination, both because of his perfect Sonship and his fullness of grace. By the grace of the Holy Spirit, which flows to all through Christ's humanity, those who imitate Christ receive a "participated likeness" of his Sonship (*ST* III.24.3). The eternal plan of election thus has Christ as its form.

Second, Christ is the cause of the predestination of the entire people of God. How can Christ's predestination, which pertains to his humanity (the humanity of the Word), be the cause of something that only God can cause? Aquinas answers that God eternally wills to achieve our salvation in and through the (predestined) humanity of Christ (*ST* III.24.4). Here Aquinas relies upon Ephesians 1:5-6: "He [God the Father] destined us in love to be his sons through Jesus Christ, according to the purpose of his will, to the praise of his glorious grace which he freely bestowed on us in the Beloved" (*ST* III.24.4 *sed contra*). In this sense, as Ephesians goes on to say, we are "created in Christ Jesus for good works, which God prepared beforehand, that we should walk in them" (Eph. 2:10).

Within the plan of divine providence, predestination/election is found in the effects of grace, through which the Holy Spirit elevates rational creatures to the Trinitarian life. Aquinas defines God's providence as the divine knowledge from eternity of the ordering of all things to the end for which they are created (ultimately God's goodness) (*ST* I.22.1). If Christ is the exemplar and cause of divine predestination, what, then, is Christ's role in divine providence? In the Word, God knows the ordering of all things, a knowledge that, when joined to God's will, is causal: "The first creation of things was made by the power of God the Father through the Word" (*ST* III.3.8 *ad* 2). The "first creation" in the Word already contains God's providence, whose aim God reveals through Christ: "For he [God the Father] has made known to us in all wisdom and insight the mystery of his will, according to his purpose which he set forth in Christ as a plan for the fulness of time, to unite all things in him, things in heaven and things on earth" (Eph. 1:9-10). This central place of the Word Christ Jesus, Aquinas suggests, befits a wise providential order: "[H]ence the second creation ought to have been brought about through the Word, by the power of God the Father, in order that restoration should correspond to creation" (*ST* III.3.8 *ad* 2).

## III. Conclusion

Aquinas holds that the reality of God's providence can be known philosophically, though pagan philosophers were generally unable to reach this conclusion.[24] Yet affirming the mystery of providence in a full manner ultimately requires theological faith, not only because the mystery of providence includes the existence of horrific and inexplicable suffering (which makes strictly philosophical affirmation of providence scandalous to those who do not know of the resurrection of the body), but also because the mystery of providence has Christ Jesus — God's answer to human suffering — at its center. For this reason Aquinas, following Hebrews 11:6, holds that people who do not know Christ can be united to him through faith in providence: "[T]hough they did not believe in Him [Christ Jesus] explicitly, they did, nevertheless, have implicit faith through believing in divine providence, since they believed that God would deliver mankind in whatever way was pleasing to Him" (*ST* II-II.2.7 *ad* 3). It follows that those who seek to understand divine providence and, at the same time, deliberately "look away from the God of electing grace revealed in Jesus Christ" (as McCormack says in a different context) will not find what they seek ("Seek God," p. 77). In this respect, McCormack and Aquinas can agree. As McCormack says, then, let us "seek God where he may be found" — but not without the help of classical metaphysics.

24. As shown by his train of argument in *ST* I.22.1.

# III. Implications for Ethics Today

## 12. The Gospel of True Prosperity: Our Best Life in the Triune God Now and Not Yet

*Paul Louis Metzger*

Certainly one of the most important aspects of humanity and a cardinal virtue of American culture is the notion of freedom. Yet we often find very different conceptions of freedom in the American church today: from the widespread "prosperity-gospel" movement illustrated by Joel Osteen to the civil rights movement and community development enterprise epitomized by Martin Luther King, Jr. and John M. Perkins, respectively. Notwithstanding the significance and impact of the civil rights movement and community development enterprise, the kind of sacrificial freedom idealized and embodied there is so radical that its most faithful exponents and adherents have never been viewed as mainstream in American culture, including the church. The pervasive prosperity-gospel movement emerges in overt and subtle forms, but characteristic of all its manifestations is its libertarian notion of freedom: freedom from constraints toward a "self-actualization" of the individual in isolation from the masses. And while America itself has a long history of caring for the orphaned, the "poor," the "huddled masses" from abroad "yearning to breathe free," to quote from Emma Lazarus's poem inscribed on the Statue of Liberty, its libertarian view of freedom leads America at times to advance its liberty in isolation from the world community.[1] The libertarian freedom espoused by the prosperity-gospel movement and at times the American society at large poses a fundamental problem to the well-being of the American church and culture — and the world at large.

Karl Barth identified the problematic nature of American freedom

---

1. Emma Lazarus, "The New Colossus," in *Nineteenth-Century American Women Poets: An Anthology*, ed. Paula Bernat Bennett (Oxford: Blackwell Publishers Ltd., 1998), p. 287.

during his visit to the United States in 1962. Barth did not seem to hold out much hope for the American church in terms of the development of a theology of freedom that reflects the gospel of love and grace, and that is conceived in positive terms: freedom for humanity. Can the American church today learn from the Swiss theologian's critique and move forward in advancing a prophetic theological vision of freedom that transcends the libertarian gospel in its various forms? Before proceeding further, let's listen to what Barth had to say on that U.S. visit to the American church and American theologians.

In a speech at the University of Chicago, Barth observed:

> If I myself were an American citizen and a Christian and a theologian, then I would try to elaborate a theology of freedom — a theology of freedom from, let us say, any inferiority complex over against good old Europe from whence you all came, or your fathers. You do not need to have such an inferiority complex. That is what I have learned these weeks. You may also have freedom from a superiority complex, let us say, over against Asia and Africa. That's a complex without reason. Then I may add — [your theology should also be marked by] freedom from fear of communism, Russia, inevitable nuclear warfare and generally speaking, from all the afore-mentioned principalities and powers. Freedom for which you would stand would be the freedom for — I like to say a single word — humanity. Being an American theologian, I would then look at the Statue of Liberty in the New York Harbor. I have not seen that lady, except in pictures. Next week I shall see her in person. That lady needs certainly a little or, perhaps, a good bit of demythologization. Nevertheless, maybe she may also be seen and interpreted and understood as a symbol of a true theology, not of liberty, but of freedom. Well, it would be necessarily, a theology of freedom. Of that freedom to which the Son frees us [cf. Jn 8.36], and which as His gift, is the one real human freedom.
>
> My last question for this evening is this: Will such a specific American theology one day arise? I hope so.[2]

Even if such a theology of freedom has arisen in America since Barth's historic visit, it is clear that such a theology has not yet captured the hearts, minds, and imaginations of multitudes of Christians and churches in the United States, as suggested at the outset of this paper. The prosperity-

---

2. Karl Barth, *Gespräche, 1959-1962* (Zürich: Theologischer Verlag, 1995), p. 489.

gospel movement is but one striking and pronounced indication of the problematic nature of American freedom, as typified by Joel Osteen's best-selling book *Your Best Life Now*.[3] Osteen's movement as a whole involves an uncritical appropriation of libertarian notions of free will. Freedom from poverty, for example, often ends up being freedom from the poor, as prosperity-gospel practitioners are bound over to various forms of self-love rather than the freedom for the poor that is captivated by God's self-less love disclosed in Jesus Christ.[4]

---

3. Joel Osteen, *Your Best Life Now: 7 Steps to Living at Your Full Potential* (New York: Warner Faith/Time, 2004). Hereafter, page references to this work appear in parentheses in the text and footnotes.

4. Generally speaking, it would follow from a prosperity-gospel paradigm to ignore the poor based on the prosperity-gospel conviction that the poor are that way because they lack the faith to advance beyond their dismal situation; in other words, they fail to "name and claim" prosperity for themselves. However, Osteen's message of positive thinking circum-scribes his prosperity-gospel message. Moreover, Osteen and his church have given pro-foundly to people in need during times of disaster. In fact, Osteen devotes a whole section of his #1 *New York Times* bestseller to the theme of "Live to Give!" And yet, Osteen's belief in free will (freedom from divine and human constraints to choose a certain course of action), and his exhortation to people to think positively and have faith in God to elevate themselves, open the door to the mindset that the poor are not following and trusting God if they re-main where they are for long. Not only does it follow from such prosperity-gospel thinking that the poor can be ignored, but it also follows from other claims Osteen has made that people, including the poor, can be used. Osteen claims that one should give to others — in-cluding the poor — so that one can receive a blessing from God. For example, he writes, "If you want your dreams to come to pass, help someone else fulfill his or her dreams" (pp. 222, 223); for all his critique of selfishness and narcissism (pp. 221-22), Osteen is still self-focused in his orientation. The result (perhaps unintentional) is that one ends up using the poor to ascend. It is also worth noting that the chapter on joy precedes the chapter on love and mercy in the section on giving, and the five sections that precede the section on giving focus on how to improve your own life. Osteen's framework stands in stark contrast to that of John M. Perkins, whose entire corpus is about helping the poor while living among them, motivated by God's love and compassion for one's neighbor, and with no ulterior motive. Among other things, while calling on people to move beyond a victim's mentality and to take personal responsibility (a point Osteen also makes to his readers), Perkins also is well aware of the structural realities that make it very difficult for many poor people — especially among minority populations — to move out of the vicious circle of poverty (a point that Osteen fails to grasp in its entirety). For Perkins, it requires the whole community to break the vicious circle, and it requires living among the people for whom one cares in view of God's self-sacrificial love, rather than caring for them so that the care-giver can ascend to new heights in the unbounded love of self-realization. For an exposition of Perkins's com-munity development paradigm, see his book *With Justice for All* (Ventura, CA: Regal Books, 1982).

PAUL LOUIS METZGER

Along these lines, it is worth noting what John M. Perkins, an African-American preacher, advisor to several U.S. Presidents on poverty, and founder of the Christian Community Development Association, says about the prosperity-gospel movement: "The prosperity movement is heavily accepted among the poor but has done very little in terms of real community development at the grassroots level. It takes people's attention away from the real problem, and if those people succeed it encourages them to remove themselves from the very people they ought to be identifying with and working among."[5] Perkins's claim causes one to wonder about Osteen's Lakewood Church in Houston, Texas. While it draws thousands of people from diverse economic and ethnic backgrounds due to his positive, prosperity-gospel messages, his "bloom where you're planted" perspective does not seem to encourage people who end up making it to stay and identify with those who do not yet have their "best life now."[6] Prosperity-gospel preaching in its overt and subtle forms never appears to focus primary attention on authentic community development, but rather the development and elevation of oneself (even through care for one's neighbor). In contrast, God revealed in Jesus Christ exhorts us to have the best lives we can possibly have *now* as we die to ourselves daily for the sake of our neighbors — especially the marginalized and downtrodden — in view of the consummation of God's kingdom, which has *not yet* occurred.[7]

How might God's revelation in Jesus Christ as expressed in Barth's theology shape our understanding of a theology of freedom that is truly prosperous in view of God's electing grace? Barth's incarnational theology resonates well with the apostle Paul's claim in 2 Corinthians 8:9: "For you know the grace of our Lord Jesus Christ, that though he was rich, yet for your sakes he became poor, so that you through his poverty might become rich" (NIV). Jesus, to whom Paul and Barth bear witness, circumscribes his freedom in love, and so identifies with us in our broken, fallen estate, including the poor. It follows that Jesus also challenges us to identify with those considered the "least of these" rather than abandon them in the freedom of our own self-actualization and self-advancement (see Matt. 25:31-46). Given the Barthian claim about the significance of the specificity of

5. John M. Perkins, *Beyond Charity: The Call to Christian Community Development* (Grand Rapids: Baker Books, 1993), p. 71.
6. For example, Osteen writes, "If you will keep blooming right where you are, then you can rest assured in God's perfect timing. He will transplant you" (p. 274).
7. Much of this paragraph is taken from my book *Consuming Jesus: Beyond Race and Class Divisions in a Consumer Church* (Grand Rapids: Eerdmans, 2007), pp. 85-86.

280

the gospel, it is vitally important that a volume on Barth's doctrine of election include explorations of the concrete implications of the gospel for human action, individual and social.

This chapter will speak to the significance of this book's discussion of the Trinity and election for the life of the church and kingdom witness in society at large. Special consideration will be given to God's loving freedom as applied to the widespread problematical phenomenon of the prosperity-gospel movement. I will contextualize my argument to the present discussion at a few points, but I will focus largely on the social implications arising from Barth's doctrines of the Trinity and election. I will seek to develop a theology of loving freedom rooted in Barth's doctrine of divine and human freedom framed by the triune God's electing grace revealed in Jesus Christ. I will also seek to make clear how that theology of loving freedom should shape the church's witness in the world, especially among the poor, through critical reflection on the prosperity gospel. Here we are talking of a gospel of true prosperity, involving our best life in loving freedom founded and perfected in the electing purposes of the triune God from and for all eternity — now and not yet. I will develop the argument on divine and human freedom by considering three related tendencies within the prosperity gospel movement: *individualism, consumerism,* and *escapism. I will challenge and counter these tendencies in view of the revelation of the free, electing grace of the triune God disclosed in Jesus Christ.*

First, the prosperity-gospel movement emphasizes an individualistic existence (*your* best life now). By contrast, the gospel of Jesus Christ promotes a relationally and communally based existence founded in the freedom and love disclosed in the triune life of the electing God. Second, the prosperity-gospel movement emphasizes a consumerist view of human well-being whereby our value and worth are bound up with what we acquire and purchase (your *best* life now). By contrast, the gospel of Jesus Christ declares that our worth and value are based in what we receive as relational gift as persons in loving and free covenantal communion through the electing grace of the triune God. Third, the prosperity-gospel movement emphasizes an escapist view of human action (your best life *now*). By contrast, the gospel of Jesus Christ promotes a model of sacrificial coexistence bound up with the far journey of the triune God in the electing grace of loving freedom for the world for which Christ died — a journey that includes us as we look forward to the consummation of all things in Jesus Christ at the end of history. The church is called to bear witness as a people sanctified by the loving and free grace of the electing God, and so live lives of true prosperity circumscribed by covenantal communion of relational giving and sacrificial coexistence in the world today.

The first item to counter is the prosperity-gospel movement's individualistic orientation (*your* best life now). The salvation it promises is one of self-actualization, and the assurance of one's individual salvation is based on the attainment of such self-actualization here and now. This individualistic orientation breeds insecurity.

Max Weber speaks of the Protestant movement's need (especially among Calvinists) for assurance of salvation, given its rejection of sacerdotalism and the institutional assurance offered through priestly mediation in the Roman Catholic Church.[8] Weber also notes that while Calvin was quite confident concerning the quality of his own faith, many of his followers struggled to gain such confidence.[9] Many Protestants speak of the election of individuals, and individual believers often want to be assured of being counted among the elect; many of them view the quality of their individual faith or performance of virtuous acts in the world as evidence of salvation.[10]

While many Christians have not given careful thought to the subject, this individual performance-based spirituality reflects in many if not all instances a lack of proper focus on God's revelation in Jesus Christ and confidence in Jesus Christ as the subject and object of God's electing purposes, in whom humanity participates. Individualism breeds insecurity, and insecurity breeds further insecurity the more we seek to save and assure ourselves by focusing on the quality of our faith and works rather than on God's grace, which creates and sustains faith and works. We must not place our confidence in ourselves, but in the triune God who elects us in love and freedom to be his people.[11]

8. Max Weber, *The Protestant Ethic and the Spirit of Capitalism,* with a new introduction by Anthony Giddens (New York: Charles Scribner's Sons, 1958; introduction copyright, 1976), p. 117.

9. Weber, *Protestant Ethic,* pp. 110-11.

10. Weber speaks of the efforts of many Calvinists to assure themselves of their salvation through the demonstration of strong faith and virtuous worldly activity. See *Protestant Ethic,* pp. 110-12, 121.

11. While Osteen does not specifically connect assurance of salvation or God's love to how much one is gaining and growing in faith and finances (among other things) on account of his positive-thinking message, nonetheless, given how much he focuses on gaining things, his paradigm can easily lead one in this direction. Moreover, while Osteen talks about God's unconditional love (p. 263), he still favors a quid pro quo model of a relationship with God (see, e.g., pp. 262-66). And though he will challenge a conditional model of

Just as trusting in oneself breeds insecurity and leads one to seek after assurances within oneself that one is secure, so it continues to breed deeper forms of insecurity. Whereas individualism breeds insecurity, a relational framework derived from God's gracious and free love revealed in Jesus Christ leads people beyond such self-concern. Self-concern always leads individuals to seek to enhance and advance their own capacities so that their security is bound up with such things as accumulating more wealth to assure themselves of their salvation. It also leads to a lack of concern for and even repugnance toward others, to treating them as though they were reprobate, especially if they do not embody the same rational, physical, or material capacities that the supposedly elect do.[12] (See Jer. 9:23-24, which Paul quotes in his rebuke of the Corinthian church for boasting in themselves, their capacities, and their groupings rather than in Christ Jesus and their union with him as God's people living together in unity.) The more individuals seek to assure themselves of their security and significance, the more they live in autonomy from God and others.

The prosperity-gospel movement encourages self-concern with its emphasis on the salvation of the enlightened individual and its assurance based on individual self-actualization over against covenantal communion with God and neighbor. It maintains that the more faith I have and the more self-actualized I am, the more secure I am. The prosperity gospel is simply a more banal form of the classic Protestant drive for security based on performance in religious or secular terms.

---

relationship at a few points (see, e.g., p. 263), the give-to-get orientation represents his overarching model. The same is true of Osteen's version of human freedom as total freedom from constraints (p. 178), in which it is ultimately up to you and me to fulfill our destiny. Osteen's focus really is on the individual, not on God. And if it is up to me, I am bound to become insecure and seek after assurances of my well-being and salvation.

12. Weber writes of the Calvinist position on proving one's faith in worldly activity that "[b]y founding its ethic in the doctrine of predestination, it substituted for the spiritual aristocracy of monks outside of and above the world the spiritual aristocracy of the predestined saints of God within the world. It was an aristocracy which, with its *character indelibilis*, was divided from the eternally damned remainder of humanity by a more impassable and in its invisibility more terrifying gulf, than separated the monk of the Middle Ages from the rest of the world about him, a gulf which penetrated all social relations with its sharp brutality. This consciousness of divine grace of the elect and holy was accompanied by an attitude toward the sin of one's neighbor, not of sympathetic understanding based on consciousness of one's own weakness, but of hatred and contempt for him as an enemy of God bearing the signs of eternal damnation. This sort of feeling was capable of such intensity that it sometimes resulted in the formation of sects." Weber, *Protestant Ethic,* pp. 121-22.

The prosperity-gospel movement is insufficiently attentive to the specifics of the gospel of Jesus Christ, which are made possible through the self-revealing and self-giving of the triune God's eternal being and will through Jesus Christ in the power of the Holy Spirit, and not through our own perceptions of faith or performance. Now, since it is the *triune God's* working in us that matters and not simply our perception of it, nor our performance in view of it, we cannot understand God solely in relationship to us in the economic Trinity; it is critically important that we have the revealed knowledge of God in himself and apart from us.[13] Such knowledge is ultimately what assures us that we have spoken well of God and have not constructed our images of God in light of contemporary cultural images of middle- or upper-class prosperity and the like. Such knowledge based in God's eternal and triune self-giving provides us with all the assurance we need that God is for and with us.

It is important to guard against abstractions; what we find in the revelation of God's electing purposes reflects the very being of God. In terms of the backdrop to this volume's overarching discussion, Bruce McCormack has admirably focused our attention on the close relationship of God's being and action in Barth's thought, but the notion that the decision of election serves as the Trinity's ground is problematic.[14] God's decision to elect us in Jesus Christ does not logically ground or constitute God's being. Rather, God's freedom in love circumscribed within the indissoluble relationality of the one divine subject of Father, Son, and Spirit prior to election (the priority here is logically rather than temporally conceived) grounds or constitutes election.

The question may arise at this point: How, then, do we know God is for us if God constitutes or grounds election rather than election constituting God? We can have confidence that God is for us in love and freedom because the Father and Son are one in the Spirit in indissoluble, eternal

---

13. Barth maintains — rightly — that we must not even ground our views of election in pastoral care or pedagogical or didactic value, but in revelation. See Karl Barth, *Church Dogmatics*, II/2, *The Doctrine of God*, ed. G. W. Bromiley and T. F. Torrance (Edinburgh: T. & T. Clark, 1957), pp. 37-38 (hereafter, volume, part, and page references to this work appear in parentheses in the text and footnotes).

14. Bruce L. McCormack, "Grace and Being: The Role of God's Gracious Election in Karl Barth's Theological Ontology," in *The Cambridge Companion to Karl Barth*, ed. John Webster (Cambridge: Cambridge University Press, 2000), p. 103; see also McCormack, *Orthodox and Modern: Studies in the Theology of Karl Barth* (Grand Rapids: Baker Academic, 2008), p. 194.

communion as the one divine subject of love and freedom. Such divine consideration of us flows from the constancy of the divine life in which God is true to himself. Even if we were to deny him, he would never deny us, for it would go against God's eternally triune being and character as the one who loves in freedom as one divine subject, which is expressed in his free and loving promise to be our God and for us to be his people in Jesus Christ.

God is fully present in his actions and revelation, as Jesus Christ is the fullness of God in bodily form, and in whom we find fullness (Col. 2:9-10). God does not give us a "part" of himself in his decision to be our God; God gives us himself, for God is not less than or other than himself in his revelation, as Barth maintains (*CD* II/1, p. 472). But that does not mean that God is exhausted by his revelation or his electing activity, or that God has no being apart from the eternal decision to become incarnate in Jesus Christ. God's electing purposes revealed in Jesus Christ accurately express and disclose God's eternal being and character rather than exhaust them. God is greater than what he is in revelation, though not different from it (or as Paul says in a different context, "God's love transcends knowledge" [Eph. 3:19]). God's love is inexhaustible, though not different from the knowledge of God's free and loving being disclosed in God's activity.

God is truly free in his eternal decisions of election and revelation, and not constituted by them. If, however, God were constituted by his decisions/actions (i.e., that God is triune for the sake of his revelation), it would be difficult to maintain that God is truly free, and in no way dependent on the creation for his identity. Such a God would have no ultimate space with respect to the creation, but would in effect be in danger of being collapsed into it. Moreover, such a view would not only limit God's freedom but also have a negative impact on human freedom: it would take away the necessary safeguard of our appropriate freedom within limits. Only as we understand that God's electing decision and activity revealed in Jesus Christ express and disclose rather than exhaust God's very being, and that such activity is constituted by rather than constitutive of God's being, do we have the assurance that God is truly free to love us and be our God.

Yet this is not to say that there are not many important points of agreement between the two sides of this debate. We are in widespread agreement that God is triune in and of God's own being. The point of debate is whether or not God is triune for the sake of his revelation.[15] The

15. See McCormack, *Orthodox and Modern*, pp. 192-93.

various contributors to this volume would agree that there is no competition within the Godhead. If, however, God were not eternally triune, but rather three separate and isolated individuals in eternity, our assurance would be jeopardized. One finds this faulty notion among those today in the church and society at large who resonate with Jesus but who are suspicious of the Father, perceiving Jesus to be benevolent and the Father malevolent, and viewing Jesus as seeking to snatch humanity's salvation from the hand of a reluctant deity. Our ultimate confidence rests on God being in himself from and for all eternity what he is in revelation. In other words, what we see in Jesus is what we get with God.

We will only be able to move beyond individualism and the resulting insecurity it breeds through efforts of self-actualization (bound up with freedom from constraints wherein the attempt to acquire greater levels of faith and wealth for the sake of gaining assurance of salvation is made) *if* we are confident that God is truly who we perceive him to be in revelation. If we take God's revelation in Jesus Christ seriously as the demonstration of God's eternal self-determination as the one who is complete in and of himself to be free in his love for and with us, we will realize that there is no division or competition in the divine being, no individualistic frame of reference: what we see in Jesus is indeed what we get with God. Jesus and the Father are one in their saving purposes. Thus there is no absolute decree that stands behind revelation, and which counters God's loving freedom disclosed in Jesus Christ. Barth says:

> The election of Jesus Christ is the eternal choice and decision of God. And our first assertion tells us that Jesus Christ is the electing God. We must not ask concerning any other but Him. In no depth of the Godhead shall we encounter any other but Him. There is no such thing as Godhead in itself. Godhead is always the Godhead of the Father, the Son and the Holy Spirit. But the Father is the Father of Jesus Christ and the Holy Spirit is the Spirit of the Father and the Spirit of Jesus Christ. There is no such thing as a *decretum absolutum.* There is no such thing as a will of God apart from the will of Jesus Christ. Thus Jesus Christ is not only the *manifestatio* and *speculum nostrae praedestinationis.* And He is this not simply in the sense that our election can be known to us and contemplated by us only through His election, as an election which, like His and with His, is made (or not made) by a secret and hidden will of God. On the contrary, Jesus Christ reveals to us our election as an election which is made by Him, by His will which is also the will of God.

He tells us that He Himself is the One who elects us. In the very fore-ground of our existence in history we can and should cleave wholly and with full assurance to Him because in the eternal background of history, in the beginning with God, the only decree which was passed, the only Word which was spoken and which prevails, was the decision which was executed by Him. As we believe in Him and hear His Word and hold fast by His decision, we can know with a certainty which nothing can ever shake that we are the elect of God. (*CD* II/2, pp. 115-16)[16]

Here, I should note, while Jesus reveals to us the Father's will of election, nowhere does Barth state that God's triune identity is constituted by election, but rather assumes that God's being is complete in himself from all eternity. Armed with confidence in the triune God, we can fight against the propensity to seek after an individualistic salvation expressed in self-concern involving religious (greater faith) or secular (greater wealth) self-actualization bound up with total freedom from constraints. We can also fight against the tendency to seek after an institutional salvation. Neither the individualistic nor institutional alternative is favorable, for they are not truly relational or centered in God's revelation in Jesus Christ.

In light of what I have said so far, we must not place our confidence in the institution of the church or in the individual believer's faith, but in the revelation of the triune Lord of the church and believer. The gospel of Jesus Christ promotes a relationally and communally based existence grounded in the eternal and self-determining freedom and love disclosed in the triune life of the electing God. It is precisely the knowledge of the love and freedom of the triune God, rooted in the revelation of God's eternal being and not in our perceptions of God, that frees us from the propensity to perform to gain God's favor through acquiring greater levels of individual faith and/or wealth. Through the power of God's loving freedom revealed in Jesus Christ, we are free to move out in the world to proclaim the good news of God's love so that all people might come to know God in Christ Jesus through the Spirit, and to bear witness to God's redeeming work for all people — especially the least among us, and not just ourselves.[17] Grounded in the eternal being of God, we are thus free to

16. Note what Barth says about the insecurity the absolute decree creates in people in *CD* II/2, pp. 64-65.

17. It is important to note that the representatives of the position that the triune God constitutes election must safeguard adequately the concept of the *dialectical* nature of God's love and freedom. If they champion God's freedom *from us* to the detriment of God's free-

move out in the world with a corresponding love and freedom in which we find our true identity in God and are free to work in the world without losing ourselves in the world.

We have spoken of the individualistic nature of what often passes for true freedom, including forms of freedom found in the prosperity-gospel movement, the insecurity it breeds, and how attention to the revelation of the triune God of electing grace moves us beyond insecurity rooted in our autonomy. Now we wish to consider more fully how the individualism and insecurity it breeds often leads to a consumerist impulse and need for the *acquisition* of salvation — religious or secular, as expressed in the prosperity-gospel movement. In contrast, the good news that God has elected us in Christ, and that we are the recipients of the triune God's free and loving gift in Christ Jesus, leads us beyond consumerist impulses. This brings us to our second point.

Osteen notes that the greatest gift of all that God has given us is God himself, and that, more than anything, God wants to restore our relationship with him.[18] While this is true and important, Osteen gives this claim inadequate consideration in *Your Best Life Now*. Instead, he focuses much of his attention on how to improve ourselves and our living conditions, such as our career, family, and health (rather than on how to grow in communion with God). Moreover, Osteen talks of how God does not force someone to do anything, but that improvement is up to the individual. Certainly, the language of "force" or compulsion is problematic, but one can speak of the sovereign determination of God in more compatible ways. Furthermore, it is equally problematic to speak of the human self-determination to choose God (which follows from Osteen's libertarian view of freedom).[19] Lasting security and transformational improvement

---

dom *for us*, they will undermine appropriate concern for community and unintentionally give license to individualism and disregard for social concern. No doubt McCormack would argue that his emphasis on God's freedom for us as reflected in his view that election constitutes God better safeguards against human isolation and the social ills bound up with individualism in contemporary culture. And yet, if God is understood in himself as only God for us, so that God has no genuine independence and freedom from us, then the being of God acquires a kind of dependence on us that might engender a corresponding *codependence* between God and human beings, as is the case if the being and essence of God and humans are determined in covenant relationships. For this reason, then, both sides in this debate need to acknowledge the need for a dialectical understanding of God's being in relationship with himself and with us.

18. Osteen, *Your Best Life Now*, p. 305.

19. When discussing why people don't change no matter how hard we pray, Osteen

do not come about from choosing God, but from God choosing us. God changes us; he alone is able to change us. If salvation and improvement were up to us, insecurity would again follow, as well as the drive to assure ourselves of our good standing through our individual performance and acquisition of greater levels of faith or perhaps material goods. Personal security is dependent on the interpersonal union and communion that God's people have in and through Jesus and his work of election.

In Osteen's work, one finds scant consideration of Jesus, his cross, or union with him.[20] If anything, Jesus functions as an exemplar for living the good life rather than as the transcendental or necessary ground for the possibility of authentic human existence; such authentic human existence is dependent on Jesus' vicarious humanity, in which we participate in the divine life through union with him in the Spirit. For Barth, living the good life always follows from knowing and participating in the life of the good God, for ethics always follows from the living subject of theology. Moreover, since we already are included in Jesus Christ through his electing of us in himself rather than through our election of him, we do not have to seek to prove our merit or worth. Instead, we bear witness to what is actually the case through our union with Christ Jesus. True freedom is bound up with God's free and eternal determination and declaration in and through Jesus to elect us in his holy love to be his people, whom he will perfect at the consummation of all things.

While Osteen speaks of our intrinsic value, and that our sense of value should only be based on the fact that we are children of God, he does not develop these points at great length (pp. 66-67). And while he says that "God's love is unconditional," that his "grace is unmerited favor," that "God gives us all many things that we don't deserve, and could not possibly earn, no matter how many good deeds we do," and that what we do for God and others simply gets "God's attention in a special way" (p. 263), nonetheless he gives rise to skeptics' challenges with statements such as this: "In your time of need, because of your generosity, God will move heaven and earth to make sure you are taken care of" (p. 262). On the contrary, God has already moved heaven and earth to take care of us. Our re-

---

writes, in a libertarian vein, "But we must also understand that God will not change another person's will. He has given every human being free will to choose which way he or she will go, whether to do right or wrong. Sometimes, no matter how hard we pray or how long we stand in faith, things don't turn out as we hope" (*Your Best Life Now*, p. 178). Elsewhere he claims, "If you will transform your mind, God will transform your life" (p. 108).

20. See *Your Best Life Now*, p. 69 (bottom) for a rare example of the latter.

sponse is simply and profoundly one of witness to what God has done and will do for us in view of his kingdom, which has dawned in our midst in Jesus Christ. Barth's critical response to the claim made at the close of Benedict's Rule has pertinence here: "It is not because and as they do this that the *regna superna* will open up to them. It is because and as the *regna superna* are opened up to them in the death of Jesus Christ that they will do this in the power of His resurrection" (*CD*, IV/2, p. 18).

Our ultimate aim here in this second section is to make clear that God's salvation is the free gift of the triune God *himself* to us: not something, but someone, as we are called forth and chosen in God's gracious love to participate in his electing purposes for us in and through the person and work of Jesus Christ in the power of the Holy Spirit.[21] God reveals God by God, and so he gives himself to us. Over against the individualistic, consumerist, and commodifying impulses of the prosperity-gospel movement and its Protestant capitalistic precursors to acquire salvation as something (greater capacities of faith or wealth), the gospel of Jesus Christ promises us salvation as the gracious gift of loving communion based in the life and action of the triune God who elects us (and not based on our choices and self-determination).

In and through the triune God, we are free to move away from trying to be saved through profit and consumption, which are bound up with our supposed freedom as autonomous individuals to choose stuff and acquire wealth; instead, God's grace frees us to respond in faith and experience the richness of vital relational union with Christ and his church. This, in turn, leads us to give of ourselves sacrificially because we are secure relationally. Individualism and insecurity in relationships lead to competition bound up with acquisition, which leads to the protection of ourselves over against self-sacrifice for the sake of others. Security in relationship derived from God's election of us in Jesus leads us to receive from others and to give ourselves sacrificially to our neighbors, especially the least among us.

Osteen affirms the love of the other, calling on the church to care for those in need; but his exhortation has as its motivating force the belief that those who care for others will be blessed. Since this is the motivating force, we must ask, What will sustain us for the long haul if the people we bless in order to be blessed do not get us the greatest bang for our earthly or heavenly buck? If we are not dealing with eschatological kingdom realities, but only

---

21. See § 67 of *CD* IV/2 for Barth's significant treatment of our participation in Jesus Christ through the Spirit.

present-tense possibilities, what is to keep us from abandoning the poor for Nietzschean heights of azure isolation?[22] Unlike Osteen and his prosperity-gospel movement, which awakens one to the possibilities of one's self-authenticated life here and now (over against the actuality of the kingdom in the present and future), the gospel of Jesus Christ awakens us to the sure reality of Jesus and his kingdom's identity in its present form in view of its eschatological consummation.[23] Thus we can have the confidence and courage to live in compassionate service to others now, for God has given us his eschatological kingdom. As Jesus says, "Do not be afraid, little flock, for your Father has been pleased to give you the kingdom. Sell your possessions and give to the poor. Provide purses for yourselves that will not wear out, a treasure in heaven that will not be exhausted, where no thief comes near and no moth destroys. For where your treasure is, there your heart will be also" (Luke 12:32-34). We can give sacrificially to others because God has given us his kingdom. Such hope drives us into the world over against those escapists who view entrance into the kingdom as an exit from the world and as an excuse to renounce concern for others, or those escapists who view entrance into the kingdom as the result of using the poor to advance their own standing and leave them behind when that is accomplished.

This brings me to the third point, namely, that the prosperity-gospel movement emphasizes an escapist view of human action (your best life *now*). By contrast, the gospel of Jesus Christ promotes a model of sacrificial coexistence bound up with the far journey of the triune God in the electing grace of loving freedom for the world for which Christ died, a journey that includes us as we look forward in complete security and total confidence to the consummation of all things in Jesus Christ at the end of history. The church is called to bear witness as a people sanctified by the loving and free grace of the electing God, and so to live lives of true prosperity through covenantal communion of relational gifting. Such relational gifting gives birth to sacrificial coexistence in the world today, as we are assured of God's love and guarantee to make all things new.

22. For a series of fascinating reflections on the nature of Christianity and how Nietzsche's vision of progress and development counters the Christian ethic, see Friedrich Nietzsche, *The Antichrist*, in *The Portable Nietzsche*, ed. Walter Kaufmann (New York: Viking, 1968), pp. 633-44; see also Nietzsche, *Ecce Homo*, in *Basic Writings of Nietzsche*, ed. Walter Kaufmann (New York: Modern Library, 1992), pp. 762, 783, 784. For Barth's response, see *CD* III/2, pp. 231-42.

23. I am indebted to Robert Redman for this point about Osteen and the prosperity-gospel movement.

When our confidence and assurance are bound up with our performance and the benefits we receive here and now, rather than in God's triune being and eternal self-determination to elect us in the gracious freedom of his love, we will likely eventually abandon those who do not gain for us our money's worth in return for the "charity" we have poured out on them. True community development among the poor is costly. We may not find that it benefits us greatly to invest in the poor, if we are thinking simply in terms of this life and our own profit margins. A giving-to-get model of engagement ultimately leads to disengagement and escapism. In this view, we often give until presently we find that we are getting nothing or very little in return. However, as the electing God and the elect human, Jesus actualizes a new form of being in the world — one that makes it possible for us not to seek our own benefit, not to seek our best life now, but to seek the best lives for those most in need regardless of what it might entail for us (*CD* II/2, pp. 115-16). As Barth says, freedom is ultimately a freedom for the other rather than a freedom from certain limitations or laws or dangers.[24] In fact, the freedom that God actualizes removes our self-imposed limitations bound up with the law of self-preservation and danger to our persons so that we might bear witness to God's ultimate act of loving freedom, wherein God laid down his life for his enemies — those not worthy of his love — including you and me.[25]

The elect human Jesus Christ, who is also the electing God, is the necessary condition for making possible authentic human existence of love and freedom. In view of Jesus Christ, we no longer need to conspire and compete with our fellow humans, seeking to ascend above them toward self-actualization in search of security before God, even using them to get there if that is what it will take. Instead, we are secure in the divine and human freedom and love revealed in Jesus Christ to descend and give our lives for our neighbors in sacrificial service to them — especially the least of these, as we bear our crosses for Christ. Only when we live fully for God and our neighbor, dying to ourselves in view of what God has done, is doing, and will do for us in Jesus Christ will we live life to the fullest now and forever. We can give sacrificially because the triune God has chosen us to

---

24. Karl Barth, "The Gift of Freedom: Foundation of Evangelical Ethics," in *The Humanity of God* (Atlanta: John Knox Press, 1960), p. 78.

25. Along similar lines, Barth interpreted the command to "love one's neighbor as oneself" as the rejection of self-love, with the affirmation of love of neighbor in place of self-love. See *CD*, I/2, pp. 387-88.

be participants in the gospel of true prosperity in his kingdom of interpersonal communion now and — even more so — not yet.

While Osteen's message of hope has ministered to countless people and has been used of God to impact and transform them in profound ways (moving people beyond various addictions and forms of victimization), his message is not hopeful or profound enough. Osteen offers people a good life, not the best life imaginable. Osteen is right to exhort people to move beyond mediocrity and the mentality of a victim; but he fails to focus on the centrality of the cross in living the best life imaginable now, and on our future glory in and through the crucified and resurrected Lord, to which no other glory can ever compare.

Now, for all my talk about self-sacrifice in the course of this essay, which is bound up with bearing our crosses for Christ in the present, we must also account for the resurrection. To be sure, the Christian life and crown does not come without the cross, for the crown of jeweled glory is made of thorns. But we must never forget that our present sufferings cannot compare with the glory that will be revealed in us through our resurrected Lord (Rom. 8:18). Barth explains that "the crown of life" is more than the cross. The cross's "dignity" is "provisional, indicating the provisional nature of the Christian existence and all sanctification," and its time is limited. Our cross's term

> . . . will cease at the very point to which the suffering of Jesus points in the power of His resurrection, and therefore to which our suffering also points in company with His. It is not our cross which is eternal, but, when we have borne it, the future life revealed by the crucifixion of Jesus. Rev. 21:4 will then be a present reality: "And God shall wipe away all tears from their eyes; and there shall be no more death, neither sorrow nor crying, neither shall there be any more pain: for the former things are passed away." P. Gerhardt is thus right when he says: "Our Christian cross is brief and bounded, One day 'twill have an ending. When hushed is snowy winter's voice, Beauteous summer comes again; Thus 'twill be with human pain. Let those who have this hope rejoice." There cannot lack a foretaste of joy even in the intermediate time of waiting, in the time of sanctification, and therefore in the time of the cross. (*CD*, IV/2, p. 613)

Following Barth's lead, we have great cause for rejoicing, for we delight in God's eternal self-determination in the freedom of his love to be our God and to make us his people in the crucified and risen Jesus through the Spirit. And so, we presently live out the best life imaginable in the Lord Jesus as we bear our crosses in view of the unimaginable glory that has not yet been disclosed but will certainly be revealed in Jesus at the consummation of the ages.

# Contributors

**Michael T. Dempsey** is Associate Professor of Theology at St. John's University in New York.

**Nicholas M. Healy** is Professor of Theology and Religious Studies and Associate Dean in the College of Liberal Arts and Sciences at St. John's University in New York.

**Kevin W. Hector** is Assistant Professor of Theology and of the Philosophy of Religions at the Divinity School of the University of Chicago.

**Christopher Holmes** is Senior Lecturer in Systematic Theology in the Department of Theology and Religion at the University of Otago, New Zealand.

**George Hunsinger** is the Hazel Thompson McCord Professor of Systematic Theology at Princeton Theological Seminary and president of the Karl Barth Society of North America.

**Paul Dafydd Jones** is Assistant Professor of Western Religious Thought at the University of Virginia.

**Matthew Levering** is Professor of Theology at the University of Dayton and coeditor of *Nova et Vetera*.

**Bruce L. McCormack** is the Frederick and Margaret L. Weyerhaeuser Professor of Systematic Theology at Princeton Theological Seminary.

**Paul Louis Metzger** is Professor of Christian Theology and the Theology of Culture at Multnomah Biblical Seminary in Portland, Oregon, and director of the Institute for the Theology of Culture.

**Paul D. Molnar** is Professor of Theology at St. John's University in New York.

**Paul T. Nimmo** is the Meldrum Lecturer in Theology at the University of Edinburgh and associate editor of the *International Journal of Systematic Theology.*

**Aaron T. Smith** is Assistant Professor of Theology at Colorado Christian University, Lakewood, Colorado.

# Index